MAN and
the
MOVIES

MAN and
the
MOVIES

edited by
W. R. ROBINSON

with assistance from
GEORGE GARRETT

LOUISIANA STATE
UNIVERSITY PRESS
BATON ROUGE

The essays in this collection were all originally written for *Man and the Movies*. Somewhat different versions of some of them have appeared in *Paris Review, Rapier, University, Virginia Quarterly Review,* and *Yale Review*.

Library of Congress Catalog Card Number: 67–24549
Manufactured in the United States of America by
Thos. J. Moran's Sons, Inc.

Designed by Robert L. Nance

For ROY HARVEY PEARCE,

who taught me the full range

of the humanities.

CONTENTS

THE PERSONAL ENCOUNTER

ILLUSTRATIONS

following page 182

MAN and
the
MOVIES

Introduction

Everybody loves a story. Children mesmerized for hours before a television set watching cartoons they are seeing for the fifth or sixth time, or long lines of shivering moviegoers outside a theater on a winter night, convincingly demonstrate that truth. And today the love of story, as these examples suggest, is requited much more often than not with a narrative told in visual images.

Anyone doubting the predominance of visual images as a vehicle for storytelling need only consider recent estimates that the typical college freshman in 1966 had seen five hundred movies, twenty times the number of novels he had read, and had put in fifteen thousand hours watching television, more time than he had spent in school to that point. And if those figures aren't convincing, the skeptic can ponder those in the 1965 *United Nations Statistical Yearbook,* from which he will learn that over two thousand full-length films were made internationally that year—657 in Japan, for example, and 305 in India, an underdeveloped country still unable to feed itself. The United States, incidentally, once the movie capital of the world, with 155 full-length films ranked no better than fifth in movie production. These figures become yet more impressive when supplemented with those of film attendance, which ran around ten billion in the United States, the Soviet Union, and China alone. If the skeptic adds to these figures the staggering quantity of visual images used in cartoons and comics, children's illustrated books, photo-stories, and television commercials for narrative purposes, there can be no question about the supremacy of the visual image in the realm of story. The fact that images and movies have many uses besides storytelling simply adds gratuitous evidence in support of the observation that the life of the mind today receives its nourishment primarily from visual rather than verbal sources.

Clearly, in terms of sheer quantity, visual narrative is the greatest aesthetic and educational force abroad in the world today, and the movies—the largest in scale, the most graphically vivid, and the most widely diffused of the visual narrative media—qualify unchallenged as the art of our time. But that stature belongs to them in the more profound sense, too—as the most potent form of storytelling today, or of myth-making, to use the fashionable term, they express and shape the contours of the contemporary mind more effectively than any competing narrative mode.

The movies have ridden to such prominence on the back of the major trend in Western culture. Since the Renaissance, an era known best for its perspective painting and empirical science, Western man has been fascinated by the reality and delights of vision. That fascination has grown until today we buy the package, so we are told by psychologists, rather than the substantive product; we vote in presidential campaigns for the image rather than the ideology; and we care more about our own images than our names, and as a consequence suffer from agonizing identity crises. Twentieth-century technology has not initiated but only helped to increase the authority of sight over modern man's mind and heart. A child of empiricism and technology, a descendant of the telescope and microscope, the movies magnify man's visual power, and in doing so they reflect and derive their stature from the stress on sight now traditional in our ocularly oriented culture.

No one has ever seriously doubted that the movies are a powerful force in contemporary life. Quite the contrary. Their potential for propaganda purposes was immediately recognized and in some cases exploited, and intellectuals readily sensed their danger as a mass-produced instrument for dehumanization. The movies' potential as well as their real effect on the quality of our lives individually and collectively has been so self-evident from their beginnings that the need for a close scrutiny of what they show us has been generally recognized. That need is, of course, no greater today than it has been at any other time during the last fifty years—nor is it any less.

What has been questioned is the capacity of the movies for doing good. Youthful and perhaps too much a work horse in the cultural marketplace, they have been vulnerable to the charge that they are unable to awaken and refresh the mind. That they are still subjected to this attitude is borne out by the fact that twenty-eight philosophers recently held a two-day symposium on art and philosophy without once mentioning them, thus tacitly asserting that the movies cannot tap the deepest reaches of man's spiritual life and so, incapable of articulating anything of consequence, are at best a rudimentary art.

Yet the movies are not now as disturbing for intellectuals as they once were. One reason, no doubt, is that they are no longer, at least in the United States, *the* popular art; television has stolen the limelight. But, more importantly, a new mood prevails today in the life of the mind, less schismatic than a decade ago, favorably disposed toward a mating of high- and low-brow, elite and vernacular art forms, as evident in Pop Art and the attitude taken by intellectuals toward the Beatles and Bob Dylan. The movies have definitely benefited from the new mood. They are the "in" thing for a coterie of intellectuals on the international scene. And they have established a beachhead at the university, the domain of formal intellect, where they are represented in approximately a thousand film societies and a thousand official courses. So, at present suspended somewhere between the hell of mass culture and the heaven of high art, they are undergoing aesthetic purification, with the favorably disposed intellectuals as their advocates and the university as their purgatory.

Although the movies entered by the back door of weekly programs for diversion and extracurricular film clubs, the university is now performing for the movies, no matter how quietly and *ex officio,* the kind of function it performs for the other arts and intellectual disciplines. It is, in effect, storing, compiling, and promulgating film classics when it shows almost annually a limited repertoire of "great" movies to young men and women who are at college to become familiar with the major intellectual events in their tradition. These classics contribute to a common intellectual heritage, and, moreover, as shared experience, they focus upon the movies the sort of intellectual inquiry which thrives at the university. The result is a refinement of film vocabulary and a more systematic organization of historical and technical knowledge about films. These developments make possible a greater range and precision of practice and pave the way for formal study by scholar and critic. The overall effect is to delegate historical and moral significance to what has formerly passed as ephemeral entertainment. Whether by design or accident, the university, as a consequence, is helping the movies to become a part of the sophisticated intellectual culture we depend upon to lift us out of our mundane selves.

While they have yet to be officially admitted to the Parnassian summit, the movies are obviously receiving a new kind of attention. This collection of essays, written especially for this volume, demonstrates that if nothing else does. Not an anthology of classic pieces in film theory or reviewing, nor representative samples of approaches to the film, it is, instead, a collaborative enterprise by predominantly writer- and scholar-teachers on location at the university. When asked to write what they would on the movies, they responded eagerly, testifying to the presence of movies in their intellectual lives and to their concern regarding the movies' effects upon themselves and others. But it is not just their willingness to write on the movies that illustrates the new attention; what they say about the movies, or, more to the point, their manner of discussing them, is even more significant. They spontaneously assess them as art. These writers consistently bare an individual involvement with the movies, whether working on the inside or as spectators, even when the recollections are painful or the judgments adverse.

It is not difficult to understand why the response to the movies by the writers of these essays is personal. As the poets and fiction writers among them directly and indirectly confess, they are of a generation born to and reared upon movies. The movies are under their skin. These writers do not feel threatened or dehumanized by them because the movies were personalized for them a long time ago, before they had a choice in the matter. Involved with movies by the fact of their existence, they cannot now extirpate them from their psyche, ironically, without dehumanizing themselves.

They gave their hearts without knowing it, but they will not abandon their souls to that affection's tyranny. These essays are not maudlin reminiscences. The old quarrel with the movies continues, but with a new intimacy and without the old disdainfulness and bitterness, although a tinge of that can still appear, usually over individual disappointments and not the movies per se. Granting movies aesthetic existence without compromising their own integrity, these writers speak about something that matters to them as men. Maybe their attitude is part of the present tendency to value the individuated, concrete, and personal over the abstract, existence over the idea. To be sure, their focus illuminates what such a commitment entails and how the movies express and clarify it. Or maybe it's just an old habit persisting, the hunger engraved in their minds in youth demanding to be appeased in adulthood on a different level, the kids reared on movies developing their youthful passion into a more responsible bond.

The movies may be the art form these writers are most likely to have in common with other people, such as students, not professionally adept in their field. And it may be that movies interest them because they recognize, as teachers, that intellectual sanity in a visual culture depends upon a critical faculty wise in the ways of images, upon the capacity to distinguish trustworthy from deceitful images, that is, upon visual literacy. These factors may lend urgency to their willingness to write about the movies, but a personal commitment to the character and quality of narrative in the "literature" of our time is their presiding motive.

Although practioners and students of verbal art, the contributors to this book are decidedly not amateur commentators on the movies. They bring to their response to the movies a highly and appropriately disciplined intelligence. The movies are, after all, a composite art, and, since the talkies, have almost invariably had a literary component. Even when words have not been overly prominent in the finished work, a movie has had a verbal title and has begun with a literary property, usually a novel or a play, which is made into a script by a writer. Admittedly, although born as literature, movies metamorphose into visual art. But as long as a title and dialogue remain, the literary component is there, and these writers, equipped in both the discursive and aesthetic dimensions of language, are unparalleled critics of at least this component of movie art.

But verbal storytelling is done by means of images too, though the images are evoked indirectly before the mind's eye by words rather than being directly revealed to physical sight. Imagery is natural to literature, but modern literature, fiction as well as poetry, is structured around image clusters not primarily arranged in chronological or logical sequence. Thus it has had a pronounced cinematic quality. Furthermore, recent literary criticism has treated imagery as the golden bough for entrance into literature's secret realms. All their training, albeit unintentionally, has endowed these writers with cinematic alertness. As storytellers and students of story they are eminently acquainted with what narrative art is devoted to accomplishing aesthetically and with its means for doing so. Armed with a vocabulary and methods for handling narrative, they have a sharp eye for detecting art and aesthetic coherence. These writers, consequently, are as sensitive, accomplished, and adept as any moviegoer, whatever his background, is likely to be.

Still, this collection of essays is essentially a literary view of the movies. The writers for the most part wisely stay within their legitimate province, commenting sparingly on photographic qualities and concentrating mainly upon narrative and humanistic ones. Despite its limitations, this approach fills a large gap in criticism of the movies, counterbalancing the professional craftsman and the reviewer, and should contribute to a discussion more to the aesthetic point than has previously taken place. At any rate, it is definitely time for the humanist to have his say alongside the technician and the professional and to exert his influence alongside the businessman. Certainly, the literary point of view has been relatively unstated and deserves a hearing. Even if the movies are produced with machines and are a business subject to corporate and financial pressures, they are also, inevitably, a human enterprise, and it is by their human relevance that they must, in the end, prove their worthiness.

What these essays collectively attest to more than anything else, then, is that the movies—their making, their audience, and their criticism—are undergoing personalization and thus humanization. The overall pressure of the essays is an insistent demand that the movies are and can be something more than rhetoric, a sincere, trustworthy vision committed to nothing but the truth, talking honestly and with heartfelt passion. In spite of the industry's inherent resistance, progress has been made in this direction. Much remains to be accomplished, however. Since we have to live with the movies, we would prefer not to be embarrassed by them; we want the chance to exercise our humanity in and through the movies, and so we persist in demanding that the movies make more room for man within their aesthetic boundaries.

We would not, by any means, take the fun out of movies in order to fit them into the traditional earnestness associated with education. What remains of crass commercialism and middle-class dowdiness which once sapped the strength of the movies is dispensable, but the aim is, and should be, a higher hedonism which more profoundly entertains the heart and mind. With the existing film classics and the fifteen to twenty a year from around the world capable of captivating attention—probably as high a proportion as in the other arts—there are enough good and great movies for us to grow by. The movies can arouse the mind and soul when given undivided attention. And they can be shaped in turn by those who will speak up, pressing toward greater dignity and excellence for both maker and viewer through such a humanistic dialogue as is conducted by the contributors to this book.

W.R.R.

the ART
and ITS
FORMS

ALAN S. DOWNER

The Monitor Image

In 1933 Henry J. Forman fulminated in print about *Our Movie-Made Children.* I must at once confess that I am a member of that unhappy group. The weeks of my childhood were marked off first by Saturday matinees and then by Friday nights at the Elmwood Theater in Syracuse, by Mary Pickford and Douglas Fairbanks, and by Tom Mix and Hoot Gibson. Later, Harvard was the nucleus of a ring of neighborhood cinemas where the double features were changed twice weekly. You went to the movies every night, you saw everything. The good ones you laughed and cried with, you talked back to the bad ones. Movies were a part of your routine like Shredded

13

Wheat or the subway to Boston. A few solemn sociology majors talked about middle-class myths and one or two avant-gardists exchanged references to Eisenstein and René Claire, but the habitual audience was indifferent to anything beyond the necessity of being in the presence of any movie at all.

It is a little startling for a member of the movie-made generation to discover that the idle pastime of his youth is an art and to be taken seriously. And it is difficult for him to know how to be serious about movies. I am sometimes tempted to suspect that serious movie criticism in this country began with the release of Eric von Stroheim's film treatment of Frank Norris' *McTeague* in 1923, twenty years after narrative films began being generally distributed. Von Stroheim's film, *Greed,* set out to capture Norris' naturalistic attitude—to deal with the lowly, in their grubby milieu, without glamor, and to present human motivation in its ugliest, anti-heroic undress. The hero is a dentist caught up by a passion for gold which eventually destroys him and all who come in contact with him. To complete the visual realization of his message, von Stroheim turned to color—not technicolor (the film was shot in black and white), but hand-tinting. Every object in the picture that was yellow by nature appeared in hand-tinted yellow on the screen. Gold teeth, gold canary in the dentist's office; gold money changed hands; the heroine, corrupted, buries herself in a shower of yellow coins; the final scene of murder and vengeance occurs on a desert under a glaring golden sun. Even newspaper reviewers could not miss the theme—or the device by which it was reinforced. They discovered that the movies employed *symbolism,* and once you are able to use the word *symbol* you are in business as a critic.

Since *Greed* there has been a flood of books about the movies— many are fan-oriented and fan-written and can be dismissed as criticism; many are written by sociologists and psychologists and can be dismissed as criticism; but many are intended to establish and develop a critical approach to evaluation and cannot be lightly dismissed. Indeed they cannot be lightly read, or lightly understood, because they are not lightly written. Many of them are written by men who profess to know what they call the grammar of the film,

but who don't seem to care much about the grammar of English.
I am perhaps somewhat out of step with the times in believing that
the function of the critic is to open paths *into* his subject, rather
than to erect a maze to be penetrated only by persistence or good
fortune. The best criticism is always an act of love, written with
enthusiasm and belief—and sometimes sorrow: the film criticism of
James Agee, for instance. I would have to set this kind of criticism
against the constipated aestheticism which used to come out of Germany or the nebulous incantations of the current French *cinéastes.*

How do you talk about a film anyway? We know several useful
ways of talking about a poem, or a drama, or a painting, or a
concerto. Why not apply them to the film? For one simple reason—in
the other media there is always one stage on which it is possible
to focus as the work of a creator—the unperformed score, the unproduced play script. A film can only be discussed in its projected
totality: the collaborative product of the talent and creative inspiration of screenwright, director, cameraman, composer, editor (and
many other contributing Indians; these are only the chiefs). It is
true that a concerto or a play performed brings other talents into
collaboration with the original creator: yet it is generally true (if
the original creator is on hand to keep a watchful eye on his work)
that these other talents are seeking to flesh out, interpret, express
what has been entrusted to them—the composer, the playwright remains the ultimate controlling force.

But in the process of film-making, though there is sometimes, but
not always, something called a screenplay which is referred to by
film-makers, the personality of the star may determine the nature of
the leading character, the director may determine the tone, the
cameraman the empathy, the composer the emotion, and the editor
or cutter the final structure.

Thus the process of film-making complicates immeasurably that
function which the critic of literature takes to be his first business,
the discovery of the unity and style of the work confronting him. This
may account for the arguments about the morality of James Bond,
the sociological implications of the adventures of Doris Day, or the
mystic revelations of the western which take the place of criticism,

in the conventional literary sense, of such films. Yet in the process of film-making lie the beginnings of an approach to film criticism.

Some years ago I was permitted a ten-minute audience with a great film producer, just two weeks before he was to become a great ex-producer. And he gave me the phrase which provided a key for my own understanding of the art of the film in general. He declared that style and unity in a film depend upon all the creative talents constantly looking at the same *monitor image*. He was referring, of course, to the bank of screens in the director's room of a television studio, each screen connected with a single camera which is concentrating on its own particular segment of the total scene or angle shot of the performers. From these multiple images the director selects the one which is to be transmitted to the spectator.

Monitor image is doubly useful. First, because it insists on the multiple points of view which are the constant danger to the unity of a work of film art, and second, because it insists on the film as an art primarily visual, to be seen. The relevance of the phrase and its implications become particularly apparent when you re-experience old films on the Late Show, the great cinema repertory theater. Despite the impertinent intrusions of mentholated waterfalls, eager-eater dogs, foundation garments, and deodorants, how readily certain films re-involve the spectator, resume their tone and tension as if no interruption had occurred. In part, such films are inviolable because the camera eye has never been permitted to stray from the monitor image, which is the inward eye of the creative film-maker.

Such is John Huston, and when he is performing as a true film artist, he has created a number of inviolable works of film art. The monitor image of *The Maltese Falcon* is unwavering because it is his, firmly his, throughout, however much he may have made use of Dashiell Hammett and Humphrey Bogart. The achievement of *Treasure of the Sierra Madre* evolves from his instinct for visual conception and expression.

Huston entered the films as a writer, but as a writer who worked best with a collaborator. As he once said, when he put pencil to paper he found himself sketching, turning to visual rather than verbal expression. In *What Makes Sammy Run,* the best work ever written about the movies, Budd Schulberg inserted a true and illuminating anecdote about the first Hollywood producer to bring first-rate writers to the service of the screen. He had engaged a leading novelist and playwright to develop a scenario about a philandering husband. It was to open by exposing the fact that husband and wife were growing apart. In two weeks the novelist produced a twenty-page scene of brilliantly written dialogue establishing this initial premise. Not a line could be cut; it was sharp, clear, amusing, and full of character. The author was somewhat disconcerted when the producer pointed out that, brilliant though it was, it was wholly unsuited for the medium. He then summoned an old movie hand who could hardly write a coherent sentence, but who had begun his career in the great talent nursery of Mack Sennett. Within an hour the scenarist handed them an envelope on the back of which he had written:

INTERIOR ELEVATOR MEDIUM SHOT
Husband and wife in evening clothes. Husband wearing a top hat.
REVERSE ANGLE
As elevator door opens and classy dame enters.
CLOSE SHOT HUSBAND AND WIFE
Get husband's reaction to new dame. Removes hat with a flourish. Wife looks from dame to husband's hat to husband. Then glares at him as we
CUT.

Particularly since the advent of sound, moviemakers have constantly to be reminded that their art is primarily visual, that words are expendable. This was a lesson that John Huston never had to learn. He was a natural-born film-maker.

In itself, of course, to be a natural-born film-maker is no guarantee of the quality of the final product. Some are born great, but few achieve greatness, and one had greatness thrust upon him. Charlie Chaplin and Henry King were innate film-makers, completely unselfconscious about technical skill but with a clear conception of character and consequence. John Ford became great through a fortunate collaboration with a serious writer and the discovery of a theme at

which both could work with conviction. D. W. Griffith had greatness
thrust upon him by critics fascinated and instructed by his inventive
use of the camera and willing to ignore his abysmal sentimentality
and his disconcerting propensity for turning up on the wrong side
of any issue he chanced to deal with.

Without making a value judgment at this point, I would place
Huston in the Chaplin-King category. He was visually oriented, he
was an experienced writer, and he had seen enough of the world to
be able to write about it seriously. Before going to Hollywood he had
been a boxer, a reporter, and a Mexican cavalryman. He had published short stories in *The American Mercury,* written a folk play,
Frankie and Johnny, and directed several Broadway shows. He had
also written a strong, semidocumentary drama, *In Time to Come,*
about Woodrow Wilson and the League of Nations in collaboration
with Howard Koch. The collaborator kept Huston's pencil from
sketching.

He was thus prepared for the madhouse of "writers' row" at Warner
Brothers. Here scripts were regularly written by teams and rewritten
(and sometimes again and again) by different teams. A shooting
script might be the laminations of six or ten writers' work (carefully
distinguished in the final product—each revised page inserted by a
particular team being typed on a particular colored paper). There
was no attempt to hide collaboration; the great emperor L. B. Mayer
had pointed out that "The number one book of the ages was written
by a committee, and it was called the Bible."

Huston wrote a number of scripts committee fashion, among them
High Sierra, in which Humphrey Bogart was starred. Bogart was a
happy accident for Huston—the hero could just as well have been
Edward G. Robinson or James Cagney, or John Garfield. Then Huston
and his teammate Allen Rivkin were assigned the dramatization of
Dashiel Hammett's *The Maltese Falcon.* Rivkin protested that Warner Brothers had already made one version of the novel, but Huston
declared that that script hadn't touched the essential nature of Hammett's work (not that this bothered screenwriters in general, but
Huston was clearly up to something). Rivkin and Huston set to work
at the first task, which was to break the story exactly as written by

Hammett into shots, scenes, and dialogue as the basis for future development. Somehow a copy got into the hands of the studio boss, who
read it and told Huston to get the script before the cameras at once.

Huston took his cue for the picture from the mistake of his master.
In a letter some years later he reduced the long process of making a
film to three paragraphs:

> The Maltese Falcon was produced three times before I did it, never with
> very much success, so I decided on a radical procedure: to *follow* the book
> rather than depart from it. This was practically an unheard of thing to do
> with any picture taken from a novel, and marks the beginning of a great
> epoch in picture making.
>
> More seriously speaking, it seems to me that each and every picture sub-
> ject calls for a specific technique. Obviously a horror tale and a pastoral
> should not be photographed through the same lenses. I attempted, in making
> The Falcon, to transpose Dashiell Hammett's highly individual prose style
> into camera terms: i.e. sharp photography, geographically exact camera
> movements; striking, if not shocking, set-ups.
>
> One other thing may bear pointing out: as the book is told entirely from
> the standpoint of Sam Spade so also is the picture. Spade is in every scene
> save one (the murder of his partner). The audience knows no more and no
> less than he does. All the other characters in the story are introduced only
> as they meet Spade, and the attempt was made, upon their appearance, to
> photograph them through his eyes, as it were. This, too, was something of an
> innovation at that time. Since then, of course, the camera itself has served
> as protagonist.

The real collaboration in *The Maltese Falcon* was between Huston
and Hammett, though I am not aware that they ever met. It resulted
in, possibly, the most successful screen realization of a novel ever
achieved. Sometimes, if you have not read a particular novel for
many years, *Great Expectations,* say, the screen version may seem
very successful. If you reread the novel after seeing the film, however,
you may become disgruntled—the movie brings out all the essentially
melodramatic character of a Dickens plot without the ameliorating
power of Dickens' style, his deliberate discursiveness. But read *The
Maltese Falcon* even several months after you have seen the film and
the very vocal mannerisms and intonations of Bogart and Greenstreet
and Lorre speak to you from the printed page.

Scene for scene, character for character, speech for speech, and often gesture for gesture, Huston is rigorously faithful to Hammett. The first part of the novel is virtually the shooting script. However, as he approaches his climax Huston permits himself a few cuts. The political overtones written into Spade's interview with the district attorney are excised—but not for political reasons. Gutman's daughter disappears and the relations between Cairo and the gunsel are not mentioned—but not for reasons of modesty. The spectator is not told why Spade is sent to the empty lot in Burlingame, or how the La Paloma caught fire—but not for reasons of careless plotting. Huston never forgot that he was building a dramatic experience and, having opened with a driving tempo, he could not allow the pace to slacken in the last reels. A few critics did complain about loose ends, but not audiences—unless on second thought. The screenwright, like the playwright, is concerned with immediate experience, not second thoughts. And perhaps the best film criticism reflects *first thoughts*.

Much of the success of *The Maltese Falcon* can be assigned to the principle of the monitor image. Huston wrote it, cast it, directed it, supervised the camera setups. If he did not edit the final product, he gave the editor shots so tightly composed that there was little chance that the monitor would be blurred. Critics began at once talking about the "Huston style."

The *Falcon* does have a style, but it is a style dictated by the matter and the intent of the original writer, Hammett. *Across the Pacific*, written by Richard Macaulay and produced in the next year with the same photographers and very nearly the same cast as *Falcon*, has a very different style. The intent was to show that the Japanese were dangerous, clever, and very much in possession, to create an understanding in the audience that the enemy was dangerous precisely because of a way of life, a culture, an ancient pride that credibly commands respect and heroic loyalty. The characters are presented with deliberate ambiguity. Bogart plays Bogart, and the audience is allowed to guess whether he will be Bogart the renegade, Bogart the scheming gangster, Bogart the misunderstood hero. Mary Astor could be distressed maiden, smart adventuress, Mata Hari. She had been those things in the past without altering an expression or a hairdo. Huston deliberately takes advantage of the limitations of the Hollywood actor: that the evaluation of his character in a given picture depends on what happens to him, rather than how he plays a role, since he always projects his own personality. By such means Huston imposed a style on *Across the Pacific*, which, aside from its concluding sequence, makes it a highly credible film, even today after the drastic shifts in political alignments since the war.

Huston made *Treasure of the Sierra Madre* after the break in his career during which he served in the armed forces and made a number of remarkable documentaries for the War Department. And *Treasure* reveals a different "Huston style"—ruthless, naturalistic, to be sure, but essentially different from the sharp economy of *Falcon*. And this time the style is imposed by the director on the original story. The novel is loosely written, careless or obscure about time and place or the definition of character. B. Traven, the mysterious novelist, is said to have written from his own experience, but the resultant story is a minor pastime loaded with Marxism, while the film is an unforgettable experience loaded with humanity.

The monitor image is again unwavering. Script, casting, directing—all are Huston's, and it would be difficult to cite a more painstakingly constructed scenario. Traven's theme, if he has one, is that only the laborer is worthy of respect. Huston completely reinterpreted the action with the broader theme of gold as corrupter. He is at great pains to dignify his hero (Fred C. Dobbs), to show him as an honorable, considerate man. He shows him using some of the money he has cadged for a shave; when he beats senseless a man who owes him money, he plunders his wallet but scornfully returns what is not owing him; when his lottery ticket turns up a winner, he generously contributes more than his share to get the expedition going.

In the novel the comrades quarrel just from the monotony of being together; Huston makes the quarrel the first sign of the breakdown of an admirable man. He adds the memorable sequence in which each man goes to see if his "goods" are untouched in the night. To increase the dramatic tension he next adds the iguana scene as a climax of this stage in the revelation of his theme.

Critics complained of the excessive violence of the brawl in the cantina, but is not this (like the sergeant's report of Macbeth's battle performance) a first hint of the instability of Fred C. Dobbs? So, too, Huston shifts the bandit attack on the train from late in the novel, where it is narrated by the newcomer to create suspense, to the second sequence of the film as the comrades are en route to their point of departure. Dobbs is so overcome with nervous excite-ment—elation?—that he does not hear the conductor reveal that the enemy has been driven off by a brigade of soldiers assigned to the train, and cannot understand Howard as he calmly resumes his dis-cussion of the terrain they are about to encounter.

One other Huston addition affects the style of the film. In the novel Dobbs, returning alone to the village, stops to rest and is overtaken by bandits. The scene in the film is unforgettable—the thirst-crazed hero plunging his face into the brackish pool, the sudden appearance of the reflected face of the chief bandit beside his own. This is not melodrama, for it is meant to reveal, not to startle. But if it is symbolism, it is so subsumed into the actuality of the film as to increase tension without destroying mood.

Like many artists whose work is valued for its technical facility, Huston disclaims interest in technique as a matter of study or plan-ning. "It is a curious thing," he once said, "that so many people ascribe to me a distinct style. Believe me I am not conscious of any such thing. Whenever I undertake to direct a film, I do so out of the deep feeling it inspires in me. It is precisely this feeling that dic-tates the way in which I direct a picture. It is a matter of spontaneous sensitivity."

In discussing film style I have introduced elements that seem to have to do with characterization, preparation, development of the story line, whereas in the study of literature style is more usually restricted to diction and syntax. Perhaps it is not necessary to point out that each of the elements I have cited is pictorially, not verbally, presented. Style in the film is determined by the shots the director chooses to photograph, the setup and duration of these shots, and their organization into the larger units of the total picture.

It is not difficult to recognize the difference between literary and theatrical style. What the writer effects by control of language is transferred to what the performing arts call "visuals." Thus most television viewers would recognize the "Dragnet style": the intercutting of extreme close-ups to match precisely the monosyllabic give-and-take of the dialogue, a deliberate de-romanticizing of the whodunit, the chief romantic form of twentieth-century fiction. And so, less correctly, moviegoers might describe the "DeMille style": the spectacular interweaving of a thousand camels, half a thousand dancing girls, and acres of cyclopean architecture. It is worth pointing out that this is not the DeMille style at all.

DeMille knew that spectacle is both breathtaking and, ultimately, without emotional content, and he knew that the success of a film depended on the response of the mass audience to the emotional content of his scenes. So he first establishes the spectacular in a series of long shots—the flight of the Israelites, the street parade of the Greatest Show on Earth—and then, with almost mathematical calculation, he intercuts close shots of the individuals who compose the spectacle: a lost child, crying; an old woman tugging at a burro; a tattered clown. It was a trick first explored by Griffith (for example, the Gettysburg sequence of *The Birth of a Nation*), but it became the trademark of DeMille.

In discussing their own work artists are frequently blowing out a smoke screen to cover their ignorance of what they have actually done. But Huston's practice (aside from *Falcon*) seems to correspond exactly to his statements. Most of what is written about him in the serious, or pseudo-serious, film journals is a record of a visit to some location where he happens to be shooting and a somewhat bewildered description of his procedure. In a medium that has relied more and more on pre-planning as it has become more and more financially perilous, Huston alone seems to preserve the silent film technique of shooting off the cuff, adding new scenes ad-lib to the script as the shooting proceeds. But when the monitor image is firm, the new inventions are pertinent and sometimes add texture or reinforcement to the theme.

The most fully reported of all Huston's pictures-in-the-making, *The Red Badge of Courage,* provides two instances of happy improvisation. The monitor image of the film, at least for a while, was the equal unreasonableness of both cowardice and heroism, and the basic script, prepared by Huston, developed the outlines of the idea very clearly. But a film must find many visual ways of reinforcing its theme.

During the day when the climactic charge across the hayfield was being shot, Huston noticed one young soldier wearing steel-rimmed spectacles. The soldier had been chosen to stumble and be shot during the charge. Suddenly Huston called a halt to the large scene and went over and talked with the soldier. Then he summoned the cameraman and set up a close shot for which the company was completely unprepared. On the screen the charge is interrupted by a head and shoulders view of the soldier kneeling, fumbling for his lost glasses, finding them, hooking them carefully over his ears, and then collapsing in death. A completely cinematic—wordless—presentation of the theme.

Or again, on location, Huston suddenly felt the desire to underline the contrast between the timorous heroics of the volunteers and the cynicism of the veterans. He improvised a sequence in which the general rides from one encampment of volunteers to another throughout the battle line. To each group he speaks words of praise and encouragement and concludes by promising that he will take supper with them when the battle is over. Finally he comes to a group of veterans with whom he shares his meager supplies. As the general rides off, a mocking voice rises out of the band of professionals, "Ain't you goin' to take supper with us after the battle?"

To project an idea in image and action is the particular problem of the film-maker, and it is not surprising that—only after the actual shooting commences—even the most experienced can discover how little he has been relying on the camera to make his points.

In the simplest terms *The Maltese Falcon* and *Treasure of the Sierra Madre* are the same story, seen through different lenses. Both are based on the most cinematic of all plots, a chase—specifically a quest for treasure (a jeweled bird, bags of gold) —ultimately frustrated. They are what in France are now called *films noirs:* brutal, misogynistic, outside the purlieus of domesticated justice and the law. The hero is equivocal, though his ultimate object is unequivocally money; the heroine (only in *Falcon,* of course) is worthy of neither love nor respect. Huston's ultimate interest in this basic plot is not in the quest but in the frustration, in how the quester "takes it." And his admiration obviously is for the Howard of *Treasure* who is man enough to laugh at the maliciousness of fate.

Falcon is complex in plot, or at least in the ordering of its situations, but not very complex in characterization. The spare, simple style and the clean, streamlined driving tempo depended, as Huston said, upon "setups," the posing and lighting of the actors for each shot. In the routine film a scene or a sequence will begin with an establishing shot, likely as not a shot of the setting in which the early action will develop. But in the *Falcon* each scene begins with action in process.

To introduce Bogart as Sam Spade the camera pans down from an office window (with the sign "Spade and Archer") to the actor's back as he is swinging around in his chair to face the lens. Scenes begin with characters halfway through an opening door or in the midst of a telephone conversation. As we return to Bogart after he has been beaten senseless in Greenstreet's apartment, he is already shifting on his elbows. In the same fashion scenes end before the action has been quite concluded. The camera fades out as it zooms in on a burning paper with Mary Astor's address and fades in at once on a car coming to a stop at her apartment. Events occur without preparation; as Spade is phoning in a close shot, Iva's arm enters the screen. In a similar shot, Spade is again on the phone with Cairo's hand holding an umbrella in the foreground. The umbrella disappears and a reverse angle shot shows Cairo brandishing a pistol at Spade.

By such setups Huston maintains the point of view on Spade and captures the driving pace of the novel. There is a good deal of trickery in the film, which might be just a gimmicky private-eye tale were it not for the structural emphasis on Sam Spade's reactions throughout. For example, Huston is constantly raising and lowering the camera's viewpoint in looking at characters. With Greenstreet this is an organic device; with some of the other characters it seems a device to stimulate the audience's eye.

However, two other kinds of setups powerfully affect the inner dramatic quality of the film and will prove adaptable to more serious purposes. In a three shot, Mary Astor on the left faces Peter Lorre on the right as they discuss the past; Bogart, in the background between them, looks up quizically as if to decide which is the more skillful liar. This setup is employed with greater pertinence to both plot development and character revelation in *Treasure:* in the flophouse old Howard sits on his cot, having delivered his worldly wise lecture on greed, and looks first at Curtin and then at Dobbs as they declare their immunity from such passions. The setup declares the theme more effectively than a paragraph of commentary and raises the dramatic question which it is the business of the rest of the film to answer.

Again, as the *Falcon* approaches its climax, Huston suddenly stops its breathless advance and treats in quite another fashion the long night which the strangely assorted characters must spend together. He places them in Spade's apartment, fixes them into a receding triangle—and holds the camera on them for shots of unusual duration, particularly after the crisp movement that has preceded. The tension, uneasiness, explosiveness of their relationship become almost tangible, and the spectator is persuaded that the next speech may ignite the catastrophe, perhaps even before the falcon is brought in. A film shot of long duration without change of angle or setup is risky; it may suggest theater rather than cinema, may lose rather than engage the spectator. The trick, as Huston reveals, is to use it at that moment in the action when it is the only suitable device for conveying the emotional content of a situation. But the greater trick, available only to the natural-born film-maker, is to know when the moment has arrived. Moviemaking, like any art, has its mysteries that neither critical rules nor the most subtle analysis can penetrate.

Treasure confronted Huston with three problems, his solution to which defined his achievement as a film-maker. Two of the problems are not unusual in dealing with a popular art form that tends to repeat patterns and situations: to find a fresh way to handle conventional situations *and* to develop the story by the emotional rather than the intellectual content of scenes. The third problem was more special—how to avoid turning the film into an allegory.

Classifying the film as a chase suggests the familiarity of the pattern; it begins with *The Great Train Robbery* in 1903 and is the characteristic action of a thousand westerns and slapstick comedies and of many of the films that are landmarks in cinematic history: *The Birth of a Nation, Tol'able David, Robin Hood, Greed, The Covered Wagon, The Informer.* One instance of Huston's ability to new-coin an expected situation visually, without relying on dialogue, is the barroom brawl, the cinéquanon of the genre. Most directors are content with the action of the scene itself—breakaway tables, shattered mirrors, gunned-out kerosene lamps, a two-man quarrel developing into a general melee of satisfying but meaningless destruction. Huston never loses sight of his monitor image; whatever happens is directly pertinent to the action and meaning of the total film.

No one is involved in the fight except Dobbs, Curtin, and their enemy. The cantina is empty. And the cantina is not destroyed; no tables are shattered by quaint devices, and the glassware is untouched. Dobbs and Curtin are simply and singly out to get what is owing them. But this is no slugging match from *The Spoilers,* either; it is seen from within. The versatile and penetrating camera rises high to look down on Bogart skidding across the floor on his buttocks, peers closely from below as McCormack's fist smashes into Curtin's throat, and then draws back for a long shot along the bar as McCormack spins back and forth between his victims, propelled by their machine-like, unemotional blows: a preparation for Dobbs' refusal to take more money than is coming to him.

Since *Treasure* was composed from a firmly moral point of view, there was always the temptation to "say what you mean" rather than to "show what you mean." Huston's ability to devise fresh visuals whose emotional content is their meaning could be illustrated in nearly every scene of the film: after shooting Curtin, Dobbs returns to the fire, to sleep; through the ragged rising and falling of the flame we see his eye—open, staring. So, when the first gold is shared

out, the setup of Dobbs' close-up is so lighted that his eyes become
hard and glittering. To the discovery of the gold Howard responds
with a wild, animal-like dance. The windstorm sweeps the gold dust
back to its element.

The third problem, the avoidance of allegory, was certainly faced,
if not completely solved. In his alterations of the original novel
Huston was most particular in developing the character of Dobbs. In
the novel he is little more than a name moving through paragraphs
of action. In a dramatization he could come dangerously close to being
Everyman or Greed. Huston tries to insist on the reality and the
individuality of his hero. In the opening sequence he is cadging
money in the marketplace of a Latin American village. A tall man
in a white suit gives him a coin. A few scenes later he approaches
the same man with the same request, but when the man rebuffs him,
he is frank: "I just looked at your hand." In a later sequence a
young urchin tries to sell Dobbs a lottery ticket. Dobbs refuses, the
boy persists, Dobbs threatens, the boy persists, Dobbs douses him with
water, the boy still persists, and Dobbs, in admiration, surrenders.
Most important is the relationship established between Dobbs and
Howard, the old prospector. It begins on a level of generosity and
devil-may-care fellowship; only the acquisition of property, of a future, leads to its destruction. The emphasis is on irony, not on allegory.

Allegory is a particular temptation in *Treasure,* but symbolism is
a constant threat to film art. For one thing it may become so noticeable that audiences will observe the symbols and ignore the film. It
is a threat because any narrative that works with visuals is in a sense
symbolic. Even *Falcon,* ruthlessly realistic as it may be, ends with a
close-up of Mary Astor, prison bound, as the iron bars of an elevator
door close across her face. And perhaps the empty bag of gold
caught in the cactus plant at the end of *Treasure* is a symbolic statement. It is easy to make the symbol into an overstatement.

A symbol can avoid calling attention to itself and still perform its
function. In *Treasure,* after the bandits have been executed, a rising
wind blows the leader's big straw hat into the grave he has dug for
himself. But the hat has threaded its way through the entire film in

various moments of significant action (it is not here first introduced for symbolic purposes), and the rising wind is the first sign of the "Norther" that will bring about the end of the quest.

If *Treasure of the Sierra Madre* is not a masterpiece or a landmark in American film history, it is at least a superior performance, and each viewing enriches the spectator's experience. And it is a great advance over the skill displayed in *Falcon*. The earlier film was content with a masterly working out of a complex story; *Treasure*, essentially a simple story, is concerned with the effect of action and experience or character on the gradual revelation of general human truth.

I said earlier that Huston was successful when he was behaving like the natural-born film-maker he is. The sad fact is that he is more often unsuccessful. He is quickly bored with projects; two-thirds of the way through a current film he will begin planning on another. Worse still, he is capable of letting his own eye wander from the monitor.

The Red Badge of Courage has become a classic instance, because of Lillian Ross's account of its production. Although Huston began with a firm idea, he allowed himself to be distracted. First the central idea was that courage was as unreasoning as cowardice. Later it became the pointlessness of the hero's courage in helping to capture a fragment of wall (the *Treasure* theme). Then it was that the youth was simply a victim of fate; he gets on a sort of roulette wheel for a few days and is finally flung off. As the patchwork picture emerged from the MGM factory, the audience was told, in solemn narration, that this was the story of how a youth became a man. Thus deprived of a monitor image, *The Red Badge of Courage* could have neither style nor unity and, questions of art aside, could not yield a satisfying dramatic experience to its audience.

One recalls, regretfully, the great visuals that went to waste for the lack of this monitor image: the death of the tall soldier; the youth, carrying his flag, stalking the dying confederate flag bearer; the two flags crossed over the dying Reb. And all for what—what's Reb or youth to us, that we should weep for them?

In a very productive career Huston has had enough successes to assure himself a place on the Late Show for many years to come, but he has also sinned against his talent. Is he the lesser artist for this? I think not. The artist who chooses to work in a popular medium inevitably manufactures much that is better forgotten after its immediate purpose has been served—Dickens, Trollope, Hemingway: they too had their lesser moments. Their great moments were composed for the same great audience, whose vitality and appetite were both challenge and reward.

MARTIN C. BATTESTIN

Osborne's *Tom Jones*: Adapting a Classic

The announcement in the late summer of 1962 that Britain's "Angry Young Men" of the theater—John Osborne and Tony Richardson—were making a movie of Henry Fielding's masterpiece occasioned among my colleagues, the professional Augustans of the academy, a reaction closer to shock than surprise. Neither was there much comfort in the knowledge that Albert Finney, fresh from his role in that equally angry film *Saturday Night and Sunday Morning*, was to appear (think of it!) as Fielding's open-hearted and bumptious hero. When one allowed oneself to think of it at all, one had only uneasy expectations of the rowdy and irreverent treatment Fielding's classic was in for. Instead, what one saw on the screen was one of the most successful cinematic adaptations of a novel ever made, and, what is more, one of the most imaginative of comic films, a classic in its own right.

To understand the success of this film as an adaptation of the novel is, fundamentally at least, to notice the curious fact that some of the best writers of our own times have found congenial the literary modes and methods of the English Augustan Age—of which Fielding's comic epic of low life was the last major achievement. We are ourselves in a new age of satire, witnessing the dubious victories of what R. W. B. Lewis has called "the picaresque saint." Saul Bellow in *The Adventures of Augie March,* Jack Kerouac in *On the Road,* John Barth in *The Sot-Weed Factor* have exploited in various ways and for various effects the conventional form of the journey novel. George Garrett, whose recent book *Do, Lord, Remember Me* is a masterful comic celebration of the boundless possibilities of the human spirit for folly and degradation, and for love and glory, has traced the source of his inspiration to Chaucer and to Fielding. The spirit of Swift in *Gulliver's Travels* is not far from that of the "theater of the absurd," from Ionesco's rhinoceroses or Beckett's endgame—the symbolic fantasies of a fallen and dehumanized world. But the appeal of Fielding's comic vision for the contemporary writer has been nowhere better seen than in Kingsley Amis' healthy satire of the Establishment, *Lucky Jim,* and nowhere better expressed than by Bowen, the young writer of Amis' *I Like It Here,* who, standing before the white stone sarcophagus in which the author of *Tom Jones* rests near Lisbon, reflects on the significance of the master:

Bowen thought about Fielding. Perhaps it was worth dying in your forties if two hundred years later you were the only non-contemporary novelist who could be read with unaffected and wholehearted interest, the only one who never had to be apologised for or excused on the grounds of changing taste. And how enviable to live in the world of his novels, where duty was plain, evil arose out of malevolence and a starving wayfarer could be invited indoors without hesitation and without fear. Did that make it a simplified world? Perhaps, but that hardly mattered beside the existence of a moral seriousness that could be made apparent without the aid of evangelical puffing and blowing.

There is, it would seem, a fundamental rapport between Bowen and his kind and the master novelist of an age which found satiric laughter the most congenial antidote to the perversion of order and the corruption of the Establishment, the most effective way of protesting the betrayal of humane ideals by the forces of venality and barbarism.

To say, however, that the film *Tom Jones* is a successful adaptation of the novel is not to equate the two works in purpose or effect. One of the most distinguished eighteenth-century scholars of our time—a man of eminent wit and urbanity—told me that he walked out of the premiere New York showing of the movie (October, 1963) dejected and irritated at how widely Osborne and Richardson had missed the point of Fielding's book. What my friend failed to find in the film was not Fielding's panoramic impression of English life two centuries ago, nor was it Fielding's hearty, brawling comedy, which the film so admirably captures. What is missing from the film is exactly that quality which Amis' hero singled out as the distinctive characteristic of Fielding's fictional world—namely, that "moral seriousness" which underlies all of Fielding's humor and his satire and which makes of *Tom Jones* not merely a frivolous, if delightful, romp through English society, but a complex symbolic expression of its author's Christian vision of life. Fielding's vision is comic in an ultimate sense: it sees the human drama being enacted within a cosmic system of order and of ascertainable moral values, a system in which the great frame of the universe and of human society is presided over by a just and benign Providence, which rewards the charitable and the virtuous and punishes the selfish and the hypocritical. It is a vision perhaps most succinctly summarized in these lines from the best philosophical poem of that age:

> All Nature is but Art, unknown to thee;
> All Chance, Direction, which thou canst not see;
> All Discord, Harmony, not understood;
> All partial Evil, universal Good. . . .

What occurs in the film—and, with the exception of Garrett's book, in those other modern works we have mentioned—is close to the superficial impulse of Augustan satire, in which human folly or depravity is the object either of olympian amusement or of savage indignation; but what is lacking is the faith in an ultimate moral and providential design which serves as a foil to vice and to social chaos. One cannot properly understand Pope's *Dunciad* without knowing that it was written by the author of the *Essay on Man*; one cannot understand *Gulliver's Travels* without knowing that its author was Dean of St. Patrick's; one cannot understand *Tom Jones* without being aware that its author was a staunch defender of the established Church and government—and that he believed wholeheartedly in the responsibility of the individual both to discipline his own passionate nature and to behave charitably toward his fellow men. To the writers of our new age of satire, Osborne among them, such faith in the order and coherency of things is naive; theirs is not, as Bowen put it, "a simplified world." Thus, whereas Fielding's novel is designed to fulfill his promise to recommend "the cause of religion and virtue" by endeavoring "to laugh mankind out of their favourite follies and vices," Osborne's film can make no more of this purpose than to prefer Tom's animal vitality and ingenuousness to the conniving of Blifil, or the pretentious metaphysics of Square, or the brutal pharisaism of Thwackum, or the jaded sexuality of Lady Bellaston. This moral opposition is, of course, very much a part of Fielding's own didactic intent, but in the novel a much larger and (to the dismay of self-complacent moderns let it be said) much less simplistic vision is operating. Ideally Fielding saw life, as he saw art, not merely as energy but as order: what he admired in men and in the natural world was a sort of benign exuberance rationally controlled and directed toward the achievement of a desirable end. The world of *Tom Jones* is dynamic, charged, as Coleridge remarked, with the energy of sunshine and laughter and love; and it is at the same time a celebration of that rational design which gives meaning to vitality, and which in fact alone makes it a source of joy and of wonder. *Tom Jones* is, on different levels, an assertion of the shaping powers of the Creator, of the artist (who, as Thackeray long ago observed, appears in this novel as a surrogate Providence), and of the moral man—the exemplar of what Fielding referred to in *Amelia* as "the Art of Life." Even the form of Fielding's novel embodies this meaning: the famous plot (Coleridge called it one of the three most perfect in all literature) in which every character and every event are organically interconnected and conspire to lead inexorably to the denouement; the much-discussed "hourglass structure" of the book, in which even the axioms of neo-classical aesthetics and architecture are scrupulously observed, producing a work balanced, symmetrical, proportionate, with the adventures at Upton standing as the keystone of the arch; the constant supervision of the narrative by the intrusive and omniscient author—such formal devices make the very fabric and texture of the novel a tacit assertion of the reality and value of design and order in the world.

The story itself is calculated to dramatize this lesson by depicting the near disastrous career of a young man possessed of every social and private virtue but one: Tom Jones is honest, brave, and generous, but he is imprudent. And prudence, as Allworthy explains, "is indeed the duty which we owe to ourselves"; it is the supreme rational virtue of both classical and Christian philosophy; it is the essence of wisdom, enabling the individual correctly to distinguish truth from appearances and to estimate the ultimate consequences of his actions. For want of this virtue Fielding's hero is cast out of "Paradise Hall," commits one good-natured indiscretion after another, and finds himself at last clapped into prison, rejected by Sophia and his foster father, and guilty (for all he knows) of incest and murder. In broad outline and in implication Jones's story is not unlike that of Spenser's Redcross Knight, who must also acquire prudence before he may be united with the fair Una—or, in Tom's case, with the "divine Sophia," whose name signifies that wisdom he has lacked. For Fielding a good heart and sexual prowess were much indeed, but they were not everything; for Osborne, apparently, they are all that really matters. In the film there is no sense of the hero's maturation, for there is never any question of his responsibility for what happens to him. In prison, having been informed that the woman he slept with at Upton was his own mother, Fielding's hero arrives at a crucial moment of self-recognition: "Sure . . . Fortune will never have done with me till she hath driven me to distraction. But why do I blame Fortune? I am myself the cause of all my misery. All the dreadful mischiefs which have befallen me are the consequences only of my own folly and vice." In the film, however, Jones is never informed of the supposed identity of Mrs. Waters, nor is he made to acknowledge his folly. His reunion with Sophie is not earned, nor, heralded by one of Finney's mischievous winks at the camera, does it have the joyous dignity and symbolic significance that Fielding invests it with. Osborne's happy ending is gratuitous, vintage Hollywood; Fielding's is— given the moral dimension which his comedy constantly implies— appropriate and necessary. Within the terms of his comic vision of an ordered and benign universe it is the only possible apocalypse. At the moment when Fielding's hero confesses his folly and learns the lesson of prudence, the prison doors miraculously open, his "crimes" are undone, his enemies exposed, his true identity discovered. His reconciliation with Allworthy and Sophia, the only father he has known and the only woman he has loved, follows inevitably.

My friend's feelings of dismay at the American première of the film were, one must grant, understandable. But if Osborne and Richardson missed a major intention behind Fielding's novel, they fully grasped and brilliantly recreated its essential spirit and manner. It is fruitless, of course, to require that the film reproduce the novel in its every scene and character. The problem of the adapter of fiction to the screen is more difficult by far than that of the translator of a novel or a play from one language to another. For one thing the rhetoric of the two art forms is fundamentally different: the arrangement of words in sequence is the business of the novelist, but the maker of a film deals in the arrangement of images. A second basic difference between the two forms is that of scope: Fielding may write on, as he does in *Tom Jones,* for a thousand pages or more, requiring the reader's attention for hours on end; Osborne and Richardson can expect us to lend them our eyes and ears for only a fraction of an evening, in this instance a little more than two hours. The two forms are similar, however, in that they may both be used for narrative purposes—for telling, or showing, a story—and they may adopt similar attitudes toward their subject and similar techniques of expression. They may be similar, but never identical. The "naturalism" of Zola in *Germinal,* let us say, is comparable to the stark realism of Rossellini's *Open City*; the symbolic fantasies of Kafka are comparable to the surrealism of Fellini's *8½*: on the one hand, the manner of expression is close to the factual, expository method of the historian; on the other hand, it approaches the supra-logical techniques of the poet.

Analogy is the key. To judge whether or not a film is a success-ful adaptation of a novel is to evaluate the skill of its makers in striking analogous attitudes and in finding analogous rhetorical tech-niques. From this point of view Osborne and Richardson produced in *Tom Jones* one of the most successful and imaginative adapta-tions in the brief history of film. This, as we have seen, is less true with regard to the authorial attitudes and ultimate thematic intentions of the two works. The real genius of the film as adapta-tion is in its brilliantly imaginative imitation of the *art* of the novel. Those "gimmicks" that so much surprised and delighted audiences may be seen as technical analogues of Fielding's own most dis-tinctive devices.

Consider, for example, the opening sequence of the film. Before the title and credits we are presented with a rapid succession of scenes done in affected mimicry of the manner of the silent film, with subtitles supplying both commentary and dialogue (even Mrs. Wilkins' "aah!" as she sees Allworthy in his nightshirt), and with John Addi-son's spirited harpsichord setting the mood in the manner of the upright of the old "flicker" days. The device serves several practical purposes, of course: exposition which required the better part of two books in the novel is presented here swiftly and economically; a playful comic tone is at once established; and the reminiscence of the earliest era of the cinema also serves to remind us that Fielding's book appeared at a comparable moment in the history of that other peculiarly modern genre, the novel. Less obviously, in the use of out-dated acting styles, exaggerated reactions and posturing, and sub-titles, Richardson and Osborne have translated into the medium of the cinema two aspects of Fielding's technique which contribute to the comic effect and distance. The overstated acting of the silent-film era is analogous to what may be called the "Hogarthian" manner (Fielding himself often made the comparison) of characterization in the novel. Even after spoken dialogue has been introduced (after the credits) and the need for pantomime is no longer present, Richardson continues to elicit heightened and hyperbolic performances from his actors—a style which, as in Hogarth and Fielding, serves not only to amuse, as caricature does, but also to reveal and accentuate the essential natures of the characters. As Fielding declared in *Joseph Andrews* (III, i), he described "not men, but manners; not an individual, but a species." Richardson's actors rarely behave in the understated, naturalistic manner of the conventional film: smiles become leers, glances become ogles, gestures are heightened into stances, posturings. Similarly Fielding's characters, like Hogarth's, verge on caricature: they do not ask, as Moll Flanders or Clarissa Harlowe or Dorothea Brooke or Emma Bovary asks, to be accepted as real people, but rather as types and emblems of human nature; they have the reality of symbol rather than of fact.

Just as the miming of the actors during the opening sequence establishes the hyperbolic style of the performances throughout, so Osborne's initial use of subtitles prepares us for the spoken commentary of the narrator, whose voice is the first we hear in the film and who will accompany us throughout as an invisible guide and observer. Osborne's commentator is a clever adaptation of Fielding's celebrated omniscient narrator, whose presence is constantly felt in *Tom Jones,* describing the action, making apposite observations on the characters' motives and deeds, entertaining us with his wit and learning, controlling our attitudes and responses. It has been remarked that the most important "character" in Fielding's novel is the author-narrator himself, whose genial and judicious spirit pervades the entire work, presiding providentially over the world of the novel and reminding us at every point that the creation we behold is his own. He it is who, more than any character in the story itself—more than Tom, more even than Allworthy—provides the moral center of the book. Osborne's commentator functions correspondingly: when first we see Tom, now a full-grown young scamp prowling for nocturnal sport in the woods, the over-voice of the commentator informs us that Tom is "far happier in the woods than in the study," that he is "as bad a hero as may be," that he is very much a member of the generation of Adam. Like Fielding's, Osborne's narrator presents his fallible hero, but the tone of wry amusement and clear affection for the character controls our own attitude, establishes that tolerant morality which makes Tom's peccadilloes far less important than his honest, warm-hearted zest for life. Though Fielding's narrator has the advantage of being continually present, Osborne's commentator is heard often enough so that his own relationship with the audience is sustained, and with each intrusion his own "personality" becomes more sharply defined: in matters of morality he is tolerant of everything but hypocrisy and inhumanity; he knows his Bible and his Ovid; he can recite a verse or apply an adage; he has a becoming sense of decorum in turning the camera away from a bawdy tumble in the bushes. Though necessarily a faint echo, he is very much the counterpart of Fielding's authorial voice.

A further effect of the constant intrusion of the narrator in both the film and the novel is to insure that the audience remains aloof and detached from the drama. We are never allowed to forget that this is not a slice of life, but only a tale told (or shown). The narrator is always there between the audience and the images on the screen, preventing the sort of empathic involvement which generally occurs in movies, or in fiction. Such detachment is very much a part of Fielding's comic purpose: his fictional world never pretends to be an imitation of life in any realistic sense, but is offered to us as a consciously contrived and symbolic representation of human nature and society. We are asked to behold it from a distance, at arm's length, as it were, to enjoy it and to learn from it.

The use of type characters and a self-conscious narrator are, moreover, only two of the means by which Fielding achieves this comic distance. The style of *Tom Jones* is itself highly mannered, not unlike the artful compositions of Hogarth, and it is often deliberately "rhetorical," not unlike the poetic diction of Pope and Gay. To reproduce this feature of Fielding's book, Osborne and Richardson similarly flaunt every conceivable device in the rhetoric of their own medium. Just as Fielding indulges in amplifications, ironies, similes, mock-heroics, parodies, etc., so the film exploits for comic effect a circusful of wipes, freezes, flips, speed-ups, narrowed focuses—in short, the entire battery of camera tricks. The effect of this is again to call attention to the skill of the artist, to the intelligence manipulating the pen or the camera, as the case may be. Particularly remarkable in this respect is the most celebrated of Richardson's tricks—his deliberate violation of the convention that actors must never take notice of the camera, because to do so is to dispel the illusion of life on the screen, to call attention to the fact that what the audience is seeing is a play being acted before a camera. But Richardson's actors are constantly winking at us, appealing to us to settle their disputes, thrusting their hats before our eyes, etc. The effect, paradoxically, is not to involve us in their drama, but to remind us of the presence of the camera and, consequently, to prevent us, in our darkened seats, from achieving that customary magical identification with the vicarious world unfolding on the screen. In just this way Fielding's rhetorical somersaults keep us aware that his own fictional world, like the macrocosm itself, is being supervised and manipulated by a controlling and ultimately benign intelligence. This, though tacitly achieved, is the supreme statement of his comedy.

The brilliance of Osborne's adaptation may be seen not only in the general handling of character, narrator, and rhetoric, but in his treatment of particular scenes from the novel as well. Certainly one of the most delightful and significant of these is the sequence in which Tom, concerned that he has got Molly Seagrim with child, pays an unexpected visit to her in her garret bedroom, only to find that he has been sharing her favors with the philosopher Square. At the critical moment a curtain falls away and the august metaphysician—who has made a career of denouncing the body— stands revealed in his hiding place, clad only in a blush and Molly's nightcap. In both the novel and the film this scene is shaped as a sort of parabolic dramatization of Fielding's satiric theory and practice: satire, as he had pointed out in the preface to *Joseph Andrews,* deals with "the true Ridiculous," which was his term for affectation and pretense—for those whose deeds did not match their professions. As a graphic enactment of this comic theory—the hilarious revelation of the naked truth behind the drapery—the exposure of Square is the quintessential scene in all of Fielding's fiction.

But the most impressive single instance of Osborne's and Richardson's genius in translating Fielding's style, attitudes, and intentions into their own medium is the famous eating scene at Upton. It may surprise those whose memory of the novel is vague that virtually every gesture and every grimace in the film sequence—and, indeed, its basic metaphorical equation of lust and appetite—originated with Fielding. The passage in question is Book ix, Chapter v, entitled "An apology for all heroes who have good stomachs, with a description of a battle of the amorous kind." The chapter begins with the reluctant admission that even the most accomplished of heroes have more of the mortal than the divine about them: even Ulysses must eat. When Jones and Mrs. Waters sit down to satisfy their appetites—he by devouring three pounds of beef to break a fast of twenty-four hours, she by feasting her eyes on her companion's handsome face—Fielding proceeds to define love, according to the modern understanding of the word, as "that preference which we give to one kind of food rather than to another." Jones loved his steak and ale; Mrs. Waters loved Jones. During the course of the meal the temptress brings to bear on her companion "the whole artillery of love," with an efficacy increasing in direct proportion to Jones's progress in appeasing his hunger. Fielding, invoking the Graces, describes the lady's artful seduction of his hero in the amplified, hyperbolic terms of a mock-epic battle: "First, from two lovely blue eyes, whose bright orbs flashed lightning at their discharge, flew forth two pointed ogles; but happily for our hero, hit only a vast piece of beef which he was then conveying into his plate, and harmless spent their force. . . ." Mrs. Waters heaves an epic sigh, but this is lost in "the coarse bubbling of some bottled ale." The assault continues as, "having planted her right eye sidewise against Mr. Jones, she shot from its corner a most penetrating glance. . . ." Perceiving the effect of this ogle, the fair one coyly lowers her glance and then, having made her meaning clear even to the unassuming Jones, lifts her eyes again and discharges "a voley of small charms at once from her whole countenance" in an affectionate smile which our hero receives "full in his eyes." Jones, already staggering, succumbs when his delicious adversary unmasks "the royal battery, by carelessly letting her handkerchief drop from her neck. . . ." No one who has seen the film will need to be reminded how brilliantly Joyce Redman and Finney conveyed, in images only, the sense of Fielding's metaphor of lust and appetite and how well Miss Redman visually rendered the epic sighs and ogles and leers of Mrs. Waters. This scene is not only the funniest in the film; it is a triumph of the art of cinematic translation. Both the form of the adaptation and the supremely comic effect could have been achieved in this way in no other genre: they are, in other words, the result of the collaborative exploitation (by writer, director, photographer, actors, and editor) of peculiarly cinematographic techniques—here, specifically, a series of close-ups arranged and controlled by expert cutting. An entirely verbal effect in the novel has been rendered in the film entirely in terms of visual images.

Consideration of the ways in which the film is a successful imitation of Fielding's novel can go no farther than this scene of amorous gastronomics at Upton. Let us turn, then, briefly, to an analysis of the film as a skillful work of art in its own right, for ultimately, of course, it is meant to be judged as such. Here perhaps it will be best to discuss those elements and techniques for which there is only the barest suggestion in the book. Most impressive of these is the use of visual contrasts in setting and situation for symbolic purposes. For instance, to establish at once the difference in nature between Jones and Blifil—the one free and wild and open-hearted, the other stiff and artful and cold—Osborne introduces each character in diametrically opposing situations. We first see Jones as he prowls in the wild woods at night, breaking the game laws and tumbling in the bushes with Molly: Tom is at home with the fox and the beaver; he returns the wink of an owl; and Molly, dark and dishevelled, flips a fern as she lures him to another kind of illicit sport. Blifil, on the other hand, is first seen in Allworthy's sun-drenched formal garden: he is dressed in formal frock coat and walks sedately, holding a book in his fastidious hands and obsequiously following those twin custodians of virtue and religion, the deist

Square and Thwackum the divine. The contrast between Tom's two sweethearts, the profane and the sacred, is equally deliberate. After we have been shown another night scene of Tom and Molly among the bushes, the camera shifts abruptly to a bright, idyllic setting: we see Sophia's image reflected in a pond; swans swim gracefully about, and Sophie is as fair and white as they. When Tom appears, bringing her a caged song bird (nature not wild, but tame and lovely), the lovers run from opposite sides of the water to meet at the center of a bridge. Sophie has been presented as the very image of purity and light, the proper emblem of that chastity of spirit which (in Fielding's story at least) Tom must learn to seek and find. The film is visually organized according to a scheme of such contrasts—Allworthy's formal estate with Western's sprawling, boisterous barnyard; Molly's disordered bedroom with Sophie's chaste boudoir. Even such a fundamental element as the color itself is varied in this way to signal the shift from the naturalness and simplicity of the country to the affectation and luxury, and man-made squalor, of London: the scenes in the country are done predominantly in greens and browns, and in black, grey, and white; but London is revealed in a shock of violent colors. The entry of Tom and Partridge into town is meant to recall the stark and vicious scenes of Hogarth's "Rake's Progress" and "Gin Lane." And soon thereafter the screen is flushed with reds, purples, and oranges as Tom enters the gaudy masquerade at Vauxhall, where he will meet Lady Bellaston.

Such contrasts are based, of course, on similar oppositions, thematic and structural, in the novel. For two of the film's most effective sequences, however, Osborne had scarcely any help from Fielding at all, and yet both these scenes serve independently to convey attitudes and themes consonant with Fielding's intentions and essential to the film Osborne is making. The first of these sequences is the stag hunt, for which there was no basis in the novel, except for the fact that Fielding represents Squire Western as almost monomaniacal in his devotion to the chase. In general effect the hunt serves a function similar to the shots of Western's licentious table manners or of the gastronomic encounter between Tom and Mrs. Waters: it serves, in other words, visually to emphasize the brutal, predatory, appetitive quality of life in the provinces two centuries ago. It is, as Osborne meant it to be, "no pretty Christmas calendar affair." No one who has seen this chase will forget the furious pace of it, the sadistic elation of the hunters—the lashing of horses, the spurt of crimson as spur digs into flesh, the tumbling of mounts and riders, the barnyard and the broken-necked goose trampled in the pursuit, the uncontrollable surge of the dogs as they tear the stag's throat out, and Western's triumphant display of the bloody prey. This, surely, is one of the most perfectly conceived and skillfully realized sequences in the film.

In sharp antithesis to the violence of this passage is the lyricism of the montage sequence portraying the courtship and deepening love of Tom and Sophie as Tom recovers from his broken arm on Western's estate. Richardson has achieved here a sense of arcadia—an unfallen, Edenic world of bright flowers and placid waters, of gaiety and innocence. The growing intimacy and communion of the lovers is expressed in a series of playful images in which their roles are interchanged or identified: first Sophie poles Tom around the lake while he lolls and smokes a pipe, then their positions are reversed; Sophie appears on horseback followed by Tom awkwardly straddling an ass, then vice versa, then they both appear on the same horse; Sophie shaves Tom, and Tom later wades into mud chest-deep to fetch her a blossom. They sing, skip, and lark about together. When at length they do silently declare their love with a deep exchange of glances and a kiss, the tone of the sequence is softly modulated from the frivolous to the sincere. The entire passage is altogether brilliant, done with exquisite sensitivity and a nice control. Richardson has managed to communicate in a few frames skillfully juxtaposed the way it feels to fall in love. From this moment we can never doubt the rightness and warmth of Tom and Sophie's affection—not even when, afterwards, Tom will succumb to the temptations of Molly, Mrs. Waters, and the demi-rep Lady Bellaston.

It is pleasant to think of this film, a comic masterpiece of our new Age of Satire, standing in the same relation to Fielding's classic as, say, Pope's free imitations of Horace stand in relation to their original. In an impressive variety of ways, both technical and thematic, Osborne and Richardson's *Tom Jones* is a triumph in the creative adaptation of a novel to the very different medium of the cinema. Ultimately, of course, the film is not the novel, nor, doubtless, was it meant to be. It does capture an essential part of Fielding's spirit and intention in its depiction of the sweep and quality of eighteenth-century English life, in its celebration of vitality and an open heart, and in its ridicule of vanity and sham. But Osborne's vision is narrower than Fielding's: this is a function partly of the necessary limitations of scope in the film, partly of commercial pressures precluding "moral seriousness" in a work designed to entertain millions, and partly of the different *Weltanschauung* of the twentieth century. We are not left with a sense of Fielding's balanced and ordered universe, nor are we made aware of the lesson Fielding meant to impart in the progress of his lovable, but imperfect hero. And because the vision behind the film is different in kind, even those techniques of characterization, narration, and rhetoric which have been so effectively adapted from the novel do not serve, as they do in Fielding, as the perfect formal expression of theme. Despite these limitations and discrepancies, however, Osborne's *Tom Jones* is a splendid illustration of what can be done in the intelligent adaptation of fiction to the screen.

LARRY McMURTRY

Cowboys, Movies, Myths, and Cadillacs: Realism in the Western

In 1961 I published a novel with cowboys in it, in 1963 it was made into the movie *Hud,* and ever since then people have been asking me if I think movies and television portray the American cowboy as he really is. I think, of course, that they do not, and personally I have no great desire to see them try. My questioners apparently assume that realism in movies is something more than a method; for them it is a kind of moral imperative. In their view documentary similitude equals truth, equals art, and the western should quit falsifying and become a responsible genre.

For my part, fond as I am of responsible genres, I am not at all sure I want the western to be one. Until I read Robert Warshow's celebrated essay on the westerner, I had been quite content to think of the western simply as a mode of entertainment, a mode in which the only "real" things were the horses and the landscape. I used westerns as I used the Maciste movies, as a means of disengaging myself from life for a couple of hours. I am seldom in the mood to look down my nose at such a cheap, convenient escape, and even seldomer in the mood to wonder whether the escape is art. I identify easily, and if I go to a movie that is even slightly real I am apt to find myself more engaged with life than ever; if it is a great movie the engagement may result in a sense of purgation, but great movies are few and far between, and if the film is all-too-believable and only middling good I often regret that I didn't choose a western.

The kind of escapes one chooses is significant, no doubt, but our culture provides such a variety that one's curiosity about them is apt to be somewhat blunted. Until *Hud* was made I had never thought much about the western as art, but it had dawned on me that there was a certain lack of similitude in Hollywood's treatment of cowboy life. Now and then, watching a western, I would see evidence that some director had got together with his technical adviser and made an earnest attempt to get his actors to looking like so-called "real" cowboys; the result, usually, was pretty much mixed pickles, with a few good details overbalanced by numerous examples of ignorance, negligence, or disinterest. In the interests of particularity I might point out three actions that are almost never performed on the screen as they would be on the range. Screen cowboys usually hold their bridle reins in their fists, as if they were gripping bouquets of flowers, whereas range cowboys normally control them with thumb, index finger, and middle finger. Second, screen cowboys spur their horses behind the girths, working cowboys forward of the girths and sometimes as high as the shoulders. Finally, there is the trotting-cattle syndrome, a recurrent screen phenomenon. The moviegoer usually sees cattle being driven across the screen at a pace so rapid that even the wiriest longhorn could not sustain it the length of Hollywood Boulevard without suffering a collapse; the great trail herds of the 1870's and 1880's were eased and grazed along at a sedate eight

to ten miles a day. Since they often had to go all the way from
Texas to Kansas (or in some cases even Montana), anything faster
would have been economically disastrous.

Warshow, of course, was right in pointing out that the working cowboy has never been very important in the western movie. The gunfighter has been the central figure, and, as numerous historical narratives point out, cowboys and gunfighters were rather different breeds,
neither being very good at the other's specialties. A western may start
out with a cowboy hero, but nine times out of ten the plot will require
him to become a gunfighter before the end of the film. Recently,
there have been signs that this is changing, especially on television.
The domestic western is becoming more and more popular (*Bonanza, The Big Valley*, even, I should say, *Gunsmoke*), whereas TV's
most impressive old-style gunfighter, Paladin, is seen no more.

At any rate, in citing discrepancies in Hollywood's treatment of
cowboy life I did not mean to imply that directors of westerns should
get my list and rigorously eliminate trotting cattle and bridle reins
held like bouquets. The effectiveness of the western as a genre has
scarcely depended upon fidelity of detail or, for that matter, upon
emotional validity. Hollywood surely would have been foolish to attempt to do the American cowboy or the winning of the West realistically; applying an anti-romantic technique to an essentially romantic
subject would have amounted to a sort of alchemical reverse
English; it would have been deliberately turning gold into lead. The
cowboy (or the gunfighter), whatever he may be like in real life,
lives in the American imagination as a mythic figure, or at least a
figure of high romance; his legend, however remotely it may relate to
his day-to-day existence, is still one of the most widely compelling of
our diminishing number of national legends. Not even kids want to
be Indians anymore, and only kids want to be soldiers. The myth of
the noble redman is kaput, and the myth of the American poor boy,
though it may linger on in figures like Robert E. Lee Prewitt, has
lost most of its appeal. Johnny Reb and Billy Yank have faded out;
G. I. Joe will follow. The jazzman's appeal has always been too
precious, and the teen-ager's, I hope, will always be too teen-age.
There are movie stars, sports kings, and rock and roll singers, but

here legends tend to accrue around the individual, not around the type. The cowboy, however, absorbed the more general figure of the pioneer or frontiersman, and so far has held his own.

The appeal cannot last forever, of course: a good mythic figure must be susceptible of being woven into the national destiny, and since the West definitely has been won the cowboy must someday fade. Indeed, a certain change has already taken place, and was taking place when Warshow wrote his essay (1954). If one can properly apply to the western the terminology which Northrop Frye develops in his essay on fictional modes, we might say that in the 1950's the western (or at least the "serious" western, the only kind Warshow considers) was working its way down from the levels of myth and romance toward the ironic level which it has only recently reached. Westerns like *Shane, The Searchers,* and *Warlock* are in the high mimetic mode; the hero is still superior to other men and to his environment. In *The Gunfighter* this is not the case and we are in the low mimentic mode, just as we are in *Hud.* The latter, indeed, approaches the ironic mode, and we have recently seen an actor (Lee Marvin) win an oscar for a role that parodies the figure of the gunfighter. No doubt high mimetic westerns will continue to be made as long as John Wayne is acting—he wouldn't fit in any other mode—but in number they are declining. The last ten years have witnessed a very sharp drop-off in the production of B and C westerns of the kind that were a Saturday afternoon staple during the 1940's. It is clear that the figure of the westerner is being replaced by more modern figures, principally that of the secret agent. In time, of course, we can expect to see the conquest of space (if we really conquer it) take over the place in the American mythos now held by the winning of the West, but that day has not come. If one agrees with Warshow— and I do—that the western has maintained its hold on our imagination because it offers an acceptable orientation to violence, then it is easy to see why the secret agent is so popular just now. An urban age demands an urban figure; the secret agent, like the westerner a sort of insider-outsider, is an updated type of gunfighter. The secret agent has appropriated the style of the gunfighter and has added urbanity and cosmopolitanism. Napoleon Solo and Matt Dillon both work

for the betterment of civilization, but the man from U.N.C.L.E. makes
the marshal seem as old-fashioned and domestic as Fibber McGee and
Molly. To be widely acceptable, the violence must be satisfactorily
aestheticized and brought into line with the times. If only there are
some bad Indians out there in space, on a planet we need, then
eventually the spaceman's hour will come.

The cowboy's golden age was the last third of the nineteenth century, and Hollywood has been fairly effective in its treatment of the
ending of the golden age. The treatment had already begun when
Warshow wrote his essay (indeed, it provided him most of his examples—*The Gunfighter, Shane,* and *High Noon*) and has been extended, perhaps most successfully in the excellent sequence of westerns Kirk Douglas has made (*Gunfight at the OK Corral, Last Train
from Gun Hill, Lonely Are the Brave*). What happened in the West
after the age ended has yet to be dealt with, though a picture such as
Hud is a beginning.

Hud, a twentieth-century westerner, is a gunfighter who lacks both
guns and opponents. The land itself is the same—just as powerful,
just as imprisoning—but the social context has changed so radically
that Hud's impulse to violence has to turn inward on himself and
his family. Hud Bannon is wild in a well-established tradition of western wildness that involves drinking, gambling, fighting, fast and reckless riding and/or driving (Hud has a Cadillac), and, of course, se-
ducing. The tradition is not bogus; the character is pretty much in
line with actuality. The cowboy, on screen and off, has generally been
distinguished for his daring and his contempt of the middle-class way
of life (he remains acutely conscious of the mores of his peers). Though
nowadays most cowboys are solidly middle-class in their values, the
values sit more lightly on them than on their white-collar cousins.

Hud, of course, is not simply a cowboy; if he were, he could never
afford the Cadillac. It is his gun, in a sense, and he can afford it
because he is the son of a well-to-do rancher, and a wheeler in his
own right. Cowboys and ranchers differ primarily in their economic
resources: a rancher is a cowboy who, through some combination of
work, luck, judgment, or inheritance, has made good. To a rancher
a Cadillac has a dual usefulness, just as the gunfighter's gun once

had: it is an obvious and completely acceptable status symbol, and also it is capable of making the long, high-speed drives that are frequently necessary in cattle country; it will do the work. The cowboy proper could no more afford Hud's car than he could afford Hud's women, though granted the latter might vary considerably in expensiveness. In spite of his reputation for going on wild binges the cowboy has usually had to accustom himself to rather Spartan living conditions; indeed, there has always been an element of asceticism in the cowboy's makeup, though it is an asceticism that has tended to wither rather badly when faced with the continuous blasts of sensuality this century has provided. Even so the cowboy's life has not yet become lush; he still gets by with far fewer creature comforts than most Americans have.

In addition to the wildness, Hud also exhibits other characteristics which are typically cowboy: independence is first among them, then pride, stoicism, directness, restlessness. The cowboy also has his own astringent brand of humor, but I have never seen this touched, either in fiction or on the screen. The cowboy's temperament has not changed much since the nineteenth century, but his world has changed a great deal. It has steadily shrunk. There are no more trail herds, no more wide-open cattle towns; no more is there the vast stretch of unfenced land between Laredo and Calgary. If a cowboy is to be really footloose these days, he must take to the rodeo circuit. Rodeo was given one excellent low-mimetic treatment in *The Lusty Men* (1952), but, except for the rodeo sequence in *The Misfits,* has not been used by the movies. (Television, of course, had *Stoney Burke* for awhile.) The big western ranches are now gradually breaking down into smaller and smaller ranches, and with the advent of pickups and horse trailers it is no longer necessary to spend long weeks on the roundup. The principal effect this has had has been to lessen considerably the isolation of the cowboy, to diminish his sense of himself as a man alone. He is gradually being drawn toward the town.

There will be a very poignant story to be told about the cowboy, should Hollywood care to tell it: the story of his gradual metamorphosis into a suburbanite. The story contains an element of paradox, for the bloated urbanism that makes the wild, free cowboy so very attractive to those already urbanized will eventually result in his being absorbed by his audience. In a sense he has been already: nobody watches TV westerns more avidly than cowboys. Of course in this respect legend and fact had long ago begun to intermingle; nature imitated art, to a degree, and the cowboy, however much he might profess to scorn Hollywood, was secretly delighted to believe the romantic things Hollywood told him about himself. Even in his most golden days the cowboy lived within the emotional limits of the western movie and the hillbilly song. Hud Bannon's West is a sort of new lost frontier, and Hud is one of the many people whose capacities no longer fit his situation. He needs more room and less company, and he is unlikely to get either. Someday the ranches of America will all be Southern California size, and all the cattle, perhaps, will be grown in the great feedlots of the Middle West. The descendants of the trail hands will be driving beer trucks in the suburbs of San Antonio, Dodge City, Cheyenne, and a hundred other towns whose names once held a different sort of promise. By that time Hollywood will have grown tired of parodying the gunfighter, the ironic mode may give way to the mythic and the Lone Ranger ride again. Romance will succeed realism, and Gary Cooper (as in *The Plainsman,* say) will be as remote and appealing a figure of romance as Roland or King Arthur. Hud Bannon, by that time, will have traded in his big pink Caddy and left the ranch forever, to become a secret agent, or an astronaut.

Twenty-Six Propositions about Skin Flicks

1. That *cheapness* as an aesthetic judgment is purely literary and applies only to the psychological dimensions of the work in hand. That no movie is properly called cheap, because all are: mere depthless images which flicker one after another over a darkened surface. *Cheapness:* nothing to do with subject matter . . . How many fine novels are sordid at heart! *Madame Bovary, Sanctuary, Anna Karenina, An American Tragedy,* and so forth.

2. To expect a "great movie" is to insult the eye. The business of the eye is to suck the surface images off all objects, to skewer them, to glut the brain. The business of the eye is to suspend critical judg-

ment. (Think how we choose our mates.) The question the nudie movie broaches is, why isn't the eye satisfied with these images?

3. Watching a Rock Hudson–Doris Day movie, one feels hurt and ashamed that he is seeing something he should not, that he has been forced to peep into the bathroom of the American imagination. But in the nudie movies they have real bathrooms, into which the camera literally peeps; and, watching, one is not embarrassed, but wise. He feels that Rock and Doris have prepared him adequately. Here is the bathroom, all right, but there are no prescription or patent medicines, no aspirin, no toilet paper (no toilet), no used razor blades, no hot water bottles, no frazzled toothbrushes. There is much Soap; there is a Naked Girl.

4. As a theoretical premise: that all kinds of art are aesthetically equal. That there could be a "great" western novel, a "great" detective novel, a "great" erotic poem. Let us make a "great" skin movie; let us make Books iv and v of *Paradise Lost*. We will have a grave, impassioned stylization, like Eisenstein's. For our Father and Mother we shall have examples of those noble, dreamy people who have undergone electric shock therapy. We shall omit God as a character or as an off-stage voice, but retain Him as visible nature, to which Adam and Eve belong. Merely pondering the project, one is shocked. This is not the way the essential goodness of the body is revealed to the camera.

5. Let us make a skin flick; let us make *The Odd Sex,* which will purport to be a study of voyeurism. It will alternate alarmingly between technicolor and black and white. The film will be scratched and splotched, and the sound will be out of synchronization. The actors will be mumblers and stammerers, idiots. The actresses will be bar girls. A typical scene: He, sweaty and bloodshot, peers through the bedroom curtains, which in the next few frames will magically disappear. She is readying for bed. Slowly unzips the dress, but quickly over her head with it. No slip. Preens herself before the dressing-table mirror. Red brassiere and panties. Preens. At last unhooks the brassiere (deftly!), cuddles it to her for a moment. Drops it, exposing breasts, largish, with unaroused nipples. Half-turns to left and right. Smiles. Hooks her thumbs into the band of her panties and slides

them down, keeping the cleavage of her ass importantly toward us. The top edge of the dressing table cuts away the front view. Preens...

How the innocence of the body overcomes all obstacles, emerges inviolate (though dulled) and matter-of-factly.

6. If the whole of history, with its prostitution and unrelenting degradation, has not violated women in their essence, how shall the camera accomplish it?

7. From the Greensboro *Daily News* of July 16, 1966, from an article headlined "High Point Council Seeks Law Banning Bare Bosoms." (High Point is a small city near Greensboro.)

An ordinance which would ban bare bosoms from motion picture screens in this city was unveiled Tuesday. . . . The proposed ordinance states simply: "It shall be unlawful for any person, film or corporation to project, cause to be projected or permit to be projected upon any public motion picture screen within the city limits, any picture of a female person over the age of 12 years whose breast or breasts are nude. . . ." In voicing his approval of the proposed ordinance, Councilman Walter Huber, chairman of the Law and Public Safety Committee, said it was "high time" the council was doing something about the situation. He said he was sure the theater [a local drive-in featuring skin flicks] was "responsible for the increased immorality, broken and unhappy marriages and moral decay," which he said was afoot in the city. He said the theater was "the worst cesspool we have."

8. A friend, Max Steele, thought that a first purpose of literature is to discover evil, the sense of evil having atrophied in our time. To which I would have added, also to discover innocence, not then understanding that while evil can be discovered—sought out and revealed—innocence can be found only accidentally. Indeed, the whole use of innocence lies in its obscurity, an obscurity not produced by modesty; for surely innocence is neither modest nor immodest. But it is obscure and can only be chanced upon. Innocence can be found accidentally in skin flicks, in the poetry of William Carlos Williams and in Dreiser's rhetorical passages, in the tired reveries of spinster shop girls, in some kinds of pornography, perhaps.

Which is to say that innocence can never be a literary "property"; it can be pointed toward but not dealt with, not "managed."

9. Which is also to say that innocence can be—often is—a by-product

of the sordid. The sordid, the cheap, is perhaps the only setting in which this inestimably hard diamond is dressed to advantage . . . What else is the sordid but the usual petty truths we don't want to be reminded of? One definition of innocence: a possible way of living we don't want to be reminded of.

10.   In *Passion Holiday,* an awkward passage. Four girls are bathing naked in the sea. They spy approaching in a rowboat their enemies, two gangsters. They run clumsily to the shore and gather up their bikinis, which they haven't time to put on. They clutch the suits to their genitals and scamper into the forest . . . The superstition of the skin flicks is that sexuality resides in the pubic fleece, which is never to be admitted on screen. A pathetic enough thread of idea, but one is reminded by it in these films that love has hair on it, yes, and teeth in it too. Here where the camera falters, the moral sense vaults, apprehensive and exacerbated, every nerve of it aglare. One is certain that something terrible is going to be revealed, that an unguessed image, inimical and blood-feeding, will stare back . . . The girls don their suits, smiling now, demure in the foliage.

11.   In almost all nudie films there is a true but unarticulated idea (actually, in most of the films, especially the nudist camp films, they make the mistaken reverse of the idea the thesis) : that physical nature itself is corrupt, has in itself the possibilities for its destruction; and is always (unwittingly) shown corrupted, flimsy under the grasp of society. But the human body, often exhibited as sadistically and masochistically degraded, as soiled and contemptible, burns through whatever attitudes the film tries to enclose it in. It maintains its integrity. Veins, pores, blemishes, follicles are stoutly independent and inform us that this kind of indignity is temporary, that the nonchalance of merely being defeats a superficial morality.

12.   Does that girl's body (she's in her mid-thirties, tending toward the pendulous, has shrieking blonde hair) also resist the imagination? It's not a malleable material for the camera, cannot be moralized or attitudinized. But it can be placed. It cannot be made shocking, nor more interesting than it already is. But it can invest its surroundings with some measure of stateliness or, at the least, with the brassy taste of the incongruous.

13. Innocence is not to be found among the Ranters. It is not in Henry Miller or Kerouac or Ginsberg or any of those people. It is not in Cecil B. DeMille or John Ford. It is not in any movie about the Bible or History.

14. The single most salient element of skin flicks is poverty of the imagination. Obvious enough. But sometimes it operates as a curious virtue. In a great many skin flicks there is absolutely no way to tell what image will be thrown on the screen next. Cocteau—who had imagination—would have envied the skin movie this quality. It gives to the film audience a restive apprehension. One emerges from the theater exhausted and exasperated, not because of the pictures of simple bodies, but because of uncontrolled tension.

15. Russ Meyer is a director who began by making nudie movies. *Lorna* was one. But in Meyer somewhere was the black seed of the artist, and he became bored. So that now, although his movies are advertised as skin movies, they are not, but are instead very odd "serious attempts," full of big, gloomy archetypes and Gothic puzzlements. One of his movies, *Faster, Pussycat, Kill, Kill!* is blood brother to *The Spanish Tragedy.* Meyer *is* Thomas Kyd, just as if no other movies had ever been made; he threw away almost every sophisticated cinematic advance—whether out of stupidity or not I don't know— and began all over with the absolutely primitive. These movies *(Faster, Pussycat; Cycle Mania; Rope of Flesh)* will be preserved and someday will be shown at a Grand Archetype Film Festival, along with *Tarzan and the Mermaid,* Buster Crabbe's Flash Gordon serial, *King Kong, The Virginian,* etc.

But as his movies became more interesting, the nudes disappeared from them. The naked body as an object is recalcitrant, inaccessible to the imagination, to even a rudimentary artistry; but it is accessible to lack of imagination, a condition in which it can dictate its own terms.

16. Innocence, however, is not to be identified with absence of imagination, but rather with absence of irony.

17. Ough, the girls in these films . . . Shopworn, nerveless girls with whole epochs of misery behind and before them. One or two of them, I noticed, have the little triangular dot tattoos (. · .) high on the

right breast, indicating that they were the properties at one time or another of *pachucos*. Occasionally a band-aid will cover a name tattoo ("Lee," "Buck"). And though the skin is troweled thick with pancake makeup, the varicose shows through, as do irregular moles and old scars and burns . . . Here, of course, is the true material for movies, for any sort of art, but disregarded. The girl must present the battered carcass impersonally, as through cellophane. The poor thing is Cheesecake; her story—the only real story—is forgotten. "Smile. That's it. Now turn . . . A little more . . . That's it, hold it now . . . Keep smiling."

And it's partly because of her misery that she is triumphant over the dazed, sullen watchers.

18.   All nudies are moralistic. Filled with naked girls and improbable sugar-tasting sexuality, they end with an admonition. To which one's reaction is, Let us burn morality. Morals and this abject misery are not compatible. Misery has a dignity which imported morality can only injure, cannot even intensify. Leave heartsickness at least its purity.

19.   Faces of the placeless men leaving the nudie movie in mid-afternoon/ heads of the cattle crammed into the slaughterhouse chutes/ a buttonless frayed shirt cuff.

20.   How can we know the dancer from the dance? In Titian, Renoir, is it the painting—pure technique—which absorbs the nude, or is it the nude which transforms painterly technique into something humane and intimate as a whisper? The nude flick answers the question. In painting the body is transformed; the audience is privy to a personal idealism; we are not given the humanity of the body, but instead the humanity of someone's artistic goals. Nuns, mothers, and painters worship images, and in the painting we witness an act of worship. In the skin flick we see the raw material that worship is exercised upon. Embarrassing, somehow, to see that it begins with flesh, bone, and blood . . . And there it should end, after a series of metamorphoses. All dreams of the soul end in a beautiful man's or woman's body.

21.   An ideal shot for a skin flick: a naked girl reflected, yellow and

splintered, in a small, aching tear. She yawns, stretches languorously; is not coy, but casual; she means no harm.

22.   For an ironic science fiction novel we shall project a background morality, extrapolated from the moral premises of nudie movies. First, sexuality is bad, a short-lived pleasure. It is bad because it is a pleasure, for all pleasure is ultimately derived from the sexual. Sexuality can never be an end in itself, and it cannot lead to another pleasurable end; its exercise is limited, constrained to grim (always) familial purposes. Pleasure begins in license and leads to license; license results in disaster, often death.

Our novel shall take place in Marsopolis in the year 2566; or, really, in Kansas in 1908.

23.   The only antidotes for the moral prurience which the skin flicks exemplify are humor and physical disease, neither of which these films allow. (There are so-called "funny" skin flicks which are successful because everyone knows that they are not funny.) There will never be a Mark Twain of the skin flicks, nor a Zola.

24.   Jim Applewhite, remarking wistfully of the immediate appeal that movies have and that poetry usually doesn't, said that every movie ought to have a nude scene in it. "That would be *one more* thing that the movies have." But perhaps his premise is wrong; perhaps poetry is the more immediate art, in the sense that it carries one immediately *into*—not toward—the flesh. If the greatest poverty is not to live in a physical world, then in a movie we are in great poverty, for that is no physical world, but merely an advertisement for one. And unfortunately (and this is especially true of skin flicks) we view these advertisements with the same distrust that we view all others. Distrust becomes unhappily a habit of the eye, a habit usurped from the critical mind. The nude movie would end by robbing the eye of half its function.

25.   The air of the skin movie house is surcharged, not with desire and frustration, but with fear and suspicion.

26. . . . A final allurement of these films: portrayal of the ineluctable weariness of the body . . .

R. H. W. DILLARD

Even a Man Who Is Pure at Heart: Poetry and Danger in the Horror Film

We are sitting, you and I, in the plush (if somewhat worn) seats of a darkened movie house—featureless, all of us seated in rows, hearing the first dark chords of a somber score, waiting for the hard grin of death's skull to chill us all to the bone that will outlast our flesh and set on end our hair that legend says will grow long after we are dead.

And on the screen, dark figures move among the mists and tilting stones of a Central European graveyard—a hunchbacked dwarf, a tall young man. There is the clank of shovels under a full moon. High scudding clouds. The action is unclear. A body is raised from its rest, and heavy clods thump on the empty coffin lid. And somehow, a stone tower, the fury of a storm, the mad harmony of thunder, lightning, and the buzzing of machines that spit and crackle life into the shrouded figure on the table. It moves, first a hand, an arm; it rises and lurches unsteadily on sewn and cumbrous limbs. And its face is the face of death, the pain and incomprehensibility of death, the death that waits for us all.

For those of you who remember, who have seen the same films and dreamed the same dreams, I offer you here a voyage of shared memories, one like that of Poe's traveler in "The Domain of Arnheim"—one which twists and winds loosely from recollection to idea, a voyage of discovery into a dark world where, maybe, with luck, we too can find a land "glittering in the red sunlight with a hundred oriels, minarets, and pinnacles; and seeming the handiwork, conjointly, of the Sylphs, of the Fairies, of the Genii, and of the Gnomes."

I

When I was nine years old, my father took me to see my first horror film, a double feature *Frankenstein* and *Dracula*—nurses in attendance at all performances and an ambulance parked and ready at the theater door. My grandmother had already frightened me with tales of the monster and his blind and destructive fury, but I was totally unprepared for what I saw: the open graves, the dead that walked, the dark as I had never pictured dark before. And heard: Count Dracula's poised and foreign voice, his mad victim crying out for spiders and dreaming of "acres and acres of rats." But, most of all, the monster, the poignancy of his reaching for the light, the horror of his wounded bellow, and the slowly dying embers of his flaming tomb.

I have shared that monster's fate more than once in my sleep, have feared him and been him in the same dream, and I suspect that perhaps even you have lived through a similar night. Or was it in the Carpathians as Count Dracula welcomed you to his webbed castle where you were to feel the light touch of teeth on your throat and were to rise at night yourself, undead and hot with a thirst for living blood? Or did you seek freedom from the wolf's curse that drove you, all shaggy hair and sharp fangs, through moonlit streets,

hungry for death and life? Or did you linger, scarred and mad, in
the catacombs of the Paris Opera, or stalk the night protecting the
mummified remains of a princess you loved 3,700 years ago? These
dreams are as much a part of us now as the doubts of Hamlet or
the frenzy of Lear. They come to us from a variety of sources—perhaps even, as Robert Eisler suggested in *Man Into Wolf,* from "the
subhuman animal strata of the 'collective unconscious.' " But certainly
they have come most clearly to us today from the films of our youth,
the horror movies we sat through eagerly, showing after showing, and
dreamed of during those hectic nights that found us shivering under
covers even in a hot and sultry summer.

There is a Shamanist myth which tells of a boy, innocent of women
yet ready for manhood, coming to his uncle, the Bwili of Lol-narong.
In a ritual rich in symbolic significance, the uncle severs the boy's
limbs from his body as they both laugh. Even the boy's head, cut
from his body, continues to laugh, and with the affirmation of the
boy's trust and of their laughter together, the uncle restores the boy
whole and a man. This primitive tale contains within it the essence
of sacrificial awakening, for in it the youth learns to live in a world
of suffering and darkness and still be able to see the light by an act
of personal faith and sacrifice and with the ministering wisdom of
an older guide. The myth is magical and certainly unrealistic, but it
is true to the essence of cruel experience if not to its daily details.
It is a work of imaginative art, concerned with intuitive and emotional
truth more than with surface fact. It satisfied those Shamanist
believers simply because, in its mystery and magic, it rang true to
life—it explained a phenomenon everyone knew but could not understand.

Frankenstein and *Dracula,* that double bill of terror, operated for
me in much the same way as the ritual of the Bwili of Lol-narong
terrified and satisfied that young boy and the other members of his
society. I am not claiming that I understood the initiation at the
time, nor is what I am saying absolutely true. Certainly those horror
films were not my sole initiation into the realities of adult life—that
initiation is a continuing one which runs from birth to death itself—but they were a part of that initiation, that fall into life which

we all must experience time and again, and they were an important part, for they helped shape my imagination to life and free my dreams to art.

James Agee, a film critic as well as a poet and novelist, seldom wrote of horror films, but on the few occasions that he did, he sensed the quality that makes the good ones real works of art. He wrote of Val Lewton's *The Body Snatcher* that it was a better film than *Isle of the Dead* (the ending of which made it "as brutally frightening and gratifying a horror movie as I can remember") because "it explodes into an even finer, and a far more poetic, horror-climax." He enjoyed being frightened, but he preferred being frightened in a "poetic" manner. And again, when he reviewed Lewton's earlier *Curse of the Cat People* (a film which is presently high in the favor of devotees of art cinema), he spoke of it as "decent and human" in its concern with "the poetry and danger of childhood." What exactly Agee meant by poetic would be difficult to say, but his use of the words *human* and *poetic* in conjunction with *horror* and *danger* is the key to what I believe to be the nature and function of the horror film as an art form.

To define *poetic* at all is a futile task, but the horror film is a part of the great imaginative tradition of art, as opposed to the realistic tradition, and as such it shares an aesthetic approach to life with works of literature as varied as Spenser and Kafka, Poe and Lewis Carroll. This imaginative tradition is not of an essentially mimetic art, but rather of a recreative art, one which fashions new worlds from the familiar pieces of the old, which gives us a world made new while still as ancient as before. As Poe, that most articulate of imaginative and gothic aesthetic theorists, puts it: "Inspired by an ecstatic prescience of the glories beyond the grave, we struggle by multiform combinations among the things and thoughts of time to attain a portion of that Loveliness whose very elements perhaps appertain to eternity alone." The poetic may not have to appertain to eternity in quite Poe's way to be of this tradition, but it does have to concern itself with the nature of being beyond the simple facts of life, with the human spirit and with what Poe called "Beauty" and Agee called "poetry and danger."

I suppose that all significant Western art, at least since the medieval period, has been directly concerned with the original fall of man and the consequent introduction of sin and death into the world. Certainly sin (or, if you prefer, human evil) and death must be the central concerns of any artist seriously involved with life; poetry can never be totally divorced from danger and still be of the highest order. The horror film is, at its best, as thoroughly and richly involved with the dark truths of sin and death as any art form has ever been, but its approach is that of parable and metaphor—an approach which enables it on occasion to achieve a metaphysical grandeur, but which also may explain why its failures are so very awful and indefensible.

Like a medieval morality play, the horror film deals with the central issue of Christian life—the struggle between the spirits of good and evil for the possession of man's immortal soul. In the morality play personified abstractions (Friendship, Knowledge, Evil Deeds, Good Deeds, Riches, Good Angel, Evil Angel, Death) argue for Vice and Virtue, and their actions free the soul to heaven or cast it down to hell. The plays were totally unrealistic and as completely serious, for they were attempts to image in the flesh on a stage the dreadful battle within the spirit between the divided forces of man's own nature—the love of God and other men versus the corrupt love of self and evil. To a medieval Catholic those plays were as true as art could ever be. The horror film is quite as unrealistic and, I believe, quite as concerned with the truth available to art.

If the morality play personified the elements of the human soul and set them forth for all to see in an instructive pageant, the horror film personifies those very elements in a dark and beautiful dream which, for all its vagueness and artificiality, is quite as instructive. The horror film is a pageant of death, the death that breeds in all things—entropy, mutability, and corruption. The morality play taught the method of salvation to which a Christian should adhere in order to pass through the temptations and sufferings of life to the peace and joy of union with God; Death was the dangerous and unexpected bailiff who cast man before the final bar of justice, and Death was, then, also the liberator to the new and true life of the spirit freed of the crippling results of the fall. The horror film teaches an acceptance of the natural order of things and an affirmation of man's ability to cope with and even prevail over the evil of life which he can never hope to understand; death is the unknown and unknowable end to life, but it is also the natural and peaceful end to the turmoil and terror of life in a fallen world. To die in irredeemable sin is the primary danger in the morality play; to be unable to die and find peace and the possibility of heaven for the suffering spirit is the great danger in the horror film.

I have certainly set the horror film a mighty task—to make us accept death as the natural ending of life, an ending to be desired. But that task is really no more possible or impossible than any of the tasks art ever attempts. The bold method of the horror film is as old as Aristotle and older; it sets out to purge us of our fear of death by exposing us to death as we have never seen it before, by distorting the fact of death into all possible contortions to help us see its simple and natural reality. The mirror the horror film holds up to death is the distorting mirror of a deserted funhouse which frightens us out of fear and frees our fancy to find the truth more surely.

Death in the horror film is most often grotesque; innocent and guilty alike are slaughtered horribly—drained of their blood by vampires, strangled or flung aside casually by a mummy's hand or the sewn hand of a monster made from dead flesh and bone, mangled by a werewolf's teeth and claws, strangled by the severed hands of a dead man, given to savage and unnatural beasts by mad and sadistic scientists, burked by a body snatcher desperate for a fresh corpse, and on and hideously on. But what is more horrible, even death and the repose of the grave are impermanent; the dead rise or are disturbed in a variety of ways: they rise as vampires thirsting for blood, their mummified remains return after nearly four thousand years to seek revenge for the desecration of a princess' tomb, they are eaten by ghouls and snatched by body snatchers, their bodies are dissected and sewn together anew as a monster, they are enslaved as zombies, and, if nothing worse, they are dug up for inspection by those left fighting whatever evil killed them.

The central figure of the film, the monster of evil whatever his particular form, suffers perhaps worst of all from the failure of death, and his grotesque death not only saves the world he inhabits from his evil, but also frees him into a natural and permanent death from the painful striving of his unnatural life. The vampire is peaceful and his features calm and even beautiful once the stake is driven through his heart, his head severed, and his mouth stuffed with garlic; the Frankenstein monster's blundering search for understanding and love in a society which is horrified by him is at the only end it could possibly have; the mummy's centuries of living death are resolved in a true death; the madman is freed of his distorting insanity; the invisible man, whose invisibility imprisoned his mind as it freed his flesh, rests quietly and visibly. This peace, the peace of death, is the object and end of the horror film; it is not merely the peace which follows the destruction of an antagonist, for it benefits the villainous opponent as well as his heroic slayers.

The werewolf story is perhaps the clearest example of this important ambiguity of death in the horror film. The werewolf, whether one considers *The Werewolf of London* or *The Wolf Man* or any of their long line of imitators, is the hero as well as the villain of the film. He is an innocent man who has been bitten by a werewolf and has, because of the supernatural properties of the bite, become a werewolf himself, doomed to change under the full moon into a wolf who must kill to stay alive. Through no action of his own the evil and madness inherent in every fallen man is released in him, or, as the gypsy's poem in *The Wolf Man* has it:

> Even a man who is pure at heart
> And says his prayers by night
> May become a wolf when the wolfbane blooms
> And the moon is full and bright.

He destroys life and hurts the one he loves, but he cannot stop himself. As a wolf, he is a creature of blind animal evil; as a man, he suffers the tortures of the damned, for he knows the evil he does and can do nothing about it. Walking through a normal environment in a business suit, he is separated only by the anguish of his face from the ordinary pattern of natural life, a life made intensely beautiful in its mundanity by his separation from it and by the alienation of his darker self from all of its standards, its humanity, its simple decencies. He can only die, as the best version of the story has it, by a wound from a silver weapon (a knife, a bullet, the head of a cane) wielded by one who loves him dearly.

This situation makes great demands of the observer, the theatergoer in his plush seat, for he must wish for the hero's victory, his release from the curse, by desiring that he die, that he be killed by someone who loves him. Death itself, our final villain, must be made the instrument of the hero's salvation. This is a paradox worthy of the highest art, for here the spiritual struggle of one man bursts out into the visible world in hair, claws, and fangs, and the cruelty of man's love for his fellows is painfully enacted in the murder of love, the sacrifice for the last victory of the soul. When Lawrence Talbot lies in the arms of his father, his evil pelt gone in death, he is no Oedipus nor poisoned Hamlet, but his story is akin to theirs—he is the victim of the nature of a fallen world, and his death restores what order there is possible to that world. The act of love that killed him was one of overwhelming sacrifice, and its victory is paradoxical and incomprehensible to the reason of our normal world. The werewolf film is a work of fantasy and thus, to eyes and minds trained by realistic standards, it seems a fragile and finally insignificant entertainment. But, whatever the merits of its performance, its form and lines are sound. Its revelation of the dark and its affirmation of redeeming love are valid; its metaphysics and its moral structure, whatever their variance from theological standards, are true to the Christian understanding and perhaps even, for those of you who demand it, to a modern existential understanding of the quality of our lives, of the way things really are.

The other central figures in the best horror films, the ones which have become a part of all our memories, are also victims as well as villains: vampires who are undead by no choice of their own, monsters who are placed in a world that doesn't want them and hates them, mummies who are driven by a curse put on them by long-dead priests of a religion which is also dead. All of these creatures find the victory of peace in the defeat of death. And we are, then, doubly relieved at their deaths and perhaps saddened, too. In this ambiguity the beauty lies, the poetry inextricably a part of the danger.

But what of the living, those who survive the horrors and live on at the end of the film? I said that the horror film (as, I suspect, all great art must) affirms man's ability to cope with evil beyond his ken and even to prevail over it. The elements of that enduring ability are two, a working combination of reason and faith, of practical understanding and belief. Neither is properly efficacious without the other. Belief alone may save one's soul, but it will give him only the direction for any temporal and practical victory. The priest and the superstitious gypsy are allied in belief, for they both know that there are things in this world beyond the scope of reason and of scientific thought. Their knowledge is ineffectual however, because it is too often fatalistic; they hold the devil in too high regard to strive to foil him; they will pray for the dead, but they can offer little beyond spiritual solace to the living. Reason, too, is ineffectual, because it denies the existence of any evil that does not fit the immutable laws of a logical and orderly universe. The myriad doctors, scientists, and believers in a rational world are baffled by occurrences which can fit in no possible way into their system; they examine the happenings of the night by daylight and cannot understand the mysteries of the dark. Theirs is a more foolish innocence than that of the superstitious peasant, for their scientific optimism often leads them to deny evil as an active force in human affairs altogether.

Evil must be known to be combated, and the knowing must lead to respect for its power but never to fearful surrender to it. He who can fuse reason and belief into an imaginative and active force is the hero of the horror film, but he is neither the tragic hero nor the comic hero. He is not even the central figure of the story, for although he restores order by his action, he does not control the movement of events at all (no Hamlet is he, nor powerful Prospero). Rather he copes with events beyond human control. He is the older and wiser guide who reveals the mystery to the votary. The usual pattern is that a young, intelligent person is suddenly faced with an evil beyond his grasp, an evil which does not usually shatter his will to resist but which does leave him stripped of illusions and unable to defend himself properly. An older man (a former teacher, a professor interested in the occult, a scientist, even on occasion a priest) arrives and teaches the young man to respect all truth no matter what its sources and to fight with what weapons are needed, whether they be the practical weapons of violent force or the incantations and rituals of primitive belief.

Edward Van Sloan is the actor who always seemed to be this heroic guide, perhaps because as Professor Abraham Van Helsing in *Dracula* he surely rendered most fully the strength of this figure—brave, intelligent, aware of the limitations of his humanity, but never faltering in his quest for securing the safety of those menaced by evil, for restoring order. He is a fully educated and practical man with an understanding of modern science and philosophy, but he never rejects the wisdom and beliefs of older orders and systems, whether they be the Transylvanian lore of vampires and werewolves, the curses of the ancient Egyptians (Van Sloan as Dr. Muller in *The Mummy*, 1932), or the old belief that there are directions in which man must not inquire and search too far without breaking the bounds set for him by God (again Van Sloan as Dr. Waldman in *Frankenstein*). He prevails over the personifications of evil, not because he is superior to it in power and appeal, but rather because he is human, weak, and fallen but continually striving to better himself and his world, to earn some of the love which is his by God's grace.

This heroic man and the young people whom he guides fight for human values and the natural order of things, the right to live freely without submitting to evil and the right to die peacefully and forever. The evil they do battle with, for all its supernatural trappings, is also human—the vampires and werewolves, monsters and mummies are all human at source and are all personifications of that potentiality for evil and sin which is so much a part of us all. Hero and villain are much the same—both human, both flawed unto death—and the complexity of their struggle and the dark nature of the order recovered by that struggle give the horror film its moral and metaphysical weight. It is a morality play for our times, approaching the very paradox of human life in its fantastic simplicity. It is religious and as mysterious as all art finally proves to be; it transmutes danger into poetry and affirms humanity in the very face of horror.

II

In *Frankenstein Meets the Space Monster* (1965), Frankenstein is no longer the tormented modern Prometheus of Mary Shelley's novel and the early films. He is the monster, and the use of the name in its popular (some say, vulgar) generic sense is typical of the modern horror film which has lost touch with its sources and usually its artistic values. Frankenstein in that recent film is a government-built android, pieced together from human corpses but with an electronic brain. Designed to be an astronaut, he is damaged in an abortive rocket shot and becomes a genuine monster, scarred and dangerous. He has a variety of adventures with ordinary people and with a group of dehumanized invaders from another planet decimated by nuclear war. Eventually Frankenstein, partially repaired by his creator, Adam Steel, saves earth from these cruel invaders by destroying their mutant monster, Mull, and their rocket ship and all aboard as well. He triumphs because he has a human heart, and even in his monstrous form he is superior to the cold, heartless aliens from that other wasteland world.

Judith Crist deplored this film in *Book Week* as typical of the loss of purity in all modern art and even modern life, and a reader of *Famous Monsters of Filmland* magazine wrote to that magazine that it was one of several films "which have twisted and cheapened the image of the classic Frankenstein monster. It is obvious that 'things' such as these are created in the hopes that the mention of Frankenstein will attract an enormous audience." Even the editors of that amazing magazine, which mixes reverence for horror films with low comedy and ads for giant ten-foot rubber snakes and monster flies, confessed a hatred for this particular movie.

I am spending such a great deal of time on *Frankenstein Meets the Space Monster* both because it has been cited as a prime example of the degeneracy of the horror film and because, along with George Garrett and John Rodenbeck, I wrote the original screenplay for it. I shall not attempt any defense of the movie as an example of the high art of the horror film, which I have been discussing, for it really is something very different, requiring an entirely different set of standards. It was written from a title supplied by the producers, and it is the best we could think to do with that title and with the requirements of such a low budget picture. It is what it is often advertised to be—a camp horror movie—and as such perhaps it is a useful object lesson to explain just why the modern horror film appears to be in the last stages of decadence. I hope, too, to use it to free my admiration for the horror film from the stigma of *I Was a Teenage Frankenstein* (1957) and its many cheap peers and of such modern metamorphoses of the old figures of darkness as that one which has recently transformed Frankenstein and Dracula into comic book super heroes.

Frankenstein Meets the Space Monster is a comedy. It has its shocks and horrors, but I cannot imagine anyone's being genuinely frightened or moved (except to laughter) by it. It is a joke, a seventy-two-minute mockery of those films which are funny without intending to be, which mock the spirit of the horror film rather than its surfaces. It is camp in reverse, and hopefully the comedy has more gut to it than most of those tittery high camp pieces which have so suddenly appeared like mushrooms after a soaking rain.

Abbott and Costello Meet Frankenstein (1948) is often cited as the last and fatal blow to the "classic" horror film, but it really was a rather loving spoof of a kind of film which was already dead, a recognition that the serious American horror film in its "purity" had already run its course. The creative period in the horror film covers roughly the years between 1931 and 1945. There were, of course, forerunners—the German expressionist film *The Cabinet of Dr. Caligari* (1919), *The Golem* (1920), *Nosferatu* (1922), the silent *Dracula* (1922), and many of Lon Chaney's films. And there have been excellent horror films since 1945, too, but those fifteen years were what Hollywood historians would call the Golden Years, the years when the horror film was as fresh and creative as any other art form.

If art is a making new, then art itself must be constantly changing, taking on new forms and manners in order to freshen and recreate the ancient truths, the eternal verities. In the 1930's and early 1940's, the Hollywood film was the most available and universal form of literary, dramatic, and pictorial art. During the depression years the movie house was the social and entertainment center for millions; they would come out to see anything, and Hollywood gave them everything. Among the serious "dramas of social significance" which were the prestige films of those years and the rootless comedies designed to cheer up a disheartened public came the horror films, which, in very many respects, carried much of the burden of art in the period. Big studios with one of those amazing conjunctions of money to spend and the necessary talent made them possible, and they were good and fresh and truly new.

And art, of course, grew on beyond them. By the mid-forties the horror film was bogged down in dwindling sequels; its major directors were no longer working; its major actors were unable to carry the load themselves, for a film is much too complicated an effort for one element to do the job alone. The films of the 1950's, like that dark and hysterical decade itself, were uninspired and cheap. There have been several real efforts to revive the horror film, chiefly those of Britain's Hammer Productions, but the pure form is dead, although its bits and pieces walk on in countless hideous mutations like those undead and mutilated monsters themselves.

The collapse of the horror film does not negate its artistic values, however, for they are as permanent as any we are allowed in this mutable world. Those few excellent films remain excellent; their dull imitations we should well ignore simply as inferior copies of better things, cheaply designed and cheaply made. My approach and that of my colleagues to *Frankenstein Meets the Space Monster* is one that I advise everyone who cares for serious art to take in regard to the contemporary cheap horror film. Laugh, mock, and enjoy, and all the while rejoice that the great ones were made and are still there for us to seek out and experience to the full.

III

I saw the great horror films in the late 1940's, after the war and the period of their creation, when they were about my age, ten to fifteen years old. In Roanoke, Virginia, my friend Jack Starkey and

I went often to the Park Theatre, which was a small rerun house and is now a parking lot so no ghosts haunt its rows of empty seats. We were always eager, our tennis shoes scrubbing the backs of the seats in front of us as we waited for the dim house lights to go out altogether and for our transmigration to that dark and misty world to begin. I remember the walls and seats of the old Park with the devotion of an aging priest for the cathedral of his ordination, and I remember the intensity of our impatience as it became sweet anticipation while the reel of film on the screen cranked and coiled *Realart* slowly across to its mate, from left to right in a script I would recognize in the most unlikely place even today. And then we were cast into a world of pure delight, tickled by a fear we knew was artificial, and at the same time initiated into the mystery of this life and world and into the true wonder of the free imagination.

Jack Starkey is now a computer expert, while I am a teacher and a writer, but both of us treasure the gift received in those afternoons spent out of the sun in the gloomy Park. I watch those old films today whenever I can, split and skewered by commercials and the costumed mockery of bored announcers, and I can still feel the old thrill, the old magic of the moonstruck Carpathians and those dirt-floored coffins in the vaults of Carfax Abbey. That both my friend and I can still feel a sense of genuine necromancy about those films, despite the variance in the patterns of our lives, is, barring that we both may merely be victims of exaggerated nostalgia, evidence of the imaginative force of those films. I have attempted already a kind of metaphysic of the horror film to explain their appeal and value, but now I should like to shuffle the worn but still bright cards of my memory and consider some of the films in a more detailed fashion. This will be no analysis, but rather an associative ramble through the myths of the American horror film, that part of our voyage of discovery when details of the view bump and jostle for attention and during which each of us will see and recall his own details but, I hope, the same general vista.

Disregarding the demands of all ghouls and zombies, shaggy beasts and hulking reptiles, crawling severed hands and evil eyes, I shall talk about the four primary figures who have entered all our minds from the horror film, for they are the most complex and interesting figures in these modern moralities, evil and innocent, villains and victims—the werewolf, the mummy, the vampire, and Frankenstein's tortured monster.

I have already discussed the cinematic myth of the werewolf and the pathos of the irreconcilable split in his very self. The two films directly concerned with the werewolf are *The Werewolf of London* (1935) and *The Wolf Man* (1941), the first with Henry Hull as the central figure and the second with Lon Chaney, Jr. Both are good films, although *The Wolf Man* focuses more truly on the tragedy of the tormented werewolf and is, thus, the better of the two. The earlier film has a more complicated plot, revolving around a Himalayan plant which can control the disease and the struggle for that plant by the hero and the werewolf (Warner Oland) who bit him and gave him his curse, and who has followed him from the Himalayas to London. Exotic evil is loose in the city in the person of a respectable young man. As he stalks the dark streets, man in figure, wolf in surfaces and mind, he is the emblem of urban evil and urban fear. In this film the fear lies in those nightly ventures, the dangerous shape under the window, the fragility of safety in the huddled herd when the wolf prowls to pick from among them. And when the evil and its bearer and victim are laid to rest, the city has been hurt but is unchanged.

The werewolf is a sympathetic figure as well as a frightening one, but the emphasis in *The Werewolf of London* is more on danger than on poetry. Henry Hull's scrambling, desperate battles with the other werewolf are frenzied and bestial, whether the antagonists are human or wolf at the time; the hero is corrupted and his two natures merge. With that merging much of the poetry is lost, and the story disintegrates into a hunt for something purely evil. But not quite—the werewolf is still a man and his death is still a blessing to himself as well as to his possible victims. The film as a whole is really about the environment, however, and what remains most vividly with me is not the hero's struggle to maintain his idea and his humanity but the image of that shaggy figure, trapped by tall brick walls and paved streets, at war with the city, society, and humanity itself. It is a striking image that the rest of the film cannot sustain.

George Waggner's *The Wolf Man* is, in many ways, a slick film, but it is a full playing out of the werewolf myth and achieves much of the great psychic impact of that myth. It reveals the abyss in truth and shows it most clearly in the worn features and weary voice of Lon Chaney, Jr. It is Chaney's picture, as it should be, and I fear we forget how well he handled himself in the clutter of repetitions of the role which he was forced to make in a variety of inferior sequels: *Frankenstein Meets the Wolf Man* (1943), *House of Frankenstein* (1944), and *House of Dracula* (1946). But even in those poor films Chaney gave Lawrence Talbot a feeling of genuine sadness, of utter hopelessness, which remains emotionally and aesthetically valid despite the sideshow context.

The anguish of Chaney's face and voice, this we remember set against a background as dark and light as the two sides of his doomed nature—the daylight town, Chaney's tweed suits, his budding love; the moonlit night, the gypsy camp where he was bitten and made accursed, the small dry face and voice of Marya Ouspenskaya; her voice played off against the rich and rational voice of Claude Rains, Talbot's father. The texture of the film is rich, and its ending is poignant, for the wolf man is the most human and the most sympathetic of the central figures of the horror film. In the wolf man, driven by an evil lust he never even knew existed and repelled from that part of himself by his goodness and his desire for love, we see our dual selves; his story is the story of us all, exaggerated into parable and myth, but how very true all the same. The shock on Talbot's face at the moment when he sees the hair spreading on the backs of his hands is a register of that primordial fall itself; it is a shock we all must share.

The mummy, Im-ho-tep or Kharis, forced to guard in living death the tomb of his princess, is also a figure we all know. Less human than the werewolf and less sympathetic despite the religious source of his evil, he appears in five films worth considering briefly: *The Mummy*

(1932), *The Mummy's Hand* (1940), *The Mummy's Tomb* (1942), *The Mummy's Ghost* (1944), and *The Mummy's Curse* (1945). Each of these films, and especially the last four, follows a single pattern with a rigidity enforced by the myth. There can be as many variations on the vampire or werewolf as there are new and distinctive characters to face the danger or the horror of becoming one of these two figures, but the mummy is one character, who must forever guard one princess' tomb or at best attempt to revive her spirit in some living woman. He is inflexibly the same, film after film, because he has but one story and that a simple one. All of the myths of the horror films are very limited, perhaps because they are myths, but the mummy's identity is so restricting that the limitations are as binding as the decayed wrappings of his brittle flesh itself.

The Mummy is the first and best of these films, but it has fewer of the familiar elements associated with the mummy story: the Egyptian priest, the Tana leaves, the stalking figure dragging a foot and with only one good arm, covered with pulpy rotten bandages. Im-ho-tep, played by Boris Karloff with all of his usual skill and grace, appears as a wrapped mummy only at the beginning of the film; later he masquerades as Ardath Bey, a living man, wrinkled and dry in appearance, but no hulking, powerful creature. He uses the force of mind and magic in his attempt to recreate his lost princess in a living girl, and his failure is not accomplished by human effort but by the very gods who cursed him to his long living death. He was punished initially for defying the gods and attempting to bring his lost love, the Princess Anck-es-en-amon, back to life after her untimely death; he dies at the end of the film at the hands of the goddess Isis, who responds to the pleas of the girl with whom he is attempting the same blasphemy once again. The rules and justice of God, whatever his name, never vary, and only a final and everlasting death can free man from his eternal folly and desire to rebel.

The Mummy is the best film of its genre because of the quality of its performances and the very high quality of its effects, especially Karloff's makeup, both as a mummy and as Ardath Bey. But its fatalistic story, which works itself out independent of any hero's action and with very little sympathy for the protagonist, curiously limits it.

It is the best film, but it does not exploit the full potentiality of the myth as well as its inferior successors. The one scene which strikes to the heart of its viewer's imagination and there remains is one early in the film in which the mummy's eyes flicker open for the first time in his sarcophagus as a foolish young man ignores the advice of his older and wiser colleague and reads aloud the words of the ancient scroll of Thoth, by which Isis raised Osiris from the dead. The weight of the film rests in this scene: the terror of seeing the dead awaken and rise and the moral lesson that reason apart from imagination (the young man's dismissal of the scroll's power as superstition) is unable to cope with the dark realities of being. Karloff's ever so slowly opening eye is the essence of *The Mummy*.

The later mummy films revise the names of the story slightly (the mummy, Kharis, suffers because he attempted to raise the Princess Ananka from the dead), but they change the pattern strikingly. Now the mummy is called from his tomb by a member of an underground cult who believe the Egyptian religion and are led by the priests of Karnak. He is kept alive and is controlled by Tana leaves, and he is used by the priests as a blind tool of vengeance against the defilers of the princess' tomb. Kharis remains a mummy throughout the film, nearly indestructible and of superhuman strength; his clumsiness, his slowness of movement, his one open eye, his flaking and rotten wrappings—all give him his proper mythic stature. He is no longer merely something very evil and very ancient; he is now the grave itself bursting hideously through the window, death calling in a gigantic and violently irresistible form.

The story is freer, too, more Christian and less fatalistic, for the mummy is defeated by either human courage or human greed and lust on the part of the priest, and the myth gains its moral element from the nature of that defeat. The later films are weakened, then, not by the development of the story but by a lessening of attention to detail, bad writing, and clumsy acting and direction, despite occasionally fine work by such actors as Tom Tyler (the mummy in *The Mummy's Hand*), Lon Chaney, Jr. (the mummy in the last three films), George Zucco, John Carradine, and Turhan Bey. The image of the mummy remains with us as the powerful force of death itself, stopping at no human barrier. And, paradoxically, the film speaks to us of natural death as a proper end, unlike the mummy's lingering horror of living death. The villains are generally the priests; the mummy himself is an unspeakable horror, but his evil is that of a preternatural force to be used and misused by human agencies. The man Kharis who died for love is too long lost in time and the mummy's mouldering figure to affect us like the victim of the werewolf's curse. Our feelings are clear and unmixed at his final destruction; any restoration of order here is a victory to be celebrated, for it is a victory over unleashed death and a restoration of the natural order and peace of the daily rhythm of birth and death.

If the mummy is, then, a figure of violent and walking death from whom there seems no escape short of the grave, the vampire is an even more potent figure, for he insidiously steals from his victims even the peace of death and the safety of the grave. The *struldbrugs* in *Gulliver's Travels* were meant by Swift to be a Christian moral lesson, to show his readers the foolishness of desiring eternal life on earth, when that life must be, because of the very order of things, unnatural and, therefore, grotesque and horrible. The legend of the vampire, of the undead, springs from an ancient fear of the dead and their power among the living; it has evolved to become, like the tale of the *struldbrugs,* a moral lesson concerning the absurdity of the desire for eternal life on earth. The vampire rises from the dead to walk eternally among living men, but he is not alive. He is undead, a creature bound by satanic laws to thrive on the blood of his fellow men and to lure them into the snare of living death. The vampire's strength is subtle; he woos his victims into his power; he charms them with an inversion of love (the very force of salvation) into a desire for his sharp kiss, a yearning for the damnation of the undead. The vampire comes closest of all these figures of evil in the horror film to representing sin itself, for his every action is a lure to that evil in the flawed human spirit in this fallen world to exert itself, to love the darkness and the void. He does not spring upon his prey suddenly and violently like the werewolf or the mummy, but he weaves his pattern of darkness into the light of their lives slowly and subtly and at their own invitation.

There have been a whole host of vampire films, perhaps because the myth is flexible within its rigid limitations and more open than the others to continual reinterpretation—or perhaps because sin is so much more enticing when it is shown in such elegant trappings and yet so purely bare, so shamelessly naked. Most of the films are descendants of one of the most popular plays of this century, itself an adaptation of Bram Stoker's novel *Dracula* (1897). Among those films which appeared from 1931 to 1945 are: *Dracula* (1931), *Mark of the Vampire* (1934), *Dracula's Daughter* (1936), *Son of Dracula* (1943), *Return of the Vampire* (1944), and, of course, *House of Frankenstein* (1944) and *House of Dracula* (1946). All of these but two, *Mark of the Vampire* and *Return of the Vampire,* are directly or indirectly involved with Count Dracula, the literary character who has come to be the epitome of the vampire, the dominant figure of the myth. He is Transylvanian (his name means *devil* in Rumanian), titled, suave, perversely handsome, and nearly irresistible in the appeal of his evil. Appropriately, then, the best vampire film, *Tod Browning's Dracula,* is the closest to his source, a direct adaptation of the play. And, although other actors have played the role (among them Lon Chaney, Jr., and John Carradine), Bela Lugosi, the star both of the play during much of its long run and of the film, is the finest Dracula, the haunting figure of our dreams.

Tod Browning, who, with James Whale and Val Lewton, is one of the three artists of horror film–making, shaped the stage play into an effective piece of cinema, dark with night and floating mists, the cobwebbed castle of Dracula, and the danger always lurking beyond the windows and open French doors of every well-lighted drawing room. The tone of the film, like the thin veneer of the vampire's exterior, is polite and restrained; Count Dracula, whether in his own lifeless castle attended by his wives in flowing white gowns or in the midst of London society, is the spirit of decorum and restraint. His clothes are the evening clothes of a gentleman; his manners are polished; his voice is soft and pleasingly foreign to English ears. He is an engaging figure until we notice his face—the hard eyes, the commanding nose, and the mouth which is sensual and almost obscene. It is a naked face, a face in which perverse hunger yearns in every feature. And the voice, as we hear it more, is also faintly obscene, a caress suggesting unthinkable delights, unforgivable sins. They are the face and voice of sin itself, with an appeal that is raw and primitive even in the guise of civilization and high culture.

Dracula's evil is decadent, the decay beneath the surfaces of a society which has refused to face evil and has let it fester out of sight, a late nineteenth-century evil but also a universal evil, the dark lust within us all for the perverse and the unnatural. *Dracula* is sexual, as sexual as Oscar Wilde's *The Picture of Dorian Gray,* and Browning's control and understatement of the sexuality explains much of the film's success. Later vampire films, especially the Hammer films, *The Horror of Dracula* (1958), *Brides of Dracula* (1960), and *Kiss of the Vampire* (1963), and Roger Vadim's *Blood and Roses* (1961), have exploited the perverse sexuality more fully; in the Hammer films, beautiful and innocent girls writhe breathlessly before Dracula's violent arrival and their rape into undeath, and Vadim's vampire, a beautiful young woman, kisses the blood from her equally beautiful young victim's pricked lip, a scene which was cut in America because of its Lesbian sexuality. But Browning's Dracula is a more frightening and potent figure because of his decadence, his slow and almost lifeless embrace, his light kiss behind the cover of his black coat. He is a figure of naked hunger, indeed, but his strength and his danger lie in his ability to obscure that nakedness in a haze of manners and surfaces, in the smoothness of his approach, in the subtlety of his veiled appeal. His victims never remember his caresses as he slowly drains their blood and life away; like the vampire bat, he drinks and satisfies his hunger from the throats of living beings who cannot feel his touch, who do not remember his presence even when the wounds of his teeth are revealed by the light of day. The shock of the naked truth which lies at the end of his wooing is, then, doubly horrible, a sudden glimpse of the abyss that lies forever open beneath the glittering surface of sin and the lust unto death.

Dracula is, then, truly the devil, luring us from God and the love

which is the creative force of life, wooing us away from that
natural order of life and death with the promise of an eternity, distorting the love which is life into an unnatural love of life which leads
us counter to God's will into the damnation of being neither living
nor dead, of being undead. The vampire myth is very close in
metaphysical structure to a morality play, for it warns us in a variety
of ways against the temptations of sin and rebellion against the world
of God's inexplicable order. To surrender to Dracula is to lose one's
human spirit, humanity itself. To become one of the undead is, of
course, the total inversion of humanity into inhumanity, but the film
also presents an example of the debasing effects and danger of less
than total sin—the comic absurdity of Renfield (played brilliantly by
Dwight Frye), who is a grotesque parody of the vampire lusting for
spiders and rats, his humanity made laughable, but still a useful tool
for his "master," an effective agent of sin. And, too, as any moral
work of art must, the film reveals the vulnerability of evil and gives
us an account of the suffering and sacrifice necessary for its defeat.

The force which can defeat sin and the vampire's dark appeal is
the same which can destroy the werewolf and the mummy—the action
impelled by the courage and selflessness of love and guided by the
wisdom of a union of reason and belief. The hero is no striking figure
like Count Dracula, but an ordinary human—the young lover of one
of his intended victims, her father, or a dedicated wise man like Dr.
Van Helsing of whom I have already spoken. Ordinary humans must
find the courage in themselves to expose the vampire for what he is,
to defend his helpless prey from him, and to seek him out in his lair
and drive through his heart the stake that will pin him to his coffin
and to the final rest of death. There is, as a good example, the
scene in which Van Helsing tricks Dracula into looking into a mirror
which will not reflect his image, proving him to be a vampire; Lugosi's hiss as he whips the cloak before his eyes is the anguished sound
of the primordial serpent exposed as Satan himself.

And the victory must be gained by sacrifice, too. A father may
have to drive a stake into his own daughter's heart to free her from
the demon's clutch; a lover must ignore the pleas of his beloved,
must disbelieve and imprison her to save her. Of course, the sacrifice

of Christ is always the strongest weapon with which to control the evil; the crucifix is hateful to the vampire's eyes, and he can face it no more successfully than he can live in daylight, that other symbol of life and God's creative love. And death, the vampire's source and weapon, is the agency of his destruction. Driven back to the soil of his coffin, the dust that none of us can escape, the vampire dies as we all must die, a death which is natural and which must be enforced to preserve the natural order from his perverse escape from his ordained end. Like the forces of sin and death, Count Dracula's power is destroyed by human action and God's love; the approaching dawn drives Dracula to his coffin, where his human opponents can find and finish him.

The myth is a full and rich one, human and religious, of great imaginative force. The later films capture much of that force and are often of high quality, although none approaches the stature of *Dracula*. *Mark of the Vampire* is sadly not a horror film nor a mystery film, but a rather unpleasant hybrid of the two. The other later films, although not as carefully and well made, have at least the dark power of the myth, and occasionally they use it effectively: Gloria Holden's scenes with Irving Pitchell as vampire and servant in *Dracula's Daughter,* Lon Chaney, Jr.'s scrabbling fear of the coming dawn, and the scenes between Lugosi and Matt Willis in *Return of the Vampire.* But the myth lives most fully in the original *Dracula.* It is that Count Dracula's pale and hungry face that we shall continue to see, peering from the dark shadows of ourselves, and that soft voice which we shall continue to hear, calling us to the caress of sin and to the lip of the abyss.

And they all speak of darkness—the werewolf of the darkness of sudden and inescapable madness and evil which one can observe in himself but cannot escape; the mummy of the darkness of a passionate love turned into an eternal nightmare, of death turned loose to walk the world in vengeance for forgotten sins; and the vampire of the most terrifying darkness of sin itself. And there remains the cinematic myth of Frankenstein, the one which moves me most deeply, the one which speaks of the darkness of being a fallen and flawed thing, alone in a world of hate and misunderstanding, out of harmony with the design of his creator and an offense to himself and to nature in that creator's eyes, doomed by the very flesh of his body to sin and separation and a long suffering unto death. The Frankenstein story speaks of the darkness of man in a fallen state, separated from God and seeking communion and understanding.

Certainly a simpler reading, and a valid one, is to consider the story of Dr. Frankenstein and his monster to be completely medieval in its moral basis, to understand it as the cautionary tale of a man who tampers with the laws of nature beyond the bounds set him by God and who suffers the sad consequences of his sin. Like Marlowe's Faustus, Frankenstein does seek too much knowledge and pays for his arrogance; but the story is something more than that, for it is as much the monster's as his creator's, and their relationship is the center of the story, dramatically and morally. As Mary Shelley wrote it originally, it is the completely Romantic story of "The Modern Prometheus," and, although the film manages successfully to avoid most of her Shelleian philosophical lectures, it does adhere to the complexity of that central relationship. The monster defines that relationship himself in the novel, as he pleads for Frankenstein to make him a wife, and offers a clearly Romantic interpretation of his fall and of his responsibilities to his creator and his creators' responsibilities to him:

> I am thy creature, and I will be even mild and docile to my natural lord and king, if thou wilt also perform thy part, the which thou owest me. Oh, Frankenstein, be not equitable to every other, and trample upon me alone, to whom thy justice, and even thy clemency and affection, is most due. Remember that I am thy creature, I ought to be thy Adam; but I am rather the fallen angel, whom thou drivest from joy for no misdeed. Everywhere I see bliss, from which I alone am irrevocably excluded. I was benevolent and good; misery made me a fiend. Make me happy, and I shall again be virtuous.

But is his fall so simple? And what of his creator's relationship to his Creator in turn? Mary Shelley developed her story thoroughly and skillfully, and the films follow it to some degree, especially *The Bride of Frankenstein,* but they have changed her rational and argumentative monster substantially and succeeded in transmuting a minor philosophical novel into a cinematic myth which carries the full emotional and moral impact of a major work of art. This is, unfortunately, not the place for a discussion of the similarities and differences between the novel and the film, but I should like to use one difference to serve as a starting point for my discussion of the films.

Mary Shelley's monster is in many ways the superior of his creator, morally as well as physically, but they can never gain an understanding because of Frankenstein's repugnance for that creature's ugliness and the misdeeds resulting from his ugliness and his isolation from human society. Frankenstein agrees to make the monster a mate but finally cannot because of that repugnance and the consequent strain on his conscience; he destroys her before she may live, and the monster loses his chance to begin a new life (and perhaps a new race) because of his creator's moral nature. In *The Bride of Frankenstein* the monster makes similar demands, for he has learned what it is to love and to be loved. Frankenstein agrees and creates a bride for his Adam, but the new Eve, impelled by whatever remains in her brain of her former human life, shrinks from her intended mate and shrieks in absolute disgust and terror. The monster, who has been driven away from every human contact and driven to violence and murder by his mistreatment, surrenders to despair and destroys himself and his bride.

Mary Shelley's monster dies, too, by his own hand when, after the death of his creator and the end of their long vendetta, he steps onto an ice floe and is "borne away by the waves and lost in darkness and distance." But he also dies a Romantic hero, morally superior to Frankenstein in his suffering and his refusal to yield his identity and life while his creator still lived. He speaks to the corpse of Frankenstein: "Blasted as thou wert, my agony was still superior to thine; for the bitter sting of remorse will not cease to rankle in my wounds until death shall close them forever"; he dies secure in the knowledge that his "spirit will sleep in peace; or if it thinks, it will not surely think thus."

The film monster does not die a hero's death, nor can he be sure of anything but death itself. He dies in a moment of total despair, rejected by even a creature of his own kind, driven to destroy not only himself but everything he is. His is a plunge into violent death, peaceful in contrast to his life but blacker by infinities than that quiet spiritual assurance of the novel's hero. The monster of the films is the ultimate victim, the final image of lost and suffering man, all illusions stripped away, naked in his own damnation. The horror of his death may be the most intense of all these cinematic myths, and the Frankenstein story is the most complex and, for all its darkness, finally enlightening.

There are seven films in which the monster appears in more or less his original form: two superior ones, *Frankenstein* (1931) and *The Bride of Frankenstein* (1935), both with Boris Karloff as the monster; two good ones, *The Son of Frankenstein* (1939), again with Karloff, and *The Ghost of Frankenstein* (1942) with Lon Chaney, Jr.; and three inferior ones, *Frankenstein Meets the Wolf Man* (1943), with Bela Lugosi as the monster, and *House of Frankenstein* (1944) and *House of Dracula* (1946), both with Glenn Strange. The first of these is the most familiar and the purest statement of the rudiments of the myth. It is, in many ways, the finest of the lot, a fortunate blend of talents which gives it a variety of strengths: the direction of James Whale; the acting of Boris Karloff, Dwight Frye, and Colin Clive; the monster's makeup by Jack Pierce; and the general high tone of the screenplay, the sets, and the photography. These strengths lead us to forget the voices and undeniably Hollywood accents (the flattest American imaginable) of the maids in Baron Frankenstein's home and the other lapses which are embarrassing in their baldness. What we remember is the danger (the monster's bellow in the Baron's halls, the fury of the lightning around the stone tower, the menace of the monster's hand raising toward Dr. Waldman, the face of the monster through the revolving gears in the windmill) and the poetry (the thunk of clods on a hollow coffin at night, the monster's hands reaching for light and speaking his frustration and hopelessness when it is withdrawn, the first motion of his hand indicating that he is alive, again the monster's face through the gears in the windmill).

Henry Frankenstein, as Colin Clive plays him, is a man obsessed by a vision who fails himself when the vision fails. He is a man of reason, but of reason crippled by a lack of belief. He knows that he can create life, but he does not know the real nature of this world—lacks the belief to see it plain—fallen and corrupt. His assistant, the hunchback (Dwight Frye), is a victim of an excess of belief without reason; afraid of the dark but brave with a torch when the monster proves to fear fire, he is unable to understand what happens and is, thus, directly responsible for the distortion of events. The monster is not seeking peace for his spirit here, but rather he is seeking his spirit itself, his identity, his humanity. Sewn together from the parts of many men, guided by a criminal brain because of the hunchback's fear, he is no man at all, but he appears to have the potentiality of becoming a man. Karloff's expressive hands, groping for the light, define him completely; new to a world beyond understanding, with only the echoes in his brain of another man who used it before, he gropes for the light, and the light is denied him.

The entire film is a flowing pattern of dark and light, texturally beautiful and symbolically rich. The world away from the monster is light and innocent; even Henry's clothes are light at his father's home. The monster, doomed even as he proves his potential for humanity, is dressed in black, kept in a dark dungeon, and denied any light save the threatening fire of a torch. After the initial failure of his dream Frankenstein struggles to maintain a clear division between day and night, light and dark, innocence and the dark truth. His struggle fails when the dark comes into the light and the monster walks in the spring countryside. The film pivots on this scene, for in it the monster is more nearly human than ever before or after, and his deranged brain fails his attempt to attain humanity.

The scene, as James Whale intended it, is overwhelming in its poetry and its danger. The spring woods are twinkling with light; the only darkness is the monster, who takes on a menacing poignancy as he moves through the saplings. By a pond he finds a little girl playing with her kitten; she does not fear him, and her innocence makes them both children, their world a childish Eden. She teaches the monster how to throw daisies into the water so that they float like small, bright boats. The monster is, for the only time in his life, happy; his smile is grotesque and beautiful. When the daisies are gone, he takes up the lovely child and throws her into the water to float like the flower she is. But she is not a flower; she does not float; she drowns. The monster moves away, his hands shaping in the air the horror of his deed and the futility of his ever understanding it. That moaning figure thrashing through the thin hanging bows of a willow tree is the essence of the film; black and ugly, a creature of death and darkness, he is as innocent and wounded as are we all. He is fallen, and the remainder of the film carries him on down that dark descent.

The film as it is normally shown is seriously damaged because the scene is cut abruptly as the monster, puzzlement on his features, reaches for the child. The next scene shows her father carrying her limp and very dead body into the town, through dancers and music celebrating Henry Frankenstein's wedding day, halting the gaiety and bringing the dark firmly and permanently into the light. The subtlety of that wedding of innocence and death by the water at the edge of the young forest is lost, and the monster appears purely evil for the rest of the film. A sad mistake which we may never be able to rectify, but at least we can know what was intended and experience the film fully by imaginative reconstruction.

The bulk of the rest of the film takes place in darkness—the only light, the light of torches, often reflected inverted in water. The symbols rush together and fuse in the windmill where the creator is held by his creature, the structure surrounded by the mob of frenzied and frightened townspeople. Frankenstein and his monster stare at each other through the moving bars of a wooden gear, forever at one and forever separated, neither comprehending the full horror of the moment. Frankenstein is flung out, saved by an action of death, and the monster dies by fire, the only light allowed him, destructive and hurtful. The order restored is the order of life itself, an inextricable tangle of light and dark, good and evil. The dying embers of that blaze speak the continual sacrifice of man on the pyre of his own failing. We rejoice that the danger, this small part of it, is over; the poetry is too rich for rejoicing and too true for tears.

The Bride of Frankenstein is generally considered to be James Whale's best film. Given adequate funds and actors of the quality of Karloff, Frye, Clive, Elsa Lanchester, Ernest Thesiger, and O. P. Heggie, Whale produced a film which is rhythmically and pictorially a masterpiece. Jack Pierce's makeup for the monster (now scarred by fire, his hair scorched away revealing the clumsy sutures and metal clamps above his forehead) is even more amazing in its elaborate and convincing detail than in the first picture; the black and white photography is carefully conceived and executed, and the tones and forms of the pictures are as fine as, and very similar to, those of Ingmar Bergman, especially in his *The Seventh Seal* and *Virgin Spring*. The screenplay lacks the clarity and parabolic quality of *Frankenstein,* but it makes up for it with an involved texture of expressed ideas and symbols. The film is a full expression of the possibilities of the communal art of film-making, even in so commercial a place as Hollywood, when happy circumstance frees the artists to create.

The film begins, after a brief prologue featuring Elsa Lanchester as Mary Shelley, in a primordial darkness of place and spirit, lit only by the dying embers of the burning windmill. Two old peasants have remained after the mob has left, hoping to loot the structure of whatever they can find undamaged by the fire. Their greed leads them only to the monster, who rises from the watery depths of the mill with the old woman's help; he has killed her husband below, and he kills her. Sin breeds death, and the destroyer still lives after a baptism in human violence, fire, and water. The film follows his quest for his humanity and his creator's relapse into sin, weaving their paths together in a cemetery and releasing them finally in the finished net of failure, despair, and death. The monster wanders into the world, is imprisoned, and escapes, hounded by packs of men and dogs, as hopeless in his new resurrection as in his first rebirth. He finds peace and kindness in the cabin of an old and blind man; he learns to speak and he learns to love. But he is hounded away to a cemetery, the appropriate place of focus for the film to which I shall return a bit further on.

Meanwhile, Henry Frankenstein has been lured by a Mephistophelean Dr. Pretorius, a creator of homunculi, to begin work on a mate for the monster. Pretorius, on a body-snatching visit to the cemetery, finds the monster, and they proceed to the castle laboratory for the fatal events that end the film—the monster's final rejection, despair, and self-destruction.

Perhaps the scenes between Karloff and O. P. Heggie, in which the monster and the old man move together by means of music and language are the most tenderly moving in the film; they are photographed in a misty, fairyland style—light diffuses through the entire frame of the picture. But the scene in the cemetery brings the darkness of the myth into its most tangible form; symbol and action unite in those short moments as they never do elsewhere. The monster's Eden with his blind mentor lost irrevocably, he moves in terror and rage through the cemetery, striking out at the stones, the emblems of his own lost natural death and of an immortality denied him by the process of his creation. For one frozen moment he stands at the base of a very large statue of a saint, hand raised in benediction. The monster is an image of anguish and despair, imploring salvation and striking out at it in the same gesture, human despair and yearning etched for a moment in his tilted head, his outstretched arms and bending legs—Karloff's genius at its most astounding. And to the right of this tableau, tilting with the weight of years, the cross in stone and Christ, suffering the fullest sacrifice to human blindness and cruelty, to man's fallen and sinful nature. Both Christ and the monster are victims of man—one a grotesque parody of the other, but a parody suitable to man's distortion of his own place in the harmony of God.

This scene gives us *The Bride of Frankenstein* in essence, as simply and purely as a medieval religious emblem sought to relate the truth of God. The entire film is stylized and non-realistic in tone, clearly a parable, never allowing itself to be taken as a simple tale. The monster permits his creator and his wife to escape the tower before it explodes. A noble act, the last remnant of the humanity he strove so hard to acquire, and his end is moving as the death of no simple villain can ever be—a blunt indictment of man and his wicked and cruel folly. The villain is Henry Frankenstein (and Dr. Pretorius as an externalization of his weakness and evil), a man who toyed with life, whose idealism collapsed in the face of reality, who gave and found only pain for all his efforts. He is a Faustus doomed in life, lacking even the strength of his monster to destroy what was unnatural and never should have been. And man, poor man, both villain and victim, is always the source and subject of this brilliant film.

Both films give the monster the peace of death and restore order to the world in which he could not live, but it is a painful death and a dark restoration of order. The death of the vampire or the werewolf or even the mummy seems more positive, frees a man caught in a perversion of life to the possibilities of death—of peace and even of salvation, of harmony with the real natural order. But the monster never achieves his humanity, and his death is only a blotting out, a leap from unnatural life into nothing. Where, then, is the moral lesson, the accommodation to death in this myth? It is, I think, involved in an act of love, a feeling of sympathy with the ugliest and most outcast of living creatures, an act which no human in the films is capable of making but one which each member of the audience should make. We give our feelings to the monster, suffer and die with him, even hate ourselves among the townspeople as we understand them, too.

There is the power of the Frankenstein myth, the power to inspire love for the untouchable, feeling for the violent and murderous beast, love and fear involved as they seldom are but always should be. The Frankenstein myth teaches us how fallen we are and, at the same time, how we must love one another, despite all our sins and crimes, in order to live through that world and maintain the humanity which the monster could not only not find in himself, but which he smothered in those around him with their fear and violence. If the film can rouse our sympathy for the monster and his downward path to death, it has shown us the possibility of a life which, even with death as its inevitable end, can be rich with love and alive with the human spirit.

The later films require little comment for all their virtues. The monster in them survives the destruction of the tower but loses the power of his mind. He becomes a crippled engine of destruction, impelled by memories and events beyond his understanding, still capable of showing affection and gentleness for a child but blindly violent and uncheckable. In Rowland V. Lee's *Son of Frankenstein,* he is rescued by Igor, a distorted old madman, legally dead for having survived a hanging with a broken neck. Igor and Wolf Frankenstein heal the monster, but finally Wolf kills him by kicking him into a bubbling sulphur pit. Igor is certainly the most imaginative and creative figure in the film; Bela Lugosi's performance is perhaps even finer than his rendering of Dracula. Basil Rathbone and Lionel Atwill are more than adequate, but the memorable thing in the film is the town in which the events take place, a town full of maimed people, victims of the monster's earlier violence, visualized most clearly by Lionel Atwill's salute with his wooden right arm, a replacement for his real one which was torn off by the monster. Igor, the crippled town, and, of course, Karloff, as brilliant and as brilliantly made up as ever—these remain, but both the poetry and the danger are lessened. The myth is damaged as the monster loses his humanity and becomes simply a force of death akin to the mummy.

Erle C. Kenton's *The Ghost of Frankenstein* is the poorest of the four. In it, Igor, by deception and trickery, substitutes his brain in an elaborate operation designed to give the monster a new brain and a new life. The blood in the body and that required by Igor's brain do not match; the monster speaks in Igor's voice but dies finally and ignominiously in a laboratory fire. The myth died hard, too, in the monster's final dismemberment and degradation. Perhaps it is an appropriate end; it is, in some way, moving, but it can in no way match the power and importance of the first two films. Of this film, what remains most clearly are two images: one, the monster walking through a misty cemetery, caked all over with sulphur, a ghost in the flesh, a haunting image; the other, the monster stumbling in an electric storm, arms raised, seeking the power of the lightning which gave him birth, a pathetic reference to his quest for humanity, now reduced to a desire for only life itself. Two echoes of the real myth, but echoes worthy of that myth.

The later films are unworthy. Each has a moment or two (the monster's face through the ice, emerging as the frost is scraped away, for example, in *Frankenstein Meets the Wolf Man*), but they are generally imitative and pointlessly repetitive. Glenn Strange's monster is a striking figure, but not a poetic one; Bela Lugosi's is short, clearly marked with Count Dracula's distinctive nose, and a sad failure. The only lesson these later Frankenstein films and all of the inferior sequel horror films have to offer is some evidence of the unending appeal of those imaginative myths. They speak that lesson but scarcely any other.

Of all these films of that creative time I feel the best to be *Frankenstein,* the truest meeting of form and meaning, text and texture, the one film which is most fully human in its horror and poetic in its danger. There were other fine films, of course, which I have not even mentioned, primarily those produced by Val Lewton (among them: Jacque Tourneur's *Cat People,* 1942, *I Walked with a Zombie,* 1943, and *The Leopard Man,* 1943; Gunter Fritsch and Robert Wise's *Curse of the Cat People,* 1944; and Wise's *The Body Snatcher,* 1945). And many others, too many to mention, but I believe that most of them may be remembered and understood best in the light of the ones I have discussed. These films, as much as any other American art form of their period, enacted imaginatively the dark drama and truth of the human spirit. That we have ignored them and left them to children is unfortunate but should not come as a surprise. So very often we choose to disregard the truths of the dark imagination when it is freed of realism to roam in parable the fallen essence of our being, and almost as often we give those parables to our children; think of Swift, Stevenson, Carroll, Mark Twain, Mary Shelley, Bram Stoker, and these very films. And giving them to children may be appropriate, too, for we initiate them to art and to life that way, to a very high form of art and a darkly positive understanding of life. We accommodate them to death before they see its awful face in life. We give them the dreams with which to pass the night and safely find the breaking of the day.

IV

There is one apparent contradiction in all this, one fact upon which all my pleadings stand or fall. The horror film is a meaningful and viable art form, concerned with the eternal verities, making them new. And the horror film, I have said, is almost a dead form, a genre of lifeless imitation after its one period of full blossom some twenty and more years ago.

The answer to that contradiction is simply that it is but another example of the unending paradox of art, that the very acts of making new must themselves continually be made new. The thirties and early forties were a time of social crisis and a dominance of artistic social realism. The horror film in America, much like the fiction of Kafka, Nabokov, and many of the surrealists, carried the burden of the imaginative tradition, the tradition of parable. The World War, its horrors, and the horrors of the years following it did not end the need for this kind of art; they did change its terms and forced, as the passage of time always does, another metamorphosis in the surfaces of the same familiar truths, the ones that never change however much we may try.

Oddly enough, then, one reason that the pure horror film died is that its mode of truth-making was so valid that it had to change. Another reason is that the use of the elements of fantasy and dream as a primary artistic technique has become so widespread today in all Western literature and art. Louis MacNeice noted, in his *Varieties of Parable,* that "parable writing is today the concern of only a minority. It is a growing minority and, I think, a very important one." Beckett and Golding are his examples; others are easy to find: Gunter Grass and Tommaso Landolfi, J. R. R. Tolkien, John Hawkes, and Thomas Pynchon; and in the film, Ingmar Bergman, whom Frederico Fellini has called "a conjurer—half witch and half showman," and Fellini himself. They have all explored in their art those ancient truths available to imagination beneath the surfaces of fact. These are the real descendants of James Whale and Tod Browning, Karloff and Lugosi, not the later horror films nor even their science fiction offspring, good as some of them have been.

And perhaps in another way that line of aesthetic descent has been responsible for our failure to accord the horror films of the thirties and early forties the appreciation they truly earned and deserve. The later horror films (with the exception of several of the first Hammer films and an occasional film like Mario Bava's *Black Sunday,* 1961, with the unique talents of Barbara Steele) have been so very cheap and tawdry, so thoroughly meaningless and formless, that we have forgotten the quality of their forebears. Their illegitimate but obvious line of descent obscured the honorable but subtle true line, that line running from the rituals of primitive initiation and sacrifice perhaps to the mass itself and on to the morality play, the medieval and renaissance allegory, the visions of the Romantics, the dreams of Eden of the Victorians, and on to Kafka and the moderns; in America from Poe, Hawthorne, and Melville to Mark Twain, and on to the horror film, one of our major contributions to the literature of the fallen human spirit laid bare.

The horror film does, I am sure, deserve its historical position in that long and continuing tradition, and, I feel, those few superb films are still able to make truth new to those who can come to them fresh, who can see them without the accumulated refuse of their bastard offspring. Because they were made with care and sensitivity, they maintain their imaginative force, their danger and their poetry.

And, too, there is something about us, even in an age of continually imminent nuclear destruction, that requires the particular dangers of the night and strange beasts that have prowled it in the lore of superstitition and simple belief. Those dangers, supernatural as they may be, are always human and always reflect that human evil in us all, that failure of spirit and love which is the source of all evil. The drama of nuclear disaster shifts the focus away from man to his devices and is finally unsatisfactory in its attempt to exorcise the mortal terror of the human spirit. That is art's limitation and its value; it is and must always be human, of and about the truths of the human heart.

Just before I began writing these rambling pages, I went to a horror film, *The Reptile,* a Seven Arts–Hammer film in color, new, not their best, marred by weak acting and a stiff screenplay. But it had imagination; its story of a young woman cursed by her father's prying into oriental religions to become a creature half-snake and half-human, to kill for life and to suffer for killing, is true to our knowledge of the fall. The pattern of her exposure and destruction is the familiar one, requiring sacrifice and pain before the normal human order is restored. I liked the film, but I could see its flaws; it haunts no dreams of mine these nights. But I saw the film with my wife Annie and our friend Henry Taylor, both of them imaginative people, both poets, and both of them having never seen the great horror films nor many later ones. They both became deeply involved, suffered the fear, shared the sacrifice, and felt the full weight of the ancient truth despite its clumsy telling. That night was long for them both and the dawn well earned.

The spirit yearns for the dark truth, for only through knowledge of the dark, the experience of the danger, can the light of day and the poetry be gained. If *The Reptile,* an imitation for all its virtues, can fulfill a valid aesthetic function, its success is proof of the value of the genre and of the lasting worth of the finest products of that genre. I only wish I had been able that recent night to have shared with my wife and my friend one of those brilliant films, *Frankenstein* or *Dracula* or *The Wolf Man,* that I shared with Jack Starkey in my youth, that I have tried to share with you, my fellow voyager and persevering reader. How much purer their experience would have been, and how much closer they would have been led to the bare face of truth disguised in the veils of activity and fact.

And so the Arnheim we sought proves to be nothing but the realm of art itself, valueless and as valuable as anything we have, artificial and as real as experience, false and as true as we are ever allowed to be. Its minarets and spires are man-made in a world of and not of man's making, but they express the aspirations of the human spirit in the face of man's own sin, the poetry of his struggle for good order in the face of the disorder of his own evil. The journey has led us back to ourselves, where all such voyages must start and end.

I hope I have not misled you or disappointed you by promising wonders and offering you only yourself. I shall continue to dream my dream, to drag my tall and heavy body ahead of the mob, to face a fiery end in anguish, and to find the peace of sleep and even death beyond it. The horror film is not the sum of art, but it is art. I hope we shall not forget it and lose its force and truth, its poetry and danger. Its demons are the demons of our hearts; it teaches us to recognize them well, but also to contend with them with reason and belief, not to despair, to know the strength of love and life within that very heart wherein they dwell.

RICHARD E. PECK

Films, Television, and Tennis

A work of art becomes, in the hands of an historian, an artifact, a primary document which he uses to define the culture that produced it. Developments in literature, in the plastic arts, even in handicrafts, somehow help the archaeologist or historian to understand the minds and opinions of the people whose concerns fostered them. If such an approach is valid, and I think it is, consider then the delights awaiting some future historian who turns his attention to tapes or films of today's television fare. For television—not the plastic arts, not literature, not theater, not cinema—is the characteristic art form of the 1960's.

97

It is the child of consensus. The American love for westerns, for the fake history of a distinctively American era, gave us *High Noon* and *Shane* as well as the Lash La Rue sagas, penny dreadfuls, and Randolph Scott. The same affection keeps *Bonanza* perched securely atop the Nielsen's year after plot-repeating year. As the child of consensus, it offers the reminder that ours is not an age in which satire thrives. Inez Robb's syndicated suggestion that exterminating senior citizens would obviate the need for Medicare brought shocked replies; people persist in misunderstanding Art Buchwald's wit; and witness the undeserved demise of *That Was the Week That Was. The Man From U.N.C.L.E.,* a series which initially parodied itself, has responded to the time's temper and gone more or less straight. Those shows created to satirize either die aborning, turn farce, or lose their satiric edge and drift toward expressing the Grand Consensus dominant in a Great Society. Without evaluating such a drift, one must agree that television reacts to, and thereby defines, majority opinion.

Beginning as the written word, television scripts reflect literary tastes and fads as well. The fictional anti-hero, whose contrived clumsiness and gaucheries continue to enrich publishers, spawned a televised counterpart. Under several names, Dagwood bumbles through his family's problems, a charming but incompetent man who somehow fails to fit into the world, but fits snugly within the confines of a 21-inch screen. In the case of a Gomer Pyle, he finds acceptance. But—to return to an earlier point—those anti-heroes created to satirize have the survival potential of that proverbial snowball. Every week *The Fugitive* escapes being executed by an unjust society, and his audience stays with him through thin and thin. Yet an attempt to mock his plight, as in *Run, Buddy, Run,* treats satirically a man we love: an anti-hero Buddy may be, but our affection is reserved for the real thing. The romantic habit of mind which elevates to prominence a real hero and revels in black and white morality rebels at any mockery of cherished beliefs. Anyone calling George Washington a royalist fink will be shouted down without a chance to offer his evidence.

This is not to say that television defines all Americans as puritanically stodgy. Camp, that grand phenomenon which brought back to theater screens Batman in all his serialized splendor, also eased the caped crusader and Robin into millions of homes in living, garish color. Prancing grotesquely in his snug BVD's, Batman camps through escapades designed to please the kiddies while letting all us sophisticates in on the gag to enjoy the tasteless, consciously unconscious poverty of the scripts which guide him. "Camp" becomes a national catchword; TV responds. Even *Batman's* slump in the ratings may well define the fad's finish better than anything Susan Sontag might say.

But television is not merely a mirror of the age. It is also a moving force. Just as cinema once provided for the rest of the world a specific view of American culture, television now introduces to our international neighbors the view we hold of ourselves. Some part of a national psyche is translated to television film, and such characterizing data are broadcast abroad. Broderick Crawford's *Highway Patrol* takes on new flavor dubbed in Japanese. To hear *Bonanza's* Dan Blocker addressed as "Monsieur 'oss" somehow spoils the effect of his nickname. Yet American traits survive even the silliest dubbing or translation. Foreigners learn to (mis)understand us via television. But the fondness for things American can't completely account for a show's popularity among peoples who may distrust or dislike America in the abstract; the themes treated in televised drama obviously have about them the flavor of universality. Not only our countrymen, but foreigners as well, react strongly to the strain of the heroic in televised drama. Hugh O'Brien's *Wyatt Earp,* seldom rerun any longer on domestic channels, is so popular abroad that O'Brien may be taking his life in his hands to wander unprotected through a crowd of adulatory Japanese. Captured by admiration for the heroes of American television, foreign audiences begin to identify the land which spawns these heroes as the home of violence, of cowboys and *Untouchables,* miniaturized in black and white. President Kennedy's assassination must have shocked others much less than it did us; after all, our television defines us in many eyes as gun-toting thugs.

Television's influence is equally dominant in this country, yet not entirely negative. Bill Cosby's being cast as co-lead in *I Spy* marks a significant step. A Negro, he plays a non-racial part, better educated and often more literate than his Caucasian partner-in-espionage. Initially the series did not appear on a few southern stations. Since becoming a success, it can no longer be ignored by men who react quickly to advertisers' dollars, and *I Spy* now reaches, according to *Variety*, 99 per cent of American television homes. A generation of American children, North and South, will grow up with the knowledge that Negroes are people, not merely creatures readily categorized as rapists or Uncle Toms. The impact of a national communication medium not dominated by local bias or pressure is undeniable, and healthy.

This impact makes itself felt strikingly in special circumstances. Teachers working in Project Head Start or similar programs directed toward children described by the sociologist as "culturally disadvantaged" are finding in television the greatest teaching aid yet devised. I do *not* speak of educational TV but of the garden variety of commercial programing. Children with illiterate or semiliterate parents, children from bookless homes in which newspapers or magazines are used for kindling fires rather than for reading, have their minds stretched and hard knowledge force-fed them minute by minute as they lie in front of the television set. Nor is it only children's fare like *Discovery* or *Exploring* which exerts such strong influence. First-graders have grown up with the spectacle of the U.S. space program brought home to them in a way unavailable during their parents' childhood; the parents may still be puzzled by the basic facts of aviation. Children are more fully aware of cultural and geographic distinctions than many of their ill equipped teachers, who find themselves astounded by children's curious and inquiring minds. Their vocabularies grow at an amazing rate, as several recent series of intelligence tests testify. While critics carp about the leveling tendency of any mass medium of communication, they ignore one crucial fact: much of that "leveling" takes place in an *upward* direction. And as children learn and develop, parents share, however slightly, in the whole happy process.

Those who ignore television's power and potential quite simply fail to recognize the impact with which TV drama strikes minds seldom exposed to literature, to legitimate theater, or to any cinema other than Walt Disney's canned distortions of the world. *La Dolce Vita* and *Last Year at Marienbad* are, after all, coterie pieces, say what you will about their merits. *I Spy* and *Dr. Kildare* reach and affect more people, more beneficially, than any feature film ever made. Not merely the escapist claptrap some critics dogmatically see in it, television drama relates to and defines the world for many viewers as nothing else can. In May, 1961, Jerry McNeely's teleplay *The Joke in the Valley* appeared on *The Hallmark Hall of Fame*. In that play a popular public figure is murdered. Before the murderer can be brought to justice, he too is executed, in this case by a man who sees his own action as a noble public service. The community's problem becomes one of evaluating the second murder in light of tension between motive and action, between "public good" and overriding questions of morality unrelated to the single act. "Melodrama," one might say, and there's an end to it.

Yet the repercussions which followed that show were eventually, more than immediately, impressive. McNeely found his mailbox crammed with letters and telegrams of two sorts: One group reacted favorably to the elements of a morality play whose impact struck them at once. The other comprised, predictably, crank notes accusing him of all sorts of twisted motives or unpopular beliefs.

Nor was that the end of audience response: more than two years later, following Jack Ruby's televised "execution" of Lee Harvey Oswald, the playwright discovered how strongly people had reacted to his work, how long their memories served. He received requests that the show be rerun, somewhere, somehow, for the comment it seemed to offer about an historical event. One can assume that even the cranks who had written initially now managed to convince themselves that McNeely had known of the plot and sinned by not warning the President, or found themselves wishing that he turn his soothsaying powers to something profitable like picking the winner of the next Irish Sweepstakes.

Statistics would be helpful at this point. What percentage of viewers, on seeing Ruby's action, immediately recalled *The Joke in the Valley*? How many thought of writing but knew of no way of contacting McNeely or the show's producer? I can offer only random estimates, but it seems likely that each of the letters which actually reached the playwright represents hundreds, perhaps even thousands of viewers. The point, then, is this: while some minds resort to quotations from favorite poems or novels, to the classics, or to childhood experience for illuminating analogies, others turn just as readily to interpretations of reality driven home by TV drama. Even speech patterns are dominated by popular television. Would you believe that millions of literate adults speak in terms suggested by one running joke on *Get Smart?* Thousands of teen-agers? How about one earnest writer?

The influence is undeniable and even surpasses that of cinema, if only because television reaches a broader audience. In one evening more people saw the televised appearance of *The Bridge on the River Kwai* than had paid admission to the film during the several years of its theatrical run. The appearance on TV of feature films leads many to discuss televised drama and cinema as though the two forms were somehow interchangeable. But by considering the current relationship between these two forms I can perhaps point out the major distinctions between them and underline one of television's most striking realms of influence—the power it seems to wield over cinema itself.

Television programing has come full circle, returning for its most characteristic success to sports or variety shows, the fare of the 1939 pioneer telecasts. Sportscasts and an occasional special remain almost the only examples of live television. An insatiable public appetite for entertainment became obvious early in the game, and television production moved toward film as the major vehicle. Even those few programs which may seem live, like NBC's *The Tonight Show,* are taped for delayed broadcast. The advantages of tape or film are clear: re-runs help amortize initial production costs, bloopers can be edited out, and whole segments may be swapped between shows for better balance. It is finally cheaper to film, hiring extras ("atmosphere people," in TV jargon) for a single day's shooting, than to rehearse an entire cast for weeks before a live production.

The overwhelming majority of prime-time televised drama is now filmed. The halcyon days of *Omnibus* or *Playhouse Ninety's* error-ridden live productions are long gone and longer lamented. Critics who bemoan the loss of live televised drama, whatever its quality, and the recent dominance of filmed drama do so out of noble motives. They see two theatrical genres distinctively different in conception drifting toward one another in disappointing ways.

The similarities are unmistakable. In the most general terms technical production of a one-hour television drama differs little from that of a full-length feature film. Cameras and sound equipment, lighting techniques, processing methods in the lab, editing and scoring are identical. Even our home movies may get the same treatment. So the habit of discussing television and cinema in the same breath is understandable. Both offer a series of images which express a point of view or convey information. Actors move easily from one medium to the other. James Garner's success as Bret Maverick led to his work in motion pictures, and his apprenticeship in television gave him whatever acting skills he has. Richard Chamberlain moved from television to the Broadway stage. And Richard Burton's playing of Caliban in *The Tempest* some years back lacked nothing for its being performed before TV cameras rather than on "legitimate" boards. Directors more and more often break into cinematic work through television, a medium which demands of them precision and directness not so stringently required by the relatively leisurely pace of cinema direction. A filmed narrative does not change character because of the means of its distribution—wide screen or square box.

When one turns from the media's similarities to their differences, however, one finds that television influences cinema rather than being influenced. First, television is *not* minor league cinema. Granted, many of the same techniques apply; physical equipment and processing methods are similar, if not identical. The real distinction resembles that between free verse and the sonnet. Writing free verse is, in Robert Frost's famous phrase, like playing tennis with the net down. Like free verse, cinema is more nearly an open-ended form. The restrictions which control and limit the typical teleplay are stricter, more clearly prescribed, but not necessarily debilitating. A *Tom Jones,* perhaps even more a *Dear John,* reaches the screen as the director's creation, with the merits achieved by intricate cutting and editing, fine nuance of camera work, and a shuffling of constituent parts which is impossible in the short week available for the filming, editing, and scoring of an hour teleplay. But what arbiter decides that the enormous craft demanded in the creation of an hour teleplay should be demeaned in comparison? The contrast is ridiculous, rather like the question on an aptitude test that asks which one likes better, living in the country or in the summer. I opt for the craftsman, the man who stands facing a net raised high enough for volleyball and yet plays his tennis match without begging for a change in the rules.

To use the titles *Tom Jones* and *Dear John* as I have is to approach a new attitude toward an art only now fumbling its way into prominence. *Giles Goat-Boy* is characterized in several reviews as allegory, artifice, and even craft without content. The arrangement of the material figures in random discussions of that novel much more than the material itself: What is the allegory? How many levels of meaning obtrude? Such a concern with the artifice of art dominates *Tom Jones* as well. It is impossible not to notice the techniques: speeded-up film sequences, subtitles, ornate framing, shifts into and out of brilliant color. Albert Finney even reminds the audience forcefully that they are watching a filmed narrative by hanging his hat over the lens.

To oversimplify, one can generalize about the phenomenon by suggesting that we who compose today's audience don't require "realism" any longer; we may not even respect it. Rather, we react to self-conscious art, to art forms which play with their own limitations and conventions. For that reason, television—that most stringently restricted of forms—sits perched securely atop what's happening. Perhaps by following a script from its birth as a vague idea in the writer's mind to the teleplay which results I can make my point, or at least suggest a new way of looking at a single hour of television drama.

The time necessary for revising, rewriting, editing, and correcting flaws—time which is afforded a team at work on a cinematic production—is denied the television producer. When he gets a script, he needs it ready to go. It may later be polished, or even rewritten, but at the cost of an expensive, ulcer-producing delay. Thus the whole process of shaping the final product for television falls more urgently into the writer's hands. He must follow a methodical plan. One of the best writers I know—"best" as opposed to "prolific"— employs the same series of steps for every script. He submits to the producer a five- or six-page "story treatment," a condensed plot. Given an OK for the idea, he moves on to a fifteen-page "step outline" in which he indicates breakdown into act and scene divisions, perhaps even a bit of dialogue for the flavor it will give his finished script. His work once more approved, he gets down to business.

Writing the finished teleplay, he finds himself entangled in the net I mentioned. There is no denying it—TV is formulaic; it has its own logic and rhetoric. Each show opens with a two- to five-minute "teaser," that capsule of drama which flashes on the screen to prevent our switching to Ed Sullivan or Lawrence Welk. In this brief span of time, the writer *must*: (1) Get our attention with a "hook" of unexplained action, striking character conflict, or a question important enough to make us eagerly await the answer; and (2) introduce the star or guest star for this particular episode. If he knows his business, he should also (1) introduce two or three other principal players, (2) distinguish the setting and historical period, (3) hint faintly at a secondary problem in the story to follow, and (4) conceal behind bright, forceful dialogue the fact that he is doing all this. If he is really good—and look to the all-too-rare scripts by names like Silliphant, Rose, McNeely, Mittleman, or the pseudonymous John Thomas James for examples—he will also make us laugh at, cry with, or hate a character on the screen. All this in the teaser, before the credits roll past and give permission for a quick trip to the pantry. A glassblower with hay fever has an easier job.

But the writer's problem has only begun. Ahead of him lies the creation of a four-act play whose acts average twelve to thirteen minutes. More, each act should ideally end as strongly as the teaser does, particularly the second, which coincides with the half-hour stroke of the clock and a viewer's recurrent impulse to catch at least the jugglers and the rock-and-roll band on the second half of Sullivan's spectacular. Once the viewer has switched channels he's gone to stay. He must be kept hooked, this time principally through effective dialogue. Each line of dialogue gets tested: Does it: (1) Define character? (2) Advance the plot? (3) Evoke emotional reaction from the audience? If it does not, out it comes. In the best scripts each line will achieve at least two of these ends.

Assuming that his muse does not desert him, the writer finishes in a matter of days—or weeks. But he has only a play, not a teleplay, and television differs even more from legitimate theater than from the cinema. The writer must now become director, sound technician, special effects man, even lighting and casting director. His completed script will contain comments unheard by any audience beyond the production staff. General camera directions are left to the director, but shots essential to creating a desired mood must be explicitly described in the script. The writer indicates essential sound cues, dramatically effective lighting, transitions between scenes—direct cut, slow dissolve, whatever paces his drama to best advantage. He includes with his script a summary description of sets and characters, perhaps even "typing" the characters according to what particular actor he might envision in each role.

And when he finally drops his pencil or leans back to let the typewriter cool, he has a first draft, sixty typewritten pages. Then another test: Read it aloud. To his wife, or a friend, a tape recorder, his shaving mirror, someone critical yet sympathetic. Test it. Check it. Then rewrite. And rewrite. The final version handed the director offers a full blueprint of the entire hour, subject to whatever minor changes may occur to this harried man in his tight shooting schedule.

Even after the play is filmed, editing and scoring require more time. Thus it becomes essential that a writer's ideas be explicit and readily translatable into action. Television is no medium for the improvisor who fondles and nurtures his creation to maturity; Bergman is a poor candidate for a job directing television drama. The time element assumes such major importance that a series may occasionally change because of it, shifting radically from the producer's original conception. I understand that the crew of *Maverick* found it impossible to complete episodes for that show in anything less than eight or ten days. Brother Bret, the Garner role, appeared in relief of Jack Kelly's Bart Maverick. With two production units at work on separate scripts it then became possible to meet weekly deadlines and to relieve pressure on the original company. And to many fans the show became Garner's, not Kelly's.

Given all these restrictions—time limits, formulaic act structure, economic limitations (about $140,000 for a single episode as compared with about $3,000,000 for a feature film)—television is forced into a mold. The writer exercises his craft as well as he can; an intelligent audience watches him at work, fully aware of the rhetoric he employs.

Unfortunately, that mythical "intelligent audience" does not always include men in the *business* of television or cinema. No one in the audience seriously believes any longer that feature films come off well on TV. The necessity for commercial interruptions and station breaks destroys the original tempo and mood of the film. Yet some have tried to solve the problem by writing feature-length filmscripts specifically geared to the requirements of commercial television. They do both industries a disservice. *Fame is the Name of the Game* recently fared well enough as a televised movie, but, transported into a theater as it will inevitably be, it must fail as cinema. An audience can hardly be expected to enjoy jolting through 100-plus minutes of plot in which a crisis leaps out at them every thirteen minutes to announce a commercial which never appears. And so the producers of that film define themselves as part of the group which persists in equating, and confusing, two distinct theatrical forms.

If cinema buffs complain that television turns leftover movies into Hollywood hash by mixing in liberal quantities of commercials and interruptions, how will they justify Hollywood's creating the same hash, to order? Which is now the dominant medium, cinema or television? More of these half-caste creations are promised. Perhaps their flaws will finally illustrate to all concerned that the media are essentially different. As cinema, television drama is poor stuff; just as certainly, cinema fails as television drama because it lacks the merits of conciseness, of direct and precise craftsmanship, where nothing else will serve. To consider each as *sui generis* is to recognize the merits, and shortcomings, of each. Even more, it is to admit that by confusing them one loses the virtues of both and is left with rubbish.

The formal differences between these genres begin to disappear as television extends its influence. A new sort of audience has been trained, a generation of viewers accustomed to certain technical devices and structural patterns which dominate television drama. More recently television's influence has begun to alter the rhetoric of cinema, either because producers and directors of cinema are themselves part of that great audience and succumb to a pressure they may not recognize, or because these same men *do* recognize and pander to the audience's new-found tastes. Everyone has noticed, perhaps without remarking on it, how audience reaction to a motion picture differs from that to a glowing television screen. The psychology of audience reaction is a study in itself, yet worth a brief comment here. Having paid his money and found a seat in a darkened theater, Mr. Average Cinemaddict is free to laugh or cry in general anonymity. People seated near him—all strangers—behave similarly; a great communion takes place. I laugh, you laugh, he laughs. But the same man ensconced in his favorite chair at home, in the glaring light of his living room and surrounded by his wife and kids, is reluctant to display his emotions; he feels foolish laughing alone. Understanding such a feeling, television moguls attempt to reproduce the conditions of the theater by providing accompaniment in the form of the comforting laugh track.

But this viewer's solitary reactions developed at home go with him on his next visit to a theater. He has been acclimated to technical devices and rhetorical traditions alien to cinema in its halcyon days of pre-television monopoly. To this man's mind slow dissolves from one scene to another no longer deepen mood so effectively; they presage a commercial. A transition through a gray or black screen may lose his attention completely. Witness the restless murmur that accompanies such a transition the next time you watch a feature film in a theater. Leisurely movement prevails no longer in any but the most consciously "arty" pieces.

The close-up, once reserved to give potent impact, has become such a common shot in many recent films that its virtues are lost. Within the brief span of an hour-long television drama a close-up allows the craftsman to say, "Look. This is important. Don't ignore it." He need underline a symbolic action or object only once, rather than repeating it as he might with more time available. But the fact that close-range camera work dominates TV seems little reason for its appearance in cinematic technique. *Gengis Khan* fairly screams at the viewer with close-ups of faces, spears, hands, swords, even maps and pointers: "Look. This is where we are now." I can stand a 21-inch screen full of face; thirty feet of forehead and mascaraed eyelashes overpowers unnecessarily. The influence seems clear.

Within the past half-dozen years cinema has adopted the teaser, a device essential to the peculiarities of television but worse than useless in the theater. It's not uncommon to find eight to ten minutes of plot preceding the credits on a wide screen, certainly to the detriment of the film's structural integrity. Nothing can account for such a mannerism except its accepted presence on the TV tube and the possibility of a television-trained director's having learned his lessons too well. In a theater the audience is already "hooked," has paid, and expects to be entertained. No one would consider leaving during the initial credits; no one can switch channels. A teaser under these circumstances satisfies expectations aroused in the audience not by the nature or traditions of cinema but by hours and hours of that other medium. Cinema, once blamed for too slavishly following a three-act structure inherited from the legitimate stage, deserves no less criticism for its currently frequent and illogical turn to the teaser-four-act structure of television.

"Don't give us a filmed stage play," critics once complained. And cinema moved outdoors to frolic in scenery, settings, and mobility unavailable onstage. But the public's insatiable demand for more and more televised drama forced TV producers back to the pattern of a small cast and few sets. Economics demands it; the audience accepts it, perhaps even considering it a new convention. But—once more—what law requires that cinema play follow-the-leader? *The Apartment* employs such a pattern. Only the opening sequence of a football game saves *The Fortune Cookie* from deserving the same criticism. The new traditions of television seem to sanction a return to theatrical patterns once happily discarded. For cinema it's a step backward, but one that offers an out to film producers: an audience which accepts filmed stage plays is also obviously more willing to accept talky drama, the too-frequently exercised option of repeating a pattern from the Greek theater—action offstage discussed onstage. Second-rate cinema runs the risk of becoming third-rate television by falling back on dialogue in place of action.

Let each do what it can do best. If TV deserves any attack in this circular mass of confusion, it is not because it too nearly approaches cinema but because it returns to formulas of the stage which film should long ago have overthrown. More, it leads cinema down the same garden path.

The influence of television, then, is pervasive, affecting certainly movies, if not *the film*—that common distinction of the culturati. Let me suggest, finally, that even *the film* benefits from the fact of television's very existence. Hollywood's self-congratulation for cinema's new maturity is misdirected praise. "Adult films" of today would have given the censors apoplexy not too long ago. Honesty is rampant. Illicit love affairs in vivid detail, frank language, visible brutality—all mark the new maturity. But it takes no cynic to suggest that all this "honesty" is also profitable. Television, as the family medium, has staked its claim on subject matter long the staple of Hollywood's output. I can see on TV more situation comedy than a normal stomach will take; Andy Hardy will never come back in a wide-screen version. Westerns abound on television. Detectives chase criminals from network to network. Film producers who expect cash customers to pay for longer versions of the same scripts misunderstand the audience and soon become agents instead of producers. Only insofar as films surpass television drama in frankness, or brutality, or "honesty" can they attract a mass audience. Whatever credit cinema claims for its honesty should be laid instead at TV's door. This is the final influence: if movies are better than ever, television made them so.

It all has to do with that net. When one recognizes that *the film* and *television* are different games, he can appreciate them both without resorting to comparisons which only cloud their differences. Let cinema play in its own backyard where television hasn't a chance to compete. And the next time you watch an hour teleplay pay attention to the net that gets in the TV playwright's way. It forces him to stretch a bit, to stay on his toes, a metaphorical exercise that might benefit all writers. A point harder won deserves more admiration. On its own court television serves up plenty of aces.

W. R. ROBINSON

The Movies, Too, Will Make You Free

Not too long ago there was no film theory. Today—as exemplified by the recent flood of paperbacks on the subject—it has reached the saturation point. Yet most of what passes for film theory is not, strictly speaking, theory at all; or, rather, it is applied, not pure, theory, for in it the theorizing faculty is made to defend personal causes or taste. When employed for special pleading, such theory contributes little toward identifying the necessary and sufficient properties of the movies as art.

In an argument waged at one time on the nature of cinema, for example, Sergei Eisenstein insisted that montage is the essence of film. And it may be the essence of an Eisenstein film—certainly, without his total dedication to it the intellectual cinema would have missed some of its supreme achievements. His purpose, he rightly sensed, made this device absolutely necessary to his art. But from a truly theoretical perspective, montage is, as Eisenstein himself eventually admitted, just one device in the film-maker's repertoire, useful for some purposes, not for others. What his films and theory actually prove is that montage can be used for certain effects—sensations of speed, power, hostility, alienation, disorder, violence (impressions that the world threatens to overwhelm the perceiver).

In the same vein is Alfred Hitchcock's insistence on using a shot of a glass of champagne gone flat as a metaphor for a finished love affair. Though more simple-minded than Eisenstein's theorizing, Hitchcock's attempt at defining something essential to films is actually an assertion of taste—a preference for wit, an intellectual delight in clever analogy instead of the thing itself directly seen. (This literary quality in Hitchcock's work is one reason why, despite the slightness of his films, he is a favorite among intellectuals.) The same holds true for the purist, realist, surrealist, and other sectarian definitions of the movies; these, like those of Eisenstein and Hitchcock, are rhetorical supports for a value espoused independently of the movies as an aesthetic phenomenon. In every case one aspect of the movies is singled out as definitive and assigned ontological dominance.

At work in film theory and responsible for much of the confusion that reigns in it, as the above instances illustrate, is a careless mental habit, a variation on what philosophers call the naturalistic fallacy. For a quality in art or life to be truly valuable, film theorists almost invariably assume (and they differ from no one else, including philosophers, in this respect) that it must be supported by a theory which attributes reality to it—indeed, proclaims it to be the "realest." In other words, their theorizing stems from a hunger for substance or weightiness, and their theory serves to anchor an airy moral entity to solid intellectual earth. Deeper yet, underlying this hunger, is man's most adamant presupposition: that only what endures can be really valuable—only if our souls are immortal does life have meaning and therefore value; only if love is forever is it true and good. Disguised as ontological definition but actually support for a value, the normal adaptations of theory for determining the nature of film attempt to put intellectual muscle into the ethereal in the hope of justifying it on the intellect's terms, thereby capturing intelligence for moral ends. A difference in taste is mistaken for a difference in reality, and, whether or not overtly, "reality" performs a service decidedly normative, functioning as the ultimate honorific epithet.

The principle, "the more transitory the less valuable," probably is responsible for much of the resistance against recognition of the movies as serious art, since they reek of temporality. They come and go at the theaters with great frequency and in great haste, never to return, and they are not possessable like books or paintings or records. We cannot live and grow in their immediate company or display them as status symbols. Above all, they take the transient—from Plato on, the lowliest aspect of life—as their subject. Western culture has been predominantly intellective, and so its art and criticism, following the natural propensity of the intellect, have been heavily biased toward permanence. They have always proclaimed plenitude and imperishability the summum bonum. Thus it comes as no surprise that early movie directors, especially European ones, sought a cinematic means to give body to the universal truths underlying the appearance of things or to evolve a style by which to elevate human consciousness out of time. Today that object is not so strenuously pursued, although its absence, nostalgically lamented, is still profoundly felt in the latest European films—particularly in the solemn movies of Antonioni, Visconti, Truffaut, and Resnais, but also in the more joyous ones of Bergman and Fellini.

From this traditional distaste for the ephemeral emerges the most persistent theme in Western art—the problem of appearance and reality—and the artist's most enduring challenge—to counterbalance transitoriness by formal strategies capable of articulating the truths behind the mask, a realm beyond change. Now every art or work of art with any pretensions to seriousness at least tacitly solves these problems and is to be judged by the intelligence with which it does so. Yet the movies appear to be attached to the physical and particular much more than any other art and so seem to resist cooperating quietly with the old values and the old aesthetic. For this reason they ought to be more at ease in the hands of Americans, for whom traditionally process is reality. But the American director, when he isn't a European, looks to the Old World for guidance. As American literature did, the American movie will probably come of age when it looks to other sources, native and abroad, for its inspiration and guiding principles. Its major indigenous form to date has been the western, and probably its greatest achievement is also to be found there, not because the cowboy is a mythic hero but because the western, to a large extent a drama of the solitary figure against the wilderness, combines the two main traditions in American visual art.

A bad mental habit and an aesthetic bias issuing from it, then, vitiate the art, criticism, and theory of the film. The immense quantity of "theory," contradictory and confined to a movie's obvious or accidental features, is more an obstacle to accurately understanding the movies as art than anything else. Consequently, to arrive at a true theory it is necessary to begin at the beginning, with the aesthetic phenomenon itself. What can be said in the way of theory without making a value commitment and turning theory into propaganda is decidedly limited: something like, the movies are an art of light produced by mechanical means. Beyond that you're in trouble. But you're already in trouble anyway—for the definition provokes the question: Yes, but what is art? That's obviously a moot matter. In fact, the confusion in film theory results largely from confusions in the theory of art, which in turn result from deeply imbedded fallacies in moral reasoning. So it is necessary at this juncture to enter into questions of aesthetics in order to free film theory from its many false entanglements.

As art a movie is a complex phenomenon, a multifaceted diamond whose glitter can be muted or magnified depending upon the intensity and angle of the light. This is because, as the end result of a deliberate human act, it is imbued with all the intangible emotional, intellectual, and moral attitudes man necessarily expresses in everything he does. Its material base is different from man's—one inorganic, the other organic; but, allowing for that, a movie as art is almost an incarnation of man, standing in relation to him as he has been conceived of standing in relation to his Maker. As such, it invites nearly every question that can be asked of life and even seems to promise an answer to most.

Since a movie reflects human nature, the key to its aesthetic being must be found there. Indeed, as soon as one asks any other than a technical question of it, the inquiry is about man. But man is a complex phenomenon, too. Traditionally, he has conceived of himself as a tripartite creature, with the parts variously designated as reason, passion, and desire in Plato's view; the religious, the moral, and the aesthetic in Kierkegaard's; the id, ego, and superego in Freud's, etc. And each of these three facets has its corresponding ideal, formulated by classical thought as the True, the Beautiful, and the Good. The product of human will, a movie is inevitably a composite of all three facets and so can be said to reflect the organization of man's being—the degree of his wholeness or fragmentation, his balance or madness. Moreover, the movie is expected to incorporate all three ideals simultaneously. To pass critical judgment with a perfect score it must be simultaneously Beautiful, Truthful, and Good. That is, it has to excite the senses with striking forms, satisfy what William James called "the sentiment of rationality," and confirm the imagination's intuitive sense of what is right for man.

Perfection will always elude the moviemaker. His work cannot be fully realized in every respect simply because, though all three facets are inescapably present in his art, he must emphasize one at the expense of another. His work will necessarily favor Truth over Beauty and the Good, or Beauty over the Good and Truth, and so on. None of the three ideals has a determinable priority; each opens out upon a unique vista; all, from a theoretical standpoint, are equally real and valuable. A work will always be just *a* view, never *the* view; it will always be an art of Truth or of Beauty or of the Good, never of all to the same degree. Similarly, a film "theory," and movie criticism as well, will inescapably lean toward either an aesthetic of Truth, an aesthetic of Beauty, or an aesthetic of Value, as has happened historically, with the classical era favoring an aesthetic of Beauty and the modern era an aesthetic of Truth.

A movie, it follows, is a pluralistic phenomenon of such a complexity it is undefinable. For this reason there is no such thing as "the movies," no one essential quality common to all movies; there are only movies. All essentialists—whether moviemakers, theorists, or critics—are necessarily moralists. The numerous schools and styles already on the books demonstrate beyond a doubt that as a medium the movies are alive with possibilities. Some things, to be sure, come more easily to them than others—action, comedy, and spectacle more easily than analysis, tragedy, and verbal theme. Nevertheless, the argument that good cinema can be produced by doing only what comes naturally with the camera makes a neat deduction but a poor observation. As the Modern novel illustrates—in its case a descriptive, temporal genre gets sharply wrenched in order to render an essential, atemporal reality—the most exciting artistic achievements may be generated from a tension between the medium and a view of things unnatural for it.

Movies are certainly recognizable as a distinct phenomenon, but their identity lies not in what they are but in what they do—or, more accurately, in what one chooses to do with them. Film per se is just celluloid strips, as useful for decorating posters, starting fires, or recording information as for making visual narratives. It becomes art when a choice is made to employ it for aesthetic ends. When those ends, not rhetoric, profit, or propaganda, are regarded as worth trying for, a movie becomes an end in itself, a vehicle by which the human spirit becomes free. Indeed, to choose to use the movies for the purposes of art is to make freedom the supreme value.

The most persistent and unjust criticism leveled at the movies has been that they are *sui generis* "escapist." But this critical term, the nastiest epithet conceivable within a very narrow-minded aesthetic of truth which sprung up alongside realism, absurdly distorts our sense of what art is or should be. It implies that only an art as grim and dour as the realist thought life to be under the aegis of materialism can qualify as serious aesthetic achievement. It is easy to understand why the realist would think this; inhabiting a cold, indifferent, inhospitable universe, nothing remained for him except to endure stoically the ruthless pushing about to which man seemed subjected. Yet even in the dourest realistic view truth is a human triumph; through it man transcends suffering and determinism. Nikolai Berdyaev saw this clearly when he argued that all art is a victory over heaviness. It is always escape. When a movie is called "escapist," therefore, all that can legitimately be meant is that it wins its battle too easily. Take, for instance, the simple examples of *From Russia with Love* and *Thunderball.* Every sophisticated Bond fan unquestionably preferred the former because, while still a hero, Bond fought as a human being reliant upon his human wits and strength against a formidable but vulnerable enemy. In *Thunderball,* on the other hand, he is a superhuman creature beyond being ruffled by normally overwhelming adversaries and extreme circumstances. A good movie, like a good athletic contest, offers a true test against a worthy opponent. It wins its victory after genuine struggle, with honor and dignity. And this applies to the movie itself, not just to the characters in it; the movie as art, as the result of a battle between imagination and reality, persuades us that its escape, the victory of the human spirit over the material medium, has been duly earned. If the triumph for the protagonist or the artist comes too easily, if little wit or courage is expended by them, then the human spirit has not been tried to its depths and so is not profoundly entertained and refreshed. Winning is inevitable—the existence of the work bears witness to that— but what is defeated and how the victory is won is the heart of the aesthetic matter.

The desire to escape from heaviness is so fundamental and universal a passion that it pervades everything man does and may even be the major moving force behind his culture and history. Certainly, he has cultivated the various intellectual disciplines in order to transcend his necessity, in the hope that he could "choose himself." Religion has always been devoted to making man free through liberating the soul from spiritual ignorance or guilt, while science has been employed to equip man with a powerful knowledge capable of freeing him from nature. The arts in general, the movies included, are a part of man's intellectual armament in this war to liberate himself from heaviness, but they serve in a distinctive capacity. Like religion and science, art frees man's consciousness from the pragmatic pressures of living for a moment's respite to meditate upon isolated qualities before he plunges again into the stream of life. But whereas religious dogma focuses upon the conceptual truths of the spirit and science upon those of nature, art, a conjunction of spirit and nature, takes moral truth as its province. In effect, it discovers or creates values; by incarnating the Good, a spiritual entity, in a concrete form, art frees it to be.

The primordial truth about a movie as art, then, is that it confronts its viewer with moral fact and engages him in a moral dialogue. Though ignored by theorists, the moral power of art is so evident as to have made it the center of a vociferous, protracted quarrel from Classical Greece to the present. The movies simply stepped into the middle of a centuries-old row when, as soon as they appeared on the scene, censors and critics attacked them for distracting people from their proper moral development by stirring up their lower depths. The record clearly testifies that moral reaction to the movies—and to art in general over the ages—has seldom, if ever, been free of specific moral biases, so that the true moral character of the movies has remained obscured by parochial passions. This impasse can be skirted with the observation that the most likely remarks made or heard after a movie are: "I liked it. Did you?" "That was a good movie, don't you think so?" "It was awful; it wasn't any good at all; it's worthless." Although they use more formal language, the reviewer and critic concern themselves with the same matters. In short, everyone instinctively recognizes that a movie—all art, in fact—invites him to exercise his taste in making a value judgment. He senses that a value assertion has been made and that a reply is demanded of him. And, except for the most diffident, everybody also senses that he is qualified to reply, for, despite the scholar's defense of his hard-earned learning, no special knowledge is required and no greater moral authority exists than the individual's own conscience—which must be defended at all costs, since his identity is inseparable from it.

What transpires in the moral dialogue becomes clear when the movies are contrasted with science, a companion empirical discipline. Science—pure science, that is, not applied science—clarifies phenomena. It opens our eyes to the facts of nature by concentrating our attention on objects, events, and relations not immediately obvious. What was hidden before, presto, we now behold. Its terminology literally discriminates what has been beyond our power to see. To record what he has seen for public and perhaps personal benefit, a scientist molds language (whether mathematical or verbal) into a proposition which accurately represents the state of affairs he has observed. Or, if working with models, he makes a visual metaphor to perform that task. But he has seen something—call it a fact—which acts as a criterion in molding his proposition or model. The moviemaker, a storyteller, has to have a similar principle of selection to tell him when he has got his tale right, when what he is making accurately embodies what he has perceived. That principle is not a fact, however, but a quality, for his subject is man, not nature. This moral fact, even if vague initially and clear only when his story receives its final touches, has precedence over and determines the devices he selects from the cinematic bag of tricks or creates on the spot to serve his unique purposes. The finished product is imbued in every part by the quality which it is constructed to embody, and as the scientist invites his reader to view the reality he has seen, so the moviemaker invites his audience to behold the moral fact he has discovered. A "pure" movie, like pure science, enhances awareness by bringing a hidden or vague quality out into the open.

We cannot overlook the power of a movie to strike and pierce the senses and thereby arouse passion and emotion and even awaken the soul. With its vigorously impersonal method science cools us off emotionally and morally to receive a dispassionate truth about objective matters. Its icy illuminations may be a great delight for the intellect, but they are not intended to bring joy to the heart or conscience. Perhaps the most evident thing about a movie is its power to excite; but like a church service it does so of necessity, for we can receive its insight, actually a state of being, only if it elevates us into exalted consciousness. Similarly, the demand that a movie be exciting, engaging, alive, that its moral truth be felt and feelable, springs from the intuition that a value is a vital existence, something worth living for and caring about. For a value is a sensation, or a feeling, as Susanne Langer calls it, given an objective state before consciousness. Art fixes sensations in form and thereby allows them to become

objects of knowledge and desiderata, states of being to be achieved
and returned to as a vital creature's good.

When properly employing his craft, the moviemaker does not imi-
tate, refer to, or symbolically represent a value but gives body to it
there in the movie. All he therefore has to do to become a serious
artist is to dedicate himself to making "objects of value"—not of meaning or for communication, nor of social or historical or psychological
import, nor as vehicles for avoiding greater moral clarity. A movie
which depends primarily upon a topical subject, a fashion in taste,
or rhetoric for its appeal, although considerable artistry may be expended for these purposes, has a short life span. When these lose their
interest the movie is dead. If, however, it primarily, accurately, and
vividly embodies a quality which, despite changes in taste, is an
eternal good, the movie has what used to be called universality: it is
always alive and relevant; it remains a living option.

To carry out his serious intentions the moviemaker ideally has to
have complete control over his medium, which means that as a storyteller he must master not only the narrative denotations but also the
moral connotations of the images with which he works. All the implications of character, plot, pace, lighting, camera angle, cutting, and
such highlighting elements as dialogue and music have to be within
his control. These are determined by traditional usage and are public
for the most part, although in a young art like the movies many of
the connotations are not yet clearly fixed. Thus the preview. Because most defects in craftsmanship are immediately apparent, nobody
gets damned simply for being a poor craftsman; he is just ignored. A
certain level of seriousness and craftsmanship has to be self-evident
for a movie to attract attention in the first place. No one gets excited
over the worthless; and craftsmanship, except in someone like Hitchcock, where it is all there is, receives only a passing comment. Our
central concern is values. Confronted with a certain pretension to
seriousness, as in a Jules Dassin film, we test for authenticity by looking for intellectual blindness and for moral crudity owing to vicious-
ness or insensitivity. We mean by sensitivity, in fact, the capacity for
subtle moral discriminations. Correspondingly, the sensitive movie-

maker, if truly an artist, via his imagination-conscience feels and thinks his way in and through his medium, making an ironic, romantic, realistic, or surrealistic movie, not one which abstractedly asserts the desirability of those qualities. He creates these values; he gives them flesh; he brings them to life.

The moviemaker as artist, it should now be clear, is a moral educator. Like every artist, he forges, in James Joyce's phrase, the conscience of his race. Take as an example Richard Brooke's recent movie *The Professionals,* not likely to be a classic but still a good film. This is an especially handy movie to illustrate the moral role of art because its title specifies the quality the movie is constructed to define. Professionalism as a value comes naturally to an era dominated by technology and technicians and prone to a taste for craft, camp, and the cool. But the movie is not a sociological tract, nor is it a treatise on the virtues of professionalism. Instead, it is a professional work, or at least it aspires to be. Not only are the major characters professionals in skill and temperament but the movie itself exemplifies complete knowledge and know-how. In effect, defining its value structurally, stylistically, and tonally as well as narratively, it not only identifies the good of professionalism but in doing so establishes a criterion by which the movie itself is to be judged. The movie insists that its viewers clearly perceive what professionalism is, then turn it back upon the movie, asking, "Does it measure up to the criterion it affirms? Has the director met and mastered every problem that came up in his professional bailiwick, moviemaking? Has he been cool and calm, always on top of the situation?" If art is creative, if it does add something to matter which wasn't there previously, it is this moral illumination inherent in form. Moreover, since the movie brings new qualities into existence, established criteria are irrelevant for judging it. Movie criticism and theory, always waiting upon art to educate them, stand disarmed before moral truth while the movies dig out within and bring to light in objective form new dimensions of moral reality.

The normative logic inherent in the sort of persuasion the movie attempts forces the viewer to ask whether the movie fulfills itself on its own terms. Intuitively sensed from man's first encounter with art this has always been the question art poses—does it pass the test of unity and coherence? In deciding if a movie is coherent or unified, we ask first whether it is being true to itself as art—does it embody value?—and then whether the quality has been so treated as to include everything necessary to its embodiment and nothing extraneous. In other words, we ask if it does what art is supposed to do in the way art must do it. The movie succeeds as art, it successfully embodies a value, when both conditions are fulfilled.

This role the movies play in our moral education is tacitly recognized by our educational practices. In the sciences students are not asked to read the original authors but a textbook or one authoritative work stating a commonly acknowledged public truth. And the same is true for religion, although it is not formally taught in the school system—unless students are old enough to become comparativists, they study the one true doctrine. But in the arts the original artists, and many of them, are studied, since the human-moral reality they serve as texts for is too complex to be exhaustively treated by one man. Even in school systems where one literary figure, such as Dante or Goethe, is looked upon as a national institution, that writer is not taught exclusively. Every writer is limited to construing the truth available within the purview of one moral perspective. Although within some schematic approaches the possible perspectives on moral reality may be reduced to a few categories, the wide variety of conservative and liberal, romantic and classical, middle-class and working-class perspectives, for example, is so great that an accurate sense of man's moral predicament can be arrived at only through reading widely. The fact that just a small part of the moral spectrum can be relevant to any individual's purpose is no argument against extensive reading, for to be able to choose what our own temperaments, equally committed to a specific value, need to clarify and strengthen their impulsions, we have to weigh the pros and cons of the whole moral truth.

We study the value spectrum so that we may become more precise about our specific good, with tolerance, it is hoped, as a side effect. Because the arts are habitually used to teach history, it is customary to emphasize their temporal aspect, whereas science, a body of constantly verifiable knowledge about nature, is taught independently of history. Yet the movies no less than science are devoted to the discovery and establishment of timeless truth. The movies, like the other art works created in the past and accumulated as our heritage, pass on moral knowledge from one generation to another; they thereby allow us to possess now the possibilities of good discovered by our forebears. As a body of work on the books, they, like the sciences, constitute an encyclopedia of knowledge. That heritage is not sufficient, however. Movies must be constantly in the making; old stories must be forever told anew; to remain living options, values must be continually validated within ever-changing reality—every moment requiring a new synthesis of Beauty, Truth, and the Good. Thus the movies, when art, explore on the frontiers of knowledge, refurbishing old values, refining discrimination in areas already charted, and producing new insight in areas of the moral spectrum previously ignored.

Because the movies play such a crucial role in our education, they must be free to follow moral truth wherever it may lead. This means they have to be as free from censorship as political thought and the other intellectual disciplines are. Censorship, long a bugaboo for the movies, defends the moral status quo, prohibiting search and discovery where they are most needed. Freedom of taste clearly is as important as freedom of speech. For the quality of our private and public lives depends upon their being nourished by living values, and only constant reassessment and refinement of the values we live by, through aesthetic meditation, can assure that. The complexity, nuances, and consequences of a value must be aired if the naive and pretentious ones are to be unmasked, the invidious exposed, and the confused clarified. Satirical movies, for example, quite overtly seek to demonstrate that a value cherished by some individual or the public is phony, a sham supported by nothing better than fear, ignorance, or malice. The genuine, of course, bear up under scrutiny and survive.

The moral dialogue a movie invites us to participate in, ideally a free field without favor, can, if it leads to the conclusion that taste is not disputable, beget disabling doubt about the profitableness of discussion or the trustworthiness of our own values. Cynicism arises from diffidence or from a failure to impress our reality cogently upon others—if we cannot intellectually establish what we value, then nothing is valuable; all is meaningless. Because our consciences cannot ultimately tolerate one another, critical dialogues quickly turn into ego contests leading nowhere but to ever louder shouting. The aim of the dialogue is not, and should not be, conversion, however, but clarification. Even if a moviemaker wanted to, he could not force his viewers to believe or act as he wished. As art a movie persuades by its power to illuminate. Most often, as with education in general, it facilitates rational defense of what otherwise would be called prejudice. Instead of converting, it brings into lucid focus a good that has been wrongly understood or obscured, correcting an error in reason or awareness. The dialogue initiated by the movie, whether directly or indirectly and regardless at what remove from the work itself, leads in its most aesthetically profitable instances to an understanding of what one's good truly is and wherein it truly lies. It does not incite to action; it clarifies for action, should the individual be so inclined.

Thus a movie as art objectively and vividly displays man's good. It brings moral truth into the world. Psychologically, by being out there, it confirms us, assuring us that our good is real. We go to a movie, certainly in our most serious moods, but probably on all occasions, in search of our moral truth; and when we find it, for the moment we dwell spiritually or meditatively in it, it is our fulfillment, our fullness of being. And if we don't like the movie, still, through the friction of an imperfect meeting of consciences, we become clearer about moral alternatives.

Taste may not be disputable in the sense that differences can be arbitrated by logic, but nevertheless disputing it is our means to personal and public wisdom. When the logical positivists and their disciples legislated that what cannot be empirically verified is meaningless, their logic was sound but their common sense was asleep. From a scientific perspective all cinematic or aesthetic utterances are nonsense, and all but descriptive propositions about a movie are sales pitches designed to persuade others to buy our way of packaging life. The trouble here is that movies are not utterances; they make no claim—nor does any art, as architecture and music illustrate glaringly—to propositional truth or falsity. Their province is taste; and taste, not truth, at least not truth independent of taste, is our pre-eminent concern as living creatures. To live is to act, and efficient action requires clear goals. By contributing to the enhancement of moral awareness, the movies as art help free man to know and pursue his true good. Whereas our scientific education equips us to use the world more effectively, the movies, assisting in our moral education, help prepare us to act more wisely.

And not just movies themselves but their criticism and theory, part of the moral dialogue they stimulate, contribute to the clarification of ends. In the final analysis, despite some impurities that creep in, applied theory magnifies and thereby facilitates examination of the values which particular schools, movements, directors, and critics have espoused. Their commitment and its resultant distortions, perhaps misleading to the unsuspecting mind, function as a necessary agency in our moral illumination. Thus that mental atavism of justifying taste with ontological argument, for all its logical absurdity, turns out to be the heart of the aesthetic matter. It is an instrument, as the movie itself is, to confirm man's being by giving substance and permanence to his supreme good. Although his commitment keeps him from being cool and therefore a reliable pure theorist, the applied theorist's intellectual power issues from his belief in himself, in what he has seen, and in his pressing need to justify himself and make living room for his moral kind.

The movies, via the moral dialogue they initiate and participate in, open our eyes to values. At their best they excite and refresh not simply the ordinary emotions but the profoundest feeling in our deepest moral reaches as well. To reiterate, they are one means by which man, through the powers of his imagination, perceives for himself possibilities without precedent in nature. Incarnations of the Good, providing opportunities to contemplate imaginatively concrete moral truth, they enhance and enrich consciousness. They are instruments helpful in lifting man up literally by his own bootstraps to contemplate the ideal and perhaps eventually to direct his effort towards its realization. When properly charged, their images empower men to behold and enjoy their finest life. No art does any more, and on the contemporary scene none surpasses them in scope and power, none more "realistically" confirms man's truth, none liberates or is liberated more completely.

That the movies possess the depth and breadth necessary for articulating contemporary moral reality, or the aesthetic means to bring it into vivid relief, is borne out by the difference between them and literature. Both are predominantly narrative arts employing images—one directly, the other indirectly—as vehicles for storytelling. Because of that slight difference, however, they are worlds apart. Literature and the literary imagination are metaphorical; they seek to make explicit a reality hidden to the senses. From one point of view literature, an art of words, duplicates the acts of creation by the Greek Logos or the Christian God: through it the Word, the primordial ontological power in Greek and Christian metaphysics, brings order into the world by imposing itself upon chaos. Since words are not natural or material entities, literature is inherently deductive—words issuing from the Word—both alienated from the physical and constituting a self-enclosed system which locates the source of the Good outside the physical world, within the Word, an a priori realm which validates particular words. But from another, a human, point of view, literature, originating within a worldly predicament, arises either from the longing of words to be themselves or from man's hunger to dwell in the realm of ideas or reason. Not inherently inclined to be denotative, words much prefer to consort among their own kind and, indeed, ardently long to return to their source. In any case, the literary imagination works from a fallen state and, nostalgically lamenting its paradise lost, aspires to regain verbal heaven.

Drama nicely illustrates the bias of literature and one of the ways in which it functions. In drama, at least when it is authentic art, words turn characters inside out, manifesting their inner being with language. For this reason the dialogue, in, say, *Who's Afraid of Virginia Woolf?* can be heard from a recording and still be aesthetically effective. With neither the theatrical nor cinematic spectacle distracting attention from the words, they intensively activate the hearer's imagination and turn him, too, inside out. Characters serve as the metaphorical vehicles by which the Word is made manifest. In a verbal medium such as drama the visual element complements the words and is eventually dispensable. Poetry—lyric poetry in particular—reigns supreme among the literary arts because the words are relatively unencumbered by the sensory, although in poetry, too, imagery is indispensable as metaphorical agency. Its object is, of course, to let the human spirit sing out. Verbal narrative on the other hand relies more heavily on the referential dimension of language, and words as a consequence tend to function analytically, pointing to underlying patterns, causes, or essences. Not by accident fiction favors temporal and historical explanations. Read in solitude, it cultivates the mind, and whatever the circumstances it proffers the intellectual satisfaction attained through comprehending the abstractions governing life. Nevertheless, despite being more abstract than drama or poetry, verbal narrative is also governed by the principle that literature be concrete and specific or "make sense"; and with drama and poetry it paradoxically employs words as the instrument by which man can penetrate through the mask of phenomena to the Word beyond it and transcend his finite condition. Literature and the literary imagination are bound by the laws of language, which is always metaphorical; through postulating likenesses, they put the mind in contact with intangible intellectual essences not directly perceptible.

In contrast to literature, the movies and the cinematic imagination are literal. A visual medium in which the word is complementary and dispensable, the movies illuminate sensory reality or outer form. They are empirical revelations lighting the thing itself and revealing change as nothing more than it appears to be. In their world there is no becoming, only being, or pointless change, no innate potential to be realized in time, no essence to be released from original darkness, no law to be learned and obeyed. For this reason analysis is rarely successful in the movies, *Citizen Kane* being the most famous of the very few exceptions. Even the Russian intellectual cinema, which on first impression seems analytical, at its best is hortatory—it inspires the viewer to be. Or, more specifically, in individual frames, by composition and photographic style, it endows the lowly and exploited with splendid being. Whatever a movie illuminates it has already celebrated, saying, in effect, "So be it." Its atomic constituents seem to have a greater life than the enclosing forms, while order, causality, and pattern appear arbitrarily imposed. And, with the atomistic quality so pronounced in them, the movies evoke an emotional rather than an intellectual response—the thing directly perceived is directly felt, and intellectual reflection follows upon the emotion, whereas in literature the emotion follows upon the word after the mind has made the initial encounter. Understandably, movies more perfectly satisfy Tolstoy's requirement that art appeal to the universal innate feelings in man. Consequently, they tend to be egalitarian, and literature elitist—only those who know how to read and think are admitted to its domain, while anyone with eyes qualifies as a citizen of the movie world. From these differences it is clear that literature testifies, while the movies witness. As a verbal medium, literature gives voice to the mind's lust for meaning. In seeking to commit the mind to what is not at once evident to the senses, literature demands belief; it insists that its report, always an interpretation, be trusted. The movies, on the other hand, a visual art, are immersed in the sensory, physical world, viewing it from within as a passing parade ceaselessly coming and going. They have no way, except for words, to gain a vantage point outside it. In this respect they are the archetype for the contemporary intellectual predicament characterized by the twilight of absolutes—they have no revealed word or a priori ideas, nor any criterion within experience itself, by which to ascertain reality or value; they are face to face with what is in its full multiplicity and glory. They dwell in the present, in a world all surface. Lacking a second level of reality, they are without complexity—without irony, meaning, or necessity. On the face of things appear process, activity, energy, and behind this mask is nothingness. Whereas the word is mysterious, the image is evident; everything it has is showing. Thus for movies the created world is good, not fallen; they offer no salvation through belief, as Christianity and rationalism do, but instead regard the given world as redeemed. They are existentialist, valuing the concrete, existence, or what is.

Little wonder, then, that the literary sensibility is not at home in the cinematic world and suspects movies of being superficial—without soul, intellectually impotent, and morally frivolous. One devoted to ideas, the other to particulars, one committed to transcendent truth, the other to ever-present reality, the verbal and visual modes are fated to eternal hostility. Yet despite this inherent hostility, the movies have their inevitable literary aspect—in their title and dialogue, and in the property or scenario from which they are derived. (Perhaps this literary origin raises major obstacles to successful film-making, since the film is in effect a translation and the viewer is invited— or does so out of habit—to translate it back into its original, and truer, literary prototype. The film functions, in this case, as literature did in classical theory, as a decorative illustration for a truth known through a prior and more authoritative faculty.)

There are those who lament the fact that movies must have a literary aspect; purists of a sort, they long for a return to the era of the silent film, when movies were movies and that's all there was to them. That nostalgia is understandable, for the pure movie demands a less complex response and poses less complex critical problems. The fact is, however, that the movies, allowing for the proper dominance, are an image-word medium, as is literature, and all for the better. For, despite the invidious criticism which can arise from a bias favoring either the intellect or the senses, the presence of the antagonistic elements reflects the human predicament. The tension generated between images and words in an impure movie and our ambivalent response to their interaction beget a truth that would otherwise be lost. As literature is enriched by the tension between word and image, so are the movies. The beneficent effects of this tension can be readily observed in many movies, but it has become consciously explicit in such recent ones as *Alfie,* in which a narrator terrified of death tries unsuccessfully, through directly addressing the audience or from a verbal point of view, to determine what his life comes to within a cinematic context; and *Fahrenheit 451,* in which a French director flatly and ludicrously repudiates his own art in lamenting the demise of book man.

The tension in these movies also appears, reversed, in recent literature, perhaps most notably in the work of Alain Robbe-Grillet. Words are being adapted to cinematic reality, with the result that they no longer mean anything. Readers trained in the traditional ways of words, predictably, are deeply frustrated by the literature of nothingness. Paradoxically, the impurity of the movies makes them a more perfect art, capable of more extensively exploring its own possibilities and limitations, and thereby of more profoundly and more precisely giving body to man's truth.

Once the movies are acknowledged to be art and what they unveil is taken seriously, we have to face the fact, extensively argued by Existentialists, that the word has been superseded by sensation. The movies define better than any other art what we feel today to be the relation between the intellect and the senses. Among other things they make it quite clear, to the verbalist's distress, that the word is an adjunct of the image. In their version of the play between the eye's truth and the mind's, the ancient theme of appearance versus reality is reversed. In contrast to, say, Elizabethan poetry, in which images decorate a rational framework, in the movies reason rides on the tiger back of images in motion.

This new relation between the senses and the mind is the contemporary form assumed by an ancient and enduring antagonism. For at stake ultimately in the difference between literature and the movies are the prerogatives of two moral universes, two cultures, and two ideas of creation. Both art forms, just by existing, pay tribute to their source, the power which makes them possible—literature to the Word, the movies to the Light. But beyond that, by implication when not directly, literature celebrates a God transcendent, the movies a god immanent; one affirms creation by fiat, the other creation by emanation. These inevitably hostile alternatives, if Joseph Campbell's account in *The Masks of God* is correct, led to the division of East from West some eight thousand years ago—the East following the way of the Light and the West the way of the Word—and has been the source of their mutual suspicion ever since. But the Light and the Word have also vied with one another for supremacy within Christendom. The Old and New Testament offer conflicting accounts of the instrument responsible for creation, and St. John indiscriminately mixes creation by the Word with creation by the Light. St. John's confusion, a careless mixture of Judaic and Greek attitudes, may well be the source of the traditional friction in Western culture between the Light and the Word. At any rate Judaism's existential, worldly faith has persistently contended with Greek rationalistic idealism for dominance in Western culture. The Word has been clearly dominant until recently, but as a result of science's corrosive effect upon Christianity, the Light is now in the ascendant. So the difference between the movies and literature is rooted in a fundamental anti-thesis in man's being, and the rise of the movies as an art is one sign of a profound change taking place in Western culture—a trans-formation begetting what pundits have been variously calling a post-Christian, post-rationalistic, post-typographical, or post-literary period.

The movies derive their aesthetic stature, obviously, from being a closer analogue to reality than is literature. For the alert film-maker and his audience today a movie can and should be a microcosm of life. All the world's a movie screen. Thus the director's medium is inherently closer than any other to life, and he is the most advan-tageously equipped artist for adventuring in moral reality.

The movies at their best have always performed the task of art, even when film-makers, critics, and theorists claimed that, paradoxi-cally, the movies could be art only if the imagination was weighed down by materiality. Accepting this condition in *Greed,* Erich Von Stroheim created serious art in spite of the inherent bias against the medium. Nonetheless this assumption hurt the movies in the pres-sure it exerted on moviemakers to honor piously the dominion of the mechanical, material, and casual over their art. And theorists, including such sophisticated ones as Erwin Panofsky and Susanne Langer, in their turn were impaled on a dichotomy which forced them to choose between conceptions of the movie as dream or as bound to physical reality.

The movie of the last decade, along with developments elsewhere in thought and the arts, has put this realistic assumption to rest. It was a period's taste, time has made evident—a corruption of reality. Today the movie is explicitly and confidently committed to freedom as the supreme value and truth, and the moral dialogue it is now partic-ipating in is probing the career of man's good in that direction—

whether in great, good, bad or indifferent films, in parts of films or in their entirety; in the character of the emancipated female: Mrs. Waters in *Tom Jones,* Jeanne Moreau or Brigette Bardot in *Viva Maria,* Jean Seberg in *Breathless,* or the various roles played by Natalie Wood; or the cool, resilient male: Belmondo in *Breathless* and elsewhere, Anthony Quinn in *Zorba the Greek,* or Vittorio Gassman in *The Easy Life;* or as a theme in the work of Bergman and Fellini.

The free camera, moreover, supports the free character. It has always been understood that the camera used with skill is a projection of an individual's sensibility, not a mechanical eye; foreign films especially, coming out of visual traditions different from our own, have been constant reminders of this fact. Today there is not even a shadow of a doubt that the movies, instead of being by nature or moral precept enslaved to physical reality, are a technological vehicle by which the human spirit can escape material limitations once thought to be narrowly restrictive. Not too long ago regarded as man's nemesis, technology, in the movies as well as in the airplane, enlarges his power of flight. The movies, consequently, need no longer be an illusion of the "real" but are at liberty to be artifice and even to call attention to their fictional character, as Tony Richardson does in *Tom Jones* and as Richard Lester does in *A Hard Day's Night.* A still more striking example is Mario Monicelli's *The Organizer,* in which, although the movie is ostensibly a realistic treatment of capitalistic inhumanity, the artistry draws attention to itself, contradictorily and ironically proclaiming the dominion of the imagination over substance.

But the movies' greatest contribution to today's moral dialogue over freedom does not lie in characters or camera technique. It lies, rather, in the emancipation of the image. Not long ago it was excitedly argued that the camera gave painting a new life by freeing it from photographic representation, but the camera has done even more than that: it has freed itself, too, at least from all debilitating forms of representation. This child of empiricism, repudiating its parent, has liberated form from the physical world. Marilyn Monroe, never a physical actuality for moviegoers, lives on every time the camera projects her image on the screen, and so, although physically dead, she has gained immortality. She has been released, as has the moviemaker and the viewer, and, indeed, man's mind everywhere, to dance in the imagination's heaven. Actually physics is mainly responsible for destroying the idea of substance, but the movies have done more to set the imagination free to dream upon human moral possibilities within a substanceless universe. By conclusively demonstrating that an image does not necessarily signify substance, they have destroyed the last vestige of our materialistic mental habits. Unburdening us of the hunger for and anxiety about meaning, the free movie teaches us that to be is enough; existence needs no justification. Ironically, in the new intimacy between the senses and the mind which the movie achieves, Plato's realm of forms is realized through physical vision.

Once regarded as a puerile, cowardly escape from life because they begot and simulated dreaming, the movies are now recognizable as an extension of the supreme power inherent in a universe of energy, chance, evolution, explosiveness, and creativity. In such a youthful, exuberant universe the movies' kind of dreaming gives concrete probability and direction to the ongoing drive of energy, and as a consequence what at one time was thought to be a vitiating defect is now their greatest virtue. The new freedom they reflect and extend is freedom within the world, contingent and not absolute, a heightened vision of existence through concrete form beyond abstraction. In a world of light and a light world—unanalyzable, uninterpretable, without substance or essence, meaning or direction—being and non-being magically breed existence. Out of the darkness and chaos of the theater beams a light; out of nothingness is generated brilliant form, existence suspended somewhere between the extremes of total darkness and total light. Performing its rhythmic dance to energy's tune, the movie of the imagination proves, should there be any doubt, that cinema, an art of light, contributes more than any other art today to fleshing out the possibilities for good within an imaginative universe.

the ARTIST
and HIS
WORK

O. B. HARDISON

The Rhetoric of Hitchcock's Thrillers

We can start from the axiom that Alfred Hitchcock is one of the great professionals in the movie business—probably the greatest. I use the word professional in its most favorable sense: movies are entertainment, and no one entertains more and more consistently than Hitchcock. What the Lincoln Continental is to the Fairlane 500 the Hitchcock film is to the standard production-model Hollywood thriller. The public recognizes this. Hitchcock is one of a very few producers whose name is more important at the box office than the names of his stars. But professionalism has its limits, too. Nobody would seriously compare Hitchcock to a dozen directors and producers

137

who have used the film medium as an art form. Eisenstein, Chaplin,
Ford, Bergman, Olivier, Fellini—the list could be expanded—have
qualities undreamed of in the world of cops and robbers and pseudo-
Freudian melodrama, which is the world where Hitchcock reigns
supreme.

Consider the professional a rhetorician. The purpose of art, says
Aristotle, is to give pleasure. Not any kind of pleasure, but the sort
that comes from learning. The experience of art is an insight, an illumination of the action being imitated. Rhetoric, on the other
hand, is oriented toward the marketplace. Its purpose is not illumination but persuasion, and its governing concept is that the work
produced must be adjusted to the mind of the audience. Rhetorical
art succeeds by saying what the audience has secretly known (or
wanted to know) all along. Its language is disguised flattery, its norm
fantasy, and its symbols surrogates for unconscious cravings. Given
the passionate desire that everyone has to suspend disbelief, almost
anything works, as witness the comic book and the exploits of Mike
Hammer and James Bond; but some kinds of rhetoric work better
than others. Just as there is good and bad art, there is good and
bad rhetoric.

A work of art produces insight. To experience it is to become
different. If not wiser, at least more human. Since a work of rhetoric
is shaped by its audience, it cannot *cause* insight, but its data, when
analyzed, can lead to certain useful understandings. We study a work
of art aesthetically, but the study of professional entertainment is a
branch of sociology. Professional entertainment, that is to say, goes
according to formula. A formula is simply a way of doing things that
works—that has been tried and found successful in the marketplace
and is therefore repeated as long as it retains its appeal. Seen in this
way, a formula is a psychological category created by social and
economic conditions, usually tensions. Crude rhetorical art, like that
of Mickey Spillane or Ian Fleming, is almost pure formula, and it is
fantastic because it approximates the mode of uninhibited day-
dream. Adolescents, by and large, can take their fantasy straight. They
provide the economic base for the comic book industry and its rela-
tives. Grown-ups, on the other hand, want their fantasy to be credible

simply because they so desperately want it to be true, and it is their needs that both shape and support Hitchcock's work. To put it differently, adults can enjoy Hitchcock without being *ashamed*, whereas they feel apologetic or vaguely guilty about enjoying what their children like. Intellectuals, by the way, tend to be the most in-*hibited of all groups. In the thirties movies were definitely non-U, and one still occasionally meets individuals who refuse to buy television sets. The current fad for formula entertainment with built-in satire— *The Man from U.N.C.L.E.* or *Batman*—shows that the predicament of the intellectual is widespread and quite serious. It is, in effect, a mild schizophrenia, since the entertainment it summons into being must provide both a fantasy to which one can surrender and a hostile critique of this fantasy. The values that the individual has learned are at war—and the psychological cost of this war should not be underestimated—with the needs that he has inherited from his culture.

How does one become a master rhetorician? There are doubtless any number of ways, but two or three things definitely help. First, it is good to know your audience. It is best, in fact, to have been one of them. There is a famous passage in "The Art of Fiction" in which Henry James tells how a lady artist (I believe it was George Eliot) was able to deduce the whole milieu of French Protestantism from a glimpse of some young Protestants finishing a meal with their *pasteur*; but James was talking about art and, in particular, about a moment of insight. A rhetorician does not need moments of insight. To the extent that a moment of insight suggests departure from formula, it may even prove an embarrassment. What the rhetorician needs is a sense of the formulas themselves, and this sense will be surest if he has grown up amid the conditions that produced them. Being ingrained, it will seem to emerge spontaneously in later life as talent. But talent is not enough. It must be shaped and filed by experience, and for the rhetorician the only relevant experience is the marketplace. Mastery of rhetoric, like mastery of any other skill, comes slowly. The rhetorician needs a long career allowing for experimentation, some failure, but mostly a polishing and bringing to perfection of the formulas that work and a pruning away of the ones that do not.

Alfred Hitchcock has been fortunate on both counts. No pedagogue could have invented a curriculum better suited than Hitchcock's career to the production of a master of rhetoric. George Perry's recent survey *(The Films of Alfred Hitchcock)* describes his as the ideal childhood. His father was a poulterer and greengrocer, a Catholic, and a rigid disciplinarian who once had the five-year-old Alfred locked up in the local jail for misbehaving. The lower-middle-class background is as close as possible to the average background of movie audiences of the twenties and thirties. The rigidities of pre-World War I class distinctions, of *fin de siècle* Catholic dogma, and of compulsive parental discipline are a paradigm of the dull, routine, boss-ridden, woman-ridden environments from which the Walter Mittys of this world forever plot their fantasy escapes. If they explain the flight of the young Alfred from the grocer's shop to the Bohemia of the early film industry, they also explain the recurrence (and recurrent success of) the "flight from normalcy" motif in the mature thrillers. One is reminded of James Joyce and Stephen Dedalus, and the contrast as well as the parallel is illuminating. Stephen left Ireland to forge the uncreated consciousness of his race, while Alfred left the grocer's shop for a medium that has as its self-imposed goal the easing of the race's already-created and very uncomfortable subconscious. In one way or another Hitchcock's early background projects itself into all of his best-known films. Since it is also the background of his audiences, it guarantees the rightness of his formulas and does much to account for their popular appeal.

Hitchcock arrived on the seacoast of Bohemia in 1921 and has been continuously involved in making films since then. His first thriller was a silent *(The Lodger,* 1926); he directed the first British talkie *(Blackmail,* 1929); and his most recent film, *Torn Curtain,* was produced in 1966. In retrospect his experience with silents seems especially valuable. Different directors have exploited different potentialities of the film medium, but the great ones have all recognized that it is first and foremost a way of telling a story by images. It is more a branch of visual art than of literature. The value of the silent period was that it forced early directors to rely on the camera rather than on spoken dialogue for their effects. Since World War II, in fact, many of the most striking cinematic innovations have not been discoveries so much as rediscoveries of techniques developed between 1910 and 1930 and then forgotten.

Hitchcock learned the lesson of silent films well. *The Lodger* is so eloquent visually that it was shown with only about eighty titles as against an industry average of about two hundred per picture. Its eloquence is partly a matter of baroque camera effects. Its most famous scene, for example, is one in which the hero (Ivor Novello) paces his hotel room while being photographed from above through a glass ceiling. Hitchcock's later fondness for striking camera effects may thus be traced to lessons imposed by the silent medium. But striking effects, no matter how typical, are less important than another lesson learned from the silents.

The foundation of a movie, I suggest, is not plot or character or visual excitement, but tone. The best directors have instinctively realized this, and in their films tone becomes a pervasive unifying element all the more effective for being subliminal—the epic tone of John Ford's photography, and the grainy, newsreel tone of the early Rossolini films are obvious cases in point. Hitchcock learned the secret of tone during the days of the silents and has applied it with increasing skill throughout his career. Since the tone of a movie is visual rather than verbal, it is hard to define exactly, but perhaps "authority," "quality," and "precision" will suggest what I am getting at. The quality of authority—the sense of complete mastery of technique—is, I believe, essential to Hitchcock's success. By suggesting hidden but omnipotent control, it insulates the spectator from the implications of the thriller plot, reassuring him that no matter how terrifying the present may seem, sanity will prevail in the end. "Quality" (by which I mean quality film, quality camera work, quality lighting and sound, quality sets, and the like) makes its contribution by separating a Hitchcock film as far as possible from the cruder forms of popular entertainment to which it is generically related. Finally, "precision" seems to have a double function. On the one hand, it underwrites the reality of the fantasy world. The images are sharper than life just as the situations that they reveal have a mathematical neatness unknown in ordinary experience. Like Platonic ideas, they are more

"real" than reality. On the other hand, I wonder if the extra sharp-
ness, the unnatural clarity may not also contribute, like "authority," to the protection of the spectator by suggesting, "This is real,
but it is not your reality; therefore, you can maintain your separate-
ness from it." Incidentally, Hitchcock's understanding of tone helps
explain his ability to adjust to the several technological revolutions
in film-making that eliminated so many of his competitors. For Hitchcock each new technical advance has been an added tool, a new means
of controlling tone. After bridging the gulf between silents and talkies
he has continued to show a remarkable ability not only to assimilate
but to use positively such advances as faster, less grainy film, more
versatile cameras and sound stages, and color.

The measure of Hitchcock's experience is given by the fact that
since 1926 he has directed and produced fifty-one full-length films.
Several of these were experiments that took him outside of his usual
territory. *Easy Virtue, Champagne,* and *Jamaica Inn,* while they have
interesting moments, can be discounted. *The Lodger* was Hitchcock's
first triumph. It was a thriller, and all of his best films since then
have been variations on the same genre. It is this form that offers
the most interesting lessons to a student of his work.

First of all, the thriller is different from the detective story. W. H.
Auden has outlined the English variety of the latter in "The Guilty
Vicarage," and whereas "purgation of guilt" is involved in both the
thriller and the detective story, the methods of purgation and the
environments in which they operate make all the difference. The
English detective is an intellectual. He solves problems rationally. He
is a descendant of Locke via Monsieur Dupin and Sherlock Holmes,
which is to say that he is a child of the Enlightenment. Like the
Newtonian universe, his world is sane and ordered—in the typical
country house, all the guests seem innocent and only one is guilty.
The problem is to identify and banish the interloper, after which
the remaining guests can get back to their tea, tennis, and evening
bridge. Reason restores paradise.

The thriller is both more primitive and more in line with twentieth-
century experience. Its milieu is a dream world in which the normal
rules of reason no longer apply, and its hero is often closer to

a buffoon than an intellectual. The thriller explores a spectrum of realities having the common characteristic of "strangeness" and varying from the comic through the absurd, the sinister, and the daemonic, to the explicitly insane. The theological type of this world is the Calvinist City of Man, a league of the Reprobate in which the few Elect muddle through not by reason or works but by a divine thrusting on. It is the world of the Gothic novel, of *Bleak House* and *Our Mutual Friend,* of *The City of Dreadful Night,* and—if Hitchcock's popularity shows anything—it is the psychological world of twentieth-century man.

Two defining characteristics of the thriller, then, are its setting, which is alien, and its hero, who is typically a victim rather than an agent. The third characteristic follows from the first two: the hero must be invisibly supported during his adventures. In mythic and religious literature (e.g., the *Aeneid, Paradise Lost*) the support is visible. Vulcan provides Aeneas with impregnable armor, and God sends Adam prevenient grace even before he asks for it. The twentieth century, however, is too much a product of the nineteenth to admit publicly to a belief in providence. Only the crudest forms of popular entertainment, the comic books, permit impregnable skins and X-ray vision, and even these try to hide the supernatural under a veneer of rational explanation: Superman is "a visitor from another planet." More sophisticated forms of popular entertainment, the western for example, work things out by chance: the assassin's bullet always misses, the rope is never tied quite tightly enough, at the last minute the chief's daughter betrays the plan of the Indian raid to her pale-face lover, and so forth. The point is that whatever the form, from *Superman* to *North by Northwest,* the hero is one of the Elect. This does not mean that he cannot make mistakes; he is often, like James Bond, an incompetent bungler who does nothing right. Rather, it means that no matter what he does, it turns out all right in the end. This, I take it, is an exact plot equivalent of the Calvinist doctrine of Election.

Heroic invincibility must be considered the most important characteristic of the thriller. (Notice that in the classic detective story the detective is often aloof. He does not need invincibility because he is never in danger: he is an observer, outside of the plot just as Newton was outside of nature.) The audience of the thriller identifies with the hero as he seeks a way out of the nightmare in which he finds himself. His eventual success—the eternally satisfying happy ending— is the payoff. It is a way of saying that no matter how terrible the world may seem there is a hidden benign force at work that guarantees the eventual triumph of good—the Reprobate will be punished, and the Elect will live happily ever after. To deprive the hero of invincibility would be to move from fantasy to reality, from rhetoric to art; and this is exactly what popular entertainment must not do. Hitchcock has, I will add, shown occasional insensitivity to this rhetorical imperative. In *The Lodger, Blackmail,* and *Suspicion* he originally planned unhappy endings but eventually changed his mind in all three cases in the interest of commercial success. This suggests the existence of a frustrated artist somewhere in the psyche of the master rhetorician—an artist who emerges from time to time in Hitchcock's television programs—but surely in the case of the three movies the public was right and the artist wrong. None of the three films can be taken seriously as art, but all three are splendid rhetoric.

The alien milieu in which the hero's adventures occur is as important to the thriller as the hero himself, and Hitchcock's films illustrate most of the possible variations. In *To Catch a Thief* the milieu is simply comic. In *The Thirty-Nine Steps* and its 1959 twin *North by Northwest* it alternates between the absurd and the sinister without ever becoming frightening. In *The Lodger* and *Psycho* it is daemonic, but, from the dominant point of view—that of the hero— it is still sane. In the sequence including *Spellbound, Rope, Vertigo,* and *Marnie* insanity becomes overt, and, at least in *Spellbound,* the visual image disintegrates into surrealistic dream sequences produced with the help of Salvador Dali. Each milieu is exciting and realized in meticulous detail. Several are underwritten by the use of well-known landmarks such as the dome of the British Museum *(Blackmail),* the Forth Bridge in Scotland *(The Thirty-Nine Steps),* and the Mount Rushmore Memorial *(North by Northwest).* But in every case the spectator is insulated from the milieu by Hitchcock's slick photography, by comic interludes, and by such tricks as the traditional appearance of Hitchcock himself, which, like a stage aside, engages the spectator in a private joke with the director at the expense of the drama.

In my opinion Hitchcock is at his best in the range between the comic and the sinister. Whatever its disguise, the thriller is, after all, a variant of the comic epic, and comic action goes best with comic or mock-sinister settings. Moreover, the comic is a valid way of seeing experience, and Cary Grant as an international jewel thief must provide the same sort of innocent Saturnalia for modern audiences that Falstaff provided for the Elizabethans. The darker the comic world becomes, the greater the temptation to take it seriously. I suppose that one of the delights of being a master rhetorician is seeing how far you can bend a formula without breaking it. Hitchcock's spy stories balance between the comic and the terrible with breathtaking virtuosity and never a false step. Their villains are bad without being evil, their heroes are good without being virtuous or wise, and their situations are absurd without being ridiculous. In *The Holy Sinner* Thomas Mann commented on God's habit of involving His saints in impossible predicaments in order to display His omnipotence by extricating them. The same might be said for the Hitchcock of *The Thirty-Nine Steps, The Lady Vanishes,* and *North by Northwest.* In fact, the parallel is exact because the unstated point of the hairbreadth escape is the operation of providence.

Rope and *Psycho* carry the thriller world about as far as it can go without being taken seriously. Actually, both films received a good deal of criticism (i.e., some people took them seriously)—the first for its rather crude reworking of the Leopold and Loeb case, and the second for the brutality of the initial murder scene. In my opinion the criticisms of *Rope* were justified. Hitchcock's effort to make his characters credible by equipping them with cut-rate Nietzschean philosophy introduced a lump of serious material that his formulas simply could not assimilate, a point that becomes perfectly clear when *Rope* is contrasted to *Compulsion. Psycho,* on the other hand, is reasonably good fun if one can get over the murder scene, which, like Nietzschean philosophy, calls for a more serious follow-up than the movie wants to deliver. The psychological thrillers, in which the

milieu varies from daemonic to insane, are the weakest. Ingrid Bergman's flimsy Freudian ministrations to Gregory Peck's equally flimsy
symptoms provide, I suppose, a rationale for the providential cure that
climaxes *Spellbound*. Freud provides a scientific equivalent of prevenient grace in *Paradise Lost*. The formula is followed, but it fails
precisely because Hitchcock has gone to such tedious lengths to make
it convincing. Anybody who knows enough Freud to appreciate
what Hitchcock is doing knows enough to realize that the psychologizing is sentimental and false. The same can be said for the miracu-
lous cure at the end of *Marnie*. In the thriller, guns, spears, fists,
rocks, broken bottles—anything, in fact, is better than understanding.
Success should come not because of intelligence but in spite of it.
After all, in the wars between good and evil, it is the enemy who
has all the brains.

Aside from the obvious point that they are impregnable, Hitchcock's protagonists are a various lot. All of them have sexual con-
sorts, and in the earlier films the relations between the sexes are
generally orthodox. In the later films the relations become more exotic.
The woman is dominant and maternal (*Spellbound*), a seasoned
predator and sexually more experienced than the hero (*North by
Northwest*), alternately frigid and passionate (*To Catch a Thief*), or
frigid and dependent (*Marnie*). This may simply reflect the relaxa-
tion of censorship after World War II, but since the unorthodox
sexual relations are correlated to Hitchcock's increasing obsession
with the daemonic and the insane, their appearance may be related
to Hitchcock's personal life or to new appetites on the part of the
audience. Heterosexual fun and games have always been a part of
the comic epic and its variants, as witness the picaresque. The sudden
change of a female character from prude to wench is also familiar
and particularly effective when portrayed by such an icily refined
actress as Grace Kelly. The more unorthodox relations explored by
Hitchcock, however, create the same problems as his psychologizing.
Do they come from the artist still buried in the rhetorician? Or do
they simply ring the changes on the Oedipal situation to make sure
that everybody has his share?

Another feature of Hitchcock's protagonists is their strong class identity. The class theme emerges first in *Murder*. The hero is titled and is played by Herbert Marshall, whose public image has always been that of an aristocrat. Marshall plays a "good" aristocrat—he saves the heroine from being executed for a crime she did not commit. On the other hand, there is considerable undercutting of the image. Marshall plays an actor (a hint of self-parody), and in two scenes he wantonly insults lower-class characters. The treatment reveals a mixture of admiration and hostility and doubtless reflects attitudes toward his betters that young Alfred took with him from the grocer's shop. *The Thirty-Nine Steps* is less ambiguous. It toys with the same class attitudes explored by Graham Greene in *This Gun for Hire*. Although he is not a lower-class character like Greene's gunman, Hitchcock's hero is definitely an outsider, while the villain is an aristocrat and inhabits a baronial country house in Scotland. Ambiguities aside, *Murder* defines one standard type of Hitchcock thriller—*noblesse oblige*—while *The Thirty-Nine Steps* defines its antitype, which might be called "local boy makes good." In the first type the upper class is benign—a source of deliverance; in the second it is malign—a source of evil—and must be destroyed by the middle-class hero.

That the class theme has remained strong in Hitchcock's American films is evident from his stars. The *noblesse oblige* roles have consistently been given to actors whose upper-class identity is established by accent (modified British) as well as publicity. Ray Milland and Cary Grant are Hitchcock's favorite male stars, with Cary Grant clearly running first. Grant has both class and *sprezzatura*. He embodies, I suppose, what every grocer's clerk wants to be rather than what he hates. (Hitchcock's malign aristocrats, identified by lack of *sprezzatura*, have been played by such Hollywood heavies as Joseph Cotten, Claude Rains, and James Mason.) The class interest is equally evident in Hitchcock's female leads. Madeline Caroll, Joan Fontaine, and Ingrid Bergman are all typed as Ladies by casting and publicity.

The class tagging is especially obvious in Grace Kelly, who might almost be called Hitchcock's invention. Miss Kelly's credentials include Philadelphia and family wealth plus a successful career as a fashion model. The latter is especially significant, as is shown by the fact that Eva Marie Saint (*North by Northwest*) and "Tippi" Hedren (*Marnie*) also came to Hitchcock via modeling. High fashion is unabashedly snobbish, and its models must consciously learn to project the upper-class image in posture, gesture, and expression, as well as in dress. (Since high fashion is mostly posing for stills, speech and accent are unimportant: thus Hitchcock's heroines lack the hint of British inflection characteristic of Milland and Grant.) The pairing of the ideal Hitchcock leads—Cary Grant and Grace Kelly—in *To Catch a Thief* helps explain its near-perfect finish. Interestingly, the film also projects an entirely benign image of class relations. Grace Kelly plays a true blue blood and Cary Grant a self-made thief (an echo of local boy makes good?). Miss Kelly's initial frigidity carries with it a suggestion of class hostility, and her capitulation to Grant a trace of middle-class wish-fulfillment or class revenge (the Lady Chatterly motif). But Grant is, himself, so much the complete gentleman that it is impossible to take his criminal background seriously. The picture is simply a romp, luxuriating in fantasies of Riviera high life and beautiful people whose only worry is the whereabouts of the family jewels.

Additional variation on the thriller formula is provided by dominance of either the male or female lead. In *Murder* and *Blackmail* the male is dominant while the female is helpless. Hitchcock inherited this stereotype from melodrama. It is a perfectly satisfactory arrangement, but, just as he explored new twists to the thriller plot, he began early in the thirties to experiment with more original deployments of characters. In *The Thirty-Nine Steps* the male-female relationship is equalized, and there are several episodes where the equality becomes overt antagonism. This is a reworking of the Beatrice-Benedick theme, so it cannot be called an innovation, but it is certainly less commonplace than the melodrama convention. Predictably, the antagonism eventually turns to love and hence to the surrender of the female. *Spellbound* and *To Catch a Thief* shift the balance of the relationship still further. In both films the female is dominant and the male dependent. Particularly in *Spellbound* the female has an Oedipal function, being both mother surrogate and object of sexual desire. The Oedipal basis of the fantasy becomes overt in the scene in which Gregory Peck stands over the sleeping Bergman with an open razor and the spectator is left in suspense as to whether he will make love to her or cut her throat. In *North by Northwest,* Cary Grant again plays a dependent part. He is equipped at the beginning of the film with a domineering mother, a nagging secretary, and not one but two ex-wives with alimony claims. When the chase begins, mother, secretary, and wives are replaced by Eva Marie Saint, who first saves him by concealing him in the upper berth of a pullman compartment and then seduces him. Later she is shown to be the mistress of the villain, who, in this situation, can only be understood as a father surrogate. Although Grant eventually bestirs himself enough to rescue Miss Saint from the villain, he resumes his dependent role in the final scene, where she is shown climbing into the upper bunk with him, evidently preparing for that special kind of sexual fun known as Turkish Delight.

Hitchcock's recent film *Marnie* (1964) appears on first inspection to be a return to the melodrama formula of the dependent heroine and *noblesse oblige.* Outwardly, Marnie seems to be a self-possessed, sexually experienced, and highly successful thief, a female counterpart of Cary Grant in *To Catch a Thief.* Having been caught in the act by the wealthy hero (Sean Connery of James Bond fame), she agrees to marry him. He soon discovers that she is virginal and sexually frigid, that her thieving is a neurotic compulsion, and that she comes from a lower-class background. As in *Spellbound,* an informal psychoanalysis ensues. Her trauma is duly discovered (her mother was a Baltimore prostitute, and Marnie was involved in the killing of one of the customers), and she is restored, as the analysts say, to a full and normal life. George Perry has already observed, however, that this apparently innocent fantasy has perverse undertones. The hero's marriage to a woman whom he knows to be a thief is curious to say the least. The suggestion of perverse relations is further underscored by the overt jealousy of the hero's sister. If the film is considered fantasy, it is a playing out of the Electra complex. But if it is judged on any other basis, the hero is at least as sick as the woman he is trying to cure.

Because Hitchcock has continued to produce successful thrillers for over thirty years, his films are a kind of contour map of the middle-class mind during this period. The early films indicate an audience restless, in search of escape, fascinated with crime and sudden death, and subconsciously considering its environment absurd or sinister. This is not, in itself, surprising or unique to the twentieth century. What is disturbing is the increasing morbidity of Hitchcock's handling of the formulas. In the fifties and sixties—that is, in the period following World War II, which one would like to consider a period of relaxed tensions—the Hitchcock world becomes darker. The dominant movement is away from the comic and toward the daemonic or the overtly insane. For the most part, the daemonic and insane are still held in the frame of the comic epic, but there is an increasing challenge to the frame itself, as in *Rope, Psycho,* and *Marnie.* The evil threatens to become real, the brutality becomes ugly, and the source of deliverance turns out to be as corrupt as the forces that it is opposing. To the degree that the controlling force of the thriller plot is providence, this represents an erosion of faith. The fantasy is becoming progressively harder to accept; a reality principle constantly threatens to destroy it. And to the degree that the thriller involves audience identification with the hero, it suggests a kind of self-revulsion. In spite of obvious tendencies toward sadism and masochism, Mike Hammer remains officially innocent in Mickey Spillane's novels. Because he is of the Elect, acts that would be evil in others become sanctified in him. This is not the case in *Marnie.* In spite of Sean Connery's rather wooden performance, Hitchcock's undercutting is too plain to be missed. The heroic image is intentionally tarnished. Instead of seeing an idealized version of his ego, the spectator finds something deformed and rather ugly. Something, that is, more like himself.

These threats to the comic epic frame of the thriller become explicit in *The Birds,* which is Hitchcock's most honest examination of his themes. The film is an art film in the sense that it brings into the open both the assumptions and the trends evident in the thrillers. Instead of being concealed, the supernatural operates overtly: the birds suddenly become possessed (no rational explanation is offered) and attack the inhabitants of a small California village. The transformation of protagonist to villain is also evident. "Tippi" Hedren, the female lead, plays a wealthy, restless girl in search of sexual adventure. It is her arrival at the village that triggers the attacks of the birds, and she is the most obvious focus of their hatred. In one scene she is brutally pecked and clawed. The motif of self-revulsion which is only a suggestion in *Marnie* is the main point of *The Birds*. Nature becomes the agent of an avenging providence. Only man is vile, and before being destroyed he must be stalked, terrorized, and physically tortured to expiate his sins. All this being fairly clear, the movie ought to be a good one. Unfortunately, it is not. The problem, I think, is tone. The tone of *The Birds* is too much that of the thrillers, and for this reason the film's denotation jars badly with its connotation. In the end, the chief interest of *The Birds* is the light it throws on Hitchcock's thrillers. I will add that *The Birds* made a poor showing at the box office. Audiences who went expecting rhetoric were disappointed, while audiences accustomed to Bergman and Rossolini could not take Hitchcock's pretensions seriously.

Whatever one thinks about *The Birds,* the increasing threat to the thriller formulas that is evident in Hitchcock's work of the fifties and sixties is significant and must, I think, reflect cultural tensions. That Hitchcock has continued—except for *The Birds*—to use the formulas and that they have continued to work at the box office are also significant. A dream, Freud discovered, is a device to help the dreamer avoid waking up. It is benign, curative. Subjects experimentally prevented from dreaming experience a rapid deterioration of personality, leading eventually to psychosis.

A culture is like an individual. It needs its dreams as well as its waking periods, and they are supplied by the rhetoric of popular entertainment. If it is becoming harder to dream, we should be all the more grateful to Hitchcock for bending the formulas so that it at least remains possible. There may not be a pot of gold (or a virginal slut) at the end of the rainbow as the comic epic maintains. It may be that the City of Dreadful Night is truly dark and truly possessed by daemons and that there is nothing to distinguish the

Elect from the Reprobate. In an absolute sense we are doubtless more like Sisyphus than stout Cortez with eagle eye, but if we truly believed this, it is hard to see how we could continue to push the stone up the hill. In the psyche the instinct for survival has to be a little stronger than the death wish. No matter how we may plot our situation on the charts of reason, the subconscious needs to view life as an epic quest through alien territories and the domains of strange gods, underwritten by providence and with the payoff guaranteed. Hitchcock's thrillers present this fantasy in palatable modern guise. If they are rhetoric and shaped by the needs of the audience, they are just as significant as art and just as necessary. We may scoff at popular entertainment, we may be ashamed of it; but when a Hitchcock film is revived at the local theater or on the late show, we usually find ourselves watching it. We usually find our friends there, too.

GEORGE E. DORRIS

Griffith in Retrospect

When the Museum of Modern Art announced its D. W. Griffith retrospective in the spring of 1965,* I decided to attend the complete series. But I had no real idea of what I was letting myself in for. Like most filmgoers, I knew the legend of the shattered titan, living out the last years of his life as a virtual recluse. I had seen *The Birth of a Nation* and *Intolerance* and been moved by the beauty, the dramatic sweep, and the emotional power of these remarkable

*Between April 25 and July 31, 1965, the Museum of Modern Art Film Library showed forty-one Griffith films, including fifteen of the nearly five hundred one-reel films he made for Biograph between 1909 and 1913, one two-reel and one four-reel film, and twenty-four full-length (six- to fourteen-reel) films.

153

films. But of Griffith's other work I knew nothing. I had no prejudice against silent films, having admired many of the classic Russian and German silents as well as a few French and American ones. But, with the exception of the Eisenstein films, I had rarely seen an extensive showing of a single director and never of one who produced mainly silent films. Therefore I was unprepared for what I discovered during those three months when at least twice a week I descended to the small theater in the basement of the museum.

Like any retrospective showing of an important figure, the Griffith cycle tested the art, the artist, and the audience. At times all were found wanting, but it remained a finely conceived tribute to a true artist, although too often it brought out flaws in the audience which were unconnected with the flaws in the artist. From it emerged, finally, an understanding of Griffith's art, still too often misunderstood, and a feeling of pity that such a man could be forced into silence and humiliation by the Hollywood studios and financiers; when he died in 1948, it had been seventeen years since he had completed his last film, *The Struggle,* which revealed his powers virtually unimpaired. What remains is the monument he created, the films themselves, for his greatness is to be found not only in the few famous ones—*The Birth of a Nation, Intolerance, Broken Blossoms, Way Down East, Orphans of the Storm*—but in nearly all he touched.

Griffith remains one of the few masters of the film. From the often primitive one-reelers (technically and artistically primitive), the form he inherited from Edwin S. Porter, he created a style which transcended the anecdotal nature of the twelve-minute film. As he developed actors sensitized to his style, subtleties of detail, of characterization, and of form emerged. Between 1909 and 1913 he built the nucleus of a film repertory company—Blanche Sweet, Mae Marsh, Lillian Gish, Henry Walthall, Robert Harron—performers on whom he could experiment emotionally as his cameraman Billy Bitzer was experimenting technically. At the same time Griffith was also experimenting with cutting, creating the film as an artistic entity. Between *The Lonely Villa, A Corner in Wheat,* and *The Usurer* (1909–10) and *The Lonedale Operator, The Goddess of Sagebrush*

Gulch, and *The Musketeers of Pig Alley* (1911–12), as his touch became surer, the films became more complex and emotionally richer.
Eventually Griffith overcame most of the problems inherent in the
one-reel form, creating suspense, humor, and pathos by his handling
of the story and of his developing actors and by his manipulation
of the techniques of film.

 In these early films many of the traits of the later Griffith can
be seen; suspense, humor, and pathos were to remain his stock-in-
trade. Most of his later films culminate in one version or another of
the big chase, however transformed in *Way Down East* or *Isn't Life
Wonderful.* Equally typical is a gentle, sometimes pastoral, humor,
from the first intellectual's discovery of weapons in *Man's Genesis*
(1911) to the warm picture of rural life in *True Heart Susie*
(1919). Comedy of the Sennett or Chaplin variety was not Griffith's
strength, but his gentler vein could be warm and effective. The pathos
speaks for itself, growing from the deep emotionalism of the melodramatic tradition from which Griffith came (he had been both actor
and playwright) and which he transformed. Another aspect of this is
the idealism which at times leads Griffith to see his characters as
Good or Evil, symbolic and often explicitly allegorical. Like the
angels who transfigure a battlefield at the end of *The Birth of a
Nation* and the pitchfork devil prodding damned souls in *Dream
Street* (1921) —a film of Limehouse life in which Good is symbolized
by the elder Tyrone Power as an itinerant street preacher and Evil
by Morgan Wallace as a masked violinist—his fancy-dress allegories
and visionary recreations of Christian symbols are often extremely
literal. But they spring directly from his idealism and the deep view
of emotion which it reflects and which he hoped to give visual form,
moving from a narrative to a moral statement. Conventionality,
naïveté, and literalness are the inevitable flaws, early and late, but
they are usually suffused with a disarming sincerity.

 One other significant aspect of Griffith's thought, seen early in its
pristine condition, is a conventional tendency to view social ills as
the primary result of individual actions. In *A Corner in Wheat*
(1909) the prohibitive price of bread is the direct and sole result of
financial manipulation by one greedy man, suitably and symbolically

punished by suffocating in a wheat bin; in *The Birth of a Nation* Austin Stoneman's passion for his mulatto mistress leads to the excesses of Reconstruction; the scorned priest of Bel betrays Babylon in *Intolerance;* the British-Indian atrocities during the Revolution are exclusively attributed to the lascivious Walter Butler in *America* (1924) ; and out of personal pique Robespierre condemns the lovers— and by implication thousands of others—to the guillotine in *Orphans of the Storm.* The lovers' rescue by Danton suggests the other side of this individual view of history and social forces, which is perhaps seen most clearly in the warm treatment of Lincoln both in *The Birth of a Nation* and in the very late *Abraham Lincoln* (1930). Only *Isn't Life Wonderful,* of the social films, is free of this social-biographical simplification: when the starving workers steal the unfortunate lovers' first harvest, they cry, "Yes, beasts we are, beasts they have made us." Here Griffith rises to a maturity of outlook unexpected in his essentially non-intellectual art, suggesting the maturity of the developing artist.

Isn't Life Wonderful (1924), his picture of a family crushed by the inflation in Germany after World War I, is a late masterpiece, a superb work of social realism, almost documentary in its approach and power. Still it seems untypical of the usually more romantic Griffith. With his tendency to push warmth and emotion toward sentimentality and his often faltering comic interludes—Griffith's greatest faults— goes his distrust of adult physical passion, for which he too often substitutes coyness. But these flaws do not cancel out the emotional power of the great scenes and the exquisite pathos seen especially in the roles designed for Lillian Gish and Mae Marsh, superb actresses who brought out the best in Griffith as he did in them.

In his tendency to emotional excess, as in his equally typical emotional delicacy, his warmth, his ability to create and define character, and his superb feeling for fitting the exact detail and small personal scene into a sweeping action, in both his excess and restraint, virtues and flaws, Griffith is closely comparable to Dickens. Modern audiences seem to fear deep emotion, and anyone who is unwilling to overlook the sentimentality and the comic excesses typical of Dickens and Griffith, in order to find the emotional richness and subtlety beyond, is well advised to avoid both of them. Those who are willing to accept these conventional flaws are abundantly rewarded by the range and power of the world each creates*

Not all of Griffith's films are masterpieces. Like Dickens, he produced too much, perhaps too rapidly. But as also is the case with Dickens, from this profusion came some of his best work. In 1919 and 1920, at the peak of his career, he released ten films, from *The Girl Who Stayed at Home,* the last of his war films, to *Way Down East,* a spectacularly successful melodrama. In the first of these he combined two strands of plot, one involving M. France, an unreconstructed Southerner who has lived abroad since the Civil War, a charmingly conceived character who comes to terms with his country through the rescue of his granddaughter and himself by the AEF; the other involves the two sons of a rich American businessman, one son conventionally noble (he rescues and marries M. France's granddaughter), while the other is transformed from "lounge lizard" to war hero and with him transforms the chorus girl he loves. Among the most revealing scenes is one in which the second boy crawls across the battlefield to report the dangerous position of the small party led by his brother; this scene is crosscut with one of his fiancée being tempted by gifts from a former admirer. As she hesitates, the boy crawls. When she overcomes temptation, he reaches safety. This point is never made explicitly, but the emotional effect is the stronger for this restraint. The treatment is typical of the way Griffith transforms a film primarily intended to encourage the war effort (and officially supported by the government) into a work independent of propaganda in its richness, charm, and effectiveness. If less moving than *Hearts of the World* (1918), an earlier

*This comparison is best explored by Eisenstein in his 1944 essay "Dickens, Griffith, and the Film Today" (reprinted in *Film Form*). His comment on the emotional power of the two masters is especially astute, as when speaking of Nancy in *Oliver Twist:* "By the way, it is characteristic for both Dickens and Griffith to have these sudden flashes of goodness in 'morally degraded' characters and, though these sentimental images verge on hokum, they are so faultlessly done that they work on the most skeptical readers and spectators!" Certainly this is true of Griffith, from the early Biograph films to his powerful last film, *The Struggle* (1931). Perhaps Eisenstein's own silent films are more readily acceptable to present-day audiences because he avoids the "sentimental images" which so often make audiences squeamish, however faultlessly done.

film exploring the horrors of war, and less gentle than *True Heart Susie,* which came soon after, *The Girl Who Stayed at Home* stands as a fine example of Griffith's craftsmanship and his ability to work creatively with his actors, especially Robert Harron and Clarine Seymour as the transformed lovers.

Even where the integration of plot fails to come off, the resulting parts can be highly effective. In *The Greatest Question* (1919) the scene in which the beloved son off at sea appears to his mother on the day he dies in action is a profoundly moving one. Such extrasensory experience may be an unfashionable subject now, although it was not following World War I, but I am unable to imagine how that scene could be improved upon or even done any differently without spoiling its simplicity and beauty. Although the Lillian Gish escape plot is largely unconnected with this whole aspect of the film, the effectiveness of each part remains. In later films these double plots are played down, so that, for example, the poor boy–rich girl subplot of *The White Rose* (1923) remains a convention and never interferes with the poor girl and rich, spoiled minister story which forms the main plot of this beautiful and moving relatively late film.

Although now most famous for the epic sweep, the vast panoramas, and the great battle scenes of *The Birth of a Nation, Intolerance,* and *Orphans of the Storm*—and properly famous, it might be added—Griffith's enduring power is also to be found in his individual emotional scenes. The mother's plea to a tired, awkward, gentle Lincoln in *The Birth of a Nation,* Mae Marsh's face as her baby is taken away from her in the modern story in *Intolerance,* and Lillian and Dorothy Gish, the two orphans in *Orphans of the Storm,* fearfully setting out for Paris and the great operation on the blind girl's eyes—these are also moments that remain.

These moments are usually held in a striking visual image, which is another aspect of Griffith's power: his ability to create a visual image which is beautiful in its own right while also embodying dramatic and emotional meaning. Perhaps the most celebrated single image in Griffith's work is the riding of the klan in *The Birth of a Nation,* the long line of white-clad horsemen galloping to the rescue of a small, embattled party. The ambiguities created by the second half of this film in the modern liberal spectator are crystallized in this scene; however much he loathes the klan, he is compelled by the hypnotic effect of suspense building in this rescue sequence to side with these towering figures as they fill the screen. The racial tensions generated by the whole film today are a belated tribute to Griffith's power, but nowhere more so than in this scene, which is so well suited to the silent screen. It is superbly visual and, when properly accompanied by music, all other sound is superfluous. One may regret that Griffith was unable to rise above the prejudices of his Kentucky background and of his age, but even *The Birth of a Nation* is suffused by the warmth and the deep humanity which he showed increasingly in such films as *Broken Blossoms* (with Richard Barthelmess as the gentle Chinese boy) and *Isn't Life Wonderful,* not to speak of *Intolerance.*

Griffith's work consists almost entirely of silent films. The aesthetic of the silent film has often been argued. There was never, of course, a literally "silent" film, supported as it was by its piano or theater orchestra accompaniment, yet the modern filmgoer outside the purlieu of the Museum's invaluable Arthur Kleiner usually sees such films in total silence. Except at the Museum they are usually seen at a slightly faster speed ("sound speed") than was intended, making fast movements jerky. Coupled with the pomposity of some of the "titles"—especially if the subject is unsuited to the silent medium—the effect can be incongruous. For the large audiences at the Museum these incongruities apparently blocked an appreciation of Griffith's richly emotional art; only the two sound films (*Abraham Lincoln* and *The Struggle*) seemed to present no such obstacles. The failure of the audience lay in this breakdown of understanding and sympathy. Unfortunately this reaction is typical of the current approach to silent films.

Of course the failure may lie with those who take Griffith and silent films seriously. But the small group of serious admirers who attended despite the behavior of a vocal part of the audience was too consistently moved and too consistently in agreement to accept such an argument. To watch an artist develop and become aware of his medium was an illumination. To see the camera begin to move, the close-up and the panoramic shots devised and brought together to create a new kind of beauty, was more than a historical thrill. Griffith loved beauty, and his films are full of it, especially when seen on the original tinted stock with its suffused blues, greens, and gold. Even in *Isn't Life Wonderful* one finds a beauty in all its starkness. Part of the pathos of the late films lies in Griffith's attempts to preserve this beauty despite the interference with his films and the inadequacy of the stories forced on him by studios. Griffith in decline takes on a symbolic quality, for much of the pathos of this retrospective view lies in the sense of waste. At the height of his powers this protean artist was trapped by the financial pressures which turned Hollywood into a factory and stifled the few artists who emerged in American films, the von Stroheims and the Welleses. He tried to come to terms with this, but inevitably he was rejected. There is no indication that the recent Griffith festival was intended as an ironic allegory; Griffith himself probably wouldn't have been amused at that idea either, despite his fondness for allegory. And perhaps the audiences were laughing to keep from crying. One can only hope, finally, that all unawares they caught some of the beauty, the emotional power, and the humanity that made the unique art of D. W. Griffith.

G. C. KINNEAR

Ingmar Bergman, Master of Illusion

Thomas Mann studied in his hero Hans Castorp the curious sense of deception and unreality experienced in watching a film: "Life flitted across the screen before their smarting eyes: life chopped into small sections, fleeting, accelerated; a restless, jerky fluctuation of appearing and disappearing, performed to a thin accompaniment of music, which set its actual *tempo* to the phantasmagoria of the past, and with the narrowest of means at its command, yet managed to evoke a whole gamut of pomp and solemnity, passion, abandon, and gurgling sensuality."

In the theater we watch life at one remove. We see the living actor mold himself to some vision of human speech and action conceived in the playwright's imagination and given an illusory life on the stage. In the film we experience a second remove from reality. We no longer see the vision through the medium of the living actor, but through his shadow, his lifeless image only, transmuted to a rapid succession of flat, abstract contrasts of dark and light: a dupe, a deception, a trick of the optical nerves. Shall we believe mind's assertion that these flickering forms can be no more than an idle hour's entertainment, a distraction, a descent from intellect's attempt to reach accurate objectivity; or shall we surrender to the heart's desire that through this medium we may find, perhaps not truth, but that uniting of speech and action, picture and rhythm which embodies reality to the imagination though we are not permitted to know it with the intellect?

Ingmar Bergman is not an artist who can settle for an easy resolution of the struggle between intellect and imagination for the domination of his soul. Neither desire nor verifiable knowledge triumphs in his films, nor do they attain a comfortable commerce. The reality lies in the struggle. He would desire to create his films as the medieval artisan created Chartres cathedral, joyously and humbly exercising his gift in worship of God or of some vision of the human imagination. But intellect protests, telling him that he is "either an imposter, or, when the audience is willing to be taken in, a conjurer."

Bergman realizes that the film is no objective recorder of reality, but a powerful, if illusory, tool capable of capturing and moving audiences. But is he a charlatan, master of illusions, or genuine magician, possessor of genuine powers of evocation and transformation? Vogler, the magician, is an embodiment of this question. His bearded and impassive face conveys power and mystery. But it is a power over the willing and accepting spirit only, not over matter or the doubting mind. In the presence of the cold and analytical Vergerus, Vogler is powerless.

And so to Vergerus, and to all minds convinced that every phenomenon is explicable, Vogler must appear a charlatan. His trick of levitation is exposed in the full light of day, just as he, perhaps in despair, later abandons the wig, beard, and silence of his outward mystery. There still remains, however, unacknowledged by Vergerus, Vogler's inward mystery, though stripped by skepticism of its power to heal and transform. The power of his mind to bind the servant Antonsson remains. His ability to frighten Vergerus by the mere sight of his face remains, first at their initial meeting, then later in the attic when he catches the nearsighted Vergerus unprepared. Below stairs, in the warm kitchen, Sara, Sanna, and Sofia desire to believe in the magical powers of Mrs. Venus Aphrodite, and their innocent and simple belief transforms them.

The mood of *The Magician* is despair, tinged with hope. Of what use are the magician's illusions for moving his audience if the effect of his inward powers may be so simply dispersed by doubting the reality of their outward manifestation? If the tricks which Bergman the director uses to sway his audience are called into question, the magic ceases to operate, and the magician stands alone, naked, foolish, and perhaps angry at the egotistical destructive intellect which he cannot for all that ignore. Yet what authority has this proud pragmatical intellect in human affairs? As Spegel, the actor in *The Magician,* says: "The author thus assumes that there is some great general thing called truth somewhere upstage. This is an illusion."

Bergman is a master of visual illusion. What the film sacrifices of real life it regains many times over in form. Light may be precisely controlled. What the director does not wish the eye to see may be excluded; what he does wish the eye to see may be more narrowly focused on, may be brought into prominence by close-up. Cuts and fades make possible the juxtaposition of characters, actions, and points of view not possible on the stage. The potential magic lies precisely in the increased artifice and discipline available to the director. He has at hand the means to compose and limit space, to obliterate or expand the orderly progression of time, to defy the physical laws of cause and effect. He has the power to make available to the senses as a simulacrum of reality imaginative visions which earlier artists could capture only in the artifice of painting or poetry. What wonder if his powers are suspect to the sober-minded?

One of Bergman's most magical passages is at the opening of *The*

Seventh Seal. The eye sees a vast panorama of turbulent clouds with behind them a hint of sunrise. The eye then moves over stony cliffs to Antonius Block and his squire as they lie on the beach. The knight kneels in anguished prayer by the water. Then his horse whinnies and Block turns his head. The camera cuts suddenly to a figure dressed in a black robe, outlined against the dull sky, his hands hidden in the robe, only his pale, scowling face visible. It is Death. Technically, it is a simple illusion, but it is emotionally powerful. We must not stop to think of the illusion, but believe instead, for the moment, that Death was not beside this knight a moment ago, and that now he has, contrary to all experience, materialized there. This is imagination's, not intellect's, truth. So it is with this scene's echo later in the film. The tumbler Jof's eyes widen with wonder as he pauses in his play with his son. A cut, and we too see Jof's vision of a smiling mother in crown and ancient courtly dress assisting her child to walk. Another cut and Jof rubs his eyes. Another, and the virgin and child are gone from the field. It is not the illusions themselves, but how they are used that is important: the counterpoint of Jof against Block, the innocent against the outcast, a vision of life against a vision of death. The illusions are the tools which create the emotions, giving them form and relationship.

Bergman composes his pictures within the area of the frame as carefully as a painter or a still photographer his scenes, but seldom for solely aesthetic ends. Aesthetic means are used to clarify and enforce emotion and idea. At the conclusion of *The Seventh Seal,* as Jof's voice relates his vision to Mia, we see in the distance, in sharp silhouette against a dawn sky, a dance of death more powerful than any medieval fresco. Bergman again uses silhouette in *The Virgin Spring* when the father goes out at dawn to vent his rage in a ritual struggle to tear down a young sapling for use in his sauna. In both scenes the carefully composed silhouette strips individuals of all but form and act, translates them into ritual idiom, exalts them to archetypal images.

Of all Bergman's films *The Silence* is the least dependent on plot, almost independent of speech. It draws all its power from visual images and the rhythm of their sequence. To conclude the film with the boy studying the translations of a few words, given him by his mother's sister, has always seemed to me an underscoring of what has already been made visually obvious. The situation is quickly stated in the film's opening scene in the railway carriage; the elder sister erect, tense, pale, and dry-skinned, coughing violently from time to time; in the opposite corner of the compartment the younger sister, sprawled loosely on the seat, in a low-cut blouse, full-bodied, with sensual face and skin covered with beads of sweat; and the boy, slender, frail, passive, with slouching posture.

The story is told once they reach the hotel. The elder sister, a scholar, is too much drawn up into her own mind. Her physical sickness is an emblem of this state, as is her constant and desperate attempt to make physical contact with her surroundings and with her sister. She is continually in motion, she smokes and drinks with violent gestures, she masturbates, trying always to flagellate her nerves, to make contact with something that is not of her own mind.

The younger sister is a splendid, thoughtless animal. We see her total lack of bodily shame, her total confidence in her sexual power, as she undresses, bathes, dresses, seduces a man, and makes love to him, all languidly and thoughtlessly. We see her son, still unformed, still uninitiated into human society, wander aimlessly about the rooms and through the halls, seeing but not comprehending, because possessed of no communion with others, no conception of himself by which to shape comprehension.

The silence is the gulf which separates the three, locking each within the compass of himself, each needing communion for wholeness and peace but lacking access to it. All this is visible in the form and rhythm of image and action.

The faces and bodies of Bergman's actors are an essential part of his vision. He has written that the ideas for some of his films grow from imagining some one or another of his actors in a certain makeup and costume. The wedding of actor and character is always imaginatively right. Whether we think of the fair, gaunt face of Max von Sydow as the despairing seeker of truth in *The Seventh Seal,* or of the dark, pregnant, sensual-faced Gunnel Lindblom as the servant girl in *The Virgin Spring,* the face and figure are the accurate correspondents of the invisible character.

Yet more remarkable is the ability of the actors and the close sympathy of actor with director which transforms the actor into the character he is playing. That remarkable actor Gunnar Bjornstrand becomes, by means of makeup and discipline, the character he plays in each film. There is scarcely any resemblance between the square-faced, coarse, cynical Jons of *The Seventh Seal,* the thin-lipped, refined man of the world Egerman of *Smiles of a Summer Night,* and the stiff, haughty, bespectacled Vergerus of *The Magician.* Bjornstrand's disappearance into his roles is typical of the transformations which Bergman draws from his company, minor miracles.

Faces alone often carry the burden of an entire scene. The faces of each of the guests at Madame Armfeldt's table in *Smiles of a Summer Night,* seen in turn, recapitulate the themes and relationships of the entire film, faces ranging from the sensuous, fiery Charlotte Malcolm to innocent Anne Egerman. The whole of the two sisters' relationship in *The Silence* may be seen in one picture: Gunnel Lindblom in profile, with full sensual lips and heavy-lidded eyes; Ingrid Thulin full face with thin lips and drawn expression. Invisible relationships take on body and form. But our overpowering sense of the reality of these characters is only in our imaginations, evoked by the magic of Bergman and his actors.

Bergman is an artist deeply troubled by the crumbling of religious belief, not as a theologian, nor out of nostalgia, but because he experiences and understands the sickly unbalance to which the human soul, bereft of all but body and objective knowledge, is abandoned. For religious knowledge is subjective, emotional, and personal. When the heart desires what the mind questions and the body denies, there can be no health, no wholeness. Bergman's two greatest characters, Antonius Block in *The Seventh Seal,* and Isak Borg in *Wild Strawberries,* are driven by death's nearness to face their souls' sickness and to search for its cure. The cure, however momentary and tenuous, lies in the outward motion of the heart, not toward any hidden and impersonal God, but toward other human beings. With this motion the uncertainties and fears of the proud self dissolve.

Block, returned from a crusade, searches through plague-ridden Sweden for an understanding of death and God, for something to return meaning to his life. But all his questioning of Death and all his demand to see some physical sign of God amid this scene of fear and cruelty and death return him no answer but the mirror image of himself, his own fear and disgust. Yet he does finally discover a meaningful act and defeat Death. He sees a meaningful life in his first meeting with the joyous and innocent couple Jof and Mia. It is, to be sure, a meaning which he feels in his heart as he watches them and takes wild strawberries and milk with them, and not the intellectual comprehension he is seeking. Yet his love for this happy family breeds his one meaningful act as, certain now of his own immediate death, he helps them to escape Death. Block is not the less a tortured soul, but he is able for a moment to find, where he had least sought it, his desired answer.

Isak Borg is not a willing searcher after health; he does not even consider himself ill. But beneath his fine old-world manners and self-satisfied humanitarianism he is cold and egotistical. Depths of himself beneath the level of his awareness begin to thrust into his consciousness troubling dreams and visions. He is first frightened by a dream of his own death. Then a visit to the house and lake where he spent his childhood vacations calls up in his mind a memory or vision of his childhood companions, especially his cousin Sara whom he had loved. A later dream brings him before a tribunal where he, physician of bodies, is accused of incompetence in matters of the heart, and before his faithless wife who accuses him of cold, false self-righteousness and failure of compassion. He has fallen into the error of believing that the impersonal intellect, so capable in medicine, is competent by itself to deal with human intercourse. The rebellion and accusation of the repressed heart prove him wrong. He begins to see his relations with mother, son, daughter-in-law, even housekeeper, with a new and humbler vision.

It is the joyous and loving nature of the young Sara, whom, with her two boyfriends, he and Marianne pick up along the road, that focuses for Isak Borg the meaning of his dreams. The image of his childhood Sara, this Sara teaches him the meaning of love. It may now be too late to alter his relations with his son Evald or his old house-keeper Agda, for the past may not be changed. This is Isak Borg's tragedy. But he is transformed within, and this is his joy.

Bergman's magic, like all magic, cannot survive too much analysis, for it dies under the anatomist's knife. It begins in some intangible imagined vision of an operative order in this shadowy life. Bergman then puts to use all the tricks and illusions of his medium to clothe and shape this vision, that we with bodily senses may see and hear what he in his imagination has seen and heard. He has no power of compulsion over our wills. Many will merely be entertained by the show. Others will choose to analyze and thereby disperse the power of his illusions. Some will admit his magic and find through it, as through all great artifice, a new access to wisdom.

JONATHAN BAUMBACH

From A to Antonioni: Hallucinations of a Movie Addict

> What interests me now is to place the character in contact with things, for it is things, objects and materials that have weight today.
>
> —Antonioni in an interview
> in the *Cahiers du Cinéma.*

In the old days, before Bergman (Ingmar) and the new wave and the art houses in the provinces, going to the movies was a form of slumming, an obsessive return to the fantasy world—lost, one feared irreparably—of our childhood. It was not, one knew, a serious addiction fit for adults. It was marijuana-candy, junk, antisocial, unimproving, and, as it was rumored, not so good for the health. Going to

movies was the public act—the celebratory ritual—of our private pleasure. The theater was a more serious (more respectable) place of
worship, and was overpriced accordingly. If the theater required
churchgoing behavior, it was all right to neck (i.e. make out) in the
movies—on Saturday night it was expected of one, the manners of
the occasion demanded it. As I think of it (in the convenience of
memory), I associate certain movies, or scenes in certain movies, with
the girl I was with, whose hand I may or may not have been holding,
with my fantasies about her.

So much for nostalgia. So much. Too much. It is a way of re-invent-
ing the past, of pretending, out of the needs of dissatisfaction, that
what is no longer, what may in fact never have been, is preferable
to what is. This is not to say that the films we loved without liking
were not worth our affection—some were, and some weren't. What
it is to say is that things have changed—in the past fifteen years the
rhythms of our lives have changed—and, whether we like it or not,
it is a condition we are obliged to live with. And movies have
changed, have undergone a minor revolution from, say, Renoir to
Godard, from Carné to Truffaut, from Rosselini to Antonioni, from
Orson Welles to Orson Welles. More importantly, our attitudes toward
movies, our ways of looking at them, have changed. Colleges, where
the students can barely read and write (I have a particular place in
mind), have film series which include works of Dreyer, Bresson,
Kurosawa, Fellini, Bergman, Olmi, Mizobuchi, Pudhovkin, Chabrol,
Godard, Resnais, and Truffaut, who were either not making films or
were unknown to all but film buffs ten years ago. What we have lost
is not the good old days of bad movies but our innocence as an
audience. We have been made aware that movies (called films or
cinema) are an art form, and generally the most vital and exciting
and immediate art form of our time. It's hard to neck in a movie
house under such pressures of obligation.

Let's come back to the idea of nostalgia. As the world becomes
more complicated and less comprehensible, the conditions of our
lives in perpetual revolution, we long inevitably for a simpler and
safer time, for less demanding, less discriminating pleasures—for the
old days—to see again with the eyes of our childhood. So our arts, like

our lives, are involved in one way or another with a world that day by day has been receding before us. The new-wave French film, with its aesthetic of a personal style, its affection for the mythic simplicity of old American movies (musicals, westerns, mysteries), tends to be nostalgic. But pop art, which also deals with the materials of the past, is not. On the contrary, much of contemporary art, whose subject is some aspect or artifact of the past, is exorcistic. It confronts us with the objects of our nostalgia, bloated and palpable, and makes them impossible for us. It destroys the fantasy that makes nostalgia possible. It destroys nostalgia.

The subject of Antonioni's films, of the trilogy in particular, is nostalgia—our uses and abuses of the past—while the style is abrasively un-nostalgic. It is one of the reasons—there are others—that his films are so much less ingratiating than the cinema of his contemporaries, of, say, Godard and Fellini. Antonioni's films are beautiful in a style uncompromisingly hard-edge, are unparaphrasable, elude patterns of interpretation, and frustrate conventional expectations of plot and theme. One admires Antonioni's films without feeling fond of them, or one resists them, turns blind to avoid seeing their beauty. The technique is alienating—shocking. The tension the films create is formal and grows out of the kind of risks Antonioni takes at the expense of conventional expectation. *Red Desert,* his first color film, has the most conventional narrative; the risk it takes is (1) in the color, and (2) in dealing with what is essentially trite subject matter—it attempts to intensify the expected (the platitudinous) into mystery. All of the films are mysteries.

All of the films are love stories. In each of the narratives, love or what passes as love turns out to be insufficient or a sham; love is dead, dying, in the death throes of willful pretense. In *L'Avventura,* Anna, the apparent heroine, wanders off from her fiancé—they have stopped off at an island during an excursion—and disappears. We are concerned, by habit of response, from years of going to movies, with the mystery of her disappearance. The film frustrates us: we never find out what's happened to Anna, she never appears again, which is disorienting and shocking. Antonioni's films teach us to see, as if we've never used our eyes before, by not allowing us our old ways of seeing. (I am speaking now primarily of the trilogy and of *Red Desert*. *Il Grido* and *Le Amiche* are good films, but they are not, like the later ones, revolutionary.)

Anna's fiancé and a friend, Sandro and Claudia, search for her. In the process they find themselves drawn to each other. The more they resist whatever it is between them—their affection for Anna perhaps—the more intensely involved they become. They become lovers. The romantic aspect of their relationship is intensified because it seems doomed, or at least endangered, by the eventuality of Anna's return. From moment to moment, with a kind of tragic forboding, we expect Anna to reappear. Her shadow, the potentiality of her presence, haunts the lovers, seems to. The ending is a revelation. Claudia, searching for Sandro who is not in his room at the hotel, obsessively afraid that he is with Anna, discovers him making love to another girl altogether—a shock for her and, given the conventional expectations of the film, for us. As Claudia is stripped of her illusions, so in effect are we. What we must admit to ourselves is that what has passed for love between Sandro and Claudia, what they've experienced as love, has been a fraud all along, a mutual self-delusion made possible by the occasion of Anna's disappearance. Sandro is a hollow man, apparently incapable of deep feeling. Claudia has been foolishly romantic, in love with a man she has willfully failed to see. At the end, in the early morning street, Claudia cries for the death of her idea of Sandro—the death of illusion, the death of love. Sandro cries. For a moment they experience themselves and perhaps each other without illusion. Without his asking Claudia forgives him. It is a terrible and touching moment. The experience of the film is cathartic, an exorcism of romantic illusions, of old ways of seeing. As metaphor Anna's disappearance is irrevocable. The form of the film is its message.

More, of course, can be said about *L'Avventura;* but I'd like to concentrate my discussion on *Red Desert* and talk about the trilogy only insofar as it looks forward to the later film. The films of the trilogy are increasingly bleak. In each, under the pressure of crisis—a dim awareness of some kind of internal dying—Antonioni's characters resort to patterns of nostalgia to revive their lives. *La Notte* is about a husband and wife, once in love, now numb to each other (and to themselves), sleepwalkers, living the death of boredom. In terms of conventional expectation, predicated on the kind of nostalgic wistfulness we bring to bear habitually as an audience, the film moves—all the romantic portents are there—toward the resurrection of their dead love. Giovanni and Lidia (Mastroianni and Moreau) move through the movie like sleepwalkers, awaiting hopefully, without the energy of hope, awakening. At the start they go to an elegantly sterile modern hospital to visit a close friend, Tomasso, who admires Giovanni and is in love with Lidia, a good-natured and gentle man who is dying of cancer. Romantic anticipation: as a result of Tomasso's death, as in effect a legacy of his devotion to Lidia, Lidia might again experience herself as someone capable of being loved; and Giovanni, when he learns of Tomasso's love, might rediscover his wife, fall in love with her again, be renewed as a man and as a writer, etc. Just below the surface of our awareness these are the expectations the film sets up. Giovanni and Lidia seek for themselves what we as an audience want for them, what we want, by habit of empathy, for ourselves. All of the forms of nostalgia are brought to bear. Lidia takes a long walk in which she encounters, as in a dream, a place where she and Giovanni used to go as lovers. Moved by nostalgia, she phones Giovanni and asks him to meet her there. Nothing comes of it. We experience a succession of factitious rebirths. Illusions fall away like dead skin. Nothing comes of nothing. The dead feelings remain. At an all-night party at the estate of a wealthy industrialist who wants to hire Giovanni (as a kind of intellectual-in-residence, a surrogate penis—a further irony since Giovanni feels impotent as a writer), the guests in a manic mood jump into the swimming pool with their clothes on and come out, one suspects, unregenerate. Giovanni seeks renewal through a love affair with the industrialist's daughter, Valentina (Monica Vitti), a sensitive and creative girl alienated from her parents' world. Nothing comes of it.

The ending is typically and masterfully audacious. The sun is coming up. Giovanni and Lidia leave the party as disconsolate and bored

apparently as they were at the beginning, yet there is the spark of
something between them. What will happen has been prophesied to
some extent in an earlier dialogue between Lidia and Valentina.

LIDIA: . . . Tonight I only feel like dying . . . It would at least put an end
to all this agony. At least something new would begin.

VALENTINA: Or maybe nothing.

LIDIA: Yes, maybe nothing.

The setting is ambiguously romantic: the golf course on the industrialist's estate, a piece of artificial nature, though it is as beautiful
in its way as real country. Lidia and Giovanni sit on the edge of a
sand trap and talk openly—she tells him that Tomasso has died. Giovanni laments that he has been selfish and blind, insists to Lidia that
he loves her. Lidia reads her husband a letter—a love letter—that
Giovanni had written to her some years back. He listens, uncompre-
hending—one wonders how Antonioni dared use a device so apparently sentimental—unable to recognize the subject of the letter or its
author. It is for both not a renewal, as we had hoped, but an inescapable recognition that love is dead between them. All illusions of hope
have been destroyed. In an agony of lust, a kind of death throe, they
make love as the dawn rises—the scene visually reminiscent of an
earlier scene in which a mad girl at the hospital attacks Giovanni. A
new day begins. The ending is painful, terrible, but also exhilarating
in that, like the characters, we are able to see things finally as they
are, unmuddied by romantic illusion. To see is a beginning, is the
end of the night.

What other illusions are left us? *Eclipse* deals with unromantic love,
love without illusions, between two modern, well-adjusted people, and
is the bleakest of the three films. I have avoided so far talking about
images which, ideally, is the way films should be talked about. In
each of Antonioni's films there is a central image—what I like to think
of as the essential setting of the action—which adumbrates the experience of the characters. I mention it now because it seems to me
the most striking thing about *Eclipse,* that objects, institutions, places,
have more weight and life in this film than the characters.

The island, where Anna disappears, where an extended and frustrating search for her takes place, is the central image-as-metaphor of
L'Avventura. The island is magnificent, desolate, mysterious, a lonely
and barren place surrounded by the sea—a natural universe divorced
from the affairs of men. The deserted country town where Sandro and
Claudia make love for the first time is an extension (metaphorically)
of the same image. It is similarly a place of loss. In *La Notte* the
modern hospital, where Tomasso lies dying under anesthetic, is the
central image—the film opens with an abrasive shot of its contour.
The frigid elegance of that palace of death and convalescence, a
metaphor for the world of the film—no births take place in that
hospital, only madness and convalescence and death—haunts our
awareness throughout. Giovanni's and Lidia's modern apartment is an
extension for us (as image) of the hospital. As Tomasso is incurable,
so in a different way are Giovanni and Lidia. The sterility of the
architecture suggests the sterility of the characters: Giovanni and
Lidia are childless, Giovanni feels he can no longer write, their feelings are moribund, etc.

In *Eclipse* the Stock Exchange, where the passions of birth and
death are enacted through the making and destroying of fortunes,
is the central image. It is an emblematic place, a microcosm of the
world. The hero (or anti-hero) Piero, a young man of exceptional
vitality and emptiness, works on the Exchange as a broker. Antonioni
films the frenetic activity of the market—another kind of death
throe—with extraordinary vividness. The most remarkable scene in
the movie, much more interesting and passionate than the love
scenes between Vittoria and Piero, is the performance of a ritual
minute of silence during a busy time on the Exchange in commemo-
ration of some official's death. The frenzy of activity stops, its energy
in tense suspension, as if everyone had suddenly died. And then, with
increased momentum—the tension released—the activity starts again
like an explosion. Ends and beginnings become one, as in the momentary darkness of an eclipse.

Eclipse goes against the grain of our expectations even more radically than *L'Avventura* and *La Notte*. The love story of Piero and Vittoria, which is the central narrative concern of the film, is dropped in

apparent midstream—the relationship neither alive nor dead, unre-
solved. We move away from the lovers, who have in effect disappeared
(like Anna), into a series of images which exist not as correlatives of
the characters' feelings but as objects, as realities, independent of the
characters. Antonioni's comment is implicit: there is no more to be
said about Vittoria and Piero—their souls are dying, they have died.
The world goes on without them, though their absence from the
last shots has a foreboding quality as if the end of something—of life
as we know it perhaps—is approaching. The images form a kind of
metaphorical history (and pre-history) of the world. The last image
is a close-up of a modern street lamp, a man-made sun, its light
blanking the screen. An ambiguous prophecy. The end and the beginning, the light and the darkness, as one.

Red Desert opens with a burst of yellow flame. A stunningly beautiful color film—the most beautiful of color films—about an excruci-
atingly neurotic woman's alienation from an ultramodern (apparently dehumanized) world. I say apparently dehumanized. When I
first saw Red Desert I felt, beautiful as it was, it was a failure—the
beauty of the color at odds with the nightmare of its theme. Bringing
to bear my own prejudices against machines and factories, I had mis-
conceived the experience of the film. What makes Antonioni a major
artist is that he creates apparently insurmountable obstacles for himself and almost, mostly, surmounts them. The result is a disorienting
and transcendently original work of art. The power of an Antonioni
film is derived from the formal risks it takes, from the tension of going
against the expected current of its own conventions. It strikes me that
the greatest art is the transcendent (and flawed) solution of an apparently impossible problem.

Red Desert is a profoundly disturbing film. Giuliana's neurosis
seemed to me an outgrowth of her struggle to survive, to become
wholly alive and human in a world which derives its rhythm, its
money and goods, from electronics. This world is not so much the
cause of Giuliana's neurosis, as I was quick to believe, as the catalyst
of its intensification. As Antonioni tells us in an interview in the
Cahiers, his heroine is "tied to life rhythms that are now out of

date." Our lives have been in the process of extraordinary change in the past twenty years, and we're feeling it—the fallout of what has been an explosive mutation in the rhythms of our lives—most intensely at the present. Change, even when less revolutionary, is frightening, and we struggle (out of old habits of survival) to retain the old ways. Antonioni is a modernist. *L'Avventura, La Notte,* and *Eclipse* are exorcistic films about dead feelings, about boredom and apathy, about the painful inadequacy of our old ways of solving problems. *Red Desert* is the next logical step—a film about the beauties (and horrors, of course, too) of the new world. The story of Giuliana's struggle to renew herself as a woman, the agony of her dislocation, is set against a background of factories, of machinery that spits flame and belches smoke like some mythological monster.

Red Desert is conceived as if no one had ever made a color film before.

If *Eclipse* is a prophecy of the end of the world, *Red Desert* is a vision of the new world to come, of the world that is apparently in the process of becoming. It is a film about—much of it projected through the disoriented psyche of Giuliana—the loss of old values and the inability to adapt to new ones. Giuliana's husband and child are at home in their world, without passion or desperation—in the modern sense, cool. That they love her is not enough. Giuliana (Monica Vitti) needs to be needed, to be loved romantically—it seems to her the only salvation.

The story Giuliana makes up for her son when the boy is in the hospital, his legs apparently paralyzed, is one of the texts of the film. The story is about a young girl, almost but not quite a woman, living an Edenic existence on a deserted island, content and lonely. One day a sailboat approaches her island and (with undefined expectancy) she swims out to it. To her surprise she discovers that no one is aboard. Before she can inspect it further the boat leaves, disappearing over the horizon. She is disappointed, though only for a moment. Then she hears someone singing, as if to her. Again there is no one there. The sound is coming from a cove of rocks—she swims over to it—the rocks like flesh. "Who was singing?" the boy asks. "Everyone," Giuliana tells him. "Everyone was singing."

It is of course the story of her life she is telling the boy, a romanticized version of it. The island is a metaphor for her isolation. The boat is an opportunity, though as it turns out an illusory one, to escape her loneliness. In that the boat is empty it suggests another kind of escape, suicide perhaps—we know that she has made an attempt in the past. There are several boats in the film—a central and recurring image—suggesting travel, change, the possibilities of a new life—in one case, where the yellow flag is raised, plague and death. It is also the symbol of Corrado (Richard Harris), who, out of romanticized restlessness, is perpetually traveling from one place to another. The singing is coming from those who love her, the fleshly forms not quite human, a kind of divine womb. She tells Corrado in the next scene, before they go to bed, that what she wants is all the people who ever loved her around her like a wall.

It turns out that the boy was pretending to be paralyzed, acting out, insofar as he understands it, his mother's sense of him. It is also conceivable that in the desperation of her need to be needed Giuliana prefers him helpless. And perhaps, if we view the episode of the boy as a paradigm, the deadness of feeling that Giuliana perceives around her is an indication of her failure to see the real life that's there. After the boy begins to walk again Giuliana runs to Corrado, who seems, in her romantic sense of him, the only one left who can help her, a last hope. Corrado's room is dark brown paneled wood, the color of earth, when Giuliana comes in. After they make love—the sex scene as nightmarish as any ever filmed—the room appears pink (flesh-colored), almost like a baby's room. Where she had seen Corrado as a strong, masculine figure, he seems to her like a child after her disillusion with him—the color, when Antonioni wants it that way, a correlative of his heroine's sense of things.

The ending of the film is inconclusive. Giuliana is with her son again as at the beginning (Antonioni likes to end as he begun) in a subdued mood—calm or inert? She has learned, like the bird she tells her son about, to avoid the poisonous yellow smoke, a step toward learning how to live in the world, a beginning. And one suspects, at the same time, something of an end. Giuliana has learned how to survive, but at what expense, and to what purpose?

Red Desert is the first color film, the most beautiful color film. To make such a film is in itself an affirmation.

An Antonioni movie presents us with a new way of seeing—that is, forces us to see against our preconception of the way things are. No other artist deals with the hang-ups and delusions and possibilities of love, which is to say life, in our time as profoundly and truthfully as Antonioni. So even if we have to give up our old myths about movies—the nostalgia that things were simpler and therefore better in the old days—it may even be worth it. Maybe not. Nostalgia dies hard: old dreams have their pleasure. In any event, resist it or not, we shall never again be as we were, which is what Antonioni has been telling us. In black and white. In films of luminous beauty. In color.

With a residual pang of nostalgia, I suppose I prefer the new days to the old. As a movie lover only, however. The world Antonioni celebrates is damned hard to live in.

ARMANDO FAVAZZA

Fellini: Analyst Without Portfolio

Fellini is in many ways a latter day Freud. By this I do not mean that he is necessarily a Freudian but simply that he has opened up the human mind with his probing camera. Now the mind is an elusive organ. It is a distinctly human trait (perhaps it is more correct to state that humanness is a trait of the ontogenetic mind) and provides no animal models; it does not secrete thoughts as the liver does bile and thus we cannot measure cognition; and it has an energy about which we know a little quantitatively and almost nothing qualitatively.

The expression of mentality is practically impossible. It would require that one become entirely empathetic with another, "one with another." If extrasensory perception is to have any value it will be this, to allow for the direct communication of mentality—cognition, affect, and fantasy. Traditionally we use words to communicate, but to reach the true *Eigenwelt* words are not enough. Nor is silence enough. Nor music. Nor art.

With all the intimated limitations we can appreciate what Fellini has done in a way that no other director has; he has opened the way, he has come the closest to communicating mentality. He has stated, "The film is the one art form with which the artist can explore the inner landscape of the human being—his thought, memories, fantasies, dreams, flickering through the mind." It is important that Fellini has used the word "explore" rather than "understand." Too often we are duped into thinking we are understanding when we are merely re-describing. Especially in the artistic fields where "meanings" are so important we tend to dupe ourselves. Let it be sufficient to warn that redescription of unconscious processes is no more a guarantee of "understanding" than is redescription of conscious ones.

Since we are not quite yet computers and since our psychic lives are limited only by the ubiquity of fantasy, we—out of necessity—must use symbols to communicate and to express ourselves. Out of the same piece of clay a priest might make a satyr's mask and a libertine a crucifix. So we should not deny Fellini his symbols because they are, with few exceptions, good combinations of cinematic skill and mental understanding. The upside-down-horse-on-the-raft symbol in *Juliet of the Spirits,* however, is an example of a contrived symbol (derived from Picasso's *Guernica*) lacking understandable substance. It cannot even be accepted on the grounds of cognitive perversity or illegitimacy and is reminiscent of Bergman.

Fellini has said that he felt close to Bergman, "the conjurer—half witch and half showman." In shadow Fellini is like Bergman, in substance he is not. One is reminded of the Wagner-Verdi arguments of years past. Cannot the words of Chapman, Nietzsche, and others about Wagner be applied to Bergman? "Among artists in general Wagner's place is with the actors"; "The Wagnerian motif does not suggest what it betokens. This is why it has to be learned"; "The essential lack in Wagner is, after all, a want of sanitary plumbing." This is not to deny Bergman's (Wagner's) greatness, but the Germanic ideal—the thorns in the crucifix, the interminable leitmotifs, the cataloguing precision and detail that oppresses, the clarity that obfuscates—lacks the splendor of the Mediterranean ideal, which has been called "the glory of the sun." The Grecian gods are flesh, the Nordic gods are fleshy shades (and basically unhappy shades at that despite their beer and Valkeries). Fellini indulges in poetic clarity. His symbols are not vague Jungian archetypes but the malignant and benign tumors of man's development from egg to casket. Were Fellini perfectly clear he would be a bore; were he perfectly truthful he would be a liar.

The early films—*Variety Lights, The White Sheik,* and others are rather unexceptional pieces. With *La Strada* Fellini made his mark, his fame, and his fortune. Yet the theme of *La Strada* is not a beautiful one—sadomasochism (complete with chains), feeblemindedness, and a saving dash of pity. It, like *Death of a Salesman,* is moving and pathetic, but so is a Walt Disney cartoon. Albeit this "shallow" Fellini film was "deeper" than most contemporary films, it was (God save me from overdeterminism, please) the first clear, public sign of Fellini's *illness.* I speak here of the illness of all creative men—Leonardo's *vulture,* Luther's *spastic colon,* Hopkin's *dappled things* (with whom he had an unholy love affair), Leopardi's *hump*—the *illness* that anchors one to reality. All men have their illnesses, but they are not hampered because they live with their disease in a parasitic symbiosis. The "sick" man must see a psychiatrist and with his help remove the parasite (a long, hard task) or else simply recover his equilibrium. The "creative" man may repress his parasite, or use it advantageously, or work it through.

What is Fellini's parasite? What themes are basic to Fellini? *Creativity* (libido) and *religion.* The larvae of the problems were laid down *in foetu* and matured over the years. The environmental origins are irrelevant to anyone but Fellini. *La Strada* was the beginning, when the parasite began to squirm. *La Dolce Vita* was a confused projection by Fellini on a society that never was. Fellini placed his problems upon others. The divertisement for *Boccaccio 70* was merely a resting period, a time to bolster his psychic boundaries with pictures of big

blicity still of Jean Harlow from the period of *Hell's Angels*. When Harlow "slipped into
mething comfortable" in *Hell's Angels*, a whole generation of moviegoers responded.

Above, Bela Lugosi as the vampire in Tod Browning's *Dracula*. As Lugosi played him, Count Dracula was the spirit of decorum and restraint, but with the face and voice of sin itself—hard eyes, a commanding nose, and a mouth which was sensual and almost obscene.

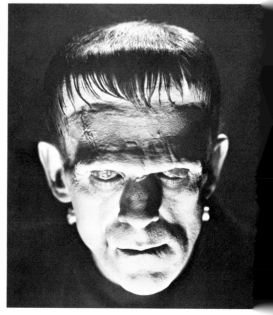

Right, Boris Karloff as the Frankenstein monster. In the films the monster is the final image of lost and suffering man, all illusions stripped away, naked in his own damnation.

Above, Albert Finney and Joyce Redman in the famous eating scene from John Osborne's movie adaptation of Fielding's *Tom Jones*.

Left, Paul Newman in a scene from *Hud*, the movie adaptation of Larry McMurtry's novel *Horseman, Pass By*. Hud is a twentieth-century rancher, not simply a cowboy, and his Cadillac is his gun, with the dual usefulness the gunfighter's gun once had: it is a status symbol and it will do the work.

Cecil B. DeMille created a visual style which transcended the anecdotal nature of the twelve-minute film.

William Faulkner and his wife Estelle with their daughter Jill riding Lady Go-lightly, at House's Glendale Stables. The photograph was taken in the summer of 1944, which Estelle and Jill spent in Hollywood with Faulkner.

Ingmar Bergman on the set of *All These Women*.

Michelangelo Antonio shooting *L'Avventura*.

Frederico Fellini directing.

_chino Visconti on the set of
ghe stelle dell'orsa. . . ._

The opening scene in the railway carriage, from Ingmar Bergman's *The Silence*. A master of visu illusion who composes his pictures within a frame as carefully as a painter, Bergman uses aesthe means to clarify and enforce emotion and idea—here to state without words the situation of t entire film.

Bhisma, the bisexual seer who advises Juliet in Frederico Fellini's *Juliet of the Spirits*. In this Fellini added the dimension of color to his communication of mentality; the harmony of rhy color, and composition at times makes *Juliet of the Spirits* seem an abortive dance.

breasts. With *8½* came the plunge, the hesitant exploration of the problem. *Juliet of the Spirits* represents a deeper commitment to working through his problem.

Creativity (libido) and religion—what vague yet essential terms. Consider *8½*. Is this anything other than the story of a man (Fellini) suffering from a pathological depression and his attempts to dispel the oppressive affect? Creativity was stifled. This was represented in many ways, e.g., marital impotence, inability to make the film. If we accept *8½* as primarily autobiographical (psychically more than physically), we see the various mechanisms Fellini used to alleviate his depression: Desensitization through recall, verbalization, and assimilation of past painful experiences; desensitization through association of experiences which have aroused anxiety with new pleasurable experiences; and, most powerfully, de-repression of past painful experiences. Reliving the depression in his film has led Fellini to gain increased supplies of respect, reassurance, and affection from other persons, a form of public approval of a personal illness.

What Fellini has given us so far is a very one-sided approach to his problem. He describes himself as a "dilettante" in psychoanalysis, "a meddler greedy to gather facts." He is at a stage of ontogenetic development which to some extent recapitulates the phylogenetic development of psychoanalysis and of every therapist. Fellini is particularly preoccupied with the various dramatic, insistent, and compelling manifestations of his drives and their consequences. This obviously is the film-maker's art. This essay, however, is concerned with what perhaps lies beneath the veneer of the screen. As Fellini matures, his interests will shift more into "ego" and "superego" psychology, and his films may well become boring dramatically. Now we see scenes of old women dressed as priests, young boys as nuns, infidelity as a way of life. We read Fellini's statements: "But she [his wife] is also a person of sufficient mystery who can embody, in relationship to me, a consuming nostalgia for innocence, for protection." "So many of us succumb passively to the laws of nature, which have been deformed by current usage, let ourselves be sucked in and swallowed up by marriage, completely overlooking its highest—and only—purpose: the attempt to realize a true union." As Fellini matures publicly, we shall get closer to the problems hinted at above. It will be, indeed, a most remarkable and unique confession with the audience as priest and absolver. To most viewers, however, the films will probably appear duller and less interesting. All of the above is predicated upon Fellini's continuing what he has started.

Fellini's religious parasite at this stage does not appear to be a profound one. Its dramatic possibilities make it compelling on the screen, however. Most Latin males have faced the same problems; a "religious" mother who would rather die than eat meat on Friday or miss Mass on Sunday unless her ankles were swollen and she couldn't wear her good shoes; priests who were not worthy of the tonsure; sexual transgressions of apostolic law; respect for the Church, even awe, but eventual abandonment (usually a gradual, undecisive move). There are few men in the churches on Sunday in Italy. In Northern Italy there is a strong anti-clerical feeling and a notion that priests carry the *mal occhio,* the Evil Eye, which can be warded off only by touching one's testicles. That is why so many Italian men have their hands in their pockets when they pass a priest. The conflict arises out of early respect for the Church. The Jesuits have always said, "Give us a child for the first six years; then, do with him what you will, he will be ours." Fellini does not seem to be undergoing any middle-age religious crisis. This is merely a part of his central creative crisis, the origin of which is in the past.

$8\frac{1}{2}$ takes place at a health spa where the movie producer has come to rest and to be "cured." He asks himself three times, "What has gone wrong?" As the movie progresses, the producer sinks into deeper and deeper depression. His mind is read by a magician, and his thoughts are written on a blackboard. The results—a series of nonsense sylla-bles. He builds a giant edifice, an austere movie set which projects his own inner emptiness. He even descends into Hades, into the bowels of the steam baths, to meet with a Prince of the Church amid vapors and dim lights. He wants an answer to his problem. He was in the bosom of the Church once, as a child, but he has lost his faith. As a child he was caught watching the hideously beslobbered Sara-ghena dance on the beach and was humiliated by the clergy. The Cardinal can only offer salvation to those who have faith; he is powerless to help the unbeliever. So the producer leaves with the homily of Origen ringing in his ears, "Outside of the Church there is no salvation." To a good Catholic this is a perfect answer; to the producer this is emptiness.

His markedly decreased libido revolves superficially around his marital relations. He is impotent with his wife. He cannot even speak with her. So he relives his conjugal experiences by using a movie-within-a-movie technique. He views different actresses portraying his wife in a series of screen tests simulating his personal relationship and tries to view it objectively to find the flaw, the turning point which has led to stagnation.

He *acts out* by taking a married woman as a mistress. He has no real feeling towards this woman—she is simply an object with whom he can sexually perform and deceive himself and thus avoid the slowing down of psychological time which characterizes depression. Even the harem scene is an attempt at self-deception. The fault cannot be his, he is desirable; woman hunger after him—all sorts of women, in every shape and size.

How is the problem resolved? Fellini does not tell us. The producer is hounded by the press and in a frightening scene is badgered into commenting on his new film. Pushed to the end of his tether, the producer puts a gun to his head and pulls the trigger.

And everything is clarified! The bang of the bullet is the turning point, the instant of the insight gained by the various mechanisms described. It comes somewhat as it does to the acolyte who is beaten by the Zen priest and at the moment of contact experiences *satori,* the gray mental opening which illuminates the depth of individuality merged with universality. "When I began to study Zen, mountains were mountains; when I thought I understood Zen, mountains were not mountains; but when I came to full knowledge of Zen, mountains were again mountains."

But Fellini does not come to full knowledge. He is brought back from the abyss of oblivion and ennui. At the point of ultimate despair his mental defense mechanisms rallied to protect him. He has not conquered his parasite; he has simply gained the momentary upper hand by achieving an insight about which we are not told.

Perhaps one cannot communicate insight, even limited insight. Fellini orders the movie set torn down. He has come to realize that it is better to destroy than to create the unessential. Creativity can continue. The cast can dance, hand in hand, so that they do not collapse like the movie set. Time flows again . . . but for how long? With *Juliet of the Spirits* Fellini has matured considerably. He is still dealing with primarily dramatic rather than ego psychology but he is more emotional and far less intellectual than in *8½* and thus gets closer to the heart of the matter. Intellectualization is often a major barrier to analysis.

Juliet has been commented upon by the American press: "An eye-filling spectacle of the psyche . . . peopled by marvelously bizarre characters, scenes wilder than 'La Dolce Vita,' stunning women in fantastic costumes, and weird, audacious situations. An eye-popping two-and-one-half hours of razzle-dazzle Fellini." "Beautiful! Hallucinatory! Extraordinary pictorial beauty!" "Fellini casts a color spell."

Even though all of this hyperbole is *true,* certainly *Juliet* must have more to offer than mere spectacle, or it would simply be another Italian *Hercules* film sans muscles. Fellini here is getting closer to the problem of *8½,* and perhaps the film should be subtitled *Fellini of the Spirits.*

One is, of course, struck by the intense visual beauty of the film. Fellini has been quoted as saying: "In *Juliet* . . . color is an essential part of the film. I don't think I could have done it in black and white. It is a type of fantasy that is developed through colored illuminations. As you know, color is a part not only of the language but also of the idea and the feeling of the dream. Colors in a dream are concepts, not approximations or memories." Thus, by adding color, Fellini has added a new extra to the communication of mentality. It must be recognized that he has harmonized rhythm and color and composition so well that at times *Juliet* seems to be an abortive dance. And another of Fellini's strengths is that his point of view is always perfectly clear. In fact, he is an intellectual's Hitchcock.

There is nothing picaresque in *Juliet,* although at first glance it might seem so. And, even though there are what seem to be elements of the absurd in Fellini's films, they certainly cannot be counted as part of the "theater of the absurd" camp. There is too much internal consistency and relationship to external harmony to ever accuse Fellini of being absurd. Perhaps *Juliet* is similar to *Hamlet*. Certainly *Hamlet* is one of the greatest dramatic creations ever, and everyone who witnesses the drama is deeply touched, although they do not understand why. There is no fully plausible *explanation* of *Hamlet*, yet it is great drama. Perhaps there is no fully plausible explanation of *Juliet* either, yet it is great cinema.

Juliet is overtly the story of a middle-aged, sweet, rather apassionate housewife's reactions to the discovery that her husband is having an affair with a Scandinavian model. This is obviously an unesoteric, commonplace, quite plausible topic. But Juliet is played by the real-life wife of Fellini, and thus the initial simplicity of the film gives way to subtle intricacy. Does it seem possible that Juliet is merely a "human commentary enriched by a seductive fantasy?" as Fellini hints with a question mark? Fellini has commented: "Although the film lends itself to esoteric, occult, psychoanalytic interpretations, I would like it to be seen in a simpler light: humane and imaginative." The film, without a doubt, is highly imaginative and humane (although I am not quite sure what "humane" means) and can be appreciated on that level. In fact, upon first viewing, this is probably the proper way to appreciate the film. But, when one goes back to *Juliet* a second and a third time, it becomes quite evident that the film is more than a humane and imaginative human commentary enriched by a seductive fantasy. The film is another step in Fellini's probing self-analysis, and by utilizing the psychic mechanism of *projection* we learn much about Fellini even though the film treats of his wife. If there is any internal weakness in *Juliet,* it is that sometimes we see Juliet as she is seen by Fellini in their daily public dialogue and sometimes she appears as Fellini himself, a *projection* which is cinematically projected.

The reason that Juliet's husband is having an affair with another woman is that he is not satisfied with Juliet. Every other woman in the film is lustful and sexually provocative. Juliet's sister is pregnant—even her pet cat is pregnant. Her mother looks hungrily at every male that passes. Her woman sculptor friend even sees God "physically, corporeally, a hero of the perfect form whom I can desire and even take as a lover." Suzy, the prostitute, wears her vagina on her lips and even makes love in a treetop. Genius, the astrologer and séance director, announces the message from the spirit, "Love for all."

Juliet is eminently "safe." In a scene of superb irony her friend Valentina comes upon Juliet stringing peppers and says: "Oh, a wreath of peppers! What a wonderful housewife you are. I can do absolutely nothing. Why am I the way I am? I feel so lost, like I'm drifting. Peppers—they seem to be nothing and yet, if I were able to prepare them, maybe I would be safe." Everyone whom Juliet loves is "lost" in a life of perpetual sex-seeking. Only Juliet is stable, and in her safety she is lonely and feels lost too. One cannot live by peppers alone. Later on the psychoanalyst tells Juliet: "But what are you afraid of? May I answer? You're afraid of being alone, of being abandoned. You're afraid that your husband is going to leave you. And yet you want nothing more than to be left alone; you want your husband to go away." The psychiatrist is speaking to Fellini also.

Juliet is led to Bhisma, the old, bisexual seer. Bhisma does not even have to see Juliet to know her problem. She-he asks: "Juliet, do you know the Kama Sutra? Sexual relations are a conflict. To be happy one must behave like a woman. The place of conflict is the body." How fortunate Bhisma is to be bisexual, for she-he can have self-conflict and, indeed, does have an orgasm while speaking to Juliet. "Love is a religion, Juliet. Your husband is your God, and you are the priestess of the cult. Your spirit, like this incense, must burn and smoke on the altar of your loving body." Bhisma then asks, "Why don't you please your husband more?" And Juliet, blind to the world, answers, "I do please him."

But Bhisma tells her that she must become like a whore and goes on to say, "You must become beautiful like me, beautiful like me, like me, like me," as she-he goes on to have a bisexual orgasm. The advice to Juliet is reminiscent of Blake's lines, "In a wife I would desire what in whores is always found, the lineaments of gratified desire."

Juliet becomes terrified and leaves. But she becomes a prostitute in fantasy. Here Fellini's genius is made manifest. He posits a whorehouse right next to Juliet's home. Of course the whorehouse does not exist except in Juliet's mind, and thus Fellini keeps the continuity of psychical fantasy and physical reality. Juliet tries to play the whore, but the orgy (a tremendous parody of Antonioni) is a terrible, psychotic failure. She tells Suzy, the prostitute, about her marriage: "I'm almost ashamed to admit it, but Giorgio was my first love. As soon as I saw him I fell in love with him and didn't want anything but to live with him, and when he asked me to marry him, I was so happy that I couldn't believe it was true. He became my whole world—my husband, my lover, my father, my friend, my house. I didn't need anything else. I thought I was happy . . ." By sheer excess of virtue Juliet has made life intolerable for her husband. And she cannot be untrue to herself so easily. She cannot make love with a Christ-like Indian lover in a gigantic bed beneath a mirror ceiling. And José, the strange Spaniard, who tells her, "No one understands the obscure magnolia in your womb," is this José really Fellini looking at himself in a different light or merely a paid intruder?

Fellini pictures Juliet's incapacity to please her husband sexually as being rooted to her religious upbringing. This is significantly portrayed in a scene where she, as a child, plays the part of a virginal Christian martyr in a convent school play. Bound and burned at the stake, she ascends to heaven—and she remains psychologically bound throughout her life. In the convent play she fails to see God; in life she fails her husband. Her joy, almost perverse, has been that of being a psychological martyr and sharing in the exquisite joy of crucifixion.

The film is resolved in the same way as $8\frac{1}{2}$. Insight leads to freedom. Only in *Juliet* Fellini documents his insight in detail. Juliet regresses to her childhood, and only when she cuts the bonds that have repressed her sexuality does she become free. The shock of cutting those bonds and releasing the spirit child leads to a brief psychotic episode—the appearance of her friend Laura who killed herself for love, the nuns, the German SS officers. This is a technically poor scene because it is impossible to portray a psychotic episode accurately, although the camera is the best means available to describe *mobility of cathexis, displacement, and condensation.*

Having taken advantage of her insight, Juliet flies to the comfort of her lecher grandfather. But then she doesn't even need him anymore. She has come of age. She has become a woman. She will try to satisfy her husband now on his terms. "Juliet walks towards the pine woods. The trees glow green and lovely in brilliant warm sunlight." Fellini has said, "In the end, Juliet's real life begins when she comes out of the shadow of Giorgio." But Juliet does not want to come out of her husband's shadow; she wants to intermingle her shadow with his, and she can do this only if she is free psychologically.

If one were asked to create an Elysian Field for cinematographers, certainly Fellini would have the loudest and most profound lyre. Apart from any deep analysis of his films, Fellini has produced highly imaginative, skillful, "professional" films. He has reached the top of his art artistically. What remains to be seen is his own personal development; the resolution of his conflict between creative detachment and depression, and his avoidance of brutality and the necessity of decay. But as Lynx-Eyes, the detective, says to Juliet, "Please understand, Signora. I always ask clients to regard everything we show them with a certain detachment. Ours is an objective point of view, and therefore limited. Reality at times may be quite different, more innocent." Perhaps Fellini is more innocent than this essay purports. Or perhaps Fellini is asking for patient understanding while he resolves the pains of a public confession.

WALTER KORTE

Vaghe stelle dell'orsa . . . :
Recent Work of a Neglected Master

The year 1965 was a most exciting, albeit somewhat disappointing, one for Italian cinema. All the critical drums were beaten to herald the arrival of the latest works of the "Big Three": Fellini's *Giulietta degli spiriti,* which after the glories of *8½* was more or less a rank failure—at best a scintillating one; Antonioni's *Il deserto rosso,* a much more important work than the Fellini, but one which fell far short, I fear, of the trilogy which had come before; and Visconti's *Vaghe stelle dell'orsa* . . . (also known as *Sandra*), a film as much maligned by American critics as the other two were overpraised lavishly.

But the reception of *Vaghe stelle* was hardly a surprise, as Luchino

191

Visconti has always been an intensely problematic director and one who has never achieved real success outside of Europe. Yet if one were to poll European film critics and scholars, and those on this side of the Atlantic who have had the opportunity to see his early works, he quite possibly would be designated one of the two or three most important living film directors. Such a verdict would not seem justifiable to American audiences, as few of his films have been shown here commercially and those few have elicited largely negative reactions. A number of factors have contributed to the unhappy fate of Visconti's works in the U.S.: political (his leftist interpretation of history, particularly in *Senso* and *Il gattopardo,* is most controversial), aesthetic (many of his films run from three to four hours in length—an elaborately constructed scheme of development and an extremely slow affective tone are key factors in his cinema), and commercial (the length of his films occasions massive cutting: the U.S. version of *Il gattopardo,* cut by nearly an hour, was all but disowned by the director; and in the last five years there have been no fewer than four versions of *Rocco e i suoi fratelli* making the rounds; also, Visconti's movies have been victims of exceptionally poor dubbing).

Visconti's first film, *Ossessione* (1942), was the spearhead of the whole neorealist movement. An extremely uneven work to be sure, it is still of enormous historical importance but cannot be shown in America due to a copyright dispute. His second film, and very possibly his masterpiece, was *La terra trema,* an adaptation of a Verga novel dealing with Sicilian fishermen. This lengthy semi-documentary, a strange blend of extreme neorealism and formal stylization, has been released only recently in America. *Bellissima,* with Anna Magnani, was released in the States around 1953 but quickly disappeared due to a flagging box office. *Senso,* Visconti's next film, starred Alida Valli, had a screenplay by Tennessee Williams and Paul Bowles, and used color in a way unmatched by any films before or since, with the possible exceptions of *Il gattopardo* and *Deserto rosso.* Unfortunately the film was considered a poor risk for the American market and, to my knowledge, was never distributed commercially. *Le notti bianche,* an adaptation of the Dostoevsky tale with Marcello Mastroianni and Maria Schell, was released in New York in 1961, four years after its production, but due to indifferent reviews it died almost immediately.

Rocco e i suoi fratelli was the only one of Visconti's works to receive excellent reviews on both sides of the Atlantic, but it was a financial disappointment in this country. Perhaps the most ambitious of his films, *Rocco* is the history of a family of emigrants from the south who travel to Milan. In the original version Visconti's sheer power as a director has never been more in evidence than in this study of disintegration by the corrupting forces of success and the city. But the film was cut so badly from its original length of over three hours that it degenerated, in its subsequent versions, into a meaningless series of climaxes in which questions of character and motive were all but impossible for an audience to answer. *Il lavoro,* Visconti's contribution to *Boccaccio 70,* was a subtle and highly mannered study of Milanese society, but one which made little sense to those unfamiliar with his style. *Il gattopardo,* a faithful adaptation of the Lampedusa novel, was a kind of grandiose *divertissement* for the director, who set out to create a visually fascinating period piece without being too concerned with the large social and political themes which loomed behind the characters. The film displayed Visconti's virtuosity with *mise-en-scéne:* each scene was staged with the rhythm of a choreographer and the composition of a painter, highly reminiscent of the French masters Duvivier and Ophuls. Although one can make a good case for *Il gattopardo's* being in many ways the most beautiful and perfect period piece the cinema has yet produced, in the U.S. it was a box office failure which even Burt Lancaster's appeal could not mollify. *Vaghe stelle dell'orsa . . . ,* our immediate concern in this article, seems fated to go down the same path: it disappeared from the commercial circuit with a speed unmatched by any other recent film except Resnais' *Muriel.*

Upon first viewing *Vaghe stelle* (the title is derived from the opening of Leopardi's *Le ricordanze*) in Rome early in the fall of 1965, I was struck immediately by its synthesis of several predominant elements in Visconti's preceding major works. It seemed to combine the *verismo* of *Rocco* with that quality of the scenographic baroque—the fantastic attention to detail—which had been *Il gattopardo's* prime characteristic. (It should be remarked in passing that in Visconti's other important artistic field, design and direction for the operatic stage, his private weakness for what might be termed "baroque decadence" has become more and more pronounced in recent times, culminating in last year's *art nouveau Rosenkavalier* at Covent Garden and the Spoleto *Salome* of some years ago, during which Herod's stepdaughter did not unveil herself but ten youths!) The intermingling of these forms gave rise to a type of movie which is hardly new, but which has been sadly neglected of late: the *cinema da camera*, or chamber film, perhaps the most *personal* of the uses of the medium. Exactly what I mean by this term will be apparent as we continue, but a few of its characteristics may be outlined now: a subject matter limited to the intensive exploration of the relationships of two or three strongly defined characters, an economy of technique and limiting of locale, and near-perfect directorial control.

Visconti is one of the very few directors who consciously develops his work from tradition. Where a Fellini or Antonioni sees or attempts to see from an angle apart from tradition, albeit a personal angle, Visconti is constantly immersed in traditions and is himself a part of them. Godard plays with the medium and many would argue that the inventive rhythms of his blocks of shadow and sound have created a new cinema; Visconti on the other hand does nothing really new in the formal use of film. *Vaghe stelle* is a compelling, hypnotic film, principally because of Visconti's presentation of patterns of emotions and manners which have long been present in the traditional arts. The story was conceived as that of a modern Electra, and, despite the many ambiguities surrounding the forces of fate, it is very much a tragedy. Whether it is a contemporary *Electra* is a matter somewhat more debatable, although an initial consideration of the characters would seem to lend credit to Visconti's claim: a sister and brother, Sandra and Gianni, immensely involved with each other on a nearly incestuous level, both harbor hatred for their mother, whom they believe betrayed their Jewish father to the Germans in the War with the help of their step-father, the official Gilardini. The forces between all the characters (with the exception of Sandra's fairly colorless American husband Andrew) and the forces behind Visconti are the Latin tragic sense of life and a conception of society as a structure of manners. Tensions arise from natural emotions set against the formalized view of living, so that at times the forces of fate are perhaps irrelevant. The emotional releases in the last reel of the film are simple and grand—operatic treatment is a necessity.

Visconti stridently alternates the heavy dark interior of the house with searing sunlight, the camera brooding over the feline, sullen movements of the brother and sister. The husband is a foreign object and becomes almost a nonentity in this smoldering world. In this milieu the upper classes are not crumbling: strength is there, but it is undirected. The neglected house suggests the power that was and the turbulent undercurrents in the family suggest the power that could be. As in most of Visconti's films, there is little sense of momentum. The occasional climax is usually a grand gesture conceived as artifice, an action coming long after the real moment of truth. The power of *Vaghe stelle* comes from the interaction of brother and sister and the translation of this by a man who is one of them. For Visconti himself is a product of what his films are about.

Vaghe stelle is not one of Visconti's minor works: in the film there is a substantial evolution of language which, on the expressive level, permits the attainment of a narrative essential and stylistic coherence— elements highly related to the director's previous problems. In his most recent films the necessity of clarifying every situation completely has often provoked a defect along the lines of structure: a large amount of narrative has been needed to make an historical, social, or psychological situation clear in all of its facets. In addition, as in the case of *Il gattopardo,* the shattering of cultural references that did not find a real unifying center impeded the resolution of the event in the historical context to which it belonged; and for the parallel progression of story and invention he favored an accidental, not a necessary, correspondence between the two elements. With *Vaghe stelle* Visconti has overcome these limitations.

He has eliminated the presence of positive characters who would indicate alternate possibilities (the character of Pietro, son of the landowner and Sandra's former lover, who has finished his studies and now has before him a brilliant future, is part of the "chorus" and does not have significance in the tragedy). Thus the respect for Aristotelian unity assumes a particular strength with regard to this investigation of the expressive essential. But it is not only in this respect that Visconti's language has changed: the real linguistic innovation lies in the new important relationship of light to the event. Lighting helps him to understand and dig into the psychology of his characters; the atmosphere that surrounds them reveals their feelings; the penumbra is their natural refuge when they fear to betray to the light the true nature of their mental states.

Let us consider the illumination of the initial scenes in Switzerland and Italy: here Sandra (Claudia Cardinale) appears normal, balanced. But, as soon as she sets foot in her home, her face appears deformed, the lines hardened, her exterior security undergoes a first shock. The husband (Michael Craig) notices the change: "This is the strangest house I've ever seen, but in a certain sense it resembles you" (and in the original version of the scenario he adds: "I can't succeed in imagining you outside this place"). Sandra seeks to avoid her husband's glance and the embarrassment which results from asking him to live always in that house. The scene of the meeting in the garden between Sandra and Gianni (Jean Sorel) also comes to mind, in which the penumbra impels an awakening of physical sensations rather than serene fraternal affections; and we note Gianni's discourse to Andrew at the city walls, pronounced with his face semi-hidden in shadow: "Provincial life . . . with its exasperated passions that seem impossible when one is far away, but which fall upon you in the very moment of your return." Sandra continually takes shelter in less illuminated areas: the certainty of her initial proposal to Andrew is compromised by the increasingly problematic actions of her brother, who, despite weakness of character, has made clear (at least to himself) the true morbid nature of his affections.

We see the first actual yielding on the part of Sandra to her brother in the cistern: she allows her ring to be removed, saying "mad . . . mad" in a more and more weak and submissive tone of voice, while, with great efficiency, a flashback takes us to the meeting with the mother (Marie Bell) and to her words of accusation: "It is I who wish to know if my children are two monsters." It may be worthwhile to consider the use of these flashbacks (three in all) which seem to me to assume a great contextual importance.

This mother who openly accuses, denouncing the same sense of guilt which strikes Gilardini (Renzo Ricci), causes those memories of the past from which Sandra cannot free herself to reappear (here the actuality of the past in the conscience of Sandra is expressed by a flashback). The mother helps us understand some of the motives for the progressive drawing closer of her children, for their voluntary rejection of any rapport with the others on the basis of a proud sense of race (we find the same motif much more articulated in Bassani's *The Garden of the Finzi Contini*). Two elements underlie their equivocal and morbid infantile affection: one implicit in their Jewish nature which, through a kind of spontaneous self-defense mechanism, cuts off all exterior relationships when confronted by a decidedly hostile world, and one originating in the prejudicial attitude of others which concretizes that character of secular "accursedness," to the formation of which Christian morality and religion have contributed in a decisive manner for centuries. "You too have Hebrew blood, like him. You are corrupt like him . . . little vices, cautious, dirty . . . secret vices," taunts Sandra's mother as soon as she sees her.

But let us return to the use of light. One thinks of the almost unbearably voluptuous scene in which Sandra reads the manuscript through which her brother reveals to her the character which certain childhood passions and disturbances actually assume for him: their faces are wrapped in a pleasing penumbra; Sandra seeks not to betray the nature of her feelings, but, despite her efforts to purify them by fleeing into childhood memories, the flame of the fireplace lays bare their sensuality. In another place a shadow surrounds, with the greatest significance, the scene which follows Andrew's departure, in which Gianni attempts to convince his sister, by appealing to any and all arguments, to stay with him and break every restraint in order to attain, even sexually, that equilibrium which she has never reached with her husband. The characters enter the shadows, then disappear completely, and one hears only the words. Sandra rejects her brother. But hers is an ambiguous resistance and the words with which she leaves him alone are not resolved: "For me you are already dead, Gianni." And Sandra's weeping after reading the words of her husband is not even cathartic; furthermore, Sandra's letter to Andrew seems imposed by production demands and hints to the spectator of the possibility of a happy resolution, of an opening toward a future reuniting. Interestingly enough, in the first scenario the whole matter does not arise at all: the film closes with definite words of farewell from Sandra. The real conclusion is seen in the last words of peace in the Rabbi's prayer, which do not serenely bring the tragedy to an end but isolate the protagonist forever in an immobile existence, without any more direction.

The narrative balance is obtained by the inclusion and fusion of two other elements: the external *ambience* of the city, fatally representative of the tragedy which it is to witness, and the extraordinary significance of gesture. This latter element reinforces our initial affirmation of a decisive linguistic evolution in Visconti: the point of departure here is a varied articulation of the temporal dimension, underlying which a maximum of freedom to represent past and present is given to gesture, conferring on it a plurality of contextually explicit values. For this reason the repeated use of the zoom shot (at first seemingly arbitrary) is justified: not only to seize a feeling in the act, as it were, but to fix it in its real and illusive duplicity. There is a scene in which Sandra, entering her mother's room for the first time, perceives the plaster cast of the hand, draws near, and sweetly caresses it. In this simple gesture Visconti sought to condense all the significance of a maternal love desired but never obtained.

It is not rare that this use of metaphorical allusion yields fairly obvious results: one notes the fixing of the camera on the pedestal of Amor and Psyche while Gianni and Sandra lie on the floor, or the banal attempt at the representation of the thoughts of the protagonists awake in their beds by the insertion of a pop song which says "you aren't happy" while the camera is fixed on Gianni.

Going back to the choice of locale, one can say that Visconti's need of presenting a kind of fatal Necessity which overwhelms men and objects and weighs on the destiny of the characters favored the choice of Volterra, an ancient Etruscan city. I do not intend to dwell excessively upon this point, but it is immediately perceived from Gianni's words to Andrew during the nocturnal walk: "Volterra is the only city inexorably condemned to die of illness, like the majority of human beings." And the choice of the Etruscan museum seems not only dictated by the necessity of making an easy archaeological reference but also desired to underline Andrew's inability to understand, his actual distance from suspicions and from the world which Gilardini points out to him.

Not even the most banal of objects escapes this law of semantic intensification—one thinks of the things represented in white for Sandra: the white linen which covers her father's monument, the white cast of her mother's hand, the white dress she wears on the anniversary of her father's death at the film's conclusion. It represents a total aspiration for the attainment of some value outside that to which she solidly clings (one recalls the way in which she embraces the monument), generated by the complete unbalance of her whole existence. It is with the unitary arrangement of these elements in the tragic dimension of the story that Visconti obtains a complete historical and psychological correspondence.

In the light of this linguistic examination along the lines which I have sought to indicate, even those defects of which we have spoken find their explanation. We find in *Vaghe stelle dell'orsa . . .* a stylistically renovated Visconti, though all the factors at play in this film are discernible in one form or another in his work from *Senso* onward. It would be difficult to imagine a film more removed from what we generally tend to think of as the neorealist tradition, yet Visconti himself laid the groundwork for this tradition a quarter of a century ago. This is but another of the paradoxes which make him one of the most fascinating directors alive.

NATHAN A. SCOTT, JR.

The New Mystique of *L'Actuelle*:
A View of Cinema
in Its Relation to Our Period-Style

I am unable—and I am unaware of anyone who is able—to certify the account that Professor Marshall McLuhan of the University of Toronto is giving us of the profound mutations that are taking place today in the character of our culture and in the constitution of humankind. Indeed, the very radical judgment that he is proposing of the revolutionary "extensions of man" by the new technology of an electronic age is doubtless marked in some measure by the afflatus of the seer and the artist, and does to that extent perhaps invite something like an aesthetic response rather than the objective measurements of empirical science. For surely the strongest impression that one carries away from such books as *The Gutenberg Galaxy* and *Understanding Media* is that of an enormously intelligent (and somewhat cranky) man whose zany and boundlessly undespairing enthusiasm for all the iconography and gadgetry of a technocratic civilization betokens what on his part has been an essentially aesthetic response, of delight and approval, to the novelties created by the electrical media.

But, whether Mr. McLuhan is taken in his capacity as sociologist of culture or as visionary, what he is saying today is commanding a good deal of attention and offers one of the more interesting new perspectives from which to survey the landscape of our time. And his fundamental contention is that the whole slant and texture of human sensibility in any age are determined by the media which the culture employs for the delivery of information. From the Renaissance to the dawn of the contemporary period, the reigning dispensation in the Western world was that of Gutenberg, for his invention of movable type established the basic terms within which reality was perceived by "alphabetic man." That is to say, the rise of a civilization based upon the wide diffusion of the printed word carried, as its major correlate, the development of an ocular sensibility, for the primary cultural reality was that of letters consecutively arranged across a page—and this in turn made for radical change in the style of man's self-interpretation and metaphysical vision. Historicity could now, for example, begin to be a part of the experienced human reality, for the cyclical categories of older mythical perspectives had now to be replaced by linear categories that more nicely comported with the linear structure of the printed page. And not only was the sense of time thus affected, but so too was the sense of space. For the fixity of the reader's position in relation to the printed page encouraged exploration of perspective in the visual arts, encouraged visual exploration of the multi-dimensionality of spatial experience, and experiments in chronological *montage* in narrative literature. And Mr. McLuhan is marvelously adept in suggesting the incalculable social and political and religious transformations that were a part of the galaxy whose center was formed by Gutenberg's innovation.

But the "Age of Writing," in his version of modern history, is now a thing of the past, and we today belong to the emerging species of "post-literate man," for reality is being codified in a new way: the culture of the book, of the printed page, is being replaced by a new vision of the world based on the grammar and syntax of the electronic image. And Mr. McLuhan is therefore announcing the death of "typographic" man. For, ever since the invention of telegraphy, the old "eye culture" has been by way of being displaced by a polity whose essential logic is an affair of new media, of electronic media, which lead men to experience reality in a new way. And thus the old social and art forms that were based in a print-culture are slipping into desuetude: a new sensibility is being born.

There is, for example, that early and widely known canvas by Picasso, done about 1912, which simply pictures a violin: it is one of the classic expressions of Cubist idiom, and its manifest intention is to eternalize in a single instant all the various possible impressions and views that we might have of a violin, from all possible angles—so that every imaginable perspective might be encompassed *at once*. And Mr. McLuhan would be inclined to take this canvas as a fine instance of the electronic image, for the electrical principle is a principle of instantaneousness and speed: so the "grammar" of Cubism—with its emphasis on *simultanéité*, on instant sensory awareness of the whole, on what Mr. McLuhan calls the "total field"—offered an early illustration in the visual art of our century of what the grammar of an electronic culture might be like. But, in order to achieve its fascinating interplay of volumes and planes, a Cubist canvas had to sacrifice that illusion of the third dimension which had been so much a part of the painter's central aim since the Renaissance; and thus, in still another particular, the work of such men as Braque and Derain and Juan Gris and the early Picasso tended to point toward the kind of general direction that art might be expected to take in an electronic age. For the depthlessness of a Cubist canvas seems presciently to augur for Mr. McLuhan that general disappearance of the dimension of depth which follows after the cultural media are once touched by the electrical principle. Depth-orientations in painting, as in literature and all the other arts, had their real roots in the culture of "alphabetic man," the man who fed his mind and spirit by solitarily reading portable books and whose isolation from his fellows in turn bred in him the habit of preoccupation with inwardness, with "depth," with the "mountains" of the soul—"cliffs of fall/Frightful, sheer, no-man-fathomed."* Which is to say, in Mr. McLuhan's patois, that the great media in the Age of Gutenberg were "hot": whereas today, deep in our electric age, they are "cool": for, "depth" no longer being a primary dimension of experience, the work of art, for example, need not itself any longer be an instrument of phenomenology, a vehicle of man's self-exploration: no, it can now once again be simply an "object," and, the horizons of the artist's world being defined by the *désacralisé*, his fundamental work takes on the character of a kind of "research" (into the sheer plasticity of his medium) which, as Susan Sontag says, is far "closer to the spirit of science than of art in the old-fashioned sense."

Mr. McLuhan's writing, like the electronic images of which he is so fond, gyrates off in so many directions at once and he so dislikes making a clean, direct statement about anything at all that it is extremely difficult to fashion a detailed synopsis of his basic argument; but something like my rough summary may approximate that argument, even if only partially. And his hypothesis, for all of its brilliantly erratic onesidedness, has at least the merit of confirming in us our tendency now to feel the cultural atmosphere of the present time as something new and strange. Indeed, it is surely so, in our own late season, that we do begin intermittently to feel a strange sense of disorientation, of belonging already perhaps to the first generation of "post-modern" people—in a period whose most authentic expressions appear to be found no longer in Hindemith and Bartok but in John Cage and Karlheinz Stockhausen and Milton Babbitt, not in Rouault and Matisse but in Jackson Pollock and Mark Rothko, not in Malraux and Faulkner but in Beckett and Robbe-Grillet, not in F. R. Leavis and Lionel Trilling but in Maurice Blanchot and Roland Barthes, not in Whitehead and Heidegger but in Wittgenstein and Merleau-Ponty. It is a new scene that we look out upon, and one for which we have not yet even begun to find any comprehensive definition.

Undoubtedly, a part of the response which it is natural for us to

*From Gerard Manley Hopkins, "No Worst, There Is None."

make was expressed a few years ago by Lionel Trilling, in an essay which he called "The Fate of Pleasure." In a tone somewhat of dismayed surprise that this should in fact have for so long been the case, Mr. Trilling was wanting to remark how firmly "our contemporary aesthetic culture" is committed to an anti-hedonist position, to a "diminished status . . . [for] the principle of pleasure"—and this as a consequence, he maintained, of the polemical intention of our literature and art to puncture the "specious good." In the tradition of modern literature, Mr. Trilling uses Dostoyevsky's *Notes from the Underground* and Ivan Karamazov's story of the Grand Inquisitor as his archetypes, and they come, of course, pat to his purpose: yet the particular cast of their anti-hedonism, though representative of the classic modern style, is something different, one feels, from what we face in the characteristic art of the present time. For in Dostoyevsky—as in Kafka and Rouault and Schoenberg and so many of the other great artists who incarnate the period-style of the modern movement—the anti-hedonist position is not so much an affair of artistic form itself as it is an affair of that account of human existence of which the writer or the painter or musician makes his art a vehicle. The love-making of K. and Frieda in *The Castle,* the prostitutes and pariahs of Rouault's *Miserere* series, and the haunting dissonances of Alban Berg's *Wozzeck* express, to be sure, a positive devaluation of the pleasure principle—but in a clarity of form so absolute as to quicken in us the sensation of great beauty. So, here, we feel that the anti-hedonism inheres not so much in the actual life of forms as in a certain estimate of the human enterprise which the artist's formal energy converts into a principle of judgment wherewith to assault a "specious good."

But, in the immediate environment of our contemporary aesthetic culture, the pervasive anti-hedonism is not an affair of ideology: it does not *follow upon* a polemical engagement with a world of specious good and is not therefore simply an affair of the experiential material with which art is informed: no, it seems rather to grow out of the very life of form itself in our time, and it is here, on this most basic level of things, that the possibility of pleasure seems to be precluded. The new music assaults the ear with a cacophony whose violence is greater even than that which was once felt in the twelve-tone constructions of Schoenberg and Webern. The painting of a Rothko or a Tobey affords no chance to enjoy convergences of perspective and spatial intervals and linear rhythms and orchestrations of plane and volume, such as the tradition accustoms us to, from Raphael to Cézanne, from de la Tour to Matisse and Chagall. And *le roman nouveau*, in the hands of a Beckett or a Robbe-Grillet or a Michel Butor, often seems, in its utter plotlessness and banality, to be only an ingeniously designed test of the reader's capacity to endure extremes of tedium.

So the denial of pleasure does indeed appear to be a hallmark of the new avant-garde. But if on one level Mr. Trilling helps us to identify what is characteristic of contemporary idioms, it is, I suspect, on a somewhat deeper level that Mr. McLuhan—or what one can piece together as to the implications of his thought—helps us toward a proper definition. For the sensation of *dis*pleasure that we are given by the new forms of art is very probably a consequence of the extent to which they have ascetically forsworn the dimension of "depth." And it is no doubt this artfully deliberate superficiality of the Muse— under the charm perhaps of the electronic image—that puts us off.

In short, disquisitions on "the fate of pleasure," though they may move into the general region of what is problematic in our aesthetic transactions today, do not, finally, take us far enough, for what is most basically frustrating in the new art of the present time is its radical *depthlessness*, its resolute refusal of what Alain Robbe-Grillet may nominate on the day after tomorrow the Anthropocentric Fallacy. Susanne Langer tells us in her great book, *Feeling and Form*, that the natural function of art is to create "forms symbolic of human feeling"—but ours *today* is an art that is determined not to create forms symbolic of *our* feeling. Indeed, John Cage, one of the chief American spokesmen for the new avant-garde in music, believes that the sounds of music should simply "be themselves rather than . . . expressions of human sentiments." So, instead of articulating the morphology of man's affective life, instead of analogically expressing the tensions and resolutions that make up the patterns of human sentience, a musical composition will simply present sounds—not

sounds going anywhere or moving through a rhythmically ordered
sequence to any sort of climax and thus satisfying expectations
aroused by the musical experience, not sounds related to one another
by any sort of *human* logic, but simply sounds, in the sheer *thereness*
of their acousticality. Mr. Cage says (in his book *Silence*) : "Wherever
we are, what we hear is mostly noise. When we ignore it, it disturbs
us. When we listen to it, we find it fascinating." And the making of
music, he maintains, is simply the "organization of sound," the organization of noise—which is precisely what the music of Christian
Wolff and Morton Feldman and Earle Brown seems to be. The principal concern, as Mr. Wolff says, is for "a kind of objectivity, almost
anonymity—sound come into its own." And it is a wonderfully exact
formula for the kind of project to which he and his friends are
committed—*sound come into its own,* a music whose most striking
feature is its radical depthlessness.

   But the spiritual depthlessness that is so noticeably characteristic
of the style being brought into existence by the new music is by no
means an isolated phenomenon in contemporary artistic life; it is an
equally striking feature of the architectural movement of which, say,
Mies van der Rohe is a major exemplar. And the movement in recent
painting with which we associate the New York School exhibits the
same quality. As John Cage wants the sounds of his music to be just
there, as sounds—come into their own—so Mies wants his Chicago
apartment-skyscrapers to be simply skeletons of steel and glass; and a
painter like the late Franz Kline wanted many of his canvases to be
simply large white fields bearing broad strokes of black: sound, glass
and steel, primed canvas and black paint—nothing more, only the
sheer thereness of the raw materials, in their unhumanized facticity.

   It is in the new *alittérature,* however, that this whole style of sensibility finds perhaps its most candid and resolute expressions, and
here the chief strategist is the French novelist-critic Alain Robbe-
Grillet. It is undoubtedly the case that such writers as Samuel Beckett
and Nathalie Sarraute and Jean Cayrol and Claude Simon and Michel Butor and M. Robbe-Grillet do not, in all respects, belong under
the same umbrella, for their stylistic and narrative procedures manifest a very considerable diversity of aim and stratagem. But, in at

least one important particular, they represent a unitary emphasis, in their conviction that narrative literature must be purged of the old "stories," the old structures of plot and character, the old eloquence: they have an equal disdain for the old "anthropomorphism"— for what M. Robbe-Grillet quite explicitly calls "the old myths of 'depth.' " So they dispense with what Claude Simon disapprovingly speaks of as "la merveilleuse illusion," for they believe that the order which the traditional "verisimilitudes" of prose fiction impose on experience does in fact falsify the existential reality. The great thing, they believe, is, as M. Robbe-Grillet says, "to look at the world which surrounds [us] with entirely unprejudiced eyes." For it is only in this way that its reality can be taken into account, since the locus of that reality is not in the various traditional "significations" of the literary imagination but is rather simply in the world's *presence*: ". . . defying the noisy pack of our animistic or protective adjectives, things *are there*." And in a time that "has renounced the omnipotence of the person" and the old "cult of the 'human,' " the principal function of literature must be that of trapping us into a kind of radical amazement at the simple *thereness* of the world and at the stubbornness with which, in its brute factuality, it resists all our traditional habits of ordering and apprehension. Our writers will become *chosistes,* connoisseurs of *things*: for "the world is neither significant nor absurd. It [simply] *is.* . . ."* And M. Robbe-Grillet, who is nothing if not consistent, develops this mystique of *l'actuelle* more radically than anyone else, producing a fiction from which the human presence has been most rigorously expunged, in which the single subject matter is formed by the novelist's descriptions of the angles and planes and surfaces of the world—its streets and houses and skies and various other appurtenances: in this way he hopes to create *le roman objectif.*

Now the program which Alain Robbe-Grillet is proposing for the new literature, in the great stringency of its emphasis, has the effect of casting into even higher relief a predominant tendency governing the central movement in the artistic culture of the present time. For, whether we turn to architecture or to painting or to music or to

---

*The quotations from M. Robbe-Grillet appear in his *For a New Novel: Essays on Fiction.*

literature, what is noticeable in the new sensibility is its impatience with "the old myth of 'depth' " and its eagerness to walk "barefoot into reality."* A musical composition does not create "forms symbolic of human feeling," but is simply so much organized sound—"come into its own." A public building is not visibly in any way a celebration of our common *humanitas* but is simply a structure of concrete or steel. A painting does not "mean" anything extrinsic to itself but is simply so much paint on a certain area of canvas. A poem, as Wallace Stevens says, is "not ideas about the thing but the thing itself." Everywhere the feeling seems to be that, "instead of making everything an object for the self, the mind must efface itself before reality, or plunge into the density of an exterior world, dispersing itself in a milieu which exceeds it and which it has not made."** The sovereign principle seems now to arise out of a new mystique of *l'actuelle*.

So our playwrights having discarded the old, well-made structures of beginning-middle-and-end and our poets wanting their poems to "be" rather than "mean" and our novelists being unwilling now any longer to tell "stories," we are often at the point of wanting querulously to complain about how "boring" the new literature is. The charge is frequently heard, of course, that the antiseptic purity of much of contemporary architecture puts one in mind of some anonymous public utility—a garage or a warehouse—even when it is a residential apartment building or a center of collegiate studies. The most ardent devotees of the new music will occasionally admit that it is a screeching, screaking vociferation. And the sense of defraudment that is provoked in the galleries devoted to the new painting and sculpture is, of course, a staple of both popular and sophisticated humor. Most of us move along older tracks of perception and taste, and the difficulty we have in following contemporary artists in their attempt to achieve a more radical penetration of *l'actuelle* brings to mind that ironic clause in T. S. Eliot's "Burnt Norton"—". . . human kind/Cannot bear very much reality."

Indeed, even the movies (long our last refuge from the rigors of

---

*Wallace Stevens, "Large Red Man Reading."
**J. Hillis Miller, *Poets of Reality*. It is Professor Miller's citations that have put me in mind of the passages from Stevens quoted above.

modern art) begin to be an extraordinarily difficult and complex form of expression, for, in the hands of many of the great new artists of this medium—Michelangelo Antonioni, Federico Fellini, Jean-Luc Godard, Alain Resnais—cinema, too, often seems to be committed to something of the same sort of effort being generally undertaken by much of contemporary art. That gifted young American critic, the late Robert Warshow, once objected to the enthusiasm which leads the *cinéaste* to say: "It is not the *movies* I go to see; it is art." And he replied in this wise:

> I have gone to the movies constantly, and at times almost compulsively, for most of my life. I should be embarrassed to attempt an estimate of how many movies I have seen and how many hours they have consumed. At the same time, I have had enough serious interest in the products of the "higher" arts to be very sharply aware that the impulse which leads me to a Humphrey Bogart movie has little in common with the impulse which leads me to the novels of Henry James or the poetry of T. S. Eliot. That there is a connection between the two impulses I do not doubt, but the connection is not adequately summed up in the statement that the Bogart movie and the Eliot poem are both forms of art.*

These lines were written in 1954, a few months before Robert Warshow's untimely death, and they do not express, one feels, the kind of lucidity which gave such high interest to much of his writing on films. For the attitude that is conveyed here, if consistently adhered to, could hardly have made for an adequate response to the best work of William Wyler and George Stevens and John Huston and Alfred Hitchcock, of Renoir and Carné and Duvivier, of David Lean and Carol Reed, of De Sica and Rossellini. Yet in 1954 an intelligent young American critic could still find it *possible* to view contemporary cinema as insufficiently serious to compete directly for the same kind of attention that cultivated people in our time give to literature and the other arts—and possible perhaps because in some measure he still belonged to what Parker Tyler calls "the eyewitness era in film fiction,"** the period when the predominant film style still found its

---

*From the "Author's Preface" to *The Immediate Experience.*
**In *The Three Faces of the Film.*

ultimate source in the ideal of film as documentary, as an eyewitness record of verifiable reality.

But, were he alive today, it is nearly inconceivable, dedicated as he was to "the tradition of the new," that Warshow would want to insist so firmly on the generic incommensurateness between a serious work of literary art and one of the more characteristic expressions of recent cinema; for the most interesting films of the last ten or fifteen years are very deeply stamped by the new film-maker's intention to be an *auteur*. And by *auteur* the ideologues of *Les Cahiers du Cinéma* mean *le directeur par excellence*; they mean the director who is so thoroughly the impresario of the entire creative process issuing in the completed film that he is indeed its primary cause and "author," having chosen his subject and superintended the preparation of his script, selected his cast and cameraman and controlled all the editing, and in fact having exercised a decisive hand in relation to every phase of the total sequence of actions whereby a film is made. The *auteur* is the master of the entire process of film creation, who uses his work as a vehicle to express a personal vision of the world. And this is indeed the role that is played today by a Truffaut, an Antonioni, a Resnais (as in an earlier time by a Welles or a Cocteau).

Like the new dramatists and novelists, the *auteur* often takes only a very slight interest in "stories." The principal focus of his interest lies rather in the *mise en scène,* in the mood and tonality of moments which by dint of audacious technical maneuvers—in photography or the use of sound or editing—can be made to become epiphanies (in something like the sense established by Joyce for prose fiction). So the model in one's mind of an *auteur*'s film is one that has forsworn most of the conventional techniques of cinematic narration, for what the director conceives his main task to be is not the exposition of a traditional linear plot but the manipulation of the forms and movements of screen images. And thus the temporality of this cinema is one which has lost the uninterrupted continuity of concrete, objective time; the new film-maker, characteristically, has little interest in developing consecutive sequences of events: for him the grammar of film has but a single tense—and the time dimension of cinematic happenings is *the radical present*. So the *auteur* tends to splice

scenes together in ways that rob the spectator of the kinds of yard-
sticks that have traditionally been provided for his equanimity; what
the director wants to do is not to carry the spectator comfortably along
through the various "logical" stages of a linear narrative but, rather,
to involve him deeply in the special quality of a given instant, and
then of another and another—and he assumes that the spectator's intelligence is agile enough to make the necessary connections. The
auteur specializes in the unexpected, the contradictory, in seeming ir-
relevancy: things are shifting, fragmentary, evanescent, because reality is felt to be dynamic and volatile, and the world is exhibited as a
place of sudden and mysterious landmarks. Cinematic structure is
conceived to be something like what Jacques Guicharnaud finds to be
the structure of a novel by Claude Simon—a structure, that is,

rather similar to a cloud, formed by the wind, which at a given moment
takes on a recognizable—or at least noticeable—shape, then changes into
another, and perhaps still another, finally becoming shapeless, lost in the
greyness of a clouded sky. Just as, in the fluid, heterogeneous and constantly
moving substance of life, there forms a kind of ephemeral coagulation, a
vague nucleus distinguishable for a short while, yet without any break in
continuity with the rest.*

The film itself, in other words, is the primary reality: this is what the
director wants us to remember that we are watching, a film and nothing but a film; and the emphasis is on spectacle and sound, on the
way things look and feel: what is striven for is an "art of appearances" whose informing spirit is that of a mystique of *l'actuelle.*

It is, I say, very much this general sort of image that one carries in
one's mind of the kind of cinema being produced by the most gifted
and the most characteristic film-makers of the present time; and,
were Robert Warshow alive today, he would, I suspect, feel compelled
to admit that this is a cinema the style of whose aesthetic pretensions
is indeed very much of a piece with the way in which the serious
art of our time generally establishes its claims upon us.

The particular film that does, for me, more nearly than any other
stand as a kind of emblem of the new period is Alain Resnais' re-

*From "Remembrance of Things Passing: Claude Simon," which appeared in the
Summer, 1959, issue of *Yale French Studies.*

markable production of 1961, *Last Year at Marienbad* (the scenario for which was prepared by Alain Robbe-Grillet). Had I to name the half-dozen (or even, the dozen) films of the last ten or fifteen years that have given me the greatest pleasure and that I regard as the most considerable achievements in the medium, there might very probably not be room for *Marienbad* on my list, for my own sense of things makes me doubtful of its meriting the rank that I would reserve, say, for Robert Bresson's *Le Journal d'un Curé de Campagne,* for Fellini's *La Strada* and *La Dolce Vita,* for Bergman's *Wild Strawberries* and *The Virgin Spring,* for Truffaut's *Les Quatre Cents Coups,* or for Resnais' own *Hiroshima mon Amour.* But, nevertheless, it is *Marienbad* that first comes to my mind when I begin to think of what is characteristically new and radical in the cinema of our time: it gives the age away, in the sense of presenting in itself a kind of summary of our period-style.

We are taken into a vast baroque hotel, cavernous in its seemingly endless labyrinth of corridors, halls silent and deserted and icy in their elaborately stuccoed and marbled elegance—where, as a neutral and monotonous male voice says (after the "credits" have been shown), "the sound of advancing footsteps is absorbed by carpets so thick and heavy that nothing can be heard . . . as if the ear itself were very far away . . . from this heavy and empty setting." After the camera has roamed through the corridors and galleries of this lugubrious palace, it moves into a faintly lit salon where the elegantly attired guests are stiffly disposed about the room, in chairs all turned in the same direction; then it focuses in on three of these personages, a woman (A) and two men (X and M). And the remainder of the film is very largely given over to the pursuit of A by X. X proposes to her that they met last year at Marienbad and had an affair there, and he insists that, though something then prevented their going away together, she agreed to meet him here a year hence and promised that this time they would go off with each other. At first A denies the entire recital and asserts that in fact they have never met before at all. But X will not be put off; he insists that they were indeed together a year ago—at Marienbad. "You never seemed to be waiting for me— but we kept meeting," he says, "at each turn of the paths—behind each bush, at the foot of each statue, near each pond. . . . One night, I went up to your room. . . . It was almost summer. . . . I remember that room very well. . . . You were sitting on the edge of the bed, in a kind of robe or bed-jacket. . . . I took you, half by force." But though for a while A insists that she has never seen him before and that he is inventing the whole tale, gradually she begins to weaken—under the force of his reiterations and his denial that M is really her husband: "Yes . . . Maybe . . ."

Meanwhile, as this strange colloquy goes on—always off screen—the restless camera is forever dwelling upon the decorative details of the great hotel, the gloomy distances spanned by its corridors, its monumental staircases, its imposing colonnades, its sumptuously appointed salons, the grandiloquent spaciousness of its geometrically formal gardens *à la française*. And this camera behaves with great eccentricity: it will shoot the same action over and again from different angles, sliding away from the persons upstage and then rushing back in upon them; or a shot will change in the middle of a speech, which then continues off screen during the shot that follows—and the change of shot is likely to be accompanied by the crash of a cymbal; or a shot will go dark and then brighten again, showing the same scene; and the camera likes to overexpose the scenes of intense emotion, in order to flood the screen with a dazzling white effect.

Indeed, the film is very largely, almost wholly, an affair of the camera alone, for very few words are actually spoken by M. Resnais' actors. What he offers is something chiefly to be seen rather than heard. And what we see are X and A and the various other people in the hotel moving up and down its vast corridors, stiff and icy in the formality of their *haute couture,* entering salons, closing doors, and, with a kind of ritualistic deliberateness, taking up positions against the background of the baroque décor, as if they were acting out an elegant charade in parody of the International Set. But we learn nothing at all about these people—not even about X and A. A, to be sure, does bit by bit, it seems, come finally to accept X's account of what happened last year at Marienbad, and at last they do apparently leave the hotel together. But who is A, really? And who is X? We never find out. And were they together last year at

Marienbad? M. Robbe-Grillet peremptorily denies that any previous meeting ever occurred, suggesting that what is involved here is simply a contest of wills which X finally wins by forcing A to accept his version of things. But M. Resnais, though he offers us the privilege of making whatever we will of the film, asserts that he could never have shot it had he not been convinced that the meeting had actually taken place. The question, of course, as to what *really* happened last year at Marienbad is very much like the question as to "how many children had Lady Macbeth?"—and along this route no great progress is likely to be made. But at least it can be fairly argued that the man X and the woman A whom we see on the screen are *there* beheld as people without any past at all: they come from nowhere; they have no backgrounds, no connections, no past and no future— and they exist discarnately amidst the ostentatious magnificence of a great hotel. And where is this hotel? Or is it, after all, really a hotel? Is it, as some have supposed, a kind of sanatorium in which X (the psychiatrist) is attempting to assist A toward some fresh repossession of herself? Or is it perhaps that this gloomy palace—like that Second Empire living room in Sartre's *No Exit*—is an image of Hell? One cannot be certain, for no "story" is told of human beings recognizably like ourselves, and the film is not "about" anything at all; it carefully forswears "the old myth of 'depth'" and wants to be simply an end in itself, a "pure" film, something utterly and absolutely autonomous. So it resists "interpretation." In its intransigent "objectivism," it offers us simply an "art of appearances" whose sole purpose is to exhibit the sheer sensuous immediacy of film images—and these are surely amongst the most captivatingly beautiful images that have ever appeared on the movie screen.

Now there are many who have a great eagerness to assail the whole style of expression embodied in cinema by *Marienbad*—or in literature by the novels of Robbe-Grillet or the poetry of Charles Olson, or in philosophy by British linguistic analysis, or in painting by the work of Franz Kline and Mark Rothko, or in music by the work of John Cage—as representing a new *trahison des clercs* which threatens a nihilistic subversion of everything humane and elevating in the received traditions of culture. The deliberate depthlessness of a cultural style whose intent is to do nothing more than describe the "appearances" of the "life-world" seems to entail a certain fore-shortening of things and a certain abdication from the *multi*-dimensionality of the real. And there is no dearth of angry, irascible traditionalists who are prepared to sound the hue and cry—of treason.

I have no doubt, of course, but that a partisanship in behalf of "the tradition of the new" which is so ardent as to exempt it from any stringently critical scrutiny must make, in the long run, for a real *trahison*. And being temperamentally more inclined perhaps toward traditionalist sympathies than toward the headiness of avant-gardist enthusiasms, I am most assuredly myself prepared to testify to a very strong sense of much being *left out* after hearing the music of Luigi Nono and Morton Feldman and remembering that of Bartok and Hindemith, or after looking at the paintings of de Kooning and Tobey and remembering the great ones of Picasso and Matisse, or after seeing Fellini's *8½* or Antonioni's *La Notte* and remembering Renoir's *La Grande Illusion* or De Sica's *Shoeshine*. But surely there is something profoundly decadent and obscurantist in that attitude of mind which prompts an outright denunciation of new forms of art because they commit what is presumed to be the great sin of simply being unlike older forms of art. And I suspect that what it is most important for us to do today, before attempting any measurements of the new idioms in accordance with inherited norms, is to ask what genuinely creative and valuable function it may be which is performed by an art that has rigorously forsworn the dimension of "depth" for the sake of fidelity to "appearances."

And it is at this point that I am immediately put in mind of that great old phrase occurring in the sixth-century *Commentary* by Simplicius on Aristotle's *De Caelo*—"to save the appearances."* For this, one begins to feel, is what it is a major impulse of the most characteristic contemporary art to try to do—to *save* the appearances, or to do what Goethe told Schiller (in a letter dated February 10, 1798) it is "the better part of human nature" to attempt: namely, to try "to bestow upon the concrete the honor of the idea." From Goethe and

*The phrase has fascinated me ever since I first read the discussion of Simplicius occurring in Owen Barfield's *Saving the Appearances*.

Blake to Bergson and D. H. Lawrence there is, of course, a persistent movement of protest in the modern period against what Alfred North Whitehead (in *Science and the Modern World*) called the Fallacy of Misplaced Concreteness. Whether one turns, say, in philosophic tradition, to Kierkegaard or to Merleau-Ponty, or, in literary tradition, to Hopkins or to Wallace Stevens, one can sense a recurrent anxiety of the modern imagination that, in the course of our growing enslavement to the disruptiveness of the analytical passions, we may altogether lose any living contact with the existential reality of the world we actually inhabit, its smells and sounds and sights and tactilities—becoming entangled, finally, in nothing more than an arid morass of utter abstractions. The great specter which has recurrently haunted many of the most sensitive men of the last two hundred years is that there may eventually come a time when all the richness and amplitude of Creation will simply pass through the eyes of a man into his head and there be turned by the brain into some sort of formula or equation.* But this tradition of protest against what Lawrence called "mentalism" has been, by and large, a minority movement, for we are a people so committed to the Idea (and thus to the Will) as not to have been able, except intermittently, really to accept the possibility that the mind might occasionally need to abandon its imperialist ambitions, might need even for a while to consent to be dumb and stupid before reality, in order once again to win access to "the dearest freshness deep down things."

Our generation begins increasingly to fear, however, that the analytical passions, grown swollen and rampant, may, through their demonic ingeniousness, be simply promoting "the vain and desperate fidgetings of the good intention to make hell a better place to live in."** A holocaustal glow is descried in the not too distant skies. And so, expressing no doubt a deep drive of our age, the contemporary artist wants very much, as it were, to return to the earth—remem-

---

*My own sentence derives from the sentence in Flannery O'Connor's novel *The Violent Bear It Away* in which Old Tarwater furiously splutters out the charge against his schoolteacher-nephew Rayber that "every living thing that passed through . . . [his] eyes into his head was turned by his brain into a book or a paper or a chart."

**Erich Heller, *The Disinherited Mind*.

bering perhaps the word of Hölderlin, that this is indeed where man
dwells, at least poetically: "upon the earth." In an age whose abstractions begin to promise death to civilization and to the human
spirit and to the very earth itself, the motion that the artist begins
now to perform with a new seriousness is a motion of digging away
at and recovering those elemental givens of experience in which, as
Wallace Stevens says, "we awake,/Within the very object that we
seek,/Participants of its being." The aim, again quoting Stevens, is
to see "the very thing and nothing else": the principal search (in
painting and music and literature and the cinema) is for what Goethe
called the *Urphänomen*—and, in this way, it is hoped that by *impaling*
the imagination on the very things of earth themselves, by saving "the
appearances," we may save ourselves. It is, I suspect, in some such
terms as these that we must finally understand the new mystique in
the artistic life of our period, the mystique of *l'actuelle*.

The campaign, however, which is generally under way in contemporary art is of a kind that will constantly skirt inanity and inocuous-
ness if it be not remembered, as Goethe insisted in his *Theory of
Colors,* that "the mere looking at a thing is of no use whatsoever.
Looking at a thing gradually merges into contemplation, contemplation into thinking, thinking is establishing connections, and thus it is
possible to say that every attentive glance which we cast on the world
is [ultimately] an act of theorizing." * The mere looking at a thing is
of no use whatsoever; to gaze deeply at any reality is already to be by
way of beginning to perform an act of theorizing; this is a profound
lesson which has been thoroughly mastered by those artists, even
those most radically committed to "the very thing itself," who make
the greatest impress upon us, for they are artists—a Benjamin Britten,
a Francis Bacon, a Bert Brecht, a Marianne Moore, an Ingmar Bergman—who show (as Mr. Trilling rightly predicts that they will**) that
they are "aware of rhetoric, which is to say, of the intellectual content
of their work." And Goethe's lesson is, I suspect, the great lesson
that much of contemporary art needs to be learning anew, that strict
attention to what the poet Richard Wilbur calls the "things of this

---

*This passage is quoted by Erich Heller in *The Disinherited Mind.*
**In *The Liberal Imagination.*

world" needs finally to lead to a kind of "theorizing," a theorizing, as
Goethe says, which will be immensely "ironic" but which will, nevertheless, entail for the artist a kind of double reversal—*away* from
"the idea" to "the things themselves" but at last *back* to "the idea."
This is the way that a Robbe-Grillet needs to take, that a John Cage
needs to take, that surely must begin to be taken by the new painters
if they are to avoid that absolute impasse towards which they often
seem today to be heading.

   And this is even, I should say, the lesson that our new film-makers
will be having to learn, if the rich promise in much of their work is
to find any large fulfillment. Indeed, it is what I take to be the
major implication of a now classic essay on contemporary cinema, the
piece that the French critic Alexandre Astruc contributed to *L'Écran
Français* in 1948 called "Le Caméra Stylo." In likening the camera to a
fountain pen, M. Astruc meant to suggest that the cinema is in fact
a kind of language, a form of writing. "By a language," he said, "I
mean the form in which and through which an artist can express
his thoughts, however abstract they may be, or translate his obsessions,
just as in an essay or a novel. . . . The film will gradually free itself
from the tyranny of the visual, of the image for its own sake, of
the immediate anecdote, of the concrete, to become a means of
writing as supple and as subtle as that of written language. . . .
What interests us in the cinema today is the creation of this language." But, of course, M. Astruc's conception of the camera as a
fountain pen with which one *writes* may now perhaps be seen to
have been less a prediction of things immediately to come than a
recommendation to film-makers of what *ought* to be their intended
course; and I say that it seems now to have been less a prediction
than a recommendation because, in the intervening years, the reigning principle in so much of avant-garde cinema has continued to be
largely an affair of "the tyranny of the visual, of the image for its
own sake," of an "art of appearances." Yet I am certain that M. Astruc
is basically right in believing that the artist of film must also be a
rhetorician—as was a Chaplin, a Cocteau, a Renoir; or as is a Bergman,
a Tony Richardson, a Fellini in his finest work. And thus I suspect
that, for all of its visual beauty, such a film as *Last Year at Marienbad,*

in its inordinate fascination with "the concrete," comes closer to ex-
emplifying what is problematic in cinema today than it does to
charting a course toward larger possibilities of expression. For the
concrete begins to take on radical significance only when it can be
seen to be leading into the "concrete universal." And this is a route
today taken too infrequently.

the PERSONAL
ENCOUNTER

RICHARD WILBUR

A Poet and the Movies

It is hard to say offhand how much one's art may have been tinctured by one's seeing of motion pictures, because watching film is (for me, for most) so much less judicial and analytic than other art experience. The conventions are transparent, the molding of the imagination is insidious. Even the worst movie has much of the authority of the actual, and quite without knowing it one comes out of the theater brainwashed into scanning the world through the norms of the camera. The enthusiasts of the pittoresco at the close of the eighteenth century, rapturously arranging the landscape in their Claude glasses, were conscious of the imposition; the moviegoer walks about taking shots and sequences unaware. The same entrancement characterizes the moviegoer's acquisition of personal style; to put on an Old Vic accent, to ape the gestures of a stage actor or actress— these involve some deliberate imposture, but to smoke like George Raft, to lift the eyebrows like Cary Grant—that is another and more hypnotized order of imitation. The mannerisms of movie stars, unconsciously borrowed and recognized without specific reminiscence, have for us something of the universality of the Italian vocabulary of gestures, though of course they are more transitory.

Knowing how far my mind's eye must have been conditioned by motion pictures, I venture with diffidence the opinion that certain pre-Edison poetry was genuinely cinematic. Whenever, for example, I read *Paradise Lost*, I, 44–58 (the long shot of Satan's fall from Heaven to Hell, the panorama of the rebels rolling in the lake of fire, the sudden close-up of Satan's afflicted eyes), I feel that I am experiencing a passage which, though its effects may have been suggested by the spatial surprises of Baroque architecture, is facilitated for me, and not misleadingly, by my familiarity with screen techniques. If this reaction is not anachronistic foolishness, it follows that one must be wary in attributing this or that aspect of any contemporary work to the influence of film.

But glancing at my own poems, as the editor has invited me to do, I find in a number of pieces—"Marginalia" for instance—what may owe as much to the camera as to the sharp noticing of poets like Hopkins and Ponge: a close and rapid scanning of details, an insubordination of authenticating particulars, abrupt shifting in lieu of the full-dress rhetorical transition. Here is a bit of the poem mentioned:

> Things concentrate at the edges; the pond-surface
> Is bourne to fish and man and it is spread
> In textile scum and damask light, on which
> The lily-pads are set; and there are also
>   Inlaid ruddy twigs, becalmed pine-leaves,
>   Air-baubles, and the chain mail of froth . . .

I notice in the first line of another poem ("Haze, char, and the

weather of all souls") what may be an effort at the instant scenic
fullness of an opening shot. Move as it may, the picture on the
screen gives enviably much at once, and the moviegoing poet, im-
patient of his prolix medium, may sometimes try for a lightning com-
pleteness, a descriptive *coup*. Finally, I wonder if the first four
lines of "An Event" are not indebted to trick photography:

> As if a cast of grain leapt back to the hand,
> A landscapeful of small black birds, intent
> On the far south, convene at some command
> At once in the middle of the air . . .

All of the above is doubtful, but there is no doubt about two of
my poems, "Beasts" and "The Undead." Each owes something to a
particular horror film, in respect of mood, matter, and images. "Beasts"
takes some of its third and fourth stanzas from *Frankenstein Meets
the Wolf Man*, and "The Undead" obviously derives in part from
Bela Lugosi's *Dracula*. Neither of these films is great art, though the
latter comes close, but both are good enough to haunt the memory
with the double force of reality and dream, to remind one of a
deeper Gothic on which they draw, and to start the mind building
around them. One would have to be brooding on a film to produce
such a visual pun as "Their black shapes cropped into sudden bats."

THE UNDEAD

> Even as children they were late sleepers,
> Preferring their dreams, even when quick with monsters,
> To the world with all its breakable toys,
> Its compacts with the dying;
>
> From the stretched arms of withered trees
> They turned, fearing contagion of the mortal,
> And even under the plums of summer
> Drifted like winter moons.
>
> Secret, unfriendly, pale, possessed
> Of the one wish, the thirst for mere survival,
> They came, as all extremists do
> In time, to a sort of grandeur:
>
> Now, to their Balkan battlements
> Above the vulgar town of their first lives,

They rise at the moon's rising. Strange
   That their utter self-concern
Should, in the end, have left them selfless:
Mirrors fail to perceive them as they float
   Through the great hall and up the staircase;
      Nor are the cobwebs broken.

Into the pallid night emerging,
Wrapped in their flapping capes, routinely maddened
   By a wolf's cry, they stand for a moment
      Stoking the mind's eye

With lewd thoughts of the pressed flowers
And bric-a-brac of rooms with something to lose,—
   Of love-dismembered dolls, and children
      Buried in quilted sleep.

Then they are off in a negative frenzy,
Their black shapes cropped into sudden bats
   That swarm, burst, and are gone. Thinking
      Of a thrush cold in the leaves

Who has sung his few summers truly,
Or an old scholar resting his eyes at last,
   We cannot be much impressed with vampires,
      Colorful though they are;

Nevertheless, their pain is real,
And requires our pity. Think how sad it must be
   To thirst always for a scorned elixir,
      The salt quotidian blood

Which, if mistrusted, has no savor;
To prey on life forever and not possess it,
   As rock-hollows, tide after tide,
      Glassily strand the sea.

Don't Make Waves

Not how to begin. For at the beginning I had no knowledge of how it would be or what it would be like. Not enough knowledge, it seemed, even to imagine what would be expected of me, let alone the feel of working in a new form. Each kind and form of writing is, after all, different, with a different energy. Different muscles to stretch and kink. Same senses to use and words, always the words to wrestle with, but each time different even as within one form, a short story for example, each beginning is always new and different, a brand new ball game. Unless, of course, consciously or merely by habit, you write the same story over and over again.

227

Put it this way. Coming to the writing of pictures, I had enough experience with other kinds of writing, other forms, to know that I did not know and would not know until the real doing and making were under way.

But this is only partly true. I would learn, as I already knew, that I knew more than I was willing to allow. And less, too, much less than I should have.

I told myself to wait and see.

Only partly true. Because I had written for film, for *filmed* television, back when that was fairly new and most of the shows were still being done live. The job was to adapt a short story of my own, and since it developed that they had an outline of how they wanted it done anyway, the work was mechanical, tedious, and quickly forgotten. From that experience I possessed only memories, anecdotes. Of the literary kind. My first encounter with Show Biz. My initiation, all self-consciously observed. I would bring back something—at least an anecdote or two.

I was teaching at Wesleyan then, a beginning teacher too. Agent called from New York and said to be there at a time and place. There was a chance we could sell a story to TV and perhaps even get the right to adapt it. Brand new series looking for new young writers. Arrived. He seemed relaxed, matter of fact, loose and cool, for a man with a tough selling job. Up a shiny pilotless elevator to the dim heights of a building. Down corridors, past guards and shiny receptionists. Through a room, awkward and noisy, that seemed full of all kinds of freaks. Impression of a trio of midgets juggling, a child in Fauntleroy outfit practicing a tap dance, a very fat woman, sheet music in her lap, her hands soft and folded demurely in her lap. Beautifully patient. Impression of several nervous little round men. Equally nervous lean and gray ones. A large Negro smiling to himself and fooling with a harmonica. A fading blond touching up her make-up at a mirror. A room packed, smoky, noisy, rich and redolent with the odor of humanity. It could have been a sealed boxcar rolling east. A glance only at the inevitable Receptionist as we simply passed through the room. She neither cool nor shiny. Not likely to smile even if we did have the right murmured name or card. In fact ignoring us, as we entered from one blank door, crossed the room briskly with the Agent in the lead, and went out through another blank door. She ignoring us, though no one else did. Questions, judgment, indignation, injustice, worry in their eyes. We might be anybody. Or nobody. . . A glance at her as she ignored our passing. Neither cool nor shiny. Granite instead, roughly, carelessly chipped and hewn. Glass-eyed, utterly indifferent. Silent with the repose of a jagged rock. You would never speak to her unless spoken to.

We closed the door behind us. Another little hall. The Agent stopped, leaned close and confidential. Which was his way, always, even if only to ask the time of day or to remark on the weather.

"The show is new and hasn't got permanent space yet," he said. "We have to go through the waiting room for that talent scout show."

This an afterthought, after the experience.

"Is that where they get the talent?"

"No," he said. "It's all set up, but they have to go through the motions, you know."

"You mean none of those people will ever get on the show?"

A look not so much of scorn as of genuine astonishment. Perhaps I was slow-witted.

"Did you see those creeps?" he asked. Then to my nod: "They go through the motions. It's like—public relations."

"Do they know that?"

"If they don't, it's their own fault."

Through a door into a large bullpen kind of room with partitions. The frosty, questioning look, both plucked eyebrows, like the savage chevrons of a new P.F.C., rising, of Miss Cool and Shiny. Nothing now. The Agent merely ignores her holding open a little half-gate for me as we go by her desk. Out of vision's corners I see the eyebrows fall and the smile suddenly brighten as if illuminated from within, a flash of inner light. She's new, I think, doesn't know the Agent but in some simple way he has communicated to her that to enter and depart without her sanction is his privilege, that *he* is not new. I suspect that next time she will know his name.

We move into the room. There are a few greetings. After a moment he leads me into small cubicle with single window, venetian blinds, single blank shiny desk and two chairs. I am to wait here a few moments. I fiddle with the blinds, look down at the snarl and choke of toy traffic far below. Behind phones ring, but muted, and the whisper of electric typewriters. In a moment someone enters, introduces himself as the Story Editor. A pale man, red hair and freckles. Slight purse of the lips I associate with indigestion or an ulcer. A wan smile. He compliments me on the short story, slightly garbling the title. Mild, idle chitchat. Then: "In a few minutes you're going to see Leo. . . ."

Everything is first name here. Some are said with more style. Leo (I've already decided to call him The Lion) is said reverentially.

"Oh?"

"If he asks you who found the story, tell him I did, huh?"

"Sure."

"And just a word of advice. He'll ask you if you want coffee. You don't."

"I don't?"

"No. Nobody wants coffee."

He's gone. I return to the blind. I try the swivel chair behind the desk. I'm spinning around and around when a second man, this one dark haired and lean, enters. He introduces himself as the Story Editor. Evidently there are two. Sacred and Profane. But which is which? We repeat the identical preliminaries. He, too, garbles the title of the story, but differently.

"In a few minutes you're going to see Leo. . . ."

"In person?"

There is neither time nor the inclination for annoyance.

"If he asks you who found the story, tell him I did, huh?"

"Sure."

"He'll ask you if you want coffee."

"I'd love some coffee," I say.

A grimace. "Nobody wants coffee. Nobody ever asks for coffee." I am thinking at that moment of a certain Colonel in the Army who always asked as a kind of test if you wanted a cigarette. You knew this going in. They told you over and over again, *"Don't take a cigarette."* Usually, I prefer anonymity and am all too willing to hide behind tact. But *that* time, praise be, when the Colonel offered me the symbolic cigarette, I accepted it, then let him light it for me, then managed a questioning look.

"What do you want?" the Colonel said.

With a smile: "An ash tray." He had to send for one.

The irony is that you can't win. By that gesture I was classified by that Colonel as an independent and aggressively self-confident type. Exactly what he was looking for, for a certain job. Another story. . . .

Abruptly we are all off to see Leo. Myself and *entourage* of Agent, two men claiming to be the Story Editor, a Secretary. Perhaps even others falling into the file behind. We proceed in a kind of rush out of the bullpen and into a large office. Many windows. A rather strangely appointed room. A row of chairs along the back wall by the door facing across an expanse and some distance of thick, nondescript expensive carpeting, a desk which has been slightly raised, resting imperiously on what appears to be several layers of plywood. Small man in shirt-sleeves hunches forward in swivel chair, perhaps cushioned, over paper-strewn desk. He's busy shifting papers. Just like in the movies. I'm aware of the others, all except the Agent, taking their seats in the row along the wall. They sit in a row of straight-backed chairs. I advance toward the desk, guided by the light touch of the Agent. At the last second Leo looks up, tossing a paper all fluttering aside, smiles briefly and brightly as we are introduced. The Agent vanishes to the row in the rear.

"Have a seat," the Great Man says.

I notice now a very small chair with cutoff legs in front of the desk. I will be sitting low craning my neck to look up at Leo. I feel the flirtatious presence of that daemon from the Colonel's office.

"Oh, is this little chair for me?"

Nevertheless I sit down.

"You wouldn't care for some coffee, would you?"

I smile my best and most disarming smile as the daemon takes possession.

"Thank you, I'd love some coffee."

I hear mild gasps behind me and the creak of chairs. Leo's frown is quite real.

"Actually we're new here and not really set up yet," he says. "I suppose I *could* send down to the drugstore."

"I don't mind waiting," I say cheerfully.

The Secretary is told to get coffee. As she rises to leave, I hear myself asking for two sugars and light cream. It must be the daemon. I usually drink coffee black. As long as the unpardonable thing has been done, Leo orders coffee too and so do the others. It may be the revolution. Hurray for anarchy!

Why do I feel, somehow, I am striking a blow for those others, the creeps, waiting patiently for their phony auditions?

Soon it's all over. He, lucky for me, doesn't ask me who "found" my story. He simply assigns the credit to one to the tune of an only slightly suppressed groan from the other. He then tells me all about my story, proving beyond shadow of doubt he has read it, even getting the title approximately right. He tells me what it means and what I meant to say. He suggests the story, set in the Depression, should be "updated" to be meaningful to today's audience. He tells me, eloquent for the first time, that it is to be an artistic show, bold and daring. Quite suddenly I discover they are going to do the story and I am going to go home and adapt it for them, with aid and comfort of the Story Editor (which one?), who will help me with technique and all that. We have somehow drunk the coffee, which was cool anyway after the long trip from the drugstore. We shake hands. It is time to leave. I rise, contemplate a salute, but the daemon has gone. I nod. We leave.

Outside on the sidewalk, the Agent wishes me a pleasant trip back to Middletown.

"I'm glad it worked out," I say.

He shrugs. "Those guys are all clients of mine," he says. "I packaged the show."

I walk away down the avenue, thinking of ritual and symbolic gestures. The creeps waiting for a phony audition. The bold brave writer (or call him a college wise guy) who probably could have urinated in the wastebasket without effecting a deal which had already been made. A mere formality. Like bank robbery. I recall an article by Willie Sutton (I think) on the art of robbing a bank. The gun and the man to carry it and point it, he said, were a necessity. But above all things the gun must not be used. It must not be fired. I couple that information with words from a banker who told me that *these days* the only real reason for an armed bank guard is to meet insurance requirements. The guard must carry a loaded pistol, but is under very strict instructions not to use it. It must not be fired. Thus a bank robbery consists of a symbolic encounter of two forces, a confrontation, and, in fact, a symbolic exchange of money—since the loss is insured.

My initiation should have taught me that I was to move in a world of stylized conventions, of symbolic gestures. Not pure phonus-balonus. Merely not true.

All anecdotes must end. Let us skip to the ending, the pay telephone, by means of the suntan story.

Leo, I learned, was a Producer in the grand style. Along about Thursday of a wintry day in the City he would decide that he couldn't work there. "Let's go to Miami," he'd say, "and work in the sun around a pool." A plane would be chartered. Exactly one half of his staff, one each of the two people for every job, would be chosen for these expeditions. Some went frequently. Some never went. Some became more and more deeply tanned. Others became, by contrast, pale and troubled. Some of the pale ones, I was told, got sun lamps to counteract the visible facts of fate. And then one day, like some grand and Calvinistic God, Leo the Lion exercised his prerogative of election and damnation.

"Too goddamn many people around here goofing off. Everybody with a suntan is fired!"

Tears of joy and justice from those palefaces who had retained their pallor. Gnashing of teeth as the suntans departed.

In the end, after God knows how much expense, including the filming of some of the scripts, the show folded without ever being on the air. I was on my second script by then. The news came to me in my office, which was, literally, a converted pigeon loft on the top

floor of an old house, entered by a stairway in the closet of another
office. A quiet place, except that the pigeons, unaware of the conversion, still returned. I shared it with a friend and colleague, a playwright. Together we were tied in a dead heat for the lowest spot on
the hierarchical totem pole of the English Department of Wesleyan
University. Our windows looked high over the town, the river, the
fields beyond, affording an excellent view of the brick sprawl of
the state insane asylum.

I was called down from out splendid isolation to receive a long
distance call.

OPERATOR:
Is this George Garrett?

GARRETT:
(*grammatical in Dept. Office*)
Yes, this is he.

OPERATOR:
(*to other end*)
That will be sixty-five cents . . .
Clink, clunk, clankety-clank. Sixty-five cents in nickels
and dimes.

OPERATOR:
Go ahead.

VOICE:
George? This is Leo. I gotta talk fast. I'm calling
from the drugstore. They won't let me use the phone
over at the Network. The show is *kaput*. We're all
fired, even the typists. Stop whatever you're doing
and forget it. Don't write another line . . .

Justice? Get serious. A temporary setback. Last I heard Leo
was back again and bigger than ever.

A brief symbolic, all-too-literary episode. A beginning in show
biz.

The chance to write some for pictures came later on, miles more
on my shoes by then, old scars and new knocks. One experience,

most freshly, was of a year of working with the Alley Theater in Houston, the production of two plays—one for children and one (I thought) for grown-ups. I left for Hollywood for the first time immediately after the opening performance of my second play, the one for grown-ups. The excitement of opening night, leaving the cast party to catch the last plane to Los Angeles. Quite pleased and full of myself. Not even daunted by the Agent. He had come down from New York to see the play. After all, a full-length play and a professional production. He had to catch the last plane too, back to New York.

"Well?" I finally asked, glowing with confidence.

"It might go off-Broadway," he said. "Who needs off-Broadway?"

I mention this because I was full of the experience of working with and writing for the stage. To lead myself to the first hard lesson I had to learn, the first generalization about writing for the screen.

Except for the fact that both forms are dramatic, writing for films is very different from writing for the stage.

Very different. At least insofar as our present concept of the stage permits. And here I am speaking of our present *stage* and its conventions, not of the marketplace, its conditions and subjects. Except to say that if one does consider the marketplace, the gap between stage and film is much wider.

To talk, even briefly, of difference, I must begin with some of the similarities. Both involve directed actors speaking lines of dialogue and performing dramatic actions. Meaning that many of the tools are the same. And we can't ignore the simple fact that the structure of the modern three-act play has had a considerable influence on the way a film script is put together. Before talkies the influence would appear to have been much less. But with the introduction of real spoken and heard dialogue the influence became stronger. For one thing a great many playwrights were hired to write pictures. Testimony to this can be found in the files of old scripts in the studios. Frequently they were divided into three acts and so labelled on the typescript. To this day a great many people who make movies or work on movies speak of the structure of a movie in terms of three acts. Asked where he begins work on a script, Billy Wilder has said that he begins with "a good second act curtain."

Yet it is possible to see this, by analogy, as a little like the evolution of the automobile from a horseless carriage with an engine to a thing in itself. Yes, it has wheels and runs something like a carriage, and yes its power is still measured in horsepower. But a car, for better or worse, is not a carriage any more.

Some of the differences between stage and screen help define the screenwriter's job and craft. One of the most obvious differences in the craft is a result of the singular trickery of the film. What is seen and shown, whether large or small, is perfectly controlled. By the camera. When something happens on stage we may look at it and react if we choose, but we don't have to. We can look at the set, at other actors, or anything else. Which means, among other things, that the playwright and/or the director have got to focus audience attention in a different way. One of the simplest problems of drama, getting people on and off stage credibly and reasonably, simply does not exist for the screenwriter. In that medium he need only put the camera on what he wants the audience to see, and all else vanishes. It is in the nature of the rhetoric of the medium that *nothing except what we see (and whatever is evoked by that sight) exists at any given moment.*

From crowded room full of people to close-up on a couple of characters. The crowded room, though the characters may indeed be in it, vanishes.

Once movements and transitions, movement in place or time for example, were emphasized as they have to be on stage. In the older picture, somebody says, "Let's go to the beach." You then have shots of the characters loading gear into a car. Shots of the car going along a road. Shots establishing the sea and shore. Finally we find our characters under an umbrella having a picnic. Logical enough. But a logic of rational motivation derived from the stage—"Come and see the azaleas in the garden."

Now it is not even necessary to prepare for such a transition with dialogue or suggested intention. More likely, to return to that crowded room, the camera shows us a close-up of the characters we are concerned with, the scene ends where it ends in fact and not artificially, and the next instant our characters are under an umbrella on the beach eating cucumber sandwiches.

Supremely economical, swift and easy.

As in stage drama much work by the writer is done by *reaction*. But how easily this is conveyed on film. Something happens or is said. We go immediately to the simple, direct, and usually wordless reaction of a character. And this reaction need not take into account the literal context. That is, boy and girl are talking. Obviously girl is eager to make points with boy. Boy says, "See you around." We need not even see the boy walk away. We can go to close-up of the girl looking disappointed. A look she might not, as an actor or in real life either, allow herself precisely at that second and in his presence. His presence is finished, his departure simply assumed when we see the girl's reaction.

Very simple examples. Ordinary. But they tell us something about the different rhetoric of film and stage. Some of these things are true because the audience has seen so many movies and filmed television shows and has become increasingly sophisticated. A condition compounded by the fact that except for wider screens, sound, different kinds of films, etc., the basic elements of film technique were set and established almost from the beginning. A uniform deck of cards which can be dealt out in a number of combinations. The basic conventions are all there. Knife, fork, and spoon. And what else? Every time you see something that appears to be radically new or different in a movie, chances are that any old-timer can give you a list of precedents for whatever it is, a list as long as your arm. It's pretty safe to say that there are no new techniques, neither in the making of pictures nor in the writing of them. The result is that movies are intricately *conventional*. Highly stylized in the use and arrangement of conventions. As much so as No drama. Perhaps more.

So, inevitably, with time, with experience in making and the corresponding sophistication of the audience, short cuts and simplicity are possible.

But I think that the evolutionary analogy is only partially useful.

For the very characteristics I've mentioned (and will be mentioning) are inherent in the medium and the form. The film is becoming more truly itself. The form is being discovered and rediscovered. And as its singular identity is being discovered it is also being explored and tested.

Moreover, the rhetorical experience of the audience, its side of the dialogue, is quite different in a number of ways. We'd have to admit, I suppose, that both occasions, going to the theater and going to the movies, are unusual, special, ceremonious, different in degree, not kind, these days. With television in the house, with prices high, with the effort of getting out and going to, both are occasions. The theater only more so. The theater experience becoming increasingly rare for many. Both becoming luxuries (remember that in the Depression a part of the relief check was *for* the movies?), but the theater much more so.

Once there, though, and the experience becomes quite different. Both are *group* experiences. Any picture plays better to a full and sympathetic house. But there's a difference in the group experience and reaction. The circumstances, even with the dimming of lights and the old gesture of opening a curtain before the screen, are slightly different. One might be tempted to imagine a kind of passivity not present in a stage performance. After all no two stage performances are quite identical. Whereas the film is set, fixed to the last frame and foot. Nothing will change or happen that has not happened before identically. Nevertheless it is of the magic power of all drama that once in motion and if the original slight spell is cast, it takes a conscious effort of will and mind, a deliberate sort of suppression of the imagination, for the suspense to be dissipated. A second or third time and one is still moved at most of the same places. A condition attested to by the apparent asininity of people who react to animated cartoons and commercials as if they were real events.

There was a moment in one of the old Bob Hope–Bing Crosby *Road* movies where Dorothy Lamour was about to slip out of her celebrated sarong and go for a skinny dip in a calm lagoon. At precisely the instant that the sarong was shucked and Miss Lamour should have been revealed in all her pristine glory, there was a gag shot—a direct cut to a shot of a train whizzing past a crossing. Then back to Miss Lamour now swimming and decently concealed by the waters of the lagoon. As I remember it. I also remember Bob Hope got some mileage out of that moment. Something like: "I've been to see the picture eight times now and I'm going again. Sooner or later that train is bound to be late. . . ."

The absurdity was shared, which is why the joke worked. Something atavistic, childlike, archetypal, call it what you will, the spell and magic of the theater and of drama itself in all forms, takes over. All things are possible even in a film.

We'll come back to Miss Lamour and the locomotive. For now a simple distinction between the rhetoric of film and of stage. On stage there are real people, actors in three dimensions, alive and performing. A different kind of encounter with the audience. It would be difficult (and probably tedious) to explain this, but it seems to me that audiences at a movie react if not more quickly, then with more assurance, than audiences at a play. One finds this in one's own reactions. An example. I once sent students to see the movie of *Long Day's Journey Into Night*. They had not seen the play. The movie seemed to be, on the whole, a pretty faithful adaptation of the play. That may have been the trouble with it—maybe the trouble with any *faithful* adaptation of a play. Their unanimous reaction was that it was very boring because they knew the problem and, to an extent, the secret of each character long before it was revealed. The essence of the play was the striptease of character. The lines and situations were the same. But within the context of *cinematic* experience the characters were revealed to the audience before it was time for revelation. Partly due to cinematic convention. Due also, I think, to the simple human reaction of skepticism and the reservation of judgment in a real and personal encounter.

Though movies are not widely noted for subtlety, much that is subtle on stage can in the cold eye of the camera become blatant and bare.

Back to Dorothy. Another difference of rhetoric. The reason why film-watching is less passive than we are usually told. From my very little experience I have discovered that many people see things that were never on the film, hear lines that were never said (or written), etc. This is merely an exaggeration of the sleight-of-hand rhetoric of the film which is already built in. A gun is fired. A man grabs his chest and falls. Two separate camera shots. Most often the audience simply sees one man shoot another. The heroine starts to unbutton her blouse. The hero observes her. We see his reaction. The implication, the heroine's undressing, is *seen* by most of the audience.

Which is why, in spite of its novelty, the direct scene of nudity, in good taste or bad, is less effective than the scene of implied nudity. Point being that a large part of the experience of a movie is imaginative. The audience sees things, makes relationships. The very skillful director, say Alfred Hitchcock, builds his art on the maximum imaginative involvement of the audience, building, working and, if possible, controlling the utmost imaginative involvement. Ironically, this seems to be especially difficult when the subject matter is close to the audience, when it is most *true* and personal. Then group response is dissipated in favor of memory, the individual imagination. Often people (even critics) seem to see a hundred different versions of a single scene.

Which may be why the admirable Mr. Hitchcock prefers to avoid certain kinds of serious subject matter in favor of his fables of suspense.

Difference between the James Bond movies and *The Spy Who Came In from the Cold*. Two ways to work within the same genre.

Which is also why the writer must, from the outset, exercise extreme care and all his craft in scenes and situations which come very close to the life and problems of his audience, to "reality."

It is easier to get away with murder when there is a little "aesthetic distance."

Some of the other basic differences from the stage. Films are very much more a drama of *reaction*. To have reaction we have to have, in the context of any given scene, a witness, more or less reliable, in any case known. We can either believe the witness or we can judge his reaction by what we know of him. First a witness is established.

Something happens which he sees happen as we do. We then see his reaction. His reaction tells us about him and is a guide to, a control of, chorus-like sometimes, the reactions of the audience. This is much the same thing as, in fiction, the device critics call *point of view*. Except that it may change swiftly from scene to scene.

Maybe Hitchcock was right when he said the *literary* form most analagous to the movie was the short story. In any case, in spite of various kinds and conventions of breaks and transitions, a movie is a continuous and uninterrupted experience. The old three-act structure of the play may be helpful to directors and some writers, but it is not a form that is explicit and discernible. Thus does not really function within the film.

No one has suggested seriously what I sometimes think of as the closest literary analogy to the screenplay. A type, probably the most widely used and known, of modern poem. The contemporary lyric which consists of (quite aside from subject, form, ostensible theme) an initial statement of images, followed by the development, exploitation, and rearrangement of those images in various combinations, ending with some final rearrangement, valid within the context of the poem. The images themselves need not be rational and the logic of their arrangement may be exclusively imaginative, a "poetic" logic. A movie differs in being group rhetoric (only one person can experience a poem or book at a time), in having to be, by virtue of its collaborative creation, supremely rational. Yet the organization and architecture is often quite like that of the prevailing mode of a modern lyric poem. It is possible that poets would make the best screenwriters.

Another big difference from the stage play. The use of dialogue. More on this later. For now a general rule: A very little bit of dialogue, even good talk, goes a long way in a movie. Speeches which seem quite long are, in fact, brief to extremity when compared with stage dialogue.

First Agent I met in Hollywood. West Coast representative of the one in New York. Took me for a ride in his flashy new sports car. Said: "One thing you gotta learn. This is a business. Art is for kids."

Later, one gray dawn, I walked past a huge economy gas station. Where you save not only on quality of the gas, but by automation. You put exact change in meter at pump and fill the tank yourself. Huge concrete apron was empty that morning. Save for one flashy sports car. And the Agent filling it up.

I wished him a cheery hello. Evidently he didn't recognize me.

Not how to begin, but why.

Why at this late stage in this day and age does the schoolteacher-writer go to work writing for pictures? I wish I could say it was for money. In a sense it was, though the money was never standard or enough to do more than pay a few overdue bills. This is not, really, however personal it may be, my story. In the brief experience of working on half a dozen different projects, I had enough of the course to earn my wound stripes. I've been sued and threatened, been given bad checks, been hired and fired, been screwed, blued, and tattooed. But I had read the novels. I wasn't surprised. My Agent friend was quite right. It is very much of a business, not a very good one or a sound one or a genteel one or a sensible one for anybody concerned, but a business is what it is. Fellini's $8\frac{1}{2}$ gives an excellent and accurate peek at the whole chaos and confusion. It's not the business part that is interesting. It is the art or craft. And my subject is the screen-writer's part. A very small, but completely essential part of the immense collaboration and compromise and adjustment which goes into making a movie.

It seems first of all important to realize and recognize the nature of the making process, to be aware of it and indeed to a degree to depend on it, making collaboration the key. The collaborative parts, from the beginning, are multiplied far beyond the necessary collaboration of the stage. You have to know this and expect it. You have to know in some way and to some degree the nature of the job of many other people. But not too much. The writer must urgently avoid, for his own sake, intruding upon their precincts. Too many writers become completely fascinated by technicque, the technique of others especially. They want to *write* something. Something which can be handed to technicians and translated into film and projected on the screen. This wish, a natural one for any maker who's used to being his own boss, goes directly against the grain of the medium and the process of making. What is really needed is something that, like the relation of the finished movie to the audience, will evoke the maximum imaginative response from the other collaborators—artists, craftsmen, and technicians. Not just imaginative involvement. Also, if possible, imaginative contribution.

There are two rules I heard from old-timers which bear repeating. *If it isn't in the script, it won't be there.* The skeleton is the script. They can decorate, elaborate, bring to life, sometimes make the ordinary seem marvelous and strange, but all is at least suggested by the script. They can greatly expand it, but can never really strike out for territory beyond the border of the script.

The other: *If any of us got 60 per cent of what we were trying for, it would be the greatest picture ever made.*

The collaborative craft is like politics. Art of the possible. Choices are seldom clear-cut. Losses are frequent. Give and take. The lesser of two evils.

Still, everybody is trying.

Another: *Nobody ever tries to make a bad picture.*

In short, someone and several someones are *responsible* for every bad picture.

The odds against a good picture, just by the nature of the process of making, are enormous.

Secretary at Studio. Always a very neat and classy dresser. More East Coast than Hollywood, but always something to behold.

ME:

You look wonderful. I sure do like your clothes.

HER:

Thank you. Unlike *some* girls around this office,
I *never* wear stolen goods.

Stolen goods.
Movies, like poetry again, are a parisitical art. For better or worse

and inevitably. For worse when, with calculation and deliberation but not much thought, the second string comes along and tries to cash in on a recent success. Cf. *Moll Flanders* and *Tom Jones*. Cf. a host of spy and secret agent stories bouncing along in the groovy wake of the James Bond movies.

For better when, at the outset, those who are making the picture are aware of the genre to which the picture belongs, are aware of successes and failures within that genre and are able to build skillfully upon the audience's expectations of that particular genre. I.e., *The Bridge Over the River Kwai* is a "wartime prison camp" movie. There have been good ones and bad ones, from *The Grand Illusion* on. However they did it, those who made the good ones managed to build on that tradition using the best things, eliminating some of the mistakes others had made. The originality of *The Bridge on the River Kwai* was its skillful use of conventions.

There are two great dangers of any art form which is essentially conventional. By convention I mean a gesture that works. A cliché is an habitual and thoughtless gesture which no longer works because it no longer means anything. The first great danger is ignorance. Pictures fall in many genres. Critically, perhaps because of our romantic hangover, we like to pretend in the literary arts that genres do not exist. They do, though, in all literary forms. So with the screenplay and with the final polished product of that raw material. In screenwriting the risk of the newcomer is innocence and ignorance. The other danger, more manifest in the work of the experienced old-timer, is the weary use of the habitual. The convention becomes cliché in his hands just because it is simple and expedient.

There is a possible third danger. Too much sophistication. Knowing much too much about the form and also knowing too much to be satisfied with cliché. And caring too much to be safe and cynical. For the film-maker this is paralysis. Pathetic. He cannot even be a critic.

The screenwriter is a laborer in the corporate setup. The making of movies, a twentieth-century art form, invariably reflects the complex, hierarchical, and corporate world. Screenwriters have a union.

They have to. I remember an old-time screenwriter I was very fond of who died of a heart attack in a little men's shop in New York. He had slipped across the street from his hotel to buy a shirt, wearing perfectly decent, casual West Coast clothes at the time and, as it happened, without any identification on his person. Nobody knew him. The cops, after stealing his wristwatch, slapped him in the morgue, labelled as "Unidentified Laborer." True enough. He was one of the founders of the Screenwriters Guild, and I like to think that label might have pleased him.

No two screenplays are exactly alike in form or in stages of development. However, it is possible to describe the basic stages in a simplified outline, abstract enough to predicate only one writer. Which is rare enough.

In the beginning, *somebody,* sometimes a Very Distinguished Director, more often a Producer, the corporate chief, has an "idea." Usually based upon a "property." Novel, play, article, non-fiction book, newspaper story, or what have you. Possibly he had the "idea" before the "property."

Here a couple of parenthetical things need to be said. Only Very Successful Writers are permitted to have "ideas." And there are and always will be very, very few "originals," if by that term we mean a screenplay written of itself out of whole cloth by a writer and then duly submitted and circulated among Producers. Most so-called "originals" start as "ideas" with Producers. "Ideas" without a relevant "property" at hand. At least the Producer has to think this is so. Producer likes to feel he is "a creative person" too. Two: why bother with the acquisition of a "property"? I'm not sure I fully understand this. It is done. One of the reasons advanced is that it is a protection, staking a quick claim on a particular subject matter, in lieu of a copyright. Which can't be had until the job is finished. Another, probably more honest one, is that the Producer wants backing, money, distribution, etc. as early as he can possibly get it. He can, with luck, sometimes get these things solely with a "property."

A very large part of screenwriting, then, consists of writing a screenplay "based on" or "adapted from" something else. Usually a novel. Usually, if the "property" is a "classic," his job is much like that of a good translator. Otherwise he is free—and should be—to adapt this raw material as ruthlessly and independently as need be.

In the latter case his relative independence is assured. For most Producers have Readers. The Readers boil down the book to a synopsis. The busy Producer most often begins there, with the synopsis. If he is genuinely interested, he may read the work and he may not.

There's an old story that goes with this. Story is that when Peter Lorre first came to this country and did his first, successful picture, he was asked by The Big Boss what he wanted to do next. He suggested *Crime and Punishment*. Boss said: "Gimme a one-page synopsis and we'll see." Lorre looked around studio until he found a near moron working in the accounting office. Offered the man fifty bucks if he could deliver a one-page synopsis of *Crime and Punishment* the next day. Just skimming, hitting the high spots. Done. The synopsis read like an old-fashioned thriller (truth in that). Boss read it and, in those days when the Industry was prospering and they were making four or five times as many pictures as they do now (though no more *good* ones), Boss said to get started. Picture was almost finished before Boss got around to reading the "property" and realized, raging, he had been had.

Enough. The contemporary Boss, more like a corporation president than the pirates and robber barons of the early days, acquires a "property" and hires a writer. He, of course, wants a writer who's interested and who *cares*. A little hard to establish since all unemployed screenwriters care.

Several stages follow. The writer does a brief synopsis. This is prosy, yet associative and connotative. One of the last, the next to last, chances he has to use the full resources of language. In form, though, it must *seem* to be at least possibly dramatic. Able to be seen and acted. Most important is that it states in rough form the ostensible aim and subject of the picture.

Next comes the "treatment." Treatments vary widely in form and substance. In essence, though, they are detailed outlines, in ordinary prose, though a dramatic scene sketch or two may be thrown in, of the sequence and order of the picture. Structure, characters, motivation, etc. All these are dealt with. In one sense, the treatment is, if it is right, the last "creative" act of the writer. There is truth in the old notion that unless the treatment is right, the film won't be right. That almost inevitably flaws and missing links in the treatment will reappear firmly in the finished picture. Those producers who believe this may require a number of revisions of the treatment.

Then begins the first draft stage of the screenplay. Here, if the treatment is complete enough and right, the job is basically a mechanical translation of the treatment into numbered "master scenes" (somewhere around three hundred scenes is about average), which are a kind of score of the basic shots of the picture. It is often these days written in abstraction from a particular cast, exact budget limitations, etc.

Here a word or two is important. The screenwriter does indeed create scenes and shots and transitions. These may be in considerable detail—though at the risk of being virtually unreadable, and the script at this stage is still intended to be *read* and, hopefully, understood by actors and the other craftsmen involved. Still the screenwriter has to remember that even in the simplest, low-budget picture the scene he has written will be shot by a Cameraman at least five times for keeps from five different angles to insure adequate "coverage." That these rough cut versions will go into the hands of that most important figure, the Cutter (Film Editor) who, with the Director, ultimately responsible for all things, will rearrange the scene visually in such a way, hopefully, as to gain maximum value from the scene, the acting, etc. What the writer has created, even though he uses numbered shots and indicates type and kind of transition, is what it is called, a "master scene." Point being that other than suggesting a tone and rhythm, he has no business doing the job of the Cameraman, the Cutter, or, for that matter, the Director, in advance. Each of his scenes and shots should be *functional dramatically*. If there is no *reason* whatsoever to make a particular shot or transition in the script, better forget it. There had better be a reason, for he will be asked to explain why by everybody all along the line.

Assuming the first draft is workable and acceptable (rare), an elaborate process of revision begins. So many reasons for and kinds of revision that the whole process might be called one big Revision. Large and small changes are constant. Not necessarily in this order, for several things are apt to be happening at once. Actors are cast. Sometimes there are intensive advance rehearsals, sometimes not. In any case, the demands of the script must be at least adjusted to account for the strengths and limitations of the particular actors. As in the theater the Director begins to exercise his influence and talent. The Cutter may already have suggestions. A transition which looks fine on paper simply will not work or, conversely, is unnecessary and redundant. Sets are being built and locations found for exterior shooting. Action and dialogue must now fit into a particular place.

Why so many sets for interior scenes? Why not simply make a location out of somebody's living room? Sometimes this is done, but a large element of control is missing. Chances of lighting, sound, and everything else being right on location are poor. Too many variable factors. More time, more trouble, more expense. Moreover, ironically, because of the tricks of the camera, a real location is often likely to look more like a phony set than a phony set.

Budget and the person of the Production Manager, the top sergeant of the whole enterprise, begin to be influential. Budget can be a helpful control of the game, like a tennis net or the sonnet form. But it can require adjustments. Example: in one picture I worked on there was simply not enough money left to build two sets. One removal was a dramatic gain (I think); it also cost me two characters who appeared only in that scene. The other was more serious. We had a hallway but not the living room for a number of important scenes. I had to find a way to have all the living room scenes played in the hall. The results were rather odd and unsatisfactory.

Today, following the example and lead of Hitchcock, a great many pictures make use of *continuity sketches,* made by an artist or the Art Director. In essence these translate the script into a kind of advanced comic strip version. They are chiefly a suggested visual rendering of the script. Here, too, there are many possibilities for revision. New things, new problems develop and have to be solved.

A process of continual change. The custom is to indicate these changes by new colored pages in the script—red, blue, yellow, etc. So that often a final shooting script is as rainbow-colored as Joseph's coat. Some Producers and Directors have found that this method, while expedient, has an awkward psychological effect on cast and crew. Even if the changes are minor, the effect is of a very unsettled script. Another *Cleopatra*? These men prefer not to use the colored pages and, no matter how many changes and revisions are actually involved, operate under the pretense that the script is fixed and set once and for all. Of course, the cast and crew know this is not true, but the slight fraud is reassuring.

Finally the so-called final shooting script.

Here we have an interesting example which is readily available— *Tom Jones*. Faber and Faber published Osborne's final shooting script. Grove Press published a script based upon the finished movie. The differences may seem fairly large to the uninitiated. In fact the two scripts are quite close, surprisingly so. Much has been cut, rearranged in sequence, added as well. The general and obvious movement has been away from the verbal and toward the visual. Which is the whole process of *re*vision. When something can be or is shown visually, then the supporting words become not just superfluous, but redundant. Redundancy and repetition are the mortal diseases of the movie. It must move, by definition. Ideally, each scene and each action and each line must move forward and with one kind of suspense or another must keep the audience interested and alert.

This means a number of things to the writer. For example, most dialogue is *not* realistic. In the sense that real conversation usually begins with *reaction* to what has just been said, then explanation or elaboration. But that is looking backwards to the last line. And, if you *begin* with reaction, the suspense of what-will-the-reaction-be is dissipated. Thus screen dialogue is ideally artificial. It tries to avoid the "backlash," going back to what has already been said, even in the form of a question. It becomes pseudo-inductive, in the sense that it reverses the normal order of reaction, arriving at a reaction at the end of the line (s). And ideally it ends looking forward, with something new suggested or a demand being made for yet another reaction. *Two:* the problem of knowledge of the audience. Difficult to explain. . . . If, on stage, a private conversation takes place, out of the hearing and knowledge of a character, then some device is usually employed to indicate how that character acquired knowledge of that conversation. Such repetition does not seem to hurt anything on stage. In films, however, it appears to be disastrous to stop the action to recapitulate knowledge or to explain how someone who was not there happens to know something. *Unless, of course, the knowledge itself is vital to the plot.* As, for example, in a whodunit. A rule of thumb for the screenwriter is simply to allow the characters to know everything that the audience does, whether this is credible or not. Somehow the effect of permitting the character to explain his knowledge credibly not only causes the movement to slow down, but tends to make the character appear slow-witted. There is an assumption that somehow the characters share all information and knowledge with the audience.

Back to that script. For all practical purposes the writer is done. Revision is not over and done with, though. Directors and actors revise this and that as they go along. Sometimes wisely and well. Cutter and Director revise the rough cuts. A whole scene, for example, might be unnecessary if the point of the scene is to create an effect or reaction or decision by a character and if the actor's facial expression or some "business" makes this point explicitly. Or some fancy cutting and real inventiveness may be required for the scene where, for some reason, the actors did not manage to convey the essence and point of the scenes in lines, actions, or expression.

A problem often. Since many of the minor actors never see anything of a script except "sides," the pages where they are involved, out of sequence and without knowledge of what comes before or after or what the movie is "about."

The writer, of course, cannot anticipate brilliant acting. He must write the scene fully and in such a way that its point will come across even if it is not well played.

Revision goes on constantly at every stage. During the writing. During the filming. During the editing, which is usually a period of time roughly equivalent to the time spent shooting the picture. And even afterwards. The Composer enters the process. Music is created, scored, played, and eventually, with other sound effects, "mixed." Sometimes the music, if it is good, can cause further cutting. Functionally used (rare) music can make points and establish values in addition to reinforcing the drama of the film. Then previews. The test. The effect on an audience. Mistakes show up, unintended effects are glaring. Example. In *Man With a Gun* (which became, in the East-West game of revising other people's movies, the model for *Yojimbo*) Samuel Goldwyn, Jr., decided to play the final showdown offstage. A mild novelty in a western. It would be played on the reaction of the townspeople. Robert Mitchum, the good guy, goes into the Saloon for the final showdown. The townspeople (and the audience) wait anxiously outside. A fusillade of shots is heard. Someone falls down noisily. Then the swinging doors open and Mitchum comes out, clutching himself, looking bad. "I've been shot," he says. The preview audiences broke up in laughter. That could be cut and fixed.

Sometimes, more often than one might think, some reshooting is necessary to save a picture after a preview. There's a story about Billy Wilder, probably apochryphal, but legend enough to be accepted. Seems that very early in the game, over here, he was hired to fix up a finished and previewed picture. One with glittering international setting, charm, and, they suddenly noticed, no suspense whatsoever. He was hired to "put in some suspense"—and to do it very cheaply. His solution: Two characters in formal dress (who could be inserted anywhere) talking. One says to the other: "Things seem to be going along marvelously." The other: "Maybe, but have you seen the Turkish Ambassador?" Cut to: A close shot of the Turkish Ambassador. Very sinister man up to no good. That's all. The Turkish Ambassador Ploy. It worked. The picture had changed subtly and was a success.

Cutting, rearrangement, various kinds of revision are possible even after a picture has gone into release. Sometimes, not often, as a result of legitimate reaction by critics.

All these possibilities of revision offer much chance for polish and improvement, offer a multitude of choices. Also dangers. The danger at any stage is to become so fascinated by the possibilities as to lose the initial image, vision, or purpose. For the writer this means that he must be ready, willing, and able to change at any time, provided that the change is an improvement, that it adds and does not detract from the initial creation—the treatment.

The same rule applies to all the others. The odds against it being faithfully followed are large.

Sign on small, modern building—rather like a branch bank in a shopping center—near my Hollywood motel: "Drive-In Music Publisher."

Technique. Something that bugs the new screenwriter. He's apt to become obsessed with it. The general form and format can be learned from the example of almost any script. Within that format his writing problems—creating character, action, dialogue, dramatizing, making outward and visible signs, creating a structure for the whole—are *writing* problems, regardless of the medium.

What else does the writer have to know? Other than some knowledge, firsthand if possible (but even this is not absolutely necessary), of the parts and process. He ought to bring to his writing an awareness of the three basic shots: Close, Medium, and Long. Which are exactly what they say. He might be aware of the possibilities of High Angle and Low Angle. Which are what they say. And even though it is the Editor and not the writer who will have the last word on this, he should know something, I think, about the three basic kinds of transitions, from one shot or "master scene" to the next. This knowledge is useful because most writers I know of worry about transitions, about getting from here to there.

There are only three basic kinds of transitions (and variations thereof) used in films to indicate transition of time or space, or both. These are the Fade, the Dissolve, and the Cut. In the Fade the image disappears and the screen goes black. It is a real interruption in the sequence. Quite as formidable as the curtain coming down in a theater. For that reason it was and still is often used in much the same ways as a curtain ending an act. There is always a risk that it may break the spell; for in fact everything does stop. A Dissolve is the name given to a lab process whereby one image begins to blur and fade out while being replaced by another image simultaneously coming into focus. It is graceful, orderly, logical; a rational change. The Cut is direct and instantaneous.

Once upon a time the Cut was used for very slight changes only.

A man approaches a door. Cut. He is coming through the door from the other side. Dissolves were once used, like scene curtains, to indicate a real change of scene, time, or space. For a number of reasons, however, these practices and the meaning of the conventions themselves have changed. One is ironic commentary on how the experience of moviegoing changes the audience. After World War II, when foreign pictures began to become popular over here, it was noticeable that foreign pictures used the Dissolve very sparingly. There was a *reason* for this. At that time the lab process was prohibitively expensive in most foreign countries. They had no choice but to use direct Cuts where Dissolves might have been used. The effect, at first, was a little jagged and startling. It became associated with Art. The American audience became accustomed to the device. Our filmmakers made use of it and the audience's expectations. Meanwhile Europe recovered. Picture-making over there became Big Business. They now use Dissolves with reckless abandon, for "production value." (A term meaning obvious largesse, free spending.) Now, on the other hand, American picture-makers tend to use direct Cuts like crazy.

Aside from accidents of fashion and association, though, these basic means of transitions imply something. The Fade is for big moments, chiefly endings and beginnings. The Dissolve obviously implies an orderly universe, one of cause and effect, of graceful and sometimes subtle relationships. The Cut is still a little jagged, a sudden and harsh, often illogical transition. It can suggest the speed, disorder, and discontinuity of the world we live in.

Time: I think very little has been understood about the use of time in a motion picture. There is no time outside of that seen by and experienced by the audience. Unless a clock is being used functionally for purposes of suspense, as in *High Noon* or *The Set Up*, there is no sense of real time or the passage of time in a movie. There is only a continuous present. There is no way to measure it except as rhythm. Some scenes in context seem slow or lyrical. Others may seem jazzy and quick. Frequently these scenes will involve exactly the same number of feet of film and, thus, an identical running time. It is the *context* which creates the effect of rapidity or graceful flow.

More about dialogue. Ideally, dialogue should never be redundant, comment on observed action, or repeat information. Also, dialogue should be used very sparingly to make *plot points.* These points will be lost. Certainly dialogue can characterize. Another possible dimension, used but still not fully exploited, is the use of dialogue functionally, *against the grain* of the situation and the observed action. Which is simply to build upon certain known and valuable practices. For example, a funny character shouldn't be conscious (not in a film) that he is funny. Nor should other characters in the story react with amusement if the intention is to move the *audience* to laughter. The audience, not the other characters, should be allowed to laugh at the character's funny lines or actions. Point of view is one thing, but explicitly seeming to direct the audience response is quite another. The audience resists being told how it should feel.

Therefore the great potential function of dialogue is ironic. A counterpoint to action.

Short of that, Hitchcock may be right (again) where he says that the only dialogue we should hear is what we would have heard in silent pictures, when the characters mouths were moving. A safe rule. Even though all actors do dearly love to talk.

One other rule. Never permit a character to say: "I don't know what to say." This is a sure sign that there isn't anything to be said and no dialogue is necessary.

A chewing out. A line in a script of mine, a line in which one character on departing is supposed to assure another that he'll return soon. The line, as written, "I'll be back before you can say . . . Rumpelstiltskin." Producer reacts, upon reading.

PRODUCER:

What's with this name, this Rumplewhatsis?

ME:

Oh, nothing. Just a smart aleck way of saying "I'll be back before you know it." Of course, there's a

little dramatic irony there. And then we have this
fairy tale motif running through. . . .

PRODUCER:

(*interrupting*)
What kind of a name is that? What nationality?

ME:

Oh . . . It's a character from a famous fairy tale.

PRODUCER:

Jesus Christ, Garrett! I'm paying you for original
work and you give me fairy tales!

There is one area of film-making that is much debated by the
makers of films. I think the debate is a little silly.

Among the more conservative makers of movies, including some
very good ones, there is a kind of absolute rule that essential to the
magic spell of the picture is the sleight of hand necessary to prevent
the audience from ever being reminded that it is watching a picture.
This is a little like the Flaubert-James-Lubbock notion of fiction
still widely held by editors in publishing houses. That the author
should never intrude or the artifice of the story show. It's hopeless
to argue that the audience is fully aware that it is in the theater
observing a movie, just as a man reading a book knows that he is
reading a book. That truth will never convince them.

And we should give the devil his due. There are a goodly number
of stories and a goodly number of kinds of movies that depend, for
the magic to work, upon this kind of pretense. A shared ritual.
There are also many kinds of movies for which this sort of pseudo-
credibility is completely wrong. One can be gloriously "conscious of
the Camera" in the right context.

Any rules of the game will work, provided they are introduced
at the outset (cf. Fellini's *8½* or *Juliet of the Spirits*) in the first five
minutes or so. While the spell is taking effect. Cheating in pictures
is purely and simply the violation of the stated and self-imposed
rules of the beginning.

As always, the problem is to find the right form and genre for the story and subject. Sometimes this is easy. It's built-in. At other times it's a process of trial and error.

I've been told that the original idea and version of the script for *Cat Ballou* was, by intention, a serious Western. That didn't work.

Anecdote of the word.

A few days before the Producer of a script I was working on had turned the script over to his financial backers. If they liked it, we'd go ahead. If not, the end. A couple of days of waiting for a phone call. Then the call came. The Producer was jubilant.

PRODUCER:

Genius, baby, they love it! We got the money. Away we go!

ME:

Did they have any other comments?

PRODUCER:

Well, they did say your script has got a lot of— verisimilitude.

ME:

Oh . . .

PRODUCER:

(*after a pause, seriously*)
Verisimilitude . . . is that good?

Some basic economics.

We Americans are only making one third as many features as we did twenty years ago. To make any picture, at home or abroad, is now fantastically expensive. You could make four or five pictures before World War II for what it costs now to make an average picture. Distribution of pictures is confused, chaotic, and irrational. Apparently beyond control. Of the pictures made, a few, a very few indeed, turn a big profit for the investors. It has been estimated that 75 per cent of the features made fail to make back their cost. They lose money.

In short, it's a very bad business. Oddly enough, this is true at a time when more people go to see movies and are interested in movies than ever before.

There may be some solutions, but it's sure to get worse before it gets better.

All of which adds up to one important fact for the writer. There is less chance than ever before of getting to write a picture. And less chance to learn by doing, to experiment, take chances, etc. Once upon a time a "serious" writer could, if he could stand the heat in the kitchen, supplement his income and not do anybody any serious harm by doing some work for Hollywood. Faulkner did, and he did a good job, too.

That possibility seems much less likely now. Except for a very, very few.

The Academy may not pay much and the groves of academe may not be the best soil and climate for a writer, but at the moment at least, Hollywood is Death Valley.

No hard feelings. Just the facts.

The truth is that whether we write movies or make movies or not, none of us is really innocent or ignorant of the art. We share a great deep reservoir of common experience. We have all been to the movies so many times. The movies are our most familiar medium, perhaps *the* medium of this century. We go out to the movies and now we see countless films (interrupted by countless commericals) on the boob tube. When I think of all the ways I have killed time, I realize that I have probably spent a very large portion of that lost time pleasurably sitting in a darkened theater watching the long gold shaft of light from the projection booth splash bright images on a blank screen, images which by a process of magic and imagination, as old as human consciousness, older probably than the cave paintings of the earliest humans we know of, become briefly and sometimes unforgettably a real and dimensional world to live in. It goes back to Saturday mornings in the heart of the Depression when the *Rialto* theater offered two features, a serial, and plenty of cartoons for any kid with a nickel. I could have learned things about screenwriting then, I suppose. For example, I could have learned then how unimportant most dialogue is. Because from that first wonderful moment when the lights dimmed and went out until much later when the show was suddenly all over and we went out, a little sad and subdued for once, went outside blinking in the strange harshness of daylight in what we were told was the real world and real life, from the first to the last, we couldn't possibly have heard a dozen lines for all the whooping and hollering, all the wisecracks and whistling, the crinkling of candy-bar wrappers and Cracker Jack boxes, the rattle of popcorn bags. Nobody minded a bit. And if we really missed anything, you can't prove it by me.

The movies have gone on, continued, and moviegoing is a common experience for us. Of course the movies change as the times do. Now that I have children of my own who go to the movies and watch TV, I have a curious nostalgia for those first, early days. But I can live with it.

There's something happening now, too. As a college teacher I can see at least part of it in my students. I notice that, given something he knows well and cares about, he can bring a very high degree of intelligence and sophistication to bear on the subject. The college student of the 1960's hasn't read all the books he ought to have read. His perceptions and his remarks on *Sir Gawain and the Green Knight* or *Paradise Regained* or *Moby Dick* often are terrifying in primitive simplicity, and in the almost complete lack of awareness of relation between classic literature and his real life. Yet, more often than not, that same student can write and talk as well as any professional critic on the subject of *8½* or *Goldfinger* or *The Knack*. Show any movie on any lively college campus and watch a crowd form. Which means real interest in their literature. I think and hope we will see more teachers leading from strength, using the sources of knowledge and interest. Before long, I believe, we are going to see movies widely used in the teaching of the liberal arts.

Doing a little screenwriting hasn't hurt my teaching at all.

What about the writer? The effect is less tangible. It's a tough experience to see your mistakes, when they are your very own, recorded on celluloid. It isn't all that much fun to hear your lines over and over again, through the whole process. The few good ones get old fast and the bad ones get worse, louder, and much more obvious. I've read the reviews and learned that I will never be bugged by a newspaper or magazine review again. If it's a rave, it's for all the wrong reasons. And I have yet to see a constructive or even useful negative review. And I've learned again what every good writer in every form has always said, a thing which somehow one tries all too long to deny. There is no way in any form, even a bastard and collaborative craft like screenwriting, no way to be sure, insured, secure, no way to play it safe. You have to give what you have and do all that you can. Then you take the lumps and the consequences for it. Without excuses. Well, nobody else can take your lumps for you. That's your pride and your privilege.

Would I do it again, if the chance came along? Yes. . . . Because I am always broke and always curious. Surely *next* time I go to Hollywood somebody will tell me where the orgy is. And like everybody else these days I feel like I've got a million ideas for writing movies. Wonderful things are happening. Just when it seemed the picture show would go the way of vaudeville, burlesque, radio, and the fan dance, new and old ways of doing movies are being discovered and rediscovered. For the first time people of my generation, the ones who grew up at the picture show, are getting a chance to do something about it.

Of course it can never, ever be the same thing as a novel, a story, or a poem. It is something else, but there is always at least the hope or the illusion that it can be better than it is or has been.

Best of all, it beats working for Leo and writing for TV. As long as you don't take it too seriously. . . .

Which may be the final problem. Perhaps I don't *care* enough. Maybe no writer can.

Which leads straight into a final anecdote. The anecdote of caring. . . .

One time a Producer asked me out to his manse for a swim and dinner. Good enough. It was an improvement over the idea of a long evening in a crummy motel near the studio.

We drive out to the place, see? Great big, huge place. He parks the

XKE and we stroll inside. His handsome wife greets us with (in James Thurber's phrase) many a loud goddamn. Mad and skittish as an ant in a hot skillet. I mean, burning up about something.

"Oh well," says he, "She's having a mood. Let's have a swim."

The pool is cool and clear and gloriously located. Imagine that—a pool with a view. He's pretty glorious too, smoothly backstroking up and down the pool. Suntanned and fit. Takes good care of himself.

After a while a Governess brings four little children, lined up in order of descending height, from left to right, in identical pajamas and bathrobes. Also at the tag end a fat old dog. They have lined up to say hello and good night to Daddy, the Producer, who is still busily backstroking. Suddenly the wife appears. Silent now. No loud goddamns. A wild smile. A glint in eye. Swiftly on tiptoes she comes up behind them and, with deftly placed boot in the butt, kicks them all, kids and dog, all except the Governess, ass over teakettle into the pool. She goes away, still smiling, amid cries and consternation. It seems that three of them and the top-heavy dog can't swim. The Governess either.

I manage, gulping a lot of chlorined water, to get the kids out and over the side of the pool. The frantic dog is more of a problem. But I manage somehow and manage to get myself thoroughly scratched and clawed in the process. I hang onto the edge of the pool and watch the Governess, like a mother hen, hurry the brood back to the house for dry clothes. Then I hear a splash behind me. Turning. . . .

There he is, still doing his backstroke laps smoothly. Did he miss the whole thing?

As he passes by he smiles and speaks without once breaking the rhythm.

PRODUCER:

That was a great little piece of business. Remind me to use it in my next picture.

FADE OUT.

Faulkner in Hollywood

William Faulkner stepped off the train at Union Station in Los Angeles one day in the first week of May, 1932. Short and compact, he was dressed in tweeds and puffing one of the ever-present pipes. The striking face was already familiar from the photographs and caricatures: the short, iron-gray hair and moustache, the bent hawk-nose, and the piercing brown-black eyes. The journey had started in Oxford, Mississippi, where the inspiration had come and the work had been done for most of the large body of writing already behind him. It comprised a book of verse, a volume of short stories, six novels and a seventh in manuscript—all this in less than eight years.

Now, at age thirty-four, he was going to try a form new and strange to him: William Faulkner was going to write for the movies.

The creator of Yoknapatawpha County, from the early 1930's the most famous of Mississippi's sons, was to spend a total of nearly four years in California working for various studios. This time was accumulated during a period of twenty-two years in often painful sojourns of varying lengths: four weeks for one producer in one year, a thirteen-week stint at a studio in another, forty-four consecutive weeks in still another year, and so on. Why did he do it—the most fertile and creative of American writers in this century? What came of this forced transplanting that never really took, and how did he feel about it? And what, finally, did the balance sheet show—how much had he gained, and how much had he (and American letters) lost?

One of the answers is simple and direct. The American public never bought enough of William Faulkner's books to support him and his family until a few years before the Nobel Prize crowned his achievement in 1950. He was chronically in need of money, and in Hollywood from time to time he could earn it. The work itself, as compared with the anguishing that went into most of his novels, was slight; it was the expense of spirit that was costly for Faulkner, who wanted above all to be a serious artist.

During his career as a scenarist his name was listed in the screen credits for six films, all but one done under his friend producer-director Howard Hawks. (The best known, of course, were made from Ernest Hemingway's *To Have and Have Not* and Raymond Chandler's *The Big Sleep*.) A closer estimate, according to studio records and other evidence, is that William Faulkner worked on no less than forty-four film "properties," plus a few more turned out with collaborators on speculation but never bought by a studio. (This is a conservative figure; he may well have done more. Attribution of screen credit is still a complex process which can involve arbitration and negotiation by the Screenwriters' Guild—and during Faulkner's time it was even more loose and flexible.) The forty-four separate film projects, usually employing more than one writer, included finished movies and scripts that never got close to a camera. (Now, as then, a large percentage of scripts remain unproduced.) They ranged from half-page synopses to two-hundred-page screenplays. Over the years between Faulkner's first film work in 1932 and his last in 1954 his earnings from screenwriting were probably between $140,000 and $150,000—before the 10 per cent agents' commissions (sometimes, because of self-induced mix-ups, paid not to one but *two* agents), before income taxes, and before the expenses of maintaining two households: one for his family in Mississippi (he was clan chief for the other Faulkners too) and one for himself in California. The net, whatever it was, could hardly have been an inordinate return for his labors. The proceeds from sales of the movies rights to seven of his works were another thing. They approached the total from the screenwriting, but the larger sums came only from the time of *Intruder in the Dust* in 1948, when the need was no longer quite so acute.

Most of Faulkner's time was spent in the writers' buildings of three studios: Metro-Goldwyn-Mayer, Twentieth Century–Fox, and Warner Brothers. When he was in Hollywood, the power was concentrated in the hands of Irving Thalberg at MGM, Darryl Zanuck at Fox, and Jack Warner on the lot he and his brothers built. And they all were distinctly aware that Faulkner was there in their employ. In 1932 he spent three months of the spring and summer and nearly two months of the fall at MGM in dusty Culver City, south of Los Angeles. He returned to the West Coast in December, three years later, this time to work for Fox intermittently but for most of 1936 and on into 1937. He was unassigned for several weeks, but it was August before he was off the studio payroll and on his way back to where he wanted to be: Rowan Oak, the antebellum home he had bought and restored in his home town of Oxford. His days at Warner Brothers, north of Los Angeles in Burbank, began in July of 1942. Except for a month's leave at Christmas, the assignment stretched out for more than a year. He was back in February of 1944, departing once again in time to celebrate Christmas at home in Mississippi. He returned for a three-month assignment the following summer, but it was his last prolonged stay in Hollywood. He had done one job in July of 1934 for Universal, and in April and May of 1936 he had worked at RKO, but his long-term service had been with MGM, Fox, and Warner Brothers, in that order.

Through the varied assignments had run a strong linking thread—

his friendship with Howard Hawks. Scarcely back from Stockholm and settled in Oxford after receiving the Nobel Prize, Faulkner left for his last Hollywood assignment, a screenplay for Hawks which he finished in less than four weeks. Faulkner commemorated his relationship with Hawks many times in different ways. In late 1953, with *A Fable* about to be completed after nearly ten years of intermittent work and trouble with it, the author told his publishers at Random House that he had to depart to help make a movie in Cairo. Donald Klopfer, the firm's treasurer, was aghast. "For Chrissake, Bill, what do you want to do that for?" he asked. "You don't like movies and you don't want to go to Egypt. Why don't you stay here and finish the book?" Faulkner replied quietly but definitely, "Whenever I needed money, Mr. Hawks was always very good to me, and if he needs me now, I'm going." And he did. It was the last joint venture of the great writer and the great director.

What does the balance sheet show about how much he gained and lost? That kind of record, complex and varied, made up of disparate elements, resists arithmetical reduction and solution. But from screenplays and memos, from interviews and letters, something can be reconstructed of what Hollywood was like for William Faulkner, how it seemed to him as from Mississippi he looked back upon what he once called his "sojourn downriver."

Faulkner's novel *Sanctuary* was the *succès de scandale* of 1931, its shocking-power obscuring for all but a few the fact that it partook of the genius of *As I Lay Dying* of 1930 and *The Sound and the Fury* of the year before. Sam Marx, head of MGM's story department, knew that his friend and boss Irving Thalberg felt that "fine writing was the only way to film superiority." In December, 1931, Marx opened negotiations to obtain Faulkner's services. Faulkner delayed, hoping for enough of an advance on *Light in August,* his new novel, to stay at home. It didn't work that way, however, and on April 15, 1932, he signed a six-weeks' contract at $500 a week as a screenwriter for Metro-Goldwyn-Mayer. He would report for work on May 16. Shortly thereafter Paramount Pictures would take an option on *Sanctuary.* "Turn About," a Faulkner story bought for MGM by Howard Hawks, would

soon be in preparation for the cameras. William Faulkner's movie
career was starting with a rush, or so it seemed.

In 1932 Metro-Goldwyn-Mayer was the undisputed leader among the
film studios. Its galaxy of stars—the Barrymores, Gable, Harlow, and
Crawford brightest among them—outshone the others. MGM picture
budgets averaged $150,000 more than the other companies'. MGM's
forty feature films a year—led by productions such as *Red Dust, Ras-
putin,* and *Grand Hotel*—grossed more than $100 million a year by
playing before an estimated total world audience of a billion persons.
The sixty-two writers on the payroll earned a total of $40,000 every
week. (There were more writers in the MGM lot, commented a *Fortune* writer, than it took to produce the King James version of the
Bible.) Eighteen directors reported to six associate producers who
were directly under Thalberg, MGM's vice president in charge of
production. Faulkner was assigned to one of the associate producers
when he came to work on Saturday morning, May 7. His name was
Harry Rapf, and the production was entitled *Flesh*.

Harry Rapf was a short, paunchy, balding man who wore double-
breasted suits and who was called "Mayer's sundial" because, it was
said, of the configuration of his nose. His specialty was drama with
a smile and a tear, with most of the emphasis falling on the latter. He
was fresh from such successes as *The Sin of Madelon Claudet* and
The Champ. Wallace Beery had played the lovable pug, Jackie Cooper
had wept winsomely, and the picture had been a box office smash.
With impeccable Hollywood logic, management had decided to do it
again, but this time Beery would take his falls in the wrestling game. It
seemed like a natural, and William Faulkner in his first screen assignment would, presumably, add to *Flesh* that extra artistic touch. The
shy-seeming, soft-spoken author was installed in an office in the rickety
white frame building that had housed the publicity department before
the advent of the talkies.

In a terse memo three days later Sam Marx informed the head of
the legal department that Faulkner wanted to tear up the contract.
He had already left the studio, apparently with no intention of ever
returning. Marx had looked for him and Leland Hayward, his agent,
had gone out in search too, but Faulkner had vanished. When he

returned five days later, it was from what sounded like one of the most symbolic flights ever made in that land of rooftop chases and thundering posses. He had fled into Death Valley, he said, where he had wandered for almost a week.

Little by little, some of the details emerged. Marx remembered that on Monday morning (presumably) Faulkner had asked about his forthcoming assignments. "I've got an idea for Mickey Mouse," he said. When Marx politely said he was destined for greater things at Metro, Faulkner asked, "How about my writing newsreels?" Marx finally managed to steer him into a projection room where they would run a film so he could familiarize himself with the subtleties and nuances of the Beery style. Scarcely had the head of the story department begun to relax in his office when the projectionist appeared, alone and perturbed. Faulkner had asked him to turn the film off. "He said there was no use looking at it because he knew how it would come out," the projectionist reported. Then Faulkner had asked for the exit and left. After his return the fugitive brought himself to mention some of the reasons for his flight. "I was scared by the hullabaloo over my arrival," Faulkner said in his soft drawl, "and when they took me into a production room and kept assuring me that it was all going to be very easy, I got flustered." The studio had gone ahead without him on the production of *Flesh*, Moss Hart lucklessly drawing the writing assignment. But Marx was willing to start out with a clean slate. As of Monday morning Faulkner was back on the payroll.

In the ensuing six weeks of the contract, the novelist worked on five more properties. (In the new vocabulary he was learning, a "property" was anything that might be turned into a motion picture: an idea, a synopsis, an original story, an adaptation of an existing work, a movie-style "treatment" of one of these, or a script with dialogue and directions.) Three were originals and two were adaptations. The three originals were all predominantly somber love stories, only one of which had a happy ending. When Faulkner was next assigned to adapt a Metro-owned story, called *Flying the Mail*, his treatment of the conflict between a flying father-and-son combination suggested that he might still be trying to come through for Beery. The fifth opus was a treacly work by Winchell Smith called *Turn to the Right*. It was a bucolic morality play which resisted his efforts. In the end, none of the five works ever made it to the klieg lights. On June 25 Marx wrote the legal department that the contract would not be extended beyond its termination date of June 26, 1932.

Faulkner was back home again after a movie career which could hardly have been called distinguished. But here Hawks stepped in. He was ready to go with "Turn About," and he wanted Faulkner to do the script. The studio picked up the renewal option in the contract and Hawks summoned him back to the Coast. Faulkner made the journey west once more and a new entry appeared on his card: "On payroll July 26, 1932." His salary was slashed in half, but he was working with a man who liked him and understood what he could do in film writing better than anyone else. The tall, broad-shouldered, angular director recalls that first meeting vividly. When the novelist walked into his office, Hawks introduced himself. "Yes," Faulkner said, "I've read your name on a check." When he characteristically fell silent, Hawks began to outline the form he thought the screenplay should take. After forty minutes his visitor was still silent. Hawks asked him what he thought. "It's okay," he replied. "I'll see you in five days." In some exasperation Hawks said, "It shouldn't take that long to think about it." Faulkner answered laconically, "I mean, to write it." The session ended amicably with a large number of drinks, and Faulkner addressed himself to the task.

He brought the screenplay to Hawks in the phenomenally short time he had promised. (He could do a whole script in about two days, he later told Stephen Longstreet, "if the wind is right.") Hawks read it and took it immediately to Thalberg. The man noted for his ability to intuit movie gold said simply, "That's great." This was what Hawks wanted. "I feel as if I'd make tracks all over it if I touched it," the director said. "Shoot it as is," Thalberg told him. Predictably, however, it wasn't that simple. Gary Cooper (who was to become one of Faulkner's Hollywood friends) was available and so were Franchot Tone and Robert Young. But suddenly and unexpectedly so was Joan Crawford. "Bill," Hawks said, "we have Joan Crawford for the picture." Faulkner remained silent for a moment. "I don't seem to remember a girl in the story," he said thoughtfully.

"That's the picture business, Bill," Hawks told him. "We get the biggest stars we can, and she's a nice girl, too." With apparent equanimity Faulkner accepted the change and went to work on revisions.

Faulkner and Hawks had interests in common outside the studio as well as inside. "He's a broken-down aviator like me," Faulkner once said. Also, they both enjoyed hunting. Taking one break from the routine, they drove into the Imperial Valley for some dove hunting. Besides Faulkner, Hawks had asked another friend who liked the outdoors, Clark Gable. As he drove, Hawks began to talk to Faulkner about books. Rather than freezing, as he usually did when most people advanced literary gambits, Faulkner began to talk freely. Gable was silent for a while but then manfully began to hold up his end of the conversation."Mr. Faulkner," Hawks remembers his saying, "what do you think somebody should read if he wants to read the best modern books? Who would you say are the best living writers?" Faulkner answered, "Ernest Hemingway, Willa Cather, Thomas Mann, John Dos Passos, and William Faulkner." There was a moment's silence. "Oh," Gable said, recovering, "do you write?" "Yes, Mr. Gable," Faulkner replied. "What do you do?"

Faulkner took a long weekend to hunt mountain lions on Santa Catalina Island with Gable and Richard Schoyer, another writer. Urgent phone calls and telegrams from home were waiting for Faulkner on his return: his father had died in Oxford. When he arrived there the funeral was over, but he stayed for nearly two months to help settle his father's affairs. He continued to work on the script when he could, however, collaborating with Hawks by long distance. This did not prevent some anxiety at the studio. The studio manager, a gaunt man named M. E. Greenwood who had once earned his living as a Faro dealer in Arizona, was especially concerned. A worrier who was always convinced that writers were trying to put something over on him, Greenwood spent considerable time investigating potential frauds. He wrote Sam Marx that he had reminded Mr. Thalberg several times that Faulkner continued to draw his salary though he was away from the studio. By return memo Marx assured him that Faulkner was nonetheless working and that Hawks had approved the arrangement.

Faulkner returned in October, driving from Oxford and bringing with him his mother, "Miss Maud," and his 24-year-old youngest brother, Dean. The collaborative script was by then well-advanced. All the aerial and naval warfare that was in the story was there plus the romance that wasn't. And the dialogue was as clipped and British as that in any film since the advent of sound. The rewriting and polishing were done in less than three weeks. Miss Maud had spent most of her time in the apartment and was anxious to return home. Her eldest son, feeling flush, was glad to go off payroll on October 22 and turn the car east. Before they left, Faulkner later recalled, "Howard suggested that I stay and pick up some of that easy money. I had got $6,000 for my work. That was more money than I had ever seen, and I thought it was more than was in Mississippi. I told him I would telegraph him when I was ready to go to work again." Out of this easy, tentative arrangement grew the best-known of the Faulkner-in-Hollywood legends.

Leland Hayward remembers that at some point—perhaps when Faulkner learned of his father's death, perhaps when he turned Hawks's suggestion over in his mind before leaving that October— he asked Hayward, "Can I work at home?" Hayward says, "I called Howard and asked him, and Howard said, 'Sure.'" Faulkner had worked for Hawks in Oxford on "Turn About," and he was to be working for him there again sooner than he apparently foresaw as he left Culver City.

Back in Oxford, however, this was the farthest thing from his thoughts. He wrote his friend Ben Wasson, "I was too busy and too mad all the time I was in California to write you. But now I am home again, eating watermelon on the back porch and watching it rain." He had just finished reading the galleys of *Light in August,* and he was well-satisfied with the novel.

Faulkner said later, however, that after he had settled some debts he wired Hawks, in what must have been November, "and within a week I got a letter from William B. Hawks, his brother and my agent. Enclosed was a check for a week's work less agent's commission. These continued for a year with them thinking I was in Hollywood." Each time Faulkner told the story some of the details varied, but the record shows that he went back on the Metro-Goldwyn-Mayer payroll on November 28 at $600 a week and stayed on it—through Howard Hawks's personal intercession with L. B. Mayer himself—through May 13, 1933.

Before this hitch was up he worked on four properties, three of them originals. One, referred to as "Mythical Latin-American Kingdom Story," in a curious way suggests Fidel Castro in Cuba before the revolution went sour. The studio-owned *War Birds* and Faulkner's own short stories "Honor" and "Ad Astra" he tried to work into dramas of love and aerial combat in World War I. They all remained unproduced.

By now it was late April of 1933, and at this point in the narrative, Hollywood legend usually takes over. It goes something like this: "Meanwhile, back in Culver City, someone in the executive echelons tried to locate William Faulkner, screenwriter. They were told that he had asked, "Can I work at home?" and that he had been granted permission. When they tried to locate him, they found that he had meant precisely what he said and was at home, working for MGM in Oxford, Mississippi." (Today even Hollywood brass seems to take pleasure in the story, but not so gleefully as humbler workers in the Hollywood vineyards for whom it seems to suggest an enormous outsmarting of the whole big-studio Establishment.)

Faulkner often denied this account—"a pure lie by some press agent fella," he told Stephen Longstreet—and usually went on to give a longer and more amusing story, itself partly inaccurate too. Actually, most of the people back in Culver City, including the ever-alert Greenwood, knew where Faulkner was. "I thought they understood what I was doing," he told producer Robert Buckner. Extensions of the screenwriting-at-home scheme finally ran out, however, and he was told to go on location under director Tod Browning. Browning had directed Lon Chaney in some of the horror films, and his credits included the original *Dracula*. This time his vehicle was to be an opus alternately entitled *Louisiana Lou* and *Bride of the Bayou.* Faulkner's version of the story is that his ambiguous reply to a telegram from MGM was followed by a long distance telephone call "directing me to get on the first plane to go to New Orleans and report to director Browning. I could have got on a train in Oxford and been in New Orleans eight hours later, but I obeyed the studio and went to Memphis, where an airplane occasionally did leave for New Orleans. Three days later one arrived." Once he got to New Orleans, Faulkner said, the continuity writer refused to let him see the story until he had shown the writer some dialogue. When he placed the problem before the director, he was told not to worry and to get a good night's sleep for an early start the next morning. For days thereafter they would travel a hundred miles in a motor launch each morning to reach the elaborately built set. It was composed of Cajun huts with false fronts whose backs opened on empty space above the waters of the bayou. Browning and Faulkner would arrive just in time to have lunch and make the return trip back to New Orleans before dark. The story's climax came in the form of two telegrams. The first, Faulkner said, read, "Faulkner is fired. MGM Studio." Browning assured Faulkner that he would call the studio immediately and obtain not only his reinstatement but an apology as well. The next telegram read, "Browning is fired. MGM Studio."

The actual truth was not nearly so entertaining as this exercise in creative storytelling. By April 26 Faulkner was working on *Louisiana Lou* and by May 5 he was in New Orleans. On May 13 he was back in Oxford, where Sam Marx wrote him that because the script had to be completed in Culver City and he could not return there, he would have to take him off it. There would be a job for him in Culver City, though, whenever he wanted to return. Faulkner understandably wished to remain at home, for the birth of his first and only child was little more than a month away. What he did not know was that Browning had answered a query from the story department by saying that the writer in question was brilliant and capable, but that his dialogue was not satisfactory and that Browning couldn't approve his refusal to return to Culver City to finish the dialogue on schedule. One more detail in both accounts does check. A friend at the studio writing about the picture told Faulkner, "Tod will not direct it. So you see he got the air, too."

On May 13, 1933, William Faulkner went off the MGM payroll for the last time. It had been an eventful year. His second book of poems, *A Green Bough,* had been published in April. Paramount's version of *Sanctuary* (called *The Story of Temple Drake*) was about to be released and so was "Turn About" (now *Today We Live*). *Flesh* had been released to become what one studio veteran called "an indifferent failure."

Back in Oxford, temporarily both idle and solvent, Faulkner wrote to Howard Hawks, "I'm sitting on the porch with the rain dripping off the eaves, drinking bourbon, and I hear a wonderful sound—the toilet, and it's due to you." There were other hard goods besides new plumbing to show: he had also bought a four-place Waco monoplane. That July, newly the father of a baby girl, he told another friend, "We are all well. I have turned out three short stories since I quit the movies, so I have not forgot how to write during my sojourn downriver."

Faulkner published another volume of short stories and *Pylon,* his novel of barnstorming aviators, before he returned again to Hollywood. Critical notice given his work disappointingly still harped on his preoccupation with violence and on the disturbing complexity of his technique. By early December, 1935, Faulkner was in an infuriatingly familiar situation: the book royalties weren't enough to keep him going, and checks from the stories—even though he had placed six with the high-paying *Saturday Evening Post* in 1934— didn't raise his income to a comfortable level of subsistence. He was working furiously on *Absalom, Absalom!,* hoping to finish it in a month and at the same time casting about for a way to earn money. He had tried unsuccessfully to arrange for a movie job far enough ahead to give him the time he needed to finish the book. But the studio people, he complained bitterly, "were not going to contract for Shakespeare himself 3 months ahead. . . ." To Morton Goldman, now his literary agent, he finally wrote, "About movies, I don't care how I get a contract, just so I do."

Hawks, now moved to Twentieth Century–Fox, suddenly decided he needed him on a script already in progress and offered $1,000 a week. Faulkner took it, even though he had to pack up the novel with his clothes and report for work in less than ten days. The trip could only have been a sad one for him, grieving as he was for his brother Dean, who a month before had crashed in the Waco he had given him. Faulkner was to work at Fox, mainly with Hawks, on and off from December of 1935 until mid-August of 1937. The pictures would not be conspicuously better than those he labored over at MGM, but at least the money would.

By the time Faulkner returned to Hollywood for this second major tour of duty, Thalberg's luminous glow was fading. His health worsening, he now made no more than six pictures a year for MGM. The new resident genius whose stature had grown while Thalberg's diminished had arrived on the Fox lot five months before Faulkner. Slim, nervous, dynamic Darryl Zanuck had been brought in by his boss, Joseph M. Schenck, when Schenck left United Artists to merge his Twentieth Century Pictures with the Fox Film Corporation, then still struggling to recover from its own debacle of 1929. Its most profitable films had featured the engaging talents of Shirley Temple, the wry humor of Will Rogers, or the oriental inscrutabilities of Scandinavian Warner Oland in the Charlie Chan series. Zanuck was supposed to broaden the range. Eleven years earlier, at Warner Brothers, he had written silent canine epics for Rin Tin Tin. When he was promoted to producer he continued to write most of his own scripts. He got his best ideas from the daily papers; and his hard, quick mind had coined gold from violence with films he had made at Warner Brothers such as *Little Caesar, Public Enemy,* and *I Am a Fugitive from a Chain Gang.* Now he was to make his magic in Fox Movietone City, the most attractive lot in Hollywood, where walked such stars as Frederic March and Ronald Colman, Loretta Young and Simone Simon. Twentieth Century–Fox was second in earnings to MGM, but it was second to none in its facilities for distributing "the product," as the art works of the silver screen were then known. All that this No. 2 studio needed to forge ahead of the fat and satisfied giant of Culver City was better pictures. And Darryl Zanuck, who was said to love his writers—though he expected them to complete scripts in half the time exacted by the competition—was supposed to provide those pictures.

When Faulkner first arrived he was ushered into producer Nunnally Johnson's office. The interview has remained vivid in Johnson's memory. After they shook hands Faulkner asked, "Do you mind if I have a drink?" Johnson said that he didn't. "I have it with me," Faulkner told him and extracted a pint of whiskey from a paper bag. As Johnson instructed his secretary to bring glasses and water, Faulkner began to remove the foil from around the cap. When it sliced into his finger, Johnson offered to have his secretary get a bandage. "No," Faulkner said, "just bring me a waste basket and I'll let it drip." The basket was brought, and, the two had a drink together. Then Faulkner began to talk.

"I've been through a rough experience," he said slowly. "My brother had a plane and gave flying lessons. It had dual controls. The plane crashed and he and a student were killed." He went on to describe the grim details of his supervision of the preparations for burial and the funeral itself. (These tragic events lived in his mind with obsessive clarity, and he was to recall them in conversation several times during this stay in Hollywood.) Johnson and Faulkner finished the pint. It was many hours later before Faulkner sat down to do his part on the job at hand.

Zanuck had bought a French film called *Les croix des bois,* which was highlighted by thousands of feet of actual combat footage in which *poilus* battled *boches.* Hawks's idea was to take the triumvirate he had used in *Dawn Patrol*—three soldiers, only one of whom would survive—and change them into infantrymen in the trenches. Faulkner plunged into the work. David Hempstead, working as Johnson's assistant, remembers Faulkner's bringing in page upon page in his miniscule handwriting. Novelist Joel Sayre, Faulkner's collaborator, recalls that a producer was delighted when a writer turned in five pages of material in one day. Faulkner would bring in thirty-five. The two men could quickly complete whatever they had to do and plan their labors on what was to come next. With time on their hands, they would talk. "Bill's head was full of stories about the Snopes family," Sayre remembers. "I would look forward to going to work to hear him talk. I would say, 'Bill, tell me some more about those Snopeses.' And he would tell me about them—Vardaman, Bilbo, and Montgomery Ward Snopes. Once he said to me, 'Why, you know, they mail Snopeses to each other, take them to the station and put tags on them.' " (The student of Faulkner will here recognize the germ of "The Apache Snopeses" section of *The Town,* recounted twenty-two years before publication.)

Faulkner managed to get some of his own work done. In early January, 1936, he called David Hempstead into his office and handed him a thick batch of manuscript pages. "I want you to read this," he said. "What is it?" Hempstead asked him. "I think it's the best novel yet written by an American," Faulkner replied. "I want you to read it tonight." To his dismay Hempstead learned he was holding the only copy. "Suppose the house should burn down," he protested. "Take it," Faulkner said. So Hempstead took it home, stayed up all night reading it, and with relief returned the manuscript of *Absalom, Absalom!* the next morning.

The shooting script of Zanuck's French film, renamed *The Road to Glory,* was completed by January 14, but by then Faulkner had been off the job for a week. He had, of course, a reputation as a hard drinker, a reputation often considerably exaggerated. This time he needed whatever anodyne from grief and nervous exhaustion he could find. When his part of the script was done, he went to Hawks. "Am I through?" he asked. "Yes, Bill, you are," his friend replied. Later the record bore the notation, "Taken off temporarily due to illness." Hawks saw his friend through the illness, and ten days later he was able to leave for Mississippi.

Before Faulkner returned to Movietone City on February 26, 1936, he completed the manuscript of what some critics call his finest novel. At the bottom of the last page he wrote his name and the title, *Absalom, Absalom!* He had begun it in Mississippi and there he finished it. In black ink he wrote the place and date: "Rowanoak. 31 Jany 1936."

When he returned to Fox this time he was assigned to *Banjo on My Knee,* a romantic tale of bargemen and shantymen set on the Mississippi above Memphis. He stayed on the payroll on this job a little over a month, and it is likely that at this time another event in the Faulkner-in-Hollywood body of legend and apocrypha transpired. From time to time Faulkner dropped in at the Stanley Rose Bookshop. Located on Hollywood Boulevard, it was the Gotham Book Mart of Hollywood. Its proprietor looked like a character out of a western. A rough-talking, tough-seeming Texan, he cared passionately about literature and was open-handedly generous to many of its makers. Indifferently educated but possessing a prospector's instinct for rich veins, Rose would make his way on some days from studio to studio with a saddlebag full of books. Two authors whose works he pushed were Nathanael West and William Faulkner. A big, sad, gentle man, West had two brilliant, commercially unsuccessful novels behind him—one the classic *Miss Lonelyhearts.* Like Faulkner, he was in Hollywood to earn enough (writing westerns) so that he could afford some time to write his own books. In the bookshop the two men met. The author-to-be of *The Day of the Locust*—the most acid study of Hollywood in fiction—was a passionate hunter for whom a weekend at his favorite sport might start on Thursday and continue through until Tuesday. While the other patrons talked books and writing, Rose and West would talk hunting with Faulkner. When West proposed that he and Faulkner go wild boar hunting, Faulkner immediately agreed.

The pursuit of these dangerous and fearsome-looking beasts was a welcome if risky change from the sedentary adventuring of screenwriting. On Catalina a hunter paid $10 for the day. This provided a guide and transportation. The sportsman would then hunt wild boar or wild goat from horseback with a deer rifle. West and Faulkner later described a much more rugged sport on Santa Cruz Island. Faulkner spoke of steep narrow paths where they had to go single file, and West described struggles through tunnels of underbrush to reach their quarry. The strategy they devised was to crawl into the depressions the beasts had rooted out for themselves, lie down in them, wait for the boars to return, and then blast away. The bag that West and Faulkner made is not recorded, but they returned well satisfied.

Faulkner was dropped at his hotel, the Beverly Hills, by then a quiet residential hostelry favored by the elderly. Unshaven and still wearing his hunting shirt, Faulkner quietly entered the lobby, his borrowed weapon under his arm, to pick up his room key. Before he had crossed half the distance, the clerk had dropped behind the desk with a cry, a salesman had bolted from the room, and two spinsters had fainted. The hotel had been robbed in Faulkner's absence and his entrance was taken to be the gunman's return appearance.

He had picked up five more weeks' work over at RKO play-doctoring *Gunga Din*. Then, in mid-May, he was able to leave bargemen, shantymen, sikhs, and sahibs and return to Rowan Oak. He was home in plenty of time for the June birthday of his daughter Jill, a chubby, blonde little three-year-old with the delicate features of her mother and the straight gaze of her father. She and her mother went along when, in July, Fox beckoned once more.

In California William and Estelle Faulkner moved into an uncomfortably expensive apartment briefly before settling down in a large house in Pacific Palisades. The site was beautiful, far up from the ocean and overlooking Beverly Hills and Los Angeles. They entertained occasionally—Joel Sayre and his wife, the Gables, Mr. and Mrs. Ronald Colman—Estelle's favorites. At the studio Faulkner worked on *The Last Slaver*, which Nunnally Johnson shot as a vehicle for the talents of Warner Baxter, Wallace Beery, and Mickey Rooney. By September 5 he had a new assignment, a naval saga called *Splinter Fleet*, but he was much more concerned with another potential film property—one of his own.

He had returned the corrected galleys of *Absalom, Absalom!*, but he asked one of his publishers, Hal Smith, to send them back as soon as the printer was through with them. The same day Faulkner wrote Morty Goldman, that he was "up to my neck in moving pictures" and would be there for about a year. "I am going to undertake to sell this book myself to the pictures, first. I am going to ask one hundred thousand dollars for it or nothing, as I do not need to sell it now since I have a job." By the time the galleys arrived, he had decided to lower his price. One day Nunnally Johnson entered his office to find the galleys on his desk with a note in Faulkner's neat and difficult handwriting. It read: "Nunnally—These are the proofs of my new book. The price is $50,000. It's about miscegenation. Bill." But 1936 was not Hollywood's year for miscegenation or *Absalom, Absalom!*, and nothing came of Faulkner's sales campaign.

The producer of *Splinter Fleet* (later *Submarine Patrol*) was Gene Markey, who planned to rely on Faulkner for dialogue. Kathryn Scola, whom Markey regarded as one of Hollywood's ablest screenwriters, was to keep an eye on the storyline. This was apparently to guard against the kind of poetic freewheeling that Faulkner had done in *Banjo on My Knee*. Markey was struck by Faulkner's appearance: "Here was a handsome, trim, well-dressed little man with the grave air of a High Court justice." Markey had expected casual dress at the least, but "usually he wore neatly-tailored tweed jackets and grey flannel trousers—and his tan shoes were polished to such a gleam that I felt sure he traveled with a valet." The familiar pattern emerged: a long conference with a silent Faulkner, a return shortly thereafter with voluminous yellow pages of material. "It was good Faulknerian dialogue," Markey remembers, "but it had nothing to do with our story." Kathryn Scola worked conscientiously at her part of the assignment. Faulkner was kind and courteous. He was a man of very few words. He seemed simple but she saw that he was obviously sensitive and complex. He was not unaware, it appeared, of the difficulties with *Splinter Fleet*. "Mr. Markey told me to follow the story line," he said to her morosely one day, "but I can't find a story line." It was only the work that gave difficulty. Markey liked him; they called each other "Doctor" with "a sort of forced bonhomie." They lunched together and Markey took him twice to the races. The disjunctive dialogue kept coming in punctually, sometimes relating more to aerial than to naval warfare. "He was not happy," Markey knew, "yet he never said so." Then, for ten days there were no yellow pages. Apparently the front office was no happier with the situation than the suffering scenarist or his uncomfortable friend, the producer, for on November 30 Faulkner was taken off the picture, and three months passed before he was assigned to another.

He worked on some of his own things during the last of 1936 and early 1937. By March the Faulkners had moved to an attractive and comfortable California-Spanish-style house in Beverly Hills. Now it was a much shorter trip when he got into his gray Ford touring car to drive to Fox Movietone City. On the ninth he went to work on *Dance Hall.* Two days later he was switched over to Walter D. Edmonds' Book-of-the-Month Club success, *Drums Along the Mohawk.* He was working on it when Jill and Estelle went back to Mississippi in May. Before he went off the picture on June 16, he had spent twelve weeks on the script, though he received no screen credit for it. Thus ended his labors for Twentieth Century-Fox.

There is a persistent story that, some time before he left, Faulkner "told off" his ultimate boss, Darryl Zanuck. It is not difficult to imagine such an exchange between the high-pressure executive and the taciturn author who, though normally gentle, could disembowel an offender with one terse sentence. Back in Oxford in November, Faulkner showed no nostalgia for Hollywood or any of its works. His general impression, he told a Memphis reporter, was "that of a very wealthy, over-grown country town. In fact, it reminds me very much of a town that has sprung up as the result of an oil boom." On previous occasions he had said that he liked some of the work he had done there— *The Road to Glory,* for instance. This time it had left a bad taste in his mouth. "I don't like scenario writing because I don't know enough about it," he said. "I feel as though I can't do myself justice in that type of work, and I don't contemplate any more of it in the near future." And his own work? He was engaged in a novel he expected to complete by summer. His best novel, he said as he looked ahead, was yet to be written.

Random House published *The Unvanquished* in early 1938 and *The Wild Palms* a little less than a year later. The first was the most readable work Faulkner had given the general public, and the second contained some of his best writing and most powerful scenes. But the sales were disappointing and, as always, he had received advances against royalties so that some of the money had been spent before it was earned in across-the-counter sales. In August, 1939, there was some dickering with MGM, but nothing came of it. He had spent money he had saved for taxes to bail an Oxford friend out of financial difficulties. And the federal tax people had demanded an additional payment of $1,100 on his 1937 income—on those hard-earned Twentieth Century–Fox dollars. He made still another effort. "Have tried tentatively for Hollywood job," he wrote to his publishers. "But I am afraid that's out for me. No good for them."

By spring of 1941 he was desperate enough to accept any job-hunting help that offered itself. Stephen Longstreet, an artist-turned-novelist whom he had first met at Random House, set up a contact between him and a young Hollywood agent named William Herndon. In May, Herndon wrote Faulkner that David O. Selznick was interested in the idea of his working for his studio. Nothing came of it.

In June, 1942, Faulkner noted that only one story out of six had been sold since January. Faulkner now enlisted the help of Harold Ober, his literary agent, and Bennett Cerf at Random House. Between them they opened the way for negotiations with Robert Buckner, a producer at Warner Brothers. Faulkner authorized Harold Swanson, Ober's West Coast affiliate, to close the deal for him. Suddenly, however, on July 17, it appeared that the deal would blow up: Faulkner and Ober received angry telegrams from Herndon. He had set up the contact with Buckner months earlier, he said, and they could not now go ahead and cut him out of his commission and his contract with Faulkner. Two letters arrived from Herndon setting forth his case. Although Faulkner fiercely resented the tone and implications of Herndon's wire, he brooded and fretted over the dilemma. On the nineteenth he wrote to Ober again. He proposed to solve the problem by paying commissions to both Herndon and Swanson, then to have done with Herndon. He prepared to depart for Hollywood immediately. The bitterly distasteful squabble with the agent had taken a good deal out of him emotionally, coming after the months of worry about money and fruitless job-seeking in a place he didn't really want to be. But he was well-advised to go: for total royalties on Faulkner titles for the year 1942, Random House would report the sum of exactly $300.

On Monday, July 26, he set foot on the 135-acre Warner lot in Burbank—girded with walls like a medieval city. The head of the stenographic pool remembers this arrival. "We heard that he was coming," she says. "When we saw this little man, quiet and grey, who was sweet and kind and soft-spoken, we said, *'This* is a *talent?'* "

The employees of Warner Brothers Pictures, Inc. were accustomed to talent wrapped in more flamboyant packages. The autocratic Harry Warner and his brothers Abe and Jack had pushed their studio into the big time in 1927 when they released *The Jazz Singer.* Al Jolson's rendition of "Blue Skies" had excited audiences and signaled the arrival of the movie's greatest technological revolution. The family business had started with exhibitions of *The Great Train Robbery* in rented halls. Then they graduated to ownership of a Pennsylvania nickelodeon. In Hollywood the operation became a very substantial and permanent one. The Warners had brought sound in and they plunged with it. Ten years after *The Jazz Singer,* they had more square feet of sound stages than any other studio in the world. It was second to none in equipment, and it led them all in gross assets. But it was no lavish MGM-style operation. Abe Warner proudly thought of the studio as the Ford of the movies, leading the low-priced field and making money with a standard, reliable product. There had been a few extravaganzas, such as *Green Pastures* and *Adventures of Robin Hood,* even expensive films like *A Midsummer Night's Dream* and *Zola,* but the money was made largely through shrewdness and economy: frugal story-buying, avoidance of retakes, and iron repression of "temperament." Along the way, the Warners contributed to the history of the cinema in Hollywood. Their social realism, as one critic called it, was not limited to gangster films such as *Little Caesar.* Like the journalistic muckrakers of forty years earlier, they did exposés of injustice and corruption. Warner Brothers' pioneering also extended to the field of the new-type musical film, with pictures such as *42nd Street.* Harry Warner was to many the second man in Hollywood, preceded only by Nicholas Schenck, head of Loew's Inc., the parent of MGM.

The star performers on the Warner sound stages in comedies and musicals were often Dick Powell and Joan Blondell. Paul Muni and Kay Francis could be cast in heavier works, whereas Errol Flynn and Jimmy Cagney were available for vehicles of violence and adventure.

Other headliners were Edward G. Robinson and Humphrey Bogart. Brother Jack dealt with the talent, and to him they were employees in a factory requiring discipline rather than artists needing guidance. Muni lived with the system through a veto clause in his contract which enabled him to pick his roles. Cagney cursed Warner and sued his way out. Bogart took eleven suspensions in preference to roles Warner picked for him. Bette Davis sued and lost—expensively. When Faulkner moved into the Writers' Building, Herndon brought him a contract. Faulkner wanted a shorter one with more elasticity, but Herndon and others told him the contract was just a formality: he should sign it, and later the brothers Warner would tear the old one up and write another more to his liking. On July 27 he signed. What he had wanted was a one-year contract. When all the options were added up, however, it came to exactly the span that Jacob labored to earn the hand of Leah—seven years.

In spite of the production-line philosophy, the Warner Brothers story department employed forty of the best writers in the movie business. Dean of them all was Sam Hellman, the writer of the Academy Award-winning *Little Miss Marker.* There were western specialists like Frederick Faust (whose pen name was Max Brand) and Frank Gruber. W. R. Burnett, the author of *Little Caesar,* was there, and so was James Hilton, famous for *Lost Horizon.* Robert Rossen, Alvah Bessie, Dalton Trumbo, and Albert Maltz—later to come into the public eye at the time of the so-called "Hollywood Ten" appearance before congressional committees investigating communism—were active spirits in the story department as well as the Screenwriters' Guild. Stephen Longstreet was there. Two more of the younger writers, A. I. Bezzerides and Jo Pagano, were also to become good friends of Faulkner, who was installed on the first floor of the Writers' Building. He had a corner office in "The Ward," a group of six small offices opening off a big room in the center where the six secretaries worked. Their occupants were meant to report five days a week at 9:30 A.M. and work until 5:40 P.M. On Saturdays they could quit at one. Many of them tended to be tardy, and occasionally there would be a personal note to the miscreant from

Jack Warner: "With the money I'm paying you, the least you can do is come in on time."

There was a good deal of informality about the place, however. In violation of rules, secretaries installed hot plates and refrigerators so that there could be soup and sandwiches, coffee and highballs at appropriate times. There were gin rummy and crap games as well as much visiting and conversation. Faulkner would usually be on the fringes—silent, observing, smoking his pipe. To the Hollywood-bred writers who knew nothing else, he was a $300-a-week writer far down on the totem pole where the man at the top might be drawing a cool $2,500. To the other writers and the discerning Hollywoodites like Budd Schulberg, he was even then, as Frank Gruber puts it, "A writer who would live. He was spoken of as Hemingway was."

The deal that had brought Faulkner to Warner Brothers had indeed been complex. The brothers—Harry especially—had been known for their fierce anti-Nazi sentiments even before opinion began to be mobilized in America. And if added persuasion had been needed, they were exposed to it in Washington, it was said, when President Roosevelt entertained them and asked for their help in winning the ideological war. Robert Buckner remembers that Herndon had sold Jack Warner on a film study of Charles De Gaulle, gallant leader of the Free French. He had also, it appears, sold Faulkner with the idea. As a sample of Faulkner's talents, Herndon showed Warner a copy of "Turn About." "Say, this is good," Warner responded. "Why wasn't this brought to my attention?" Buckner, who was a logical choice as producer after doing *Mission to Moscow*, put in his bid. "I want him on this picture," he said.

After the usual conferences, Faulkner began to work, producing a sixty-six-page treatment by August 3. But he no longer came in with forty-page batches of script. Wise in the ways of Hollywood, he would call on Buckner punctually at 3:30 P.M. every Friday afternoon. "I never knew how he arrived at the ratio of twenty-five pages to $350 a week," the producer said. Faulkner worked out three parallel plot lines full of drama, Gallic bravery, and defiance to tyranny. By November 16, he had done a 153-page screenplay.

A week later he began work on a different picture. Two-thirds of the way through, Buckner recalls, a De Gaulle-Churchill dispute led to Roosevelt's cooling off on the idea of *The De Gaulle Story*. The word got to the Warner brothers, and the picture was closed down. Faulkner had apparently been interested in this film, even to the point of discussing casting the title role with Buckner. He had done research for it, while allowing his imagination full sway. There was something offbeat about his treatment of it, almost *nouvelle vague* in the manner of Fellini or Bergman. But there was also the old-style action: he had written a major tank battle into the script. "Bill," Buckner remonstrated with him, "where do you think we're going to get the money from to do a scene like that?" Faulkner was unperturbed. "I don't know," he answered, "but it was important in De Gaulle's life and I know you fellows will find a way to do it."

His aloofness hadn't changed. He was solitary often through choice, but some of his weekends were lonely. Everyone thought someone else was entertaining him, when the truth was that nobody was. He lived at a clean, cheap, dreary hotel in Hollywood called the Highland Hotel. Sometimes he would accept impromptu rides to the studio; at other times he would join a car pool. On still other occasions he would walk the three miles—through simple preference or because he didn't want to be obligated. Sometimes the Buckners would entertain him at their home in Encino. Then under contract at Warner's was actress Ruth Ford, a former Ole Miss co-ed who had dated Dean Faulkner there. Faulkner would visit her and play with her small daughter Shelley. He left an imprint on everyone, Buckner remembers, with his dignity and composure. His tweeds were in good taste, his shirts and knit ties sometimes worn but never frayed. His hair and moustache were always impeccably trimmed. He would lunch in the commissary or at the drugstore across from the main building at one of the writers' tables. He would remain quiet through the whole meal, while tough comedy writers sat there "throwing gags like knives." Then he might make one of his dry observations which would break up the whole table. Yet he was aloof without condescension, with them but not of them. "He walked," remembers Buckner, "in a cloud of his own making."

On occasion Faulkner would see his old Hollywood friends. Hawks, of course, was one. By 1942 he was a Hollywood figure. A deliberate man, he never raised his voice, yet he could set echoes ringing with a sentence which one Hollywood beauty still remembers: "Tell Mr. Warner I'd like to see him on the set." Faulkner occasionally went fishing with Hawks, his two children, and his wife, the lovely "Slim" Hawks. (Faulkner later said, "The way she cleans a fish—it's beautiful.") They also went dove shooting in Calexico, a hot, dusty town on the border. Once, the children were left at home and Clark Gable was made one of the party. They drove back to Los Angeles at night, Gable and Faulkner in the back of the station wagon, relaxing in good fellowship enhanced by bonded bourbon. But these times were the exceptions.

One brief interruption of his work on *The De Gaulle Story* had come in September. Hawks was stuck for a good final scene for his current war movie, *Air Force*. It was the death scene of the pilot of "Mary Anne," the B-17 which was the heroine of the film. He called for Faulkner, and his old collaborator again supplied what was needed. Faulkner infused drama into a weakly sentimental scene by changing it completely. His crew around him as his strength failed, the pilot went through his cockpit and takeoff checklist, dying as the plane headed west. Faulkner did one other scene. Later, when the film had been released, he wrote his stepdaughter Victoria that he had written the two scenes. She should see the picture, he said.

When he went off *The De Gaulle Story,* he went onto another called *Background to Danger,* based on Eric Ambler's *Uncommon Danger.* This assignment had run less than two weeks when he was put on another, an original to be called *Life and Death of a Bomber.* Now it was November. He tried always to be home for Jill's birthday and for the Yuletide holidays when the family gathered at Rowan Oak. He asked the studio for permission to go home on a month's leave and they granted it. Again he was working at home— and legitimately.

He was glad to be there. Five months earlier Brooks Atkinson had written about Oxford for the New York *Times,* calling it the American town least obviously affected by the war. Its sons went off to serve, but the fabric of life otherwise remained pretty much the same. There couldn't have been a greater contrast to Hollywood. Just before leaving Hollywood, Faulkner had written to his stepson Malcolm, "There is something here for an anthropologist's notebook. This is one of the richest towns in the country. As it exists today, its economy and geography were fixed and invented by the automobile. . . . The automobile (for a time, anyway) is as dead as the mastodon. Therefore the town which the automobile created, is dying. I think that a detached and impersonal spectator could watch here what some superman in a steamheated diving-bell could have watched at the beginning of the ice age, say: a doomed way of life and its seething inhabitants. . . ."

In Oxford he apparently finished most of *Life and Death of a Bomber.* It was a patriotic screenplay meant to be inspirational, and it was obvious that into it went some of Faulkner's own keen feelings of frustration at being unable to do the kind of war work being done by his fictional creations in the bomber rather than sitting in a corner office of the Writers' Building at Warner Brothers writing about them.

By late January, 1943, he was back in Hollywood. The next month he was one of a series of writers who bent their talents on a scenario of derring-do for Errol Flynn. It was called *Northern Pursuit,* in which Flynn played a Canadian Mountie engaged in counterespionage. "I am well and quite busy," Faulkner wrote one correspondent, "surrounded by snow, dogs, Indians, Red Coats, and Nazi spies." Only one bit of business contrived by him stayed in the final script. As Frank Gruber puts it, "It was not his type of story."

He worked on two screenplays in March that seemed closer to what was his type of story. *Deep Valley* juxtaposed a California convict labor camp and the mountain home of an absconded bank president, with the banker's daughter and a patriotic convict providing the love interest. Some of its sequences suggested the great scenes from "Old Man," the novella within a novel which Faulkner had used to counterpoint the title story of *The Wild Palms.* But the scenario was redone, and Faulkner got no credit for it.

The other property was a book of reminiscence by Bellamy Part-

ridge called *Country Lawyer*. The place was New York state and
the time was the half-century following the Civil War. Faulkner
changed the locale in his fifty-page treatment. He put it in Jeffer-
son, Mississippi, the seat of his own fictional Yoknapatawpha County. The protagonist was a new man establishing himself in an old
town. The areas of unity and division between the races were those
explored in Faulkner's newest book, *Go Down, Moses*, which was to
be published in May. Propinquity may be the best explanation of
Yoknapatawpha County's being in a Hollywood scenario. Galley
proof corrections must have been fresh in his mind as he wrote the
treatment. And the result must have been the reverse of what he
feared: rather than his own writing being contaminated by Hollywood stories, the stuff of his fiction had gotten into the Hollywood product in strong solution, rather than as the diluted hints
and devices previously appearing here and there. There was a kind
of logic and symmetry in the eventual result. *Country Lawyer* remained unproduced.

In April Faulkner had hoped to have enough money to leave
Hollywood temporarily to soldier or to farm. Instead, he had a
cold, "the damned worst bloody rotten bad cold in human captivity,"
as he wrote to Victoria and her husband, Bill Fielden. "But I can
still see the red lights to cross the street on, and I can still invent a
little something now and then that is photogenic, and I can still
certainly sign my name to my salary check each Saturday." This
was the day around which his studio weeks centered. Albert Erskine,
Faulkner's last editor, recalls his answer to a young writer's question, "Mr. Faulkner, how did you stand those awful story conferences
in Hollywood?" The novelist's reply was, "I just kept, saying to
myself, 'They're gonna pay me Saturday, they're gonna pay me Saturday.' "

The next picture which kept the weekly checks coming in was
called *Battle Cry*. He worked on it from April into August, collaborating chiefly with Hawks and one other writer. Costs mounted
and there was still no final shooting script. Then, early in August,
Warner Brothers shut the film down. Hawks went onto another
project: he had persuaded his friend Ernest Hemingway to sell the

studio the film rights of *To Have and Have Not.* Hawks was switched over to preparations for the new project, and Faulkner prepared to leave for Oxford.

Before he returned, however, he had unknowingly begun the most extended and laborious single project of his career as a creative artist. As Faulkner recounted it, it began one night after dinner when a producer named William Bacher described an idea of his for a picture to Henry Hathaway, the veteran director. It dealt with a reappearance of Christ, ending in his Crucifixion all over again during World War I, his sacrificial role merging with that of the Unknown Soldier. Hathaway caught fire, Faulkner later wrote his agent, and told Bacher that Faulkner was the only writer for the job. The three met and discussed it. Some of Faulkner's friends had strong reservations about the idea and urged him not to touch it, but Bacher was a brilliant, hypnotic talker and Faulkner caught his enthusiasm. The three men decided to produce the picture independently and share alike in the profits. If it was successful, Faulkner must have reasoned, he would not have to worry about screenwriting soon again.

Bacher loaned Faulkner a thousand dollars and Faulkner went home to work. While he was on leave from the studio his contract prevented him from writing scripts for anyone else. But under his agreement with his partners he had exclusive rights to a play or novel in which he might treat the idea, so he decided that he would go ahead with the story in extended, detailed synopsis form. He could do the screenplay later when his status with Warner Brothers had been resolved, hopefully under a new contract of the kind he had wanted from the start. In early November he wrote to Harold Ober from Rowan Oak: "I am working on a thing now. It will be about 10–15 thousand words. It is a fable, an indictment of war perhaps, and for that reason may not be acceptable now." He could not know that it would not become a film, that he would write not fifteen thousand but hundreds of thousands of words on *A Fable,* and that it would be eleven years before he would complete it.

Faulkner had finished his first draft and begun rewriting it a full month before his return to California on February 10, 1944. Hawks asked for him and he was put on *To Have and Have Not,* where he worked until mid-May. His collaborator was Jules Furthman, a veteran screenwriter much valued by Hawks and other directors for his adaptability and ingenuity in scenario writing. He knew the kind of movie shorthand that was to Faulkner quite simply part of another medium. Faulkner remembered twenty years later the way Furthman solved the problem of instantly characterizing the kind of girl Lauren Bacall was playing. "She looks at Bogart to light her cigaret," he said. "Bogart looks at her for a minute, sizes her up, then tosses her the matches for her to light her own cigaret." Hawks remembers that he "set the picture up on the set." The Hemingway novel underwent numerous changes, partly as a result of concern expressed by the State Department and the Hays Office. Harry Morgan's milieu was changed from Key West to Martinique, and the villains were no longer idle American rich or bad Cuban revolutionaries but instead the kind of Vichyites Faulkner had dealt with in *The De Gaulle Story.* When the film was released in October, several reviewers noted its indebtedness to *Casablanca.* They were enchanted by Hoagy Carmichael and intrigued by Lauren Bacall. But there was no praise for the script. Instead, some wondered how a book by Hemingway and a scenario at least partly done by Faulkner could have been so disappointing. There is no indication that the scenarist took this any less philosophically than other reviews of pictures he worked on, if, indeed, he was even aware of them. He had kept on drawing his check each Saturday and had come to know two more men in Hollywood whom he liked: Hoagy Carmichael and Humphrey Bogart.

He had been living in a bedroom-sitting room and bath with a private entrance in a small home in the Hollywood Hills. Housing was terribly tight because of wartime demand, but by May he thought he had found an apartment. To Victoria he wrote that he thought Jill and Estelle might enjoy "living in a city apartment with nothing to break the silence but the shriek of brakes and the crash of colliding automobiles, and police car and fire wagon sirens, and

the sounds of other tenants in the building who are not quite ready
to lay down and hush at 1 or 2 A.M. They may like it. At least
we will be together. . . ."

Estelle and Jill arrived at the pink adobe apartment house in
time to celebrate Jill's eleventh birthday on June 24. The apartment
was a small one, but much of the time Jill spent all day riding. She
would go as far as Warner Brothers with her father and then take
the bus to the home of friends who lived on the edge of Griffith
Park and owned two stables full of horses. One horse in particular
she loved: a little mare named Lady Go-lightly. At the end of the
day her father would call for her—sometimes her mother would
have spent the day there, too—and they would ride back to the
apartment in the car of an assistant to the assistant director. His
family remembers that Faulkner would come home furious, depressed,
or both after a day at the studio. Often they would go out for dinner
at Musso & Frank's, Hollywood's oldest restaurant and a favorite
among the screenwriters. At night they might go for a stroll past
the nearby Cedars of Lebanon Hospital, or they might play a round
on the miniature golf course. Faulkner noted that they were con-
spicuous on those streets: he and Estelle were the only people
walking with a child; the others had dogs on leashes. Fortunately
there was another family to share an occasional outing. A. I. Bezzerides
and his wife and daughter sometimes joined them. They might go
to the beach where Zoe and Jill, both of an age, would dive like
porpoises and their fathers would take snapshots of them.

Automobile travel was now even more curtailed than ever,
though the machine was not quite yet the dying mastodon Faulkner
had described. Often he would ride in the car pool with Longstreet,
Bezzerides, and Gruber. Sometimes his producer would serve as a
chauffeur. Jerry Wald, who had worked on *Air Force,* had moved
up in responsibility and authority, and he appeared to place something of the same kind of valuation on Faulkner's work that Hawks
did. Faulkner did one long treatment for him based in part on his
own story "The Brooch." Then he was transferred to another Wald vehicle that was ill-starred from the first. It was called *The Adventures of Don Juan,* and it starred Errol Flynn. A series of writers

were to struggle with this swashbuckler. One of them, George Oppenheimer, was later to recall delays in shooting caused when Flynn showed up on the set prepared to play the Great Drinker rather than the Great Lover.

In July and August Faulkner worked on *Fog over London,* a remake of *The Amazing Dr. Clitterhouse.* He let his imagination go in this story of a psychiatrist who becomes involved with a criminal ring. The resultant screenplay looked backward to the Jekyll-Hyde archetype and forward as well to the psychological films of the later 1940's. The other assignment was also a remake, this time of Robert Sherwood's *The Petrified Forest.* It would be called *Strangers in Our Midst,* although another tentative title was *Escape in the Desert.* But rather than just criminals on the lam, as in the play, there were to be added Nazis escaped from an internment camp. Faulkner was to give the picture class, his collaborator Bezzerides remembers, and he was to keep Faulkner in line. The two men would alternate between lethargy and anger. Occasionally they would write scenes for their own amusement. In one Bezzerides recalls, the fleeing Nazis continued their escape in a gas truck. A fusillade of police bullets produced a shattering explosion. When the police pulled up to the smoking ruins, there were the much-damaged Nazis—in blackface. One asked the police: "Which way to Memphis?" The two writers gave the scene to the director, who doubled up with laughter. Then he added regretfully, "Of course, I can't shoot this." By early August Faulkner and Bezzerides were no longer on the project.

Another assignment of that summer was an adaptation of Robert L. Scott's *God Is My Co-Pilot.* Faulkner's long, deeply serious screenplay departed radically from the book. It was never filmed. But now he was switched back into familiar company. Jack Warner liked the idea of another *To Have and Have Not.* In casting about for a subject, Hawks and Faulkner began to talk about murder mysteries. They were both fans. To Faulkner, Dashiell Hammett and Raymond Chandler were the outstanding practitioners of the form. Faulkner had tried his own hand at it in several stories later collected in *Knight's Gambit.* They were both enthusiastic about the idea of doing Chandler's *The Big Sleep.* Producer as well as director of this film,

Hawks obtained the services of Jules Furthman again. He also assigned to the script a young woman named Leigh Brackett. Hawks told his writers at the start not to analyze the characters, just to keep the story going. And they were to go ahead and take liberties with the book when they could improve it. "It won't be a great work of art," Hawks said to them, "just keep it moving."

On August 28 the collaborators began their work. It was Leigh Brackett's first film job, and she was enormously in awe of her co-worker in the adjoining office. She remembers Faulkner then as "rather a small spare man, fiercely erect, with bristly iron-gray hair and moustache, a hawk nose, and a disconcertingly piercing way of looking at, and usually through, the person he was talking to (or rather, being talked at by) . . . ." They spoke no more than a dozen words, it seemed, during the three months they were on the job, Faulkner unfailingly polite as he laid out the work in alternate sections. "He was an immensely conscientious worker," Miss Brackett remembers, "turning out masses of material, but his dialogue did not fit comfortably in the mouths of actors and was often changed on the set. Amazingly (to me, after breaking my teeth on some of his novels) he was a master at story-construction." The Chandler novel was a complicated one, and whatever architectonic skills Faulkner and his collaborators were able to bring to bear were not enough to keep some reviewers from having—like Bosley Crowther—"only the foggiest notion of who does what to whom. . . ." The confusion was little dispelled by the pell-mell pace—the writers had "kept it moving"—and by the six murders dominating the action. One patron asked Hawks who had committed one of them. Hawks replied, "I don't know. I'll ask Faulkner." When he did, Faulkner confessed that he didn't know either. Hawks then sent the question to Chandler, who answered that the butler had done it. Hawks telegraphed in reply, "Like hell he did. He was down at the beach house." In spite of the story's complexity, the Bogart-Bacall team functioned well again and the general reception was favorable.

Estelle and Jill had left Hollywood to be home in time for the opening of school. Faulkner enjoyed lunches off the set with Bogart and Hoagy Carmichael, with Steve Longstreet and John Huston, but

California seemed more than ever stale and weary to him now. One golden October afternoon as he and Longstreet stood waiting for their car pool ride, Faulkner gazed out across the Burbank hills. "Look at it, Steve," he said, "one day *one* leaf falls in a damn canyon up there, and they tell you it's winter." And the setting was alien, antipathetic to him on more than just the physical level. "It's too large for life or man," he told Longstreet; "existence evaporates, slips from your grasp in all this sunlight." Moods like this would sometimes trigger off the drinking with which he would escape temporarily situations which had become unbearable. Friends like Bezzerides would see him through the sickness; friends like Geller and Hawks would protect him from loss of the job which he bitterly detested and desperately needed. On one occasion when Hempstead expressed his concern, Faulkner looked at him, straight-faced, and said, "Dave, there's a lot of nourishment in an acre of corn."

But soon he was to win another temporary release. The last half of November he spent reworking part of a script for Wald based on James M. Cain's *Mildred Pierce*. By the time the script went before the cameras he had accumulated enough money to afford another stay at home, and the studio had agreed to a six-months' leave. He was to complete final rewriting on *The Big Sleep* there. Apparently he wanted to be free as soon as possible after he put his foot on Mississippi soil, for he began to write in the day coach that carried him home. One batch of material he datelined "Arizona, 12/12/44"; another, "New Mexico, 12/13/44"; and the last, "Oxford, Miss. 12/15/ 44." He wrote shortly thereafter to Malcolm Cowley—then at work on what would become the introduction to his *Viking Portable Faulkner*—that he was free now for a while. "I can work at Hollywood 6 months, stay home 6." And this way he could do his own work, because "am used to it now and have movie work locked off into another room." In his own room, he drove ahead on *A Fable*. Back in Hollywood Wald found in Faulkner's abandoned desk a yellow legal pad bearing the familiar miniscule pen strokes. They formed a series of formulas: "Boy meets girl . . . Boy gets girl . . . Boy loses girl . . . Boy sues girl. . . ." And so on, for pages.

As the spring of 1945 wore on, he grew morose thinking about the end of his leave from the studio in mid-June. The contract signed three years earlier still haunted him. "I might try to beg off my word to an equal—" he wrote, "a literary agent or a publisher—but not to an inferior like a moving picture corp." They had intimated again that they would tear up the old contract and write a new one. But Faulkner feared it would be for another seven years. If it was, he would insist on a one-year contract. If they refused, he would serve out the present one at the old salary scale to get quit with them. "If they had any judgment of people," he went on angrily, "they would have realised before now that they would get a damn sight more out of me by throwing away any damned written belly-clutching contract and . . . let us work together on simple good faith and decency. . . ." His contempt also extended to some of the writers. (One woman had gone to the administration building to inform management that he sometimes drank in his office.) "Hollywood," he told novelist Shelby Foote, "is the only place in the world where a man can get stabbed in the back while climbing a ladder."

He was back in Burbank again and on the payroll on June 7, assigned to adapt a novel by Longstreet called *Stallion Road*. The producer found the adaptation largely unrelated to the book, however, and engaged Longstreet to do the job himself.

Faulkner's attitude toward studio work remained the same. "The way I see it," he told Longstreet, "it's like chopping cotton or picking potato bugs off plants; you know damn well it's not painting the Sistine Chapel or winning the Kentucky Derby. But a man likes the feel of some money in his pocket." But there was one film which he worked on briefly during this period that did catch his imagination and for which he did some of his best screenwriting.

Jean Renoir was directing a film called *The Southerner* in which Zachary Scott was to score one of his finest successes. Scott remembered that Faulkner considered Renoir the finest director then working. Renoir reciprocated Faulkner's admiration, and when he learned that Faulkner was in Hollywood, he was excited at the prospect of meeting him. When they met, Faulkner began their conversation with a few words in French. He had, says Renoir, *"la galanterie."* Renoir described the troubles he was having with his script. A few days later Faulkner brought back some scenes with dialogue. The final script from which Renoir worked combined the efforts of Nunnally Johnson and Faulkner. Bezzerides remembers Faulkner's saying that he worked on the scene of the first lighting of the hearth. Zachary Scott recalled that he also contributed to the scene in which Scott caught the wily old catfish called "Lead Pencil." It is not surprising that Faulkner was more at home writing about a young family of Southern tenant farmers than about Nazis, submarines, or the Free French. It is also unsurprising that the two scenes suggested elements in *Go Down, Moses,* the Faulkner novel which had appeared just three years before.

He was working harder than ever during this period. He was staying with Bezzerides again, who had been his host for a total of seven months during 1942 and 1943. Bezzerides was working at home now, and his guest was no longer able to ride to work with him in the battered old Willys which would thunder alarmingly down the boulevard to the studio. ("Just like comin' in for a landing," Faulkner would say.) Instead, he rode the buses a total of three hours every day. He would rise early, sometimes before dawn, and put in his day's work on *A Fable* before leaving the house. Two weekends he worked with Bezzerides on an adaptation of "Barn Burning," which they hoped to sell to Hawks. But he wasn't too busy to react as usual to California. "I don't like this damn place any better than I ever did," he wrote to a friend from home. "That is one comfort: at least I can't be any sicker tomorrow for Mississippi than I was yesterday."

The Bezzerides family did everything they could for him. "They have been mighty kind to me," he wrote Estelle. He did not want to become the guest who overstayed his welcome, but he hadn't been able to find a hotel where a guest could stay more than five days. By late August he was feeling worse. Malcolm Cowley, writing him that *The Portable Faulkner* was definitely in the works, had told him that all his seventeen books, with the exception of *Sanctuary,* were out of print. He was also trying to dispense with Herndon's unwanted services, and the studio had refused to release him from the seven-year contract. "I think I have had about all of Hollywood I can stand," he said in one letter. "I feel bad, depressed, dreadful sense of wasting time, I imagine most of the symptoms of some kind of blow-up or collapse. I may be able to come back later, but I think I will finish this present job and return home. Feeling as I do, I am actually becoming afraid to stay here much longer." It was the familiar conflict, but intensified. He wanted to be home, but he was loath to bolt and lose the film income irrevocably. He would try to solve the problem of the studio and the agent so he could be home by the first of October, he informed Estelle. To Jill he wrote, "Lady is just fine. I am still working to get her home. Conditions are better now, and maybe I will be able to do so. But then we have always hoped we could get her home someday, so we will keep on hoping and I will keep on working to do that." He had resolved this the previous year when Jill said something he would recount vividly years later: "Pappy," she said, "I've got to have that horse, it hurts my heart."

He stepped up his campaign. The new head of the story department was Finlay McDermid, with whom he was on good terms. "Finlay," he said one day, "I've got a mare that's going to foal. I want it to foal in Mississippi. I've got a trailer for it, and when that mare goes back to Mississippi, I'd like to go with it." McDermid said he would see what he could do. He suspected that what Faulkner wanted was to go home and complete a novel. McDermid went to the legal department and procured from them a document which gave Faulkner a six-months' leave to write a novel on which Warner Brothers would have a claim. Bacher and Hathaway, of course, had the screen rights to *A Fable* since the three men had agreed on the project. Remembering the contract Herndon had brought him, Faulkner refused to sign. "Finlay," he said, "I've got ink poisoning." He left without signing anything, feeling vaguely threatened with reprisals, and with the contract, the agent business, and the film rights to *A Fable* still up in the air. But that would have to be enough. The next time Steve Longstreet saw him it was September 24, 1945, and he recalls that Faulkner was in his car with a two-wheeled horse trailer hitched behind. Inside it was Lady Go-lightly. "That's a mighty pregnant mare, Bill," he said. "Gotta get her to Mississippi," Faulkner replied. "No mare of mine is going to throw a foal in California."

If the flight into Death Valley was symbolic, so was this one. In letters Faulkner would sometimes liken himself as a writer to a mare who knows she can have only so many more foals. Neither he nor his mare was going to leave any progeny in California from now on if he could help it. Newt House, from whose father Faulkner had bought Lady, was going to do the driving back to Mississippi. A friend remembers that Faulkner told him he wanted to make that trip back as fast as they could.

They arrived late at night, driving slowly, pulling the horse-trailer and its occupant over the rutted, cedar-lined drive up to Rowan Oak. It was past two in the morning, but he had phoned ahead and Estelle and Jill were waiting. In her nightgown, Jill ran down the stairs of the gallery and across the driveway to the trailer. Her father stood silently and watched. "It's my horse," she said, her arms around Lady, "it's my horse!"

The next month Faulkner sent Malcolm Cowley what he had originally intended as a few pages of synopsis to preface the portion of *The Sound and the Fury* which was to go into *The Portable Faulkner*. The covering letter read in part, "I think this is all right, it took me about a week to get Hollywood out of my lungs, but I am still writing all right, I believe. . . . Maybe I am just happy that that damned west coast place has not cheapened my soul as much as I probably believed it was going to do." It was the last time he would have to go through the psychic decompression and purification chamber. Without knowing it, he had completed the last of his extended stays in Hollywood; he had all but completed his screenwriting career.

At home, the novelist continued to worry over the status of his contract and the effect of the dispute on his non-screenwriting work. He wrote to Jack Warner asking to be released from the contract. The answer—the same one as before—came back, from the legal department. Grimly he wrote to New York: "Warner seems to insist he owns everything I write, and so Faulkner won't do any writing until he finds out just how much of his soul he no longer owns."

Throughout early 1946 he worried over these problems, fearing that in a few months he would have to go back. But on March 28, 1946, the breakthrough came: Ober wired Faulkner that Warner

Brothers felt it best for him to finish his novel and agreed that they had no rights in it. When he finished the novel, he would go back to the coast and finish the contract. Meanwhile, Random House would provide a monthly advance on royalties so that he could stay in Oxford and work. The financial strain was further eased in late October when he took four weeks off to do a *sub rosa* film job. For the rest of that year and on through 1947 he worked away at *A Fable*. Then, in mid-January, 1948, he turned to what he thought would be a short murder-mystery novel.

Two months before *Intruder in the Dust* was published in September, 1948—it was Faulkner's first novel in six years—it was purchased by MGM for $50,000. (He had wanted Warner Brothers to have first refusal because they had relinquished film rights to *A Fable* and had been "amicable . . . about getting time away when I insisted. . . .") He had finally completed the kind of transaction he wanted with Hollywood since the beginning. The book sold well, too. The next year came *Knight's Gambit*; the year after that *The Collected Stories of William Faulkner*; the year after that, *Requiem for a Nun*. He was out of the woods financially. He would never be obliged to go to Hollywood again. (When *Intruder in the Dust* was filmed in Oxford in the spring of 1949, Hollywood had come to him. He helped pick a few locations and sometimes showed up on the set, but more often he was at home caulking his boat or sailing it on nearby Sardis Lake, where they would have to take their chances on seeking him out if they wanted him. He did, however, make a reluctant appearance at a cocktail party when the shooting was completed, and a more reluctant appearance later at the premiere at the Lyric Theatre.)

There were other films too: *Tarnished Angels* (adapted from *Pylon*) in 1957, *The Long Hot Summer* (from *The Hamlet*) in 1958, *The Sound and the Fury* in 1959, a remake of *Sanctuary* in 1961. These sales added up to considerably better than $300 a week, but some of it would have been nice, say, twenty years earlier.

Faulkner did a little more scenario-doctoring at home from time to time, and he did spend February, 1951, at the Beverly-Carlton in Hollywood doing a scenario called *The Left Hand of God* for Hawks.

The subject matter was somewhat different from the old fare, but Faulkner's reaction to Hollywood wasn't. To a friend he wrote, "This is a nice town full of very rich middle class people who have not yet discovered the cerebrum, or at best the soul. Beautiful damned monotonous weather, and I am getting quite tired of it, will be glad to farm again."

A camera crew came to Oxford again in November, 1952, when the television program "Omnibus" was producing a short film on William Faulkner and his work. (The director was amazed: Faulkner, he said, would be good at acting. "It's just not my type of work," the subject said.) Almost exactly a year later Faulkner evoked consternation from Donald Klopfer at Random House by interrupting the finishing touches on *A Fable* to go to Europe to help Hawks with his latest spectacular, *The Land of the Pharaohs*. He and Hawks and Harry Kurnitz put the script together in Paris, Stresa, St. Moritz, and Cairo. Faulkner's heart wasn't in the job, however, loyal as he was to Hawks. The trip was a rugged one for him, and he secured Hawks's consent to his departure ahead of schedule. He left Cairo on March 29, 1954, managed some rewriting on *A Fable* in Paris on a stopover, and was back in New York by April 20. Kurnitz had done most of the work on the screenplay, he later said. As if to compensate, he helped to publicize the film at a promotional affair held in the Hotel Gayoso in Memphis, a month before the film opened there in July, 1955. This was the kind of function Faulkner would normally have avoided as he would a room full of literary critics. Perhaps it was reaction when he said with dry amusement that the forthcoming epic was "the same movie Howard has been making for 35 years. It's *Red River* all over again. The Pharaoh is the cattle baron, his jewels are the cattle, and the Nile is the Red River. But the thing about Howard is, he knows it's the same movie, and he knows how to make it."

What had Faulkner gained during his nearly four years "in the salt mines"? Money, of course; economic survival while he struggled in his maturity to keep doing his work. He described it succinctly in the biographical sketch he sent Cowley. Of his life after 1918 he wrote simply: "worked at various odd jobs until he got a job writing movies and was able to make a living at writing." One boon, he sometimes thought, was a curious kind of protection from intrusion. He wrote again to Cowley, in anger, that he had been sought out at Rowan Oak by two foreigners and "a confounded Chicago reporter." Now a Russian wanted to descend on him. "I swear to Christ being in Hollywood was better than this where nobody knew me or cared a damn."

Had he gained any more skill in his craft? Perhaps it made the dramatic medium a little more familiar to his hand when he wrote *Requiem for a Nun,* although when it was published as a play he insisted on giving credit to Ruth Ford, the actress for whom he wrote it and who starred in it. The title page read: ". . . a play from the novel by William Faulkner, adapted to the stage by Ruth Ford." He had never said that this medium was his cup of tea. "I have always worked with some one who knows how to write for movies." Self-deprecating though it sounds, and though he did work alone on some scripts, this was basically true, whether the collaborator was the director, the producer, or another writer. It was always a joint effort, and Faulkner the artist was always the loner, "the cat who walks by himself," as he said in another context.

Had Hollywood ever contaminated his work? He never really thought so. When Jean Stein* asked him if screenwriting could be injurious, he told her, "Nothing can injure a man's writing if he's a first-rate writer." When it did get into the work, which was rarely, it got there deliberately. One instance stands out. Caddie, standing at the center of *The Sound and the Fury,* had always been, he said, "my heart's darling." When he returned to the Compson destinies in the genealogy he composed for *The Portable Faulkner,* he noted her first marriage, to a banker, which ended in divorce. She was, he wrote, "doomed and knew it. . . ." Then he went on to supply her more recent history: "Married 1920 to a minor movingpicture magnate, Hollywood California. Divorced by mutual agreement, Mexico 1925. Vanished in Paris with the German occupation, 1940, still beautiful and probably still wealthy too. . . ." But in 1943

*In her *Paris Review* interview.

she reappeared in a photo from a "slick magazine" which showed her face "hatless between a rich scarf and a seal coat, ageless and beautiful, cold serene and damned; beside her a handsome lean man of middle age in the ribbons and tabs of a German staff-general. . . ." It is surely more than coincidence that not too long before this Faulkner had been writing at *The De Gaulle Story, Northern Pursuit, Battle Cry,* and *Escape in the Desert.* And it was certainly not mere casual selection that the middle stage in Caddie's damnation and degredation—between her marriage to the banker and her liaison with the German general—was her marriage to "a minor movingpicture magnate, Hollywood California."

Faulkner felt that it did not take excessively long to get Hollywood "out of his lungs" each time he returned home. And his body of work during and after the Hollywood years—an *oeuvre* containing *Absalom, Absalom!; Go Down, Moses;* and the Snopes trilogy, to name only five—scarcely suggests a contamination or serious falling off. Nathanael West told Budd Schulberg that he didn't mind the "oaters" he was writing for Republic Pictures—he could easily write lines like, "Pardner, when you say that, smile." It was "relatively painless and I can concentrate on what I want to write for myself." Faulkner obviously employed something like the same conservation of energy, but he never stinted on his end of the bargain, as the number of pages he would turn in testified. "If I didn't take, or feel I was capable of taking, motion-picture work seriously," he told Jean Stein, "out of simple honesty to motion pictures and myself too, I would not have tried." He had the craftsman's pride in what he did as his suggestion that Victoria see *Air Force* had shown. But it went no further than that. "I know now that I will never be a good motion-picture writer," he said, "so that work will never have the urgency for me which my own medium has."

To turn the question about, had any influence flowed in the opposite direction? Had Faulkner made any impress on the film art? Hawks always thought of him as an artist at the screenplay as well as prose fiction. "He has inventiveness, taste, and great ability to characterize the visual imagination, to translate those qualities into the medium of the screen," the director told Robert Coughlan.

Faulkner "is intelligent and obliging—a master of his work who does it without fuss." Bezzerides described the touch his friend could supply: "With a script that didn't work, Bill would take a key scene and make it go. There can be one good scene, the moment that makes the picture work or not, the one good scene that spills over to the others. Sometimes a whole picture can be made in a few scenes." Besides this, there was another quality. It was a mood, a tone, a flow completely his own. It was, said both Buckner and Longstreet independently, like the New Wave film style today. But that was twenty-five years ago, and Hollywood wanted something else.

And, of course, there were friends who came with the Hollywood years. Faulkner always mentioned Hawks. In 1952, now a Nobel Laureate, he didn't "especially want to go to Hollywood for any reason." But if he should, he was "still primarily committed to Hawks, since he is the only one I have any success with. . . ." He had put in another way in an earlier letter: "Hawks has carried me in pictures, seen that I got credits I really did not deserve, that sort of thing, also he has given me chances to pick up money." There were obviously other friends. Faulkner had a gift for friendship, taciturn, withdrawn, difficult though he might often be. His warmth and kindness, his wit and decency, plus what one called this "peculiar nobility and infusing grace" inspired the love of friends here as it had elsewhere.

Of course he lost books. And it is impossible to say how many. In the period when he was "hottest," as he put it, before the first hitch in Hollywood, he published six books; they appeared between 1929 and 1932, and four of them are among the best he ever wrote. Between 1932 and 1937, when he worked at MGM and then at Twentieth Century–Fox, he published four, two composed mainly of stories and poems written earlier. During the 1942–45 period at Warner Brothers, only one appeared, and it was three years before it was followed by another. But he was older now, and he had passed the flood, though the tide would run strong for the rest of his years. Also, during these years he labored at *A Fable*. At first there were a thousand pages of the typescript, and then there were even more—enough pages to make two or three novels of the length of some of the early ones. Later, with servitude in Hollywood safely behind, the books began to flow out again—ten of them in the last fourteen years of his life. One wonders about the energy that went into the forty-odd, perhaps fifty, synopses or treatments or full-blown screenplays that sometimes ran over two hundred pages. How much would have otherwise run in the channel that produced the novels and stories and poems?

Faulkner did what he had to do. When the public would not buy his poetic and complex fiction in sufficient volume for him to meet his financial obligations, he employed his talent in helping to produce the ephemeral art of the silver screen for which the public was eager to pay, and pay handsomely. But what of the expense of spirit? Almost exactly twenty-five years after his first arrival in Hollywood, he was asked by a student how one could remain an individual today without isolating oneself from society. "Well, I will use an analogy," he answered. "There's some people who are writers who believed they had talent, they believed in the dream of perfection, they get offers to go to Hollywood where they can make a lot of money, they begin to acquire junk swimming pools and imported cars, and they can't quit their jobs because they have got to continue to own that swimming pool and the imported cars. There are others with the same dream of perfection, the same belief that maybe they can match it, that go there and they resist the money. They don't own the swimming pools, the imported cars. They will do enough work to get what they need of the money without becoming a slave to it . . . it is going to be difficult to go completely against the grain or the current of a culture. But you can compromise without selling your individuality completely to it. You've got to compromise because it makes things easier."

One wonders what else Faulkner could have done. What better compromise was there for him? Finally, there are two indisputable facts. He survived. He did his work.

LESLIE FIEDLER

What Shining Phantom: Writers and the Movies

In *The Boys in the Back Room,* a little book first published in 1941 (which is to say, at the end of the decade during which serious writers first went in large numbers to Hollywood), Edmund Wilson turns uncustomarily to verse—perhaps because for once he is moved too deeply for prose. "What shining phantom," he asks, "folds its wings before us?/ What apparition, smiling yet remote?/ Is this—so portly yet so lightly porous—/ The old friend who went west and never wrote?" And toward the end of that same book, reflecting on the then recent deaths of F. Scott Fitzgerald and Nathanael West, both friends like the anonymous non-writer in his poem, Wilson turns to prose to make explicit his intent. "Both West and Fitzgerald," he explains, "were writers of a conscience and with natural gifts rare enough in America or anywhere; and their failure to get the best out of their years may certainly be laid partly to Hollywood, with its already appalling record of talent depraved and wasted."

In prose or verse, however, what Mr. Wilson provides us is more poetry than truth, a conventional elegy rather than a series of insights, as might well be expected from a critic whose range of understanding did not extend to the world of pop culture in general, or that of the "pratfall," the "weenie," the "gag," and the "big take" (movie jargon which Mr. Wilson uses with all the unconvincingness of Walt Whitman turning on his French) in particular. What was involved in the flight of writers to Hollywood and their inevitable defeat there was not so much a series of betrayals and appropriate punishments as the first stage in a revolution—only recently defined by such commentators as Marshall McLuhan—which would make print obsolete, and the first panicked attempts of those committed to the old regime of words to come to terms with the future.

Yet once upon a time Mr. Wilson's fable (only lately reprinted without the prefatory verses in *Classics and Commercials*) was taken as literal fact; and it remains, in certain nostalgic quarters—especially where reinforced by vestiges of thirties-type liberalism—a staple of pretentious journalism. Malcolm Cowley, for instance, writing in 1966 about William Faulkner (whose example should have taught him better), submits to the old routine: ". . . Hollywood, which used to have a notorious fashion of embracing and destroying men of letters," he starts in an offhand way; and continues, "After publishing an admired book, or two or three, the writer was offered a contract by a movie studio, then he bought a house with a swimming pool and vanished from print. If he reappeared years later, it was usually with a novel designed to have the deceptive appeal of an uplift brassiere."

Perhaps it was necessary not only to have sold oneself to the movies but also to have bought a swimming pool to make it into Mr. Cowley's category of the damned; for surely the post-Hollywood novels of both Fitzgerald and West, *The Last Tycoon* and *The Day of the Locust,* have an appeal based on something more substantial than foam rubber. More specious than either, to be sure, are the Pat Hobby short stories of Fitzgerald, purely commercial ventures in which Fitzgerald travestied and stereotyped his own situation as an unsuccessful writer of scripts; and among the clichés deployed in these seventeen or more attempts at pandering to popular notions of life in Hollywood is Pat's memory of the magnificent swimming pool he possessed in his time of glory. In "A Patriotic Short" Fitzgerald tells us, ". . . when Pat had his pool in those fat days of silent pictures, it was entirely cement, unless you should count the cracks where the water stubbornly sought its own level through the mud."

West, too, however—in work considerably above the level of potboiling—is obsessed by the banal image (a motion picture image, really, its ironies obvious enough for the obtusest audience), taking time out from the grimmer concerns of *The Day of the Locust* to let us know that Claude Estee—the single successful screenwriter in the book—has the required pool with its required significances. But West, of course, redeems this cliché in the same surreal fashion he redeems so many others, by putting a dead horse (a *fake* dead horse, naturally) at the bottom of the pool. Yet even a dead horse does not help for long—disappearing, for instance, from the pool in Evelyn Waugh's *The Loved One,* to make possible once more the pristine Wilsonian sentimentality. In the course of describing the house of Sir Frances Hinsley (formerly "the only knight in Hollywood" and "chief scriptwriter in Megalopolitan Pictures"), Waugh lingers over his now-abandoned swimming pool, which, he informs us, "had once flashed like an aquarium with the limbs of long-departed beauties" before it had become "cracked and over-grown with weeds." All of which was quite literally reproduced on the screen—where it belonged to begin with—in the recent film version of Waugh's novel.

Well, swimming pools have ceased, even mythologically, to represent Hollywood, not because any banality ever wears out on its own, but because prosperity has brought that legendary pleasure from dreamland to the backyards of suburbia and what survives of its former legendary glory to that storehouse of the dreams of the thirties, Hugh Heffner's pleasure palace in Chicago. The suburban swimming pool is memorialized in a story by John Cheever called "The Swimmer," which recounts the dream-legend of a commuter who swam all the way home from the station through the pool after pool after pool of his neighbors; and even now that story is—of course, of course—in the process of becoming a movie.

Yet the legend survives its trappings; the myth of "the old friend who went west" outlives the Hollywood swimming pool. Some such "old friends" at least are still wincing, perhaps protesting too much— Daniel Fuchs, for instance, who comes closest to having lived the mythological history of Wilson's "shining phantom." Fuchs had written three novels before going off to Hollywood toward the end of the thirties—*Summer in Williamsburg, Homage to Blenholt,* and *Low Country*—none of which were much "admired" (the word is his) when they appeared. "The books didn't sell—400 copies, 400, 1200," Fuchs himself reports. "The reviews were scanty, immaterial." And so, he went to Hollywood, made it there, lived long enough to see his reputation revived, his novels reprinted in the sixties—but remained bugged all the time, it would appear, by the judgment implicit in Wilson's vision. At any rate, he uses the occasion of the re-issue of his fiction in a single volume in 1961 to go on record: "The popular notions about the movies aren't true. It takes a good deal of energy and hard sense to write stories over an extended period of time, and it would be foolish to expect writers not to want to be paid a livelihood for what they do. But we are engaged here on the same problems that perplex writers everywhere. We grapple with the daily mystery. We struggle with form, with Chimera . . . 'Poesy', my father used to call it, and I know I will keep at it as long as I can, because surely there is nothing else to do."

It would be easier to believe Fuchs if he seemed really to believe himself; but he is as much of a child of his age and Wilson's, of those mythicized and mythicizing thirties, as was James M. Cain, who had already cried out against Wilson twenty years before—and with more apparent cause, being one of the "boys in the backroom" specifically attacked by Wilson. ". . . Edmund Wilson . . . in an article he wrote about me . . .," James M. Cain complained in 1942 in a preface to three of his own novelettes, "attributed these socko twists and surprises to a leaning toward Hollywood, which is not particularly the case." And he goes on to explain that, despite the tutoring of a script-writer called Vincent Lawrence, he himself just "couldn't write pictures," which he takes to be some guarantee, we gather, of virtue as well as of ineptitude. But we remember that, though Mr. Cain may have written no successful scripts, he was the author of "Double Indemnity," as well as of *The Postman Always Rings Twice,* which is to say, of certain not very good books which *became* very good films—the sort of transitional figure between a Gutenburg era and a non-Gutenburg one (the later Hemingway would be another example, and Steinbeck most of the time), whom we have not understood very well until now, the author of embryo movies which only pretend to be books. Cain, indeed, must be given double credit since he not only provided the cue for several first-rate American screenplays, but the inspiration as well for Visconti's *Ossessione* (born of an encounter between *The Postman Always Rings Twice* and the Italian director's characteristic blend of social protest and High Camp), with which "neo-realism" was born.

All this, however, has to do not with being "depraved and wasted" in any conventional sense but with being fulfilled and completed in a quite unforeseen way. No, the notion of being "depraved and wasted" or, alternatively, "embraced and destroyed," belongs to the legendary literature of defunct "modernism"—to what we can readily see now is the realm of myth rather than that of history or sociology. It is a special development, which flourished chiefly in the thirties, of that Cult of Self Pity which underlies much of the literature of the first half of the twentieth century. The notion of society as a conspiracy against the individual and of art as a protest against that conspiracy goes back as far as the beginnings of Romanticism at least. Originally, however, the artist himself was not thought of as the sole or exclusive victim of the world, women and children and noble savages, even peasants and workers being quite understandably preferred.

After World War I, however, writers in Anglo-Saxon countries (responding belatedly to cues from the French) began to portray the poet himself as the victim *par excellence* and to shop about for the institutions most inimical to his career. To such basically European writers as James Joyce, for instance, the traditional institutions of

Christendom seemed quite satisfactory: the Family, the Church, the State; but these have struck latter-day Americans as somehow outdated compared with the newer institutions (the threat of the future rather than the incumbrance of the past) of mass culture, including mass war. But the notion of total war as particularly reprehensible because of the masterpieces it inhibits or destroys (a notion pathetically developed in, say, Dos Passos' *Three Soldiers*) seems finally a little absurd. And, in any case, our writers have chosen to think of themselves as being destroyed—more ironically than pathetically—by advanced technological substitutes for their own discipline: advertising, script-writing, publish-or-perish scholarship, television.

Besides, most men, even writers, are *drafted* into wars—raped as it were—whereas they are *tempted* into other areas of mass culture, seduced or prostituted. In Peter Viertel's *White Hunter, Black Heart,* which appeared late enough (1953) to seem a retrospective catalogue of all the anti-Hollywood clichés, a semi-fictional character, transparently modelled on John Huston, is permitted to comment at length on this metaphor, crying out, "They mean the whores, when they say Hollywood. . . . Now get this, Victor . . . whores have to sell one of the few things that shouldn't be for sale in this world: love. But there are other things that shouldn't be for sale besides love, you know . . . There are the whores who sell words and ideas and melodies . . . Now I know what I'm talking about . . . because I've hustled a little in my time, a hell of a lot more than I like to admit I have . . . Well, anyway, my point is that it's the whores who put up Hollywood as a big target, and very often they shoot at it themselves just to feel clean again . . ." Once more we find ourselves in that dim area of protest and apologetics in which muddled voices cry, "You're one, too!" or "I may be one, but not full-time," or, "not as much as you."

Money and guilt and the denial of guilt: these are, at any rate, key terms in all accounts of Hollywood, though for a long time, as a matter of fact, not "selling oneself" but "selling out" (another one of those slightly alien terms imported by Marxists into American life during the thirties), an image more sociological than erotic, possessed the minds of those who sought to make fiction of an experience already fictional in essence. The anti-Hollywood Novel—that writer's ultimate, even sometimes posthumous, revenge on his seducer-employers—is basically a depression product; for the heyday of the in-and-out writer in Hollywood, the classic period memorialized in the classic books, coincides almost exactly with that somewhat more than a decade we call the thirties.

The thirties as a social-psychological phenomenon begins with the stock market crash of late 1927, or perhaps with the execution of Sacco and Vanzetti earlier in that same year, and ends with the Japanese attack on Pearl Harbor on December 7, 1941; while the legendary era for the writer in Hollywood begins with the perfection of "talking pictures" in 1927 (with Al Jolson in *The Jazz Singer,* let's say, making it on the screen by singing the death of two worlds: the Minstrel Show and Orthodox Judaism)—and ends with the corresponding double death, the demise within a few days of each other during December, 1940, of Scott Fitzgerald and Nathanael West. The novels which comment on that era reflect inevitably, then, its fashionable class-consciousness; but since the experience which produced them had to come first, they did not begin to appear until that class-consciousness, at first vulgar and surly and truly embattled, had become attenuated and sentimental and token.

They are a sub-variety not of the Proletarian Novel proper, which belongs to pre-1935, the time of Mike Gold and Grace Lumpkin and Jack Conroy, but of the Popular Front Novel, like *Grapes of Wrath,* for instance, which arises out of a world conditioned by the rhetoric of such Hollywood politicos as Donald Ogden Stewart and which disappears back into the clichés of that world without a struggle. In the declining thirties, as a matter of fact, when writers of real eminence were deserting the ranks of their Communist fellow-travelers, hack script-writers were replacing them in the leadership of movements like the League Against War and Fascism; and the old vision of the high-paid Hollywood professional as necessarily a whore and a sell-out had to be qualified.

A division began to be made, in popular mythology and fiction alike, between the kind of successful screenwriter who joined the Screen Writers Guild and/or tried to smuggle favorable references to

Loyalist Spain and the Soviet Union into his scripts, and the kind who refused to pay dues in the workers' cause and/or give lip service to "Humanity" as defined by the Communist Party. In the encoded cant of the time the former, being only half-whores or not-quite-whores, were referred to as the "decent and progressive forces"; and it came to be believed that "decent and progressive" novelists, desiring to treat justly the environment which bred them, ought to populate their novels with a preponderance of such types. Woe unto those who did not! Even poor Budd Schulberg, who in his best-selling *What Makes Sammy Run* had rewarded his Jewish narrator-hero ("a decent, generous and gifted" screenwriter and Guild member) with the hand of an Anglo-Saxon heroine (an even more "decent, generous and gifted" screenwriter and Guild member), was abused for having insisted too much on the villainy and success of the Jewish heel who gives his book its name.

But he made amends by carrying over into his second book about the movies, *The Disenchanted,* a minor "decent, gifted, etc." character from the first, a certain Julian Blumberg, whom he permits to be kind to a sodden, aging, unsuccessful screenwriter, obviously intended to represent Scott Fitzgerald; and Schulberg appears himself, faintly disguised, to lecture the same failing lush on the virtues of "progressivism." It is all a little disheartening, but fair enough, I suppose, in light of the fact that Fitzgerald had actually flirted with left-wing politics, perhaps under the influence of Donald Ogden Stewart, with whom he had worked on a script; and had paid his respects to that flirtation in the embarrassingly bad scene in *The Last Tycoon* which describes a fist fight between the brilliant but failing Jewish producer, Monroe Stahr, and a (Jewish?) Communist organizer called Brimmer ("a little on the order of Spencer Tracy. . .," poor Fitzgerald describes him). At the close of the scene the producer lies on the floor, cold-cocked with a single symbolic punch; and to make the allegorical meanings of the encounter clear, Fitzgerald has his girl narrator, partly responsible for the conflict and a witness throughout, comment about Brimmer, ". . . afterwards I thought it looked as if he were saying, 'Is *this* all? This frail half-sick person holding up the whole thing?' "

Only Nathanael West managed to resist the temptation to redeem the Hollywood writer by reminding us that he was tithing himself for Spain or meeting secretly with others of his kind to condemn the system by which he lived; and even West felt obliged to apologize privately, in a letter to the now almost forgotten Proletarian novelist Jack Conroy: "If I put into *The Day of the Locust* any of the sincere, honest people who work here and are making such a great, progressive fight . . . the whole fabric of the peculiar half-world which I attempted to create would be badly torn by them." In the letter itself we watch his rhetoric go fashionably soft and realize that only his exclusion of those whom the age (with West assenting) conspired to think virtuous kept his novel as bleak and anti-sentimental as it had to be for truth's sake.

When the "progressive" self-deception of the Popular Front had given way to the "anti-Communist" self-righteousness of the McCarthy era, the "sincere, honest people" who had persuaded themselves that somehow they were *really* boring from within, even as they made it big in Hollywood, were disconcertingly taken at their word by congressional investigation committees; and they had, therefore, to choose between public recantation and informing on the one hand, or silence and exile on the other, exile from the industry that had for so long permitted them both swimming pools *and* clean consciences. There have been two major attempts at dealing with those who made the choice, one way or the other, the first by Norman Mailer, who deals with a recanter, and the other by Mordecai Richler, who treats those who stood firm and were exiled; and oddly enough (though perhaps not unexpectedly) the recanters come off a little better than the unreconstructed.

Mailer's *The Deer Park* begins as the outsider's dream (nurtured in part by other earlier books) of Hollywood people disporting themselves at Palm Springs and ends as a sympathetic study of the vain and gifted director Eitel, an almost hero who gives up his lifelong resistance to the world in which he flourishes when he learns first to love, then to be defeated and die. Richler, on the other hand, begins completely outside of Hollywood and its environs, portraying in *Choice of Enemies* the life in England (where Richler himself, a

Canadian by birth, is a screenwriter) of certain left-wing refugees from Hollywood who still try to play, without power and on immensely diminished funds, the old games of backbiting and ass-kissing and self-congratulation and betrayal. Both Mailer's book and Richler's, however, though obviously the products of talented younger writers, seemed even at the moment of their appearance imitations or refinements of a mode still viable, perhaps, but no longer mythically potent.

By 1955, surely, when *The Deer Park* was published, we needed no Sergius O'Shaughnessy come back from the grave to tell us the truth about Southern California and the movies; for the truth had been invented before the fact and, whatever its effectiveness once, had long since ceased to move anyone but actors. How much more remote and unconvincing, then, that same world of Mailer's seemed in 1967, when after long, long delays the play he had been making of his novel all those years finally got onto the stage, where (with true lack of discretion) it is being presented right now, not as a period piece but as something current or, at least, timeless. Such trifling with time is necessary, I suppose, if *The Deer Park* is eventually to be made a movie, since the men who make movies cannot really confess that they are dead, that all their writers are ghost-writers, their players ghost-players, and even the producers ghosts like the rest. And *The Deer Park* must be made a movie so that we can all be quit of a legend we seem to have known forever without that knowledge having ever done any of us a bit of good.

Certainly it did not help Mailer, who—knowing what he must have known, what his book reveals he knew—went anyhow to Hollywood. But, why, we ask, *why*? And not only Mailer, since delusion was built into Hollywood from the start, and no one ever went there without his eyes open. Into wars, writers may have carried for a little while illusions to be lost; and similarly the universities once dangled before them fair promises and enticing hopes, as did even the Revolutionary Movement of the Depression years and the Popular Front days which followed. But what ever drew writers to Hollywood?

The search for destruction, I am tempted to answer off the cuff, a desire to play Russian Roulette, if not to die—to act out in their own particular lives the fate of the literary art to which they have committed themselves, the fate of books in the world of Hollywood, whose normal temperature is *Farenheit 451* (the temperature at which as everyone now knows—since Ray Bradbury's book of that name has been consumed in a film, too—all paper burns). But perhaps it is much simpler than that—they go just to make money, as Wilson suggested, or to find a subject for a book, as all the rebuttals to him have really answered, whatever they pretended to say. Or maybe after all it is a mythological journey, in the full sense of the word, a descent into all that Hell used to be; for suerly "Hollywood" is just as polysemous and attractively sinister a word as any of the traditional names for the underworld, though like Hell itself it has become a cliché.

Let us try once more, then, to penetrate the cliché by turning once more to Peter Viertel's handbook of banality, *White Hunter, Black Heart,* at the place where his producer-director-villain continues to cry out in protest against platitudes:

"You see, the way Vic used the word 'Hollywood' is an insult. Now, don't contradict me. I've heard it before. In the Army, in the theatre in New York— hell, everywhere. People say 'Hollywood' when they want to insult you. But it isn't an insult, really . . . Hollywood is a place where they make a product; it's the name of a factory town, just like Detroit, or Birmingham, or Schaff-hausen. But because the cheap element in that town has been over-advertised, it is insulting to remind a man that he comes from there . . . but it doesn't bother me so much when they say it, because I know they're talking about the hustlers, and the flesh peddlers, and the pimps who sit in the sun out there, around the swimming pools . . . They're not talking about the guys who work out there, who try to do something worth while. They mean the whores . . ."

But this takes us right back to where we started, indicating that the longest way around is the only way home (or to hell, if you please), that the swimming pools and the whores are not incidental but essential to Hollywood, which, if it is indeed "a factory town," is quite unlike others in that it produces not machines but men and women, living meat for use and pleasure, though (by the canny use of machines) it manages to produce them twice over—once in what *they* take for actuality, i.e., life itself, and once on what *we* take for actuality, i.e., the screen. That these men and women, this living meat, be "hustlers, flesh-peddlers and pimps" is precisely necessary; since Hollywood is, on the first mythological level, Sodom, or—to use Mailer's alternative title—"The Deer Park": "that gorge of innocence and virtue, in which were engulfed so many victims who when they returned to society brought with them depravity, debauchery and all the vices they naturally acquired from the infamous officials of such a place. . . . Indeed who can reckon the expense of that band of pimps and madames. . . ." Now that the hand-held camera and a kind of ultimate vertical social mobility has placed the journey to hell within the reach of everyone—and we need no deer parks, no Sodom, no Hollywood—we can consider with detachment the special sexual function Hollywood once fulfilled.

In a world which had lost the secret pleasure palaces of the aristocrats as loci for fantasy and which had not yet learned fully to democratize sexual reverie as well as sexual fact, Hollywood was the place which simultaneously created—and fulfilled by proxy—the wet dreams of everyone. No wonder that there is scarcely a book which uses Hollywood for a setting which does not include scenes in a whorehouse, or encounters with a pimp, or descriptions of private showings of dirty films for the makers of public films (the movies within the movie world—at least according to the anti-Hollywood novelists—were explicitly, banally pornographic, i.e., totally unclothed). But the special fable which haunts the writers of books about the bookless world of Hollywood is the actual pursuit and possession of a female star, one of those standardized erotic objects nightly possessed in fantasy by millions—super-whores, as it were, in possessing whom in fact one joins himself in fantasy to all the other males of his world, potent or demi-potent or without even the power to dream unaided.

Sometimes, to be sure, we are presented, in the fictions made of the Hollywood experience, with the caricature of this sexual encounter, as the hero embraces or, better still, fails to embrace not some recognized and celebrated actress but the frantic anonymous slut aspiring to the role of the Love Goddess. In Mailer's *The Deer*

Park, however, or in Fitzgerald's short story "Crazy Sunday" (his
first attempt to come to terms in print with Irving Thalberg and the
alluring image of Norma Shearer who was his wife), we are given
fantasy triumphing over frustration: the universally desired women
privately (if only momentarily) possessed. This is the place where
the fiction about Hollywood aspires to poetry rather than revenge—
or rather, perhaps, where the poetry of celebration and the prose
of revenge improbably approach each other, two opposed traditions
becoming one. Ever since films became a part of our common culture, poets—who, unlike novelists, have gone not to Hollywood with
the chosen few but just to the movies with the unnumbered
many—have been singing the charms of the not-quite-unreal ladies
who move through those films: from Vachel Lindsay's coyly gallant
"Mae Marsh, Motion Picture Actress" ("She is a madonna in an
art/ As wild and young as her sweet eyes:/ A cool dew flowers
from this hot lamp/ That is today's divine surprise") to Joel Oppen-
heimers' considerably franker "Dear Miss Monroe" (". . . some
night I think, while/ I'm in bed, of how lovely your/ body must be,
and I don't mean of/ when the king's hand is sneaking/ under the
sheets while you two/ kiss, I mean of when you and I/ would
kiss . . ."). Closer to the poems than to Fitzgerald or Mailer's
evocations in prose of bitch-goddesses without minds are those transformations of Marilyn (*last,* it now becomes clear, of her once apparently inexhaustible line) at the end of Mailer's own later *An
American Dream* or in the first pages of Leonard Cohen's post-
Hollywood novel *Beautiful Losers.*

And somewhere on the other side of both poems and novels, behind the screen, as it were, where neither form of literature had
reached before, is the strange saga of the Writer and the Star that
Arthur Miller lived-wrote by first marrying Marilyn Monroe; then
casting her as the anonymous aspirant to all she actually was in *The
Misfits* (where she insisted all the same on being only what the
screen had composed, not what Miller thought he had rewritten,
loving a tree, subduing Clark Gable); then, when she was dead,
playing her story—the story Hollywood and the myth had determined
for her—on the stage, even printing it, as if he had made it up out

of the whole cloth and were waiting for the Hollywood that no longer existed to find another starlet to play it, another John Huston to
direct it, another Arthur Miller to be given the job of writing the
script; as if the whole thing could continue to go round and round,
as if the exact point of it all were not that it was finished, done
with. *Basta.*

But what fun and games we have had before it was finished; and
how our authors large and small have responded, running the whole
gamut of the ambivalence proper to our culture: from nauseated
horror (as in Faulkner's single, queasy story out of his Hollywood
experience, "Golden Land," in which the drunken and eminently
successful father of a faggot and a whore wakes to find his daughter's photograph under the headlines, APRIL LALEAR BARES ORGY
SECRETS) to the kind of wistful longing, the dumb hope that rises in
the heart of Mailer's dumb hero in *The Deer Park,* when a cynical
producer, urging him to turn actor, cries, "You think you're going
to enjoy goosing waitresses when you've been boffing the best?
Brother, I can tell you, once you've been bed-wise with high-class
pussy, it makes you ill, it makes you physically ill to take less than
the best . . ."

It is Nathanael West, however, who preserved the flavor and
balance of the ambivalence most perfectly—in the yearning of the
studio artist Tod Hackett (nearest thing to a self-portrait of West in
The Day of the Locust) for Faye Greener, the girl who will never
be a star but who embodies the erotic allure of the film heroine all
the more convincingly: available to anyone with the going price of
tail or with the face and body of a movie actor—but unobtainable
by that very token to the only one capable of imagining her, that
is, to the poor artist. A luscious seventeen-year-old in the dress of
a twelve-year-old child, she flashes across the screen, her long legs
"like swords" suggesting to Tod destruction and death; while behind
her run (in the painting Tod dreams, at least, which only can give
meaning to her life) the book's other major grotesques: a lustful
dwarf, a parody cowboy, a troupe of Eskimo acrobats; and behind
them a howling crowd of witnesses—caricatures of the passive and
resentful audience—enter at last upon the violence which they have

too long only dreamed. The title of Tod's picture is *The Burning of Los Angeles,* but the destruction of the city is only the public fantasy which masks his private dream-wish: to rape and destroy that green and golden girl (always golder and "greener" on the other side of the invisible, impassable fence between audience and screen image), or better yet to be destroyed by her: "Her invitation wasn't to pleasure, but to struggle, hard and sharp, closer to murder than to love. If you threw yourself on her, it would be like throwing yourself from the parapet of a skyscraper. You would do it with a scream. You couldn't expect to rise again. Your teeth would be driven into your skull like nails into a pine board and your back would be broken . . ."

It is such a love in such a setting that the writer has sought in Hollywood, or so at least West would have us believe, so he shrilly insists in the pages of the best book anyone has ever written about that oddest of "factory towns." In his vision the metaphorical whore, who calls himself an artist ("when the Hollywood job had come along, he had grabbed it despite the argument of his friends who were certain that he was selling out . . ."), grapples with the actual one, who calls herself an actress (" 'She's a whore!' he heard Homer grunt . . ."), even as Sodom turns to ash and the doomed avengers of all they have themselves desired and loved and despised riot in the streets: ". . . a great united front of screwballs and screwboxes to purify the land. No longer bored they sang and danced joyously in the red light of the flames."

But if, on the one hand, the force which took the American writer to Hollywood is a dark and inverted passion that makes him seek destruction in the arms of the blonde child-whore, his corrupt and death-dealing sister; on the other hand, he is moved by a more beneficent love that takes him westward in search of an alien and unlikely father—more technician than artist, more businessman than creator—but a dreamer and peddler of dreams all the same, quite like himself. The relationship resembles that of Stephen Dedalus to Leopold Bloom in *Ulysses,* that blind man's word-bound book, which, after more than half a century, someone has been bold or foolish enough to try to make a film; and, as in Joyce's novel, so in our lives the mythical father of the artist in flight from tradition to Nighttown is a Jew.

How oddly the love affair between the Gentile writer and the Jewish producer-director, the young philosemite and the aging Jew, emerges in our literature, which as late as the twenties and on into the thirties was continuing to portray chiefly anti-semitic heroes and antipathetic Jewish foils, in the poetry of Pound and Eliot as well as in the prose of Dreiser and Sherwood Anderson and Hemingway and even Fitzgerald himself. But the latter—after the first rude shock of Hollywood, after the experience of confronting the Jews on their own home grounds, as it were, in a world where not they but the Gentile author seemed the intruder—learned to create an image of the Jew vastly different from the threatening bogeyman Wolfsheim who haunts the pages of *The Great Gatsby*. Monroe Stahr, the Jewish tragic hero of *The Last Tycoon,* the wary boy gang leader from the Bronx who has made himself top-dog in Hollywood and is ready for destruction, represents for Fitzgerald not only a triumph of art but a victory over prejudice.

To *see* him, much less to love him, was not easy for Fitzgerald, whose initial reaction, as recorded in "Crazy Sunday," was to find Hollywood's Jews funny, fit subjects only for burlesque. In that story he tells how his protagonist (himself, surely) at his first big movie party begins an intendedly hilarious takeoff "in the intonations of Mr. Silverstein": " '—a story of divorce, the younger generators and the Foreign Legion . . . But we got to build it up, see? . . . —then she says she feels this sex appeal for him and he burns out and says, 'Oh, go on destroy yourself—' " But Fitzgerald's alter ego is greeted with boos and blank stares. "It was the resentment . . ." the author explains, "of the community toward the stranger, the thumbs-down of the clan." And all, of course, played out in the house of that most eminent of doomed Jews, the figure who was to become eventually Monroe Stahr.

The word "Jew" is not mentioned, to be sure, any more than it is in Nathanael West's brief retelling of what may have been the very same incident, or one very like it, introduced as background conversation during a minor episode in *The Day of the Locust*; but this time we hear it in the voice of the "clan." " 'That's right,' said another man. 'Guys like that come out here, make a lot of money, grouse all the time about the place, flop on their assignments, then . . . tell dialect stories about producers they've never met." But when Fitzgerald attempts a full-scale treatment of Stahr and his wife— the redemptive father-husband, and the dangerous actress wife who were in real life Irving Thalberg and Norma Shearer—when he turns to them again in his unfinished novel, he is on top of his own Jewish problem, to the extent at least of being able to name names; registering what may have been his own first impressions in a detached and objective way through the consciousness of a certain Prince Agge, who, sitting at lunch with the executives of a great studio, notes: "They were the money men—they were the rulers . . . Eight out of ten were Jews— . . . As a turbulent man, serving his time in the Foreign Legion, he thought that Jews were too fond of their own skins. But he was willing to concede that they might be different in America under different circumstances, and certainly he found Stahr was much of a man in every way . . ."

With Agge's final opinion the two spokesmen characters into whom Fitzgerald has split himself agree, Cecilia Brady, female and Irish and worshipper of the great, loving Stahr unabashedly for his alien masculinity; and Wylie White, WASP presumably and tyro writer, admiring him for his control of the new narrative skills which make words seem obsolete. But *The Last Tycoon* remained unfinished and Stahr exists—or better, fades away—in a confusion of other loves: one of which Fitzgerald had borrowed for him out of his own life, exploiting his then current affair with Sheila Graham, who was herself, though not until years later, to exploit both his exploitation and the affair itself (not without the help of a ghost-writer, of course) in a popular book, which, becoming a movie, brought Fitzgerald (not without the help of an actor, of course) back in triumph to the world of Hollywood from which he had died in despair. "There are no second acts in American lives," he had written in the notes to himself appended to the manuscript of *The Last Tycoon,* and "not one survived the castration." But he had forgotten about what was then still called "the silver screen."

No matter—for better or worse what exists of *The Last Tycoon* had fixed forever (or perhaps merely caught once and for all) a pattern which has been repeated over and over again in books as vastly different from each other as Christopher Isherwood's *Prater Violet,* Norman Mailer's *The Deer Park,* and Robert Penn Warren's *Flood.* Expatriate Englishman, wandering Jew, and transplanted Southern Agrarian, each portrays in his own way the romance of Celt or WASP writer and Jewish moviemaker, a sentimental allegory signifying the capitulation of High Art to Pop Art, not in terror, however, but in pity and affection. Isherwood reveals the meaning of the encounter and the surrender with an uncustomary candor (though he, for reasons of his own, eschews the word "Jew"), permitting the one of his ill-matched pair who bears his own name to comment just before the novel's close: "Mother's Boy, the comic Foreigner with the funny accent. Well, that didn't matter . . . For, beneath our disguises . . . we knew. Beneath outer consciousness, two other beings . . . had met and recognized each other, and had clasped hands. He was my father. I was his son. And I loved him very much."

But, of course, Isherwood's Herr Bergman, the director in flight from the Nazis and toward Hollywood, *is* a Jew—just as is Mailer's Charles Francis Eitel, in flight from congressional investigating committees toward death, and even Robert Pen Warren's Yasha Jones, camouflaged behind an assumed last name and oddly at loose ends in the American Deep South. Yet each of these authors plays games with the deepest mythological identity of the adopted father, who represents to each the real maker of the movies for which they aspire to be given screen credits at least. Mailer is less coy and cagey about Eitel's origins in the dramatic version of *The Deer Park* than he was in the earlier novel; but even in the later work Eitel when challenged admits only to being "half Jewish—on both sides" and in a context which makes it clear that he habitually lies about such matters. And though Brad Tolliver, the WASP writer of Warren's *Flood,* would clearly love his director to be a Jew, the author will not grant him this mythological satisfaction—insisting that Yasha Jones is a "deraciné Georgian— . . . Georgia in Russia"; and when Brad says wistfully, "I thought you were a Jew," his longed-for foreign father answers oddly, "I sometimes think I am . . . But we Georgians have a noble history, too."

Perhaps the problem arises in large part simply because, in the years since *The Last Tycoon,* the typical American novelist has ceased to be a provincial Gentile and has become himself an urban Jew, while the refugees to Hollywood (Daniel Fuchs, for instance, and West himself) were already often Jewish even in Fitzgerald's own time—so that the contrast of pre-Gutenburg Gentile and post-Gutenburg Jew was ceasing to be viable at the moment it was first being imagined. Yet how hard that mythological vision is to surrender even for Jews themselves, who, like Mailer, project *goyish* alter egos to represent their own entry into Hollywood, or, like Peter Viertel, invert the legendary romance—pitting a Jewish obsolescent writer against an Old Hollywood Pro turned super-Goy, or, more precisely maybe, super-Hemingway. Hemingway's name is, at any rate, often on the lips of Viertel's John Wilson, who views himself as having followed in the steps of the Master, only to go beyond by rendering in unspeaking images more appropriate than words the simplicity and silence which Hemingway pursued. But maybe *all* Hollywood Pros tend to think of themselves as Hemingways, even the Jews, in a penultimate irony which demands that the grave-diggers of books find a metaphor for their own lives in the career of a writer of books—who himself, in a more ultimate irony, defined his life style in imitation of that movie cowboy Gary Cooper. Fitzgerald, certainly, whose own attitudes toward Hemingway were more complex than this, thought it all a sad joke, jotting down among his notes for the background of *The Last Tycoon:* "Tragedy of these men was that nothing in their lives had really bitten deep at all. Bald Hemingway characters."

Viertel's Hemingway character is quite another matter, however, more like the author's flattering image of himself than Fitzgerald's wry vision of his bald imitators, a true communicant in the Church of Raw Experience and Mortal Danger, appropriately portrayed at play in the jungles of Africa. But he is no anti-semite like the first Hemingway, this second one turned moviemaker; and he is shown choosing to insult the latter-day Lady Brett of *White Hunter, Black Heart* rather than join her in vilification of the updated Robert Cohen, who is his companion and surrogate for the book's author. "And suddenly the lady next to me," Wilson tells his own anti-semitic lady-interlocuter, as his put-down begins, "and she was a beautiful lady, said that the one thing she didn't mind about Hitler was what he'd done to the Jews. Well, dear, I turned to her, and everyone was silent, and I said, 'Madam, I have dined with some ugly, goddamn bitches in my time. I've dined with some of the goddamnedest, ugliest bitches in the world, but you, dear, are the ugliest bitch of them all.' "

This is not just a pious political stand, a final development of Popular Front politics before it fades into general American liberalism, required of all men of good will after Hitler—though it is this in large part. It is also a declaration of allegiance to the movies themselves and the force that made them; since the movies *are* Jewish, after all: a creation of Jewish ingenuity and surplus Jewish capital, a by-product of the Jewish Garment Industry, which began by blurring away class distinctions in dress and ended by blotting out class distinctions in dreams. But the movies are, alas, ceasing to be Jewish, which is to say, they are dying—dying into something else.

These days there is scarcely a film produced which is not in fact an embryo TV program, its brief appearance in the neighborhood theater as clearly an intermediate step on the way to a lifelong run on the Late, Late Show as the appearance in hard covers of a new book by, say, James Michener, has been for a long time an intermediate step to a flick at that neighborhood theater. And (peace to Lenny Bruce, who first revealed to me the scope and depth of this distinction) as surely as chocolate is Jewish and fudge *goyish,* so are the movies Jewish and TV *goyish.* What the implications of this are beyond the fact that new mythologies of Pop Culture will have to be invented to suit new needs and that the figure of the Jew is almost sure to be absent from them I, the spiritual child of those Jewish Sages Marx and Freud, leave to those sitting even now at the feet of *goyish* Gurus like Marshall McLuhan and Norman O. Brown.

R. V. CASSILL

In the Central Blue

Ordinarily I considered it no drawback that there was no theater in our little farming town of Chesterfield. But in the case of World War I air movies I felt different. At puberty I was very airminded, and it seemed a large disaster when I missed *Wings*.

The week it played in Nebraska City spring thaws took the bottom out of the gravel road for miles east of the bridge we would have to cross to get there. Toward the end of the week when the road began to get firmer, I was struck down by fever and diarrhea. My affliction was probably brought on by anxiety about the road conditions and by arguing with my father about whether, at full power and with three boys to push, his Essex might not churn its way through the bad spots to the bridge.

My older brother and my best friend Hudson Fowler saw the picture, driving over to Nebraska City at the week's end with a truck full of other kids from Chesterfield. From an upstairs window I watched the truck pull away, crouched in my weakness, nursing the envy manifested in the uncontrollable, spastic burning of my gut. My father hunted me out to say that if I "had taken care of myself"—instead of dashing across wet lawns and fields outside of town all week without boots to prove that the earth was *not* mirey underfoot—I might now be going with the others. If I just hadn't got so excited about a darn airplane movie, I wouldn't have overtaxed my system.

The lesson was plain enough without his pointing the moral. But I wouldn't have it. In the darkness of the privy that evening I shit it away. In their wobbly, sassy little Spads, the boys had gone up there without me. The little line of dots pocked the canvas of their fuselages. Spitting black blood, their clean American faces lolled on the padded rims of the cockpits. In his black triplane with a black scarf crackling in the slipstream, the Kraut laughed at us all. Wind whistled around the ill-fitting privy door. Its mockery and the stink of my own excrement were no more offensive to me than my father's common sense judgment on my psychosomatic folly. I rebelled against them all.

So, if I had missed *Wings,* I was not going to miss *Hell's Angels.* After so long a time, I'm not sure how much later, it came to the theater in Nebraska City. It must have come at least a year afterward, because by then both my friend Hudson and I had graduated into high school, my older brother got to take the car out in the evening for dates, and I was in love with Hudson's blonde and titless cousin Betty.

I loved her ignorantly, impurely, and intermittently, sometimes unfurling toward her passions that had been cultivated for other objects and which were, no doubt, more appropriate when directed toward building model airplanes, shooting Germanic spatsies from the mulberry tree with antiaircraft fire from my Stevens' Crackshot, or working up nurse-aviator fantasies by a near simultaneous reading of *War Aces* and *Silver Screen* magazines.

Good little Betty couldn't have known what I wanted of her when I scrimmaged for a seat next to her in algebra class. At Halloween of our freshman year I caught her by accident as she was coming—costumed and masked—across the parking lot to the back entrance of the high school building to the party. She couldn't have known what I did to her then when I drew her out of the moonlight into the shadow of the fire escape and kissed her. I took off running in the direction of the Chesterfield grain elevator and went past it for a mile down the moon-glinting railroad tracks, convinced that I had done to her what Lieutenant Frank Luke did to the French nurse before he took off for his last spree of balloon busting.

So she couldn't have known what I had in store for her when I invited her to go to Nebraska City with me to see *Hell's Angels*. That is, she couldn't have guessed at thirteen—or at thirty-five for that matter, when she had boys of her own to study and wonder about—what role she had been assigned to play in my intense imaginative life. She might have expected that I would try to kiss her in the car while we were riding home from Nebraska City with my brother and his date after the movie was over. Certainly I meant to do that and probably try to put one of my hands where she would eventually have breasts like Jean Harlow's. At thirteen she was prepared to sink her nails in my impudent hand and laugh it off with a merry, "None of *that!*"

But it was not a physical assault on her that I planned or needed. I was going to ravish her mind. With the aid of this powerful movie plus a few tickles and kisses afterward, I was going to wheedle her mind right away into the realm of wish and nonsense, where I was so lonely all by myself.

I had been making myself at home there since I had first begun to understand what this movie was going to be about. Of course I hadn't seen it yet, but months before I had read about it—probably in *Silver Screen*—and seen pictures of Jean Harlow in white furs with those big, bruise-toned spots under her eyes, of the burning Zeppelin, and of the Same Browne–belted heroes who tangled with both.

There had been a bit of verse in the piece I read:

> Hell's angels,
> Soaring in the central blue,
> As though to conquer Heaven
> And plant the banner of Lucifer
> On the most high. . . .

It was the verse which provided the cipher or incantation that really took me out. Out *there*. Through the hot days of that summer there would be a lot of occasions when I was lying there with my bare naked thigh against the chill linoleum, beating away with the Harlow picture propped up in front of me, and just before I came, in that instant of focused self-awareness when I had stopped listening for the sound of my mother moving in the kitchen or my father or brother entering the house, I would say "In the central blue" and *be there*. I would be one of them. And I thought, wouldn't it be a lot happier if Betty would become one too and be out there with me, since she was a girl?

What? Beg pardon? Once again . . . ? How did I think this mating in the central blue was going to take place?

No use asking. I am no longer a mystic, so I no longer know. I repeat, merely, that in those months before my fourteenth birthday I anticipated that with the help of *Hell's Angels* I was going to ravish Betty Carnahan's mind. Too bad that I can't give a more satisfactory explanation. Anyway, it was in the hope of mental ravishment that I made the date with her two weeks before the movie came and with breathless stealth arranged that the two of us would go over to Nebraska City with my brother and his girl to see it.

Hudson Fowler behaved despicably when he heard that I was taking Betty. He acted as if it was his right to go with me if I had found a ride. "Get your mind above your belt," he said. "What do you want to do intercourse with that little nitwit for?"

"I don't," I said. I was shocked on many counts. Shocked by so much resentment from him just because I wasn't asking him along.

His odd choice of expression shocked me into awareness that there was a fishy unreality in my plans for Betty.

He saw he had me on the defensive. "You pretend you're just interested in the airplanes," he crowed.

"They're burning a two-million-dollar zeppelin in this one."

"While all the time you just want an excuse to see Jean Harlow's legs. Listen, I've got a notion to show Aunt Ellen that dirty magazine you gave me and see if she lets Betty go with you at all."

The dirty magazine he alluded to was my copy of the movie magazine with choice shots of Miss Harlow in her starring role. It could hardly have shocked Mrs. Carnahan into an interference with my date. Hudson, with unscrupulous insight into the uses I had put it to, was merely using it to discomfort me.

"All right. Go ahead and take her," he said savagely. "But just remember this. Whatever happens over there"—he made *over there* sound splendidly more like Flanders Fields than like Nebraska City— "I've already done intercourse with her."

In the face of such challenge I had to claim, "Well, so have I."

"At the family reunion in Sidney. Behind the rodeo barns."

"At the Halloween party. On the school fire escape," I said.

Then we both called each other liars and backed away, throwing sticks and bits of bark and finally good sized rocks at each other's heads.

I should have known he wouldn't let it go at that. He got to my brother and with some sort of specious implication that I, his best friend, wouldn't dream of seeing this great movie without him, he arranged to go with us. Having conned my brother, Hudson insinuated to Betty and his Aunt Ellen that I hadn't so much been asking for a date as offering to share a historical cultural experience with Betty when I invited her to the movie. I suppose that such an implication was welcome to Mrs. Carnahan, in spite of my good reputation.

At any rate, when I bounded up on the Carnahan's porch just before dusk on that cold December afternoon—freshly bathed and shivering and wearing just a dash of my mother's perfume—who should come out in answer to my knock but Betty *and* Hudson. I didn't know then what arrangements had been made behind my back. All I knew was that I couldn't stand there, practically within earshot of Mrs. Carnahan and Betty's father, and go through the argument about Betty with Hudson again. He had me.

He had me good, and the rest of the evening was just one failing attempt after another to retrieve what I could from the disastrous misunderstandings he had set going. At least on the ride over Betty sat between Hudson and me in the back seat of the Essex. I fancied that she got a whiff or two of me in spite of the strong perfume she was wearing. Hudson and I bellowed the Air Force song back and forth for her benefit. In the front seat Betheen Hesseldahl, the big, cowy girl my brother was going with then, alternately nuzzled her face in his neck and sat as far away from him as she could move, asking for a cigarette. "Not in front of the kids," he growled. "Later," he promised. I managed to get my arm up on the back of the seat behind Betty for a mile or two. The trip over wasn't so bad.

But when we went into the theater things got horribly disarranged. I hung back politely to let the others slide into their seats first, and then found that Hudson was sitting between Betty and me. I could feel my bowels begin to writhe and burn. I leaned to Hudson's ear and called him a sonofabitch.

He caught me hard in the ribs with his elbow. "Ssssh! Look! There she is. Just like in the magazine."

What was going on—as I understood later, perhaps years later, when my equilibrium was at last restored—was the famous scene in which Harlow gets into something more comfortable. That was going on for the others. I was down between the rows of seats trying to get a lock on Hudson's arm and force him out of his place. He was trying to pay no attention to me. He burst into loud cackles, whether at the sight of Jean Harlow in *negligee* or at my plight I have no idea.

The usher came to quiet us. For the rest of the movie I huddled motionless. I wouldn't have trusted myself to try to speak, even at

the break after the feature. My brother sidled out past me to get popcorn for everyone and muttered, "What's the matter with you?" but
I didn't answer him. Hudson said, "Boy, it really got me when that
little plane came in over that big dirigible. You know it was *real.*"
The sneak knew he had gone too far with me and was trying to make
up, but I didn't even turn my head.

It was my impression that I didn't see a single bit of the movie.
Only, afterward, as we were driving out of Nebraska City across that
high, silvery bridge with the dry moon coming up over the Iowa
bluffs, I began to get images that must have been before my eyes in
the theater. Between the struts of the bridge I saw the RAF insignias
and the snapping ribbons from the ailerons as the flight leader brought
his planes up alongside us. There were black, darting shapes down
where the silhouette of willows cut the reflecting glitter of ice near the
Iowa shore.

A little later—not in any sequence that would have appeared in
the film—I saw the Krauts in their zeppelin panic and prepare to cut
loose the observation car dangling a mile below them over London.
I was in that little teardrop contraption and I knew what they were
doing. There was no way to stop them. Only a fool would have let
himself in for such a mission.

And then Harlow was all over me. Her silks were jiggling like
moonlight on my retinas and that white hair was moving in like a
cloud on a high wind. The bruise-toned shadow of her cleavage was
so close to my face that my eyes crossed trying to keep it in focus.
I turned to Betty. She was leaning back quite peaceably in the crook
of Hudson's shoulder. Her eyes were open and as far as I could make
out, she was smiling. Hudson's free hand was stuck in between the
buttons of her winter coat.

What I did then was inexcusable. That is, it is the kind of thing
for which one's own psyche never, never finds a tolerable excuse, so
that when you say to yourself long afterward, "Why I was only a
fumbling, ignorant kid then," still the eye of memory averts itself.

While she leaned back in Hudson's arms, I tried to neck her. I
tried to kiss her while his face was so close to hers that I could feel

his hot breath on my cheek. I tried to unbutton her coat, not so much to get his hand out of it as to get mine in too.

"What are you little monkeys *doin'* back there?" Betheen Hessendahl wanted to know. She leaned over the back of the seat and giggled.

"You're crazy," Betty said.

"He's gone crazy," Hudson said, with maddening self-assurance. "Too much Harlow."

"Well, give everyone a cigarette," Betheen suggested.

My brother argued that the smell of tobacco would stay in the car and displease our parents. But in a minute he pulled to the side of the road and lit two. He gave one to Betheen and kept the other himself. After two drags she leaned back and passed it to us.

She passed it to Betty Carnahan, rather, and I can not describe the horror and excitement I felt when Betty leaned forward and puckered her lips to draw on it. It was not I who had had too much Harlow. It was Betty. Her mind had, somehow, been truly ravished by what she had seen. In the red glow from the cigarette a positively obscene merriment flickered over her little face. It was quite beyond anything I had meant for her. At that moment, and only then, I believed that she had been behind the rodeo barns at Sidney with her cousin.

I made up my mind then and there that after we had dropped Hudson at his house I would ask my brother to take Betty and me straight home. I knew it was his habit to take Betheen or one of his other girls to park down behind the grain elevator in an empty field at the end of his Sunday night dates, and in all the arrangements for this evening I thought it had been tacitly assumed that Betty and I might go there with them tonight. Now I didn't want to go. My mixed intentions had begun a process of depravity that had to be stopped. I wanted to go back to the innocence of that evening earlier in the fall when I had kissed Betty by the fire escape and run away.

Caught in such unfathomable hypocrisy, I hardly noticed that my brother stopped the car first in front of our house at the edge of Chesterfield.

"Good night," Betty said. "Thanks for the movie."

My brother said, "Hurry up. If the folks are awake they might look out and see we're back."

I said "No."

They coaxed, they argued, they scoffed. That is, Betheen and my brother did—for guessable motives wanting me out of the car so they could quickly leave the other two at Betty's door. And when persuasion got them nowhere, they made the mistake of trying to extract me from the rear seat by force.

I was too stubborn to see that nothing remained to be salvaged from my evening. I simply clung and kicked. I grabbed indiscriminately at the upholstery, the window cranks, and Betty. Once I caught big-shouldered Betheen under the chin with my knee. In her recoil she cracked her head on the door frame. A pretty brawl!

They were still tugging uselessly when my father came out. He was wearing his old bath robe with galoshes over his bare shins. I guess he'd thought we were having some trouble with the car when he started out into the cold.

"Why, you ought to be ashamed," he said to me as he grasped the real nature of our trouble. "Why, Betty's cousin can see that she gets home safe."

"I'd have let him come along if he hadn't put up such a fuss," my brother said. "He kicked Betheen."

"Gee, my mother will worry if I don't get home soon, 'cause tomorrow's a school day," Hudson said.

"Good night," Betty said, with just a precocious hint of sophistication.

Ah, I was ashamed all right. Ashamed of the whole sick, sorry human race as I walked through the frosty yard with my father. The tail lights of the Essex were already disappearing around the corner of the Christian church.

My father threw his arm around my shoulder. He wasn't as foolish or as hypocritical as his remark had made him sound. It was just that he, too, saw no way out of the tangle except to subtract me from it. It had gone beyond considerations of justice. All that remained was to restore order. "You'll see Hudson and Betty at school tomorrow," he said. "You'll see them every day. Thing's 'll go better if you just forget what happened tonight."

I didn't answer.

"Now then, you're too old to cry," he said.

"Well, I'm crying, you bastard."

I expected him to hit me then. In fact you might say I had invited it and would have welcomed the punishment for having been such an idiot.

But he couldn't bring himself to do it. We were standing on the porch by then, and I saw him in fuzzy silhouette against the moonlit yard. I saw him waver as though he were lifting his fist but couldn't quite make it, and then, maybe for the first time, I saw him in his human dimension, bewildered and tugged in contrary directions like me.

"We better get some rest." That was the only moral he could draw from what he had just seen.

You remember that at the end of *Hell's Angels* there is a sequence in a German prison. One of the fly-boy brothers—of course it is the one who *missed* the hanky-panky with Miss Harlow in London that night the zep came over and she got into her comfort suit—has to shoot his sibling with a pilfered Luger to keep him from betraying plans for the spring offensive to the enemy. There's a lot of poetic justice in the shooting. One is made to feel the traitor should have kept it in his pants whatever provocations the Sexual Adversary offered. Morality is vindicated with bookkeeping precision. With the Luger still smoking in his hot little hand, the killer sniffles about *mein bruder* to a baffled Hun.

It has taken me a terrific, lifelong integrative effort to resurrect a memory of that movie with even a tint of morality or poetic justice. The images that first stuck with me composed a very different pattern. That night I lay under the covers sleeplessly waiting for my brother to come home, agonizing the minutes it would take him to get rid of

Betty and Hudson, the minutes it would take to wheel down past the elevator for a quick feel and a kiss, and the other minutes to deliver Betheen home and come back.

I had no weapon to commit a physical murder with. But as plainly as if it were on a silver screen I could see myself hauling a Luger out of the bedclothes as he entered the room and began to undress. I would sneer, *"Mein bruder,"* and let him have it between the eyes. After him, the others, one by one. Then—"spinning through stardust and sunshine"—down I'd go. Down, down, down. Where, after all, my true desires had been tending.

DAVID SLAVITT

Critics and Criticism

M y daddy," says the first little first-grade kid, "is a dentist."

"Very good, Harvey," says the teacher. "And you, Edna? What does your daddy do?"

"My daddy is a grocer."

"Very good. And Jimmy, what does your daddy do?"

"My daddy plays the piano in a whorehouse."

Consternation! Shock! Fury! And off to the principal's office, where little Jimmy is asked to explain this bizarre tastelessness, and, the joke goes, he does explain, saying that actually his father reviews movies for *Time*. But he didn't want to tell that to the class because he was ashamed of it.

And the funniest part of it all is that little Jimmy is right. It isn't respectable. I could never even bring myself to say, with a straight face, that I was a "film critic," but used to admit to being a "flicker picker," which had about the right ring to it—glib and brassy—and was just puzzling enough so that, by the time people had figured out what the hell I was talking about, the shock of it had worn off a little. It wasn't *Time,* but *Newsweek,* the main difference being that *Newsweek* pays a little less.

It was a weird life. I used to see six or eight movies a week in a good week. In a bad week it could go to fourteen. Once, I think, it was twenty. Fantastic! And not entirely unattractive—I liked it, actually. It was fun to race around from screening room to screening room, accumulating cast-and-credit sheets and mimeographed synopses that were invariably inaccurate and seemed to have been translated, badly, from the Japanese. I got used to seeing cowboys shooting the hell out of each other at ten in the morning, while I smoked cigarettes and drank coffee from Jack-Mo's Delicatessen on West Forty-ninth Street. I got to like the routine of absorbing all those movies and then at the end of the week squeezing my brain like a sponge to turn out the reviews. And it did get to be a routine. It even got to the point where I was playing games with myself, the way I did when I was a youngster and had a summer job stamping textbooks for the Row Peterson Company, "Property of the Board of Education of the City of New York." At Row Peterson the game was simply one of speed—to see how many of those waxy workbooks one could stamp in three minutes. (I still remember the *Through the Green Gate* workbook: Alice, of the old Alice and Jerry duo, was bending over, and it was a refinement of the simple race to require that the stamp be right on Alice's backside.) And with movie reviews, too, I started racing with myself. I did a standard sixty-line movie review in about twenty minutes.

I have been trying to make this as homely and as vulgar as possible, because it ought to be. It was. There is not any such thing as film criticism, and that gaggle of reviewers, magazine and newspaper reviewers alike, were all faking it, one way or another. Or they were lucky enough to be such natural fakes that they could do it sincerely, take it seriously, have committment. But what good is the sincerity of a natural-born fake?

The situation is simple enough. Our best criticism, by which I mean both best written and with the greatest degree of influence, is criticism of poetry. The only people who read poetry anyway are poets and critics of poetry. It is a nice, or nicely nasty, coherent community. One writes about poetry with a comfortable certainty that one's audience shares at least a few assumptions about the value of art, and the aims of art. The art itself is sufficiently moribund to allow for brilliant demonstrations of its anatomy. Movies, however, are distressingly alive. Film is the great popular medium, with an audience of incredible size, a commercial vigor which, though somewhat diminished from the halcyon pre-television days, is still staggering, and perhaps most appallingly even an artistic potentiality that realizes itself with some frequency in works of an undeniable excellence. There are more good movies in any given year than there are good plays or good novels. Reviewing films, then, or criticizing films, is like reviewing or criticizing a blizzard or a war. The critic is laughably impotent, has no influence either with the film-makers or with the film audiences, has no suitable or adequate vocabulary with which to discuss the films for his putative reader, and, perhaps worst of all, has no position on which to stand, from which to formulate a general theory of what he is trying to do or wants to say, and no way of rationalizing his intellectual career. One cannot write about *Cleopatra* and *Otto e Mezzo* in the same week, on the same page, without going a little bit schizy. So, one makes it up, one fakes it. I suppose the formula is sociology and psychology for the pop films and belle-lettrist aestheticism for the "serious" films. But it's treacherous. Laurel and Hardy, who were always condemned by the critics, are now revived. So pop comedy is "serious." But the only pop comic working now in America is Jerry Lewis, who is terrible, but not quite terrible enough to be dismissed out of hand.

Or, to go at it from another angle, consider the only recent attempt at a general theory of film to have had any currency whatever in the past five years or so. The *auteur* theory of the *Cahiers du Cinéma* people wilfully ignores the dank jungles of personality and commerce in the depths of which directors must stalk their elusive quarry of quality. Blandly, they pin it on the director as if he were a poet, sitting at a desk somewhere with a nickel pencil and a dime pad, creating. But he isn't. None of them is. He's got a two-million-dollar pad, and a pencil with its own vanity, temper, ability, or lack of it. His success will depend on the script, of course, but on the budget, too. And on the cast, and even on the scheduling. No movie can be serious, can afford to take the risks that are a part of serious-ness, with a budget of more than ten million dollars, no matter what *auteur* you've got setting up the shots. The genesis of the theory, however, was legitimate enough. When Manny Farber observed, back in the forties, that Howard Hawks on his crummy "B" budgets was turning out nice, grainy, tough movies, and coined the phrase "un-derground films" to describe Hawks's spectacular successes, working against the very grain of the industry, he made an absolutely legiti-mate observation . . . about Hawks's films of the forties. The *auteur* theory merely generalizes from this. A Hawks film is now a good film. A Minelli film is a good film; Hitchcock is good. But it doesn't work. Hawks, Hitchcock, and Minelli have been awful, especially lately (*Hatari; The Birds* and *Marnie; The Sandpiper*) . But no matter. The question is not one of accuracy in the reviews but sanity on the part of the reviewer. It isn't just that very expensive movies tend to be bad, and cheap movies tend to be bad. That would be easy. But good movies tend to be bad. (Bresson is very pure, but boring. Fellini is theatrical, but often in a vulgar way. Antonioni, who is serious, is often both boring *and* vulgar.*) And bad movies tend to be good. (Laurel and Hardy, Busby Berkely, Bogart, Jerry Lewis, even Elvis Presley, in a slick, glycerined, unpretentious way.)

Small wonder, then, that most critics are nervous, twitchy fellows who are comfortable only in dark rooms. They manage, one way or another, to survive, but the one way is incompetence and the other is lunatic pretension.

The newspaper critics are mainly incompetent. The best of them are in New York, and the ones in New York are terrible. (Judith

*No, no, I don't mean dirty. I mean vulgar. Soap opera-ish. Extravagant. Excessive.

Crist was the only one who could pass a freshman course in expository writing in even the most obscure cow college in the country—and her paper folded.) Archer Winston knows something about film, but can't write. The important, influential critics, of course, are Bosley Crowther, for the washed, and "Kate Cameron" for the unwashed hordes. ("Kate Cameron" is a fake name, like "T.V. Dailey," who writes the "Pick of TV" column in a lot of newspapers. I forget, or have blocked out, her real name.) Mr. Crowther is a national disaster, and "Kate Cameron" is a joke. Crowther cannot write and doesn't know anything about films, but he's a nice man and tries very hard, which only makes matters worse. He is usually about two films behind everyone else, so that when *L'Avventura* came out and everyone else thought it was either good or interesting or worth something, he thought it was terrible. To make up for this he liked *Red Desert,* but by that time the tide had turned, and everyone else hated it. He detested *Dr. Strangelove,* but by the end of the year seemed to have heard that other people had liked it, and there it was at the top of his "Ten Best List."* He liked *The Longest Day,* and *Cleopatra,* and . . . but he can't help it.

The other influential critics are *Time* and *Newsweek.* The foregoing is a tortured grammatical construction, because the reality is a tortured situation. Any clown whom *Time* or *Newsweek* hires for the movie desk becomes, ex officio, the second or third most influential critic in the world (Crowther is number one). This influence is partly a function of circulation and partly the result of utter corruption in the provinces, where reviewers on out-of-town papers find out what they think by reading the Sunday New York *Times, Time,* and *Newsweek.* So, at twenty-seven, I had not only *Newsweek's* eight million or so readers, but all the readers of all the "critics" who were copying from me. (Power? No! Movie reviews don't make any difference, anyway, except on art films from Europe brought in by small distributors who don't have the money for big ad campaigns or the leverage to get the mass bookings.)

The *modus vivendi* at the "weekly newsmagazine" and the "news-

---

*Crowther's "Ten Best List" is chronological, and *Dr. Strangelove* was on top because it was released in January; it looked terrible just the same.

weekly" is a sort of freneticism of life and prose. A friend of mine, a former *Time* man who once sat in for writer Bradford Darrach, the then movie critic, while Darrach was on vacation, tells me that in the course of rummaging through Darrach's desk drawers looking for booze, candy bars, cigarettes, and other treasure, he discovered a box of three-by-five index cards of puns, which fragments Darrach had shored against his ruin. I am not sure that this is true (my friend is a great liar), but it might as well be. "Timestyle" is nowhere more extravagant than in the Cinema section, where it serves an additional function of giving the writer something to hide behind. If hyped-up prose, puns, and enjambments like "cinemoppet" are annoying after a while, they are less limiting than something like the *auteur* theory, and they serve the same function. It is a point of reference, an established attitude which the writer can take toward the bewildering variety and diversity of the films about which he writes. The *Newsweek* persona is a little less definite. Nobody ever said this to me, but I soon found out that the way to survive was to be like *Time,* only a little less so. I punned less frequently and only hyped up the prose an eentsy bit. And I found a sort of attitude, which might best be characterized as a perpetual condition of raped innocence. (Innocence, perpetually raped, cannot long survive, and after two years I was beginning to enjoy it, so I quit.) *Newsweek,* because it is less stylized than *Time,* throws the writer more and more back upon himself, which is good, but that makes for difficulties too. The copy does go through the hands of four editors, and the more self one puts into it, the more one resents changes. I remember I was furious when one of the editors changed "Feh" to "Fah" because "Feh" sounded too Jewish. They used to take out puns, too, sometimes, but I could always save them up and use them later in the *Yale Review.**

The *New Yorker* is the other special case among magazines, in that it too has an identity of a kind, a personality into which the reviewer can merge himself, and in which he can hide, when necessary. The *New Yorker* is especially fortunate in that Brendan Gill is

---

*It's worse now. The system is the same, but the reviews are signed now—so even that small moral hedge is gone.

its reviewer, and he is so successful posing for them as the world's most sophisticated man that I am willing to grant that he *is* the world's most sophisticated man. He writes well, is intelligent about movies, and is flexible enough to be able to respond on the widely different levels that the differing films demand. He can review Satyajit Ray or Nicholas Ray and not go out of his mind trying to make the jump. He makes mistakes sometimes, and likes bad movies, or dislikes good ones, but he is nearly always right, and nearly always worth reading. The point, anyway, is not to be correct in grading these movies, but to write interestingly about them. Dr. Johnson was often wrong, and was a great critic anyway. The only regrettable thing about Brendan Gill is that he is a very good novelist, but those people who have heard of him mostly think of him as the *New Yorker* movie reviewer. He won, and deserved to win, a National Book Award, but he's still the *New Yorker*'s man at the movies. Which is a shame.

For the rest, there is no mask, no mold, no disguise, and they all have to make it up for themselves. They take their cues from their magazines about the level on which they ought to try to write, but even that is precious little help. The movies themselves are so unruly as to make the mass magazine critics inadequate and the academic and scholarly quarterly critics uncomfortable. There is simply no comfortable posture to take. The *McCall's* critic is strained to fantastic intellectualism, while the *Partisan Review*'s critic is on a slumming party. Some get around it by dint of personal eccentricity. Dwight MacDonald, for instance, having come to this peculiar cultural cul-de-sac of writing about movies for *Esquire,* brought a history of political involvement which was not entirely irrelevant. Having given up on everything about the Russian Revolution except its notion of the possibilities of the film as the art form of the masses, he maintained an allegiance to Eisenstein and Pudovkin, which, with his own crankiness and good prose, was enough to get by on. Stanley Kauffmann, who was at the movie desk of the *New Republic* when I was working, got by on a strange kind of stuffiness which was leavened by lechery. His prose came alive when he addressed himself to some gut issue, as, for instance, the relative attractiveness of

Ann-Margret and Jane Fonda. If anything saved him, that did, for one cannot write about the standard Hollywood product for very long without some feeling of connection, and that was a connection. Unfortunately, he split himself, and in his anonymous reviews for *Playboy* gave more attention to the girlies—which was sensible, but which impoverished the pieces for the *New Republic* somewhat. He was stuffier there. Kauffmann has since left the *New Republic* for the drama page of the New York *Times,* and returned to the old stand to write mostly about first novels (in which no one is interested). Pauline Kael, who now deals with movies for the *New Republic,* is rangier than he was, rangier, in fact, than any American critic, responds across the board, does not flinch from using her feminine license to be bitchy, and is the only critic beside Brendan Gill whom I still read with any regularity or interest.

Perhaps the worst film criticism is in the best magazines, the intellectual quarterlies, and the serious film magazines, in which the most intelligent and the most nearly literate practitioners try to function. They are not stupid or imperceptive, but, precisely because of their deficiencies in stupidity and unfeelingness, they writhe on the wrack of unreasonableness which the medium demands. You cannot, with a straight face, examine a gesture in a film—Mastroianni, say, sucking at his tooth, or Belmondo rubbing his upper lip with his thumb—in the same way and with the same seriousness and exactitude your neighbors in the magazine display when they analyze an image in a poem or a trope in a novel. The techniques do not apply, and there is nothing more ridiculous or pathetic than the scholarly apparatus grinding away at nothing in elaborate discussions of images of triangles in *Jules and Jim.* The alternative is to go against the grain of the magazine, to be folksy, or casual, or hip, which fails too, because it is embarrassing. Or fails because it succeeds too well, and the readers are convinced not that the critic is *posing* as a lowbrow jerk, but that he *is* a lowbrow jerk, in which case to hell with him.

This is not a difficulty peculiar to film criticism. The whole boom in pop culture is a larger manifestation of this same phenomenon. One is uncomfortable on any level and is either too serious or not serious enough. Pop art and pop literature derive from comics and movies, but comics have the advantage over movies (and are therefore more important in pop art) because of their consistency. Comics are always bad, always stupid, always disreputable. To discuss comics in a serious way, to use them in painting or in fiction as if they were serious, is a simple business of bringing out into the open a taboo object. Mom, Dad, and teacher disapproved of comics. We'll show them. We'll make comics respectable. The satisfaction is the same as that derived from telling a dirty joke in mixed company for the first time and getting laughter and approval from everyone. With a large part of the movie culture you can work the same kind of kick. Mention Carmen Miranda in a serious way to a lot of intellectuals, and you're a genius. But mention Jeanne Moreau in a serious way, and you've said something merely banal and obvious. So you have to retrieve your status by going through some preposterous contortion like claiming that Moreau in *Viva Maria* was Carmen Miranda. To Brigitte Bardot's Jane Powell?

I suppose another way of putting all this would be to say that the film critic cannot take his identity from the art form, because the movies don't offer any identity. He can't take it from the magazine because, except in very special circumstances, he will be either uncomfortable or impossibly restricted. And he can't take it from literacy and intellectual fashion, because that way lies even surer madness than in the movies themselves. What he must do is what those few movie critics who have amounted to anything have done—and that is find it, somehow, somewhere, in himself. It's terribly unfair, and I can think of no other area of criticism which demands this kind of psychic integration on the part of its practitioners.

The late Robert Warshow, who was one of the few first-rate movie critics we have had, suggested that "A man watches a movie, and the critic must acknowledge that he is that man." When I first read that, I thought it was semi-opaque nonsense, but that was before I had been promoted from my position as saloon editor to the movie desk. I am amazed now at the lucidity and good sense of Warshow's observation. The critic has to admit that he was there. There is no theory to save him, no tradition to rely on, no coherence but the coherence of his soul. You sit there, in the dark, and are bombarded by images, dramatic sequences, painterly constructions, dialogue, cutting, acting, flesh, and you sip your coffee from Jack-Mo's Delicatessen and watch and listen. The medium is seductive (if you go into any movie in the middle and sit down, the first five or ten minutes is interesting, until it does something stupid or wrong), and you can't fight that, but neither can you give in to it, entirely. And then, at the end, you sort out not just whether it was any good, but whether it was good-good, or bad-good, or good-bad, or what . . . And then, when you write about it, you're not writing about the work of one man, but of fifty, and not about pure art, but about a strange soup made of money and morals and ego and, yes, art, too. And all you can do is try to be reasonably honest, not just in saying what you think, but in making sure that you do think what you think, or that you think at all.

In the end it is wearing, it is destructive, it is hopeless. It would be tolerable if movie critics were not widely read. Such a situation can be perfectly healthy. But to be read and *still* to be ignored is confusing and depressing. One learns to live with that, too. For a while.

It used to be, in the bad old days, that the movie companies would try to bribe the critics. Not directly, of course, which would have been at least honestly dishonest, but through the papers, by pulling ads from papers that had tough critics. They still do it, from time to time. But mostly it isn't necessary. The critics are a bunch of clowns promoted from covering weddings or shipping news or fires in Brooklyn to this dubious eminence. Or, occasionally, by some fluke of luck or nepotism, there is a bright, intellectual youngster all hot to write great film criticism. But the movie men have learned that, given a little time, such a bright young man is more than likely to corrupt himself.

References

The material included here is at once selected and limited. This reference section is made up of various basic books and periodicals recommended by the contributors and others, and it is intended only as a beginning, a starting place for further study of the movies from a variety of angles and viewpoints. The material is also further deliberately limited so as to include only those items which are (or should be) readily available.

Serious research, scholarly and critical, of the movies is only just beginning. Most libraries at this time have woefully inadequate collections of pertinent material. And, on the other hand, for some of the same reasons, there is much unnecessary duplication of the same sources and materials. In a short time much will have changed. Meanwhile it is hoped that this brief reference section will be useful not only to students and teachers, but also to all those who are seriously interested in the movies.

A SELECTIVE CHECKLIST OF BASIC MATERIAL

This list was prepared by George Broughton of the Department of Radio, Television, and Motion Pictures at the University of North Carolina (Chapel Hill).

Aesthetics of the Film

Arnheim, Rudolf. *Film as Art*. Berkeley: University of California Press, 1957.
A classic work in film aesthetics using primarily examples from the silent era of film. This book is a new and expanded translation of a work prepared early in the sound era.

Balazs, Bela. *Theory of the Film*. New York: Roy, 1953.
A posthumous edition of the works of one of the great European critics

345

and film-makers. The book is inclusive of all the arts; however, the art of film is given primary consideration throughout with examples from the Soviet silent films.

Bluestone, George. *Novels into Film*. Berkeley: University of California Press, 1966.
Bluestone begins with a discussion of the aesthetic as well as the practical problems of the adaptation of a film from a novel. In subsequent chapters, he discusses the problems involved in the making of films from six novels of literary merit. Each novel presents specific problems for the film-maker. Included in the specimen novels are *The Grapes of Wrath, The Ox-Bow Incident, Pride and Prejudice, Wuthering Heights, The Informer,* and *Madame Bovary*. An outstanding book.

Eisenstein, Sergei M. *Film Form*. New York: Harcourt, Brace, 1949. Paperback by Meridian, New York, 1957.
A series of essays in film theory by Sergei Eisenstein, edited and translated by Jay Leyda. This book provides insight into the theories of a great film-maker. In addition to this it is an introduction to the problems of the cinematic form.

Eisenstein, Sergei M. *The Film Sense*. New York: Harcourt, Brace, 1942. Paperback by Meridian, New York, 1957.
A highly theoretical book that makes difficult reading for the layman. Edited and translated by Jay Leyda, this book provides us with a sense of meaning for film. Leyda has also included appendices of excerpts from the works of Eisenstein.

Kracauer, Siegfried. *Theory of Film*. New York: Oxford University Press, 1960. Paperback by Galaxy, 1965.
A very complex book dealing with the theories of film. Kracauer traces the development of film from the early days of the still photograph and then follows this with an attempt to delineate a theory of film. In subsequent chapters he discusses areas and elements of film, composition of film, and film in our time. In addition to this, he includes an interlude discussion of the problems of the filmed novel.

Nicoll, Allardyce. *Film and Theatre*. New York: Crowell, 1936.
A comparison of the two media during the early days of film. Discusses the problems of filming Shakespeare.

Spottiswoode, Raymond. *A Grammar of the Film: An Analysis of Film Technique*. Berkeley: University of California Press, 1950.
A reprint of a work that first appeared in 1935, this book attempts a

formal outline of the techniques of the cinema as art. Also available in paperback.

Film Technique

Agee, James. *Agee on Film.* Boston: Beacon Press, 1964.
A paperback edition which contains five filmscripts by James Agee. Included is a foreword by John Huston. Agee was one of the first writers to recognize the cinema as a serious art medium.

Alton, John. *Painting with Light.* New York: Macmillan, 1949.
Written by one of the top photographers in Hollywood, this book is a readable account of studio camera techniques. The emphasis, however, is on lighting of both interior and exterior scenes. Illustrated throughout.

Baddeley, W. Hugh. *The Technique of Documentary Film Production.* New York: Hastings House Publishers, 1963.
This book deals with all aspects of the production of the factual film. Baddeley covers the entire process from beginning to end in a step-by-step form. A glossary is also included.

Carrick, Edward. *Designing for Moving Pictures.* Studio, 1947.
An easy-to-read account of the problems and solutions of set design.

Eisler, Hans. *Composing for the Films.* New York: Oxford University Press, 1947.
Eisler outlines a theoretical base for film music. One of the few considerations of the element of music as related to the film.

Mascelli, Joseph V. *The Five C's of Cinematography.* Hollywood: Cine/Grafic Publications, 1965.
A large format book that discusses the techniques of the film-maker. Included are chapters on camera angles, continuity, close-ups, composition, and cutting. An easy-to-read book with illustrations.

Nilsen, Vladimir. *The Cinema as a Graphic Art.* New York: Hill and Wang, 1959.
A discussion of the early Soviet films. Included are the works of Eisenstein and his collaborators. While this book is a reprint of a 1936 edition, many of the illustrations and theories are still in use today.

Oringel, Robert S. *Audio Control Handbook.* New York: Hastings House, 1963.
This book is a practical discussion of the various techniques used in every phase of audio control. The language of the book is as nontechnical as possible. An excellent book for the layman with an interest in the production of sound.

Quigley, Martin, Jr., ed. *New Screen Techniques*. Quigley, 1953.
An explanation of the mechanics, problems, and solutions of 3-D and wide-screen techniques. This book is illustrated throughout.

Spottiswoode, Raymond. *Film and Its Techniques*. Berkeley: University of California Press, 1951.
A detailed presentation of the techniques of factual film production. In-cluded are camera techniques, editing techniques, and a glossary. The book is illustrated throughout.

Trapnell, Coles. *Teleplay*. San Francisco: Chandler Publishing Co., 1966.
A very good introduction to the art of film writing. Contains the grammar, theory, preparation, and mechanics of script writing. Trapnell has included in the appendix a full length teleplay.

History of the Film

Agee, James. *Agee on Film; Reviews and Comments*. Boston: Beacon Press, 1964.
A paperback book containing the reviews written by James Agee between 1941 and 1948. During this time he was writing for *The Nation* and *Time*. Also includes an essay on comedy and a discussion of John Huston.

Balcon, Michael. *Twenty Years of British Films 1925–1945*. Falcon Press, 1947.
One of the National Cinema Series, this book includes works by several writers. It is compact, informative, and well-illustrated.

Crowther, Bosley. *The Lion's Share*. New York: Dutton, 1957.
This book is concerned mainly with the history of Metro-Goldwyn-Mayer. Of course this in effect traces the history of the growth of the American film industry.

Dickinson, Thorold, and Catherine De la Roche. *Soviet Cinema*. Falcon Press, 1948.
The history of the developing techniques of the Soviet film.

Griffith, Richard, and Arthur Mayer. *The Movies*. New York: Simon and Schuster, 1957.
A big book of pictures and text covering sixty years of film history in America. An excellent book for the layman desiring an introduction to films.

Griffith, Richard, and Paul Rotha. *The Film Till Now*. New York: Funk and Wagnalls, 1949.
A book that deals with the different movie trends in America, in their historical context. Examples are discussed in the context of the gangster

film, the western, etc. The question is raised concerning the effect of the film on society.

Hampton, Benjamin B. *A History of the Movies*. Covici, Friede, 1931.
A detailed account of the early growth of the major studios in America. A very good reference work concerning the patent wars.

Jacobs, Lewis. *The Rise of the American Film*. New York: Harcourt, Brace, 1939.
A history of the American motion-picture industry which deals with the audience, the economic factors, and the sociological factors. A very good reference work.

Jarratt, Vernon. *The Italian Cinema*. New York: Macmillian Co., 1951.
A historical and critical appraisal of the Italian film from before World War I until its rebirth after World War II.

Kracauer, Siegfried. *From Caligari to Hitler*. New York: Noonday Press, Inc., 1959.
This is a paperback book concerned with the psychological history of the German film. While being an important work on film, it is also a model for research by sociologists, psychologists, and students of "the film as propaganda." Virtually every important German film down to 1933 is discussed.

Low, Rachel. *The History of the British Film* (1896–1906, 1906–14, 1914–18) . London: Allen and Unwin, 1948–50.
Three volumes have appeared to date in what was to have been a thoroughly documented account of British film history. Undertaken by the British Film Institute and under the supervision of Roger Manvell, these volumes cover the least-known years of the British film.

Museum of Modern Art Film Library. *Film Notes,* Part I, *The Silent Film.* New York: Museum of Modern Art, 1949.
This is a publication of notes designed to accompany films. A good source, however, for researching films.

Ramsaye, Terry. *A Million and One Nights*. New York: Simon and Schuster. 1926.
A two-volume book that is concerned with the silent era of film. An excellent reference work. It is also indexed.

Sadoul, Georges. *French Film*. Falcon Press, 1953.
A concise history of the film in France through the Nazi occupation. One of the publications of the National Cinema Series.

The Film and Society

Huettig, Mae D. *Economic Control of the Motion Picture Industry.* Philadelphia: University of Pennsylvania Press, 1944.
A well-written statement of the problem of films. Although this book was written in 1944, it is still a valid contribution to the economic understanding of the film of today.

MacCann, Richard Dyer. *Film and Society.* New York: Charles Scribner's Sons, 1964.
A paperback edition of a research anthology on film. The book is a collection of written sources concerning film and its relationship to society. An excellent book for finding source material.

Manvell, Roger. *The Film and the Public.* Baltimore: Penguin Books, 1955.
A discussion of the various forms of censorship imposed upon the movie industry. Often very revealing.

Powermaker, Hortense. *Hollywood, the Dream Factory.* Boston: Little, Brown, 1950.
Dr. Powermaker is an anthropologist who attempts to apply the methods of science to the film industry. Her book uncovers the motives behind the power structure of Hollywood, a power structure which seems to encourage mediocrity.

ADDITIONAL MATERIALS RECOMMENDED BY CONTRIBUTORS

The form of listing in this section is, by design, slightly different from that employed in Section I. Brief annotations are offered only where they seem specifically relevant.

It should be remembered that a great deal of valuable criticism and information, largely uncollected, can be found in newspapers and newspaper supplements.

Useful and intelligent material dealing with specific films is regularly prepared and mailed out by the Saint Clement's Film Association (423 West 46th Street, New York City 10036).

Listings of interesting books and periodicals, foreign and domestic, new and old, are available from the Gotham Book Mart (41 West 47th Street, New York City 10036).

Two other well-known bookshops which specialize in movie books and materials are: Hampton Books, Hampton Bays, New York, and the Larry Edmunds Bookshop, 6658 Hollywood Blvd., Hollywood, California 90028.

Books

Ackerman, Forest J. (ed.). *The Best from Famous Monsters of Filmland.* New York: Paperback Library, 1964.

_____. *Famous Monsters of Filmland Strikes Back.* New York: Paperback Library, 1965.

_____. *Son of Famous Monsters of Filmland.* New York: Paperback Library, 1965.

Bogdanovich, Peter. *The Cinema of Howard Hawks.* New York: Museum of Modern Art, 1962.

_____. *The Cinema of Alfred Hitchcock.* New York: Museum of Modern Art, 1963.

_____. *The Cinema of Orson Welles.* New York: Museum of Modern Art, 1961.

Boyer, Deena. *The Two Hundred Days of 8½.* Translated by Charles Lam Markmann. Afterword by Dwight Macdonald. New York: Macmillan, 1964.

Calder-Marshall, Arthur. *The Innocent Eye: The Life of Robert J. Flaherty.* New York: Harcourt, Brace, and World, 1963.

Ceram, C. W. *Archaeology of the Cinema.* New York: Harcourt, Brace, and World, 1965.

Clarens, Carlos. *An Illustrated History of the Horror Film.* New York: Putnam, 1967. Sober, scholarly, and thorough, an encyclopedic history of the horror film.

Conway, Michael, Dion McGregor, and Mark Ricci. *The Films of Greta Garbo.* Introduced by Parker Tyler. New York: Citadel, 1963.

Cowie, Peter. *The Cinema of Orson Welles.* New York: Barnes, 1965.

_____. *Three Monographs: Antonioni, Bergman, Resnais.* New York: Barnes, 1963.

Donner, Jorn. *The Personal Vision of Ingmar Bergman.* Bloomington: Indiana University Press, 1964.

Durgnat, Raymond. *Nouvelle Vague: The First Decade.* Loughton (Essex): Motion Publications, 1966.

_____ and John Kobal. *Greta Garbo.* New York: Dutton Pictureback, 1965.

Everson, William K. *The Bad Guys: A Pictorial History of the Movie Villain.* New York: Citadel, 1964.

Fenin, George N., and William K. Everson. *The Western.* New York: Orion, 1962. A thorough, readable genre history.

Ford, Charles. *Histoire du Western.* Paris: Pierre Horay, 1964. Covers same ground as Fenin and Everson, only in French and using different stills.

Franklin, Joe. *Classics of the Silent Screen: A Pictorial Treasury.* New York: Bramhall House, 1959.

Goode, James. *The Story of* The Misfits. New York: Bobbs-Merrill, 1963.

Goodman, Ezra. *The Fifty Year Decline and Fall of Hollywood.* New York: Simon and Schuster, 1961.

Graham, Peter. *A Dictionary of the Cinema*. New York: Barnes, 1964. Contains "films-graphies" of directors, actors, writers, etc.

Griffith, Richard. *The Cinema of Gene Kelly*. New York: Museum of Modern Art, 1962.

_____. *Marlene Dietrich: Image and Legend*. New York: Museum of Modern Art, 1959.

_____. *Samuel Goldwyn: The Producer and His Films*. New York: Museum of Modern Art, 1956.

_____. *The World of Robert Flaherty*. London: Gollancz, 1953.

_____. *Fred Zinneman*. New York: Museum of Modern Art, 1958.

_____ and Arthur Mayer. *The Movies*. New York: Simon and Schuster, 1957.

Houston, Penelope. *The Contemporary Cinema*. Baltimore: Penguin, 1963.

Jacobs, Lewis (ed.). *Introduction to the Art of the Movies*. New York: Noonday, 1960. An anthology of ideas on the nature of movie art containing excerpts from the work of an impressive array of critics and theorists.

Kael, Pauline. *I Lost It at the Movies*. Boston: Little, Brown, 1965. Also available in Bantam paperback.

Knight, Arthur. *The Liveliest Art: A Panoramic History of the Movies*. New York: Macmillan, 1957. Also available in New American Library Paperback.

Lauritzen, Einar. *Swedish Films*. New York: Museum of Modern Art, 1962.

Limbacher, James L. *Feature Films on 16: A Directory of 16mm Sound Films Available for Rental from Major Distributors in the United States*. New York, Continental 16, Inc., 1966. An essential and valuable guide with full cross reference, addresses, etc., for the film society, school, or group.

McAnany, Emile G., S. J., and Robert Williams, S. J. *The Filmviewers' Handbook*. Glen Rock, N. J.: Paulist Press, 1965. Contains useful general bibliography and information about film societies.

MacCann, Richard Dyer (ed.). *Film: A Montage of Theories*. New York: Dutton, 1966. An interesting and useful collection of previously published materials. Particularly useful for rare material by European directors and critics.

McGowan, Kenneth. *Behind the Screen: The History and Techniques of the Motion Picture*. New York: Delacorte, 1965. A large and extremely useful compendium, with more than 200 illustrations, by a distinguished figure in both the theater and movie worlds.

Manvell, Roger. *New Cinema in Europe*. New York: Dutton, 1965.

Michael, Paul. *The Academy Awards: A Pictorial History*. New York: Bonanza Books, 1964.

Michael, Paul. *Humphrey Bogart: The Man and His Films*. New York: Bobbs-Merrill, 1965.

Millar, Merle, and Evan Rhodes. *Only You, Dick Darling, or How to Write One Television Script and Make $50,000,000.* New York: Bantam Books, 1964.

Montagu, Ivor. *Film World: A Guide to Cinema.* Baltimore: Penguin, 1965.

O'Leary, Liam. *The Silent Cinema.* New York: Dutton, 1965.

Perry, George. *The Films of Alfred Hitchcock.* New York: Dutton Picture-backs, 1965.

Pudovkin, V. I. *Film Technique and Film Acting.* New York: Grove, 1960.

Ray, Man. *Self Portrait.* London: Andre Deutsch, 1963.

Rhode, Eric. *Tower of Babel: Speculations on the Cinema.* New York: Chilton, 1967.

Ross, Lillian. *Picture.* New York: Rinehart, 1952. Also available in Double-day Dolphin paperback. A classic; the story of the making of *The Red Badge of Courage.*

Schumach, Murray. *The Face on the Cutting Room Floor.* New York: Morrow, 1964. A history of movie and television censorship.

Sontag, Susan. *Against Interpretation.* New York: Farrar, Straus, & Giroux, 1966.

Southern, Terry. *The Journal of* The Loved One: *The Production Log of a Motion Picture.* With photographs by William Claxton. New York: Random House, 1965.

Steiger, Brad. *Monsters, Maidens, and Mayhem: A Pictorial History of Hollywood Film Monsters.* Chicago: Camerarts, 1965.

Stevenson, Ralph, and Jean R. Debrix. *The Cinema As Art.* Baltimore: Penguin, 1965. Contains useful bibliography.

Strick, Philip. *Antonioni.* Loughton (Essex): Motion Publications, 1965.

Taylor, John Russell. *Cinema Eye, Cinema Ear: Some Key Film-makers of the Sixties.* New York: Hill and Wang, 1964.

Tyler, Parker. *Classics of the Foreign Film: A Pictorial History.* New York: The Citadel Press, 1962.

Verdone, Mario. *Roberto Rossellini.* Paris: Editions Seghers, 1963. Seghers' series, "Cinema D'Aujourd' hui," also offers book-length studies of the following directors: George Melies, M.A. Antonioni, Jacques Becker, Luis Bunuel, Alain Resnais, Orson Welles, Jacques Tati, Robert Bresson, Fritz Lang, Alexandre Astruc, Joseph Losey, Roger Vadim, Federico Fellini, and Abel Gance.

Wanger, Walter, and Joe Hyams. *My Life With Cleopatra.* New York: Bantam, 1963.

Warshow, Robert. *The Immediate Experience.* New York: Doubleday, 1962.

Weise, E. (ed. and trans.). *Enter: The Comics—Rodolphe Töpffer's Essay on Physiognomy and the True Story of Monsieur Crépin.* Lincoln: University of Nebraska Press, 1965.

Wood, Robin. *Hitchcock's Films.* New York: Barnes, 1965.

Screenplays

Antonioni, Michelangelo. *Screenplays of Michelangelo Antonioni.* New York: Orion, 1963. Contains narrative-dramatic versions of the following: *Il grido, L'avventura, La notte,* and *L'eclise.*

Bergman, Ingmar. *Four Screenplays of Ingmar Bergman.* New York: Simon and Schuster, 1960. Contains narrative-dramatic versions of the following: *Smiles of a Summer Night, The Seventh Seal, Wild Strawberries,* and *The Magician.*

Duras, Marguerite. *Hiroshima Mon Amour.* Translated by Richard Seaver. Picture Editor Robert Hughes. New York: Grove Press, 1961.

Eisenstein, S. M. *Ivan the Terrible.* New York: Simon and Schuster, 1962.

Eliot, T. S., and George Hoellering. *The Film of* Murder in the Cathedral. New York: Harcourt, Brace, 1952. Contains essay by Eliot on film art.

Fellini, Federico. *La Dolce Vita.* New York: Ballantine, 1961.

_____. *Federico Fellini's Juliet of the Spirits,* ed. by Tullio Kezich. Trans. Howard Greenfield. New York: Ballantine, 1965. Contains lengthy interview with Fellini. Especially noteworthy for offering two versions of the screenplay—the final script, then "translation" of finished film to script form.

Fry, Christopher. *The Bible.* New York: Pocket Books, 1966.

Godard, Jean-Luc. *The Married Woman.* New York: Berkeley, 1965. Contains essay on the film by Tom Milne.

Isaksson, Ulla. *The Virgin Spring.* New York: Ballantine, 1960. A "novelistic" version of the script.

Miller, Arthur. *The Misfits.* New York: Viking, 1961. A "novelistic" version of the script with comments on film art by Miller.

Osborne, John. *Tom Jones.* London: Faber, 1964. Osborne's "final shooting script."

_____. *Tom Jones: A Film Script,* ed. Robert Hughes. New York: Grove Press, 1964. This somewhat different version was "translated" from the film itself.

Rattigan, Terence. *The Prince and the Showgirl.* New York: New American Library, 1957.

Robbe-Grillet, Alain. *Last Year at Marienbad.* New York: Grove Press, 1962.

_____. *L'Immortelle.* Paris: Editions de Minuit, 1963.

Serling, Rod. *Patterns.* New York: Simon and Schuster, 1957. Contains TV plays and commentary on TV and movies.

Vadim, Roger. *Les Liaisons Dangereuses.* New York: Ballantine, 1962.

Wilder, Billy, and I. A. L. Diamond. *Irma La Douce.* New York: Midwood-Tower, 1963.

Periodicals

Amateur Cine World. 46 Chancery Lane, London, W. C. 2, England. Editor: Tony Rose. Semiannual, illustrated.

L'Avant-Scène du Cinéma. 27 Rue Saint-Andreo-des-Arts, Paris, 6, France. Editor: Robert Chandeau. Illustrated and containing detailed scripts.

Bianco e Nero. Via Antonio Musa 15, Rome, Italy. Editor: Ernesto G. Laura. A monthly, representing the Centro Sperimentale film school in Rome.

Bild Und Ton. Oraienburger Str. 67/68, 104 Berlin, Germany. Monthly, illustrated.

British Kinematography. 164 Shaftesbury Ave., London W. C. 2, England. Editor: B. J. Davies. Semiannual, illustrated.

British National Film Catalogue. 55a Welbeck St., London W. 1, England. Editor: Bernard Chibnall. Bimonthly, illustrated.

Bulletin Fipresci. Via Somani 6, Lugano, Switzerland. Published three or four times a year.

Business Screen. 7064 Sheridan Road, Chicago, Illinois 60626. Editor: O. H. Coelln, Jr. Illustrated business and trade journal. Published eight times a year.

CTVD: Cinema-TV-Digest. Hampton Books, Hampton Bays, New York. Editor: Ben Hamilton. Quarterly review, illustrated.

Cahiers du Cinéma. 8 Rue Marbeuf, Paris 8, France. Editors: J. L. Comolli and J. L. Ginibre. Illustrated.

Canadian Federation of Film Societies Bulletin. 1762 Carling Ave., Ottawa 13, Canada. Editor: Dorothy Macpherson. Quarterly.

Canadian Film Institute Bulletin. 1762 Carling Ave., Ottawa 13, Canada. Editor: Roy Little. Published six times a year, illustrated.

Castle of Frankenstein. Box 43, Hudson Heights Station, North Bergen, New Jersey. Excellent, illustrated.

Celuloide. Rua David Manuel da Fonseca 88, Rio Maior, Portugal. Editor: Fernando Duarte. Monthly, illustrated.

Chaplin. Box 913, Stockholm, Sweden. Editor: Bengt Forslund.

Cine Cubano. Calle 23 No. 1155, Havana, Cuba. Editor: Alfredo Guevara. Monthly, illustrated.

Cineforum. S. Marco 337, Venice, Italy. Editor: Francesco Dorigo. Large, illustrated, with script extracts.

Cinema. 9667 Wilshire Blvd., Beverley Hills, California. Illustrated.

La Cinématographie Française. 29 Rue Marsoulan, Paris 12, France. Editor: Laurent Ollivier. Trade magazine with useful information on festivals, films in production in France, etc.

Cinema Nuovo. Via Valvassori Peroni 55, Milan, Italy. Editor: Guido Aristarco. Bimonthly.

Cinéma 64 . . . 65, etc. 7 Rue Darboy, Paris 11, France. Editor: Pierre Billard. Reports on festivals and reviews of films released in Paris.

Cine World. Box 86, Toronto 9, Canada. Editor: K. Godzinski. Bimonthly, illustrated.

Cinema Domani. Cas. Post. N. 30 Ferrovia, Turin, Italy. Editors: R. Dotti and F. Valobra. Bimonthly, illustrated.

Cinema International. 1026 Echallens, Switzerland. Editor: Georges Kasper. Six times a year, illustrated.

Continental Film Review. 71 Stoke Newington Road, London N. 16, England. Editor: Gordon Reid. Monthly, illustrated.

Daily Cinema. 142 Wardour Street, London W. 1, England. Editor: C. H. B. Williamson. Issued three times a week, trade journal, illustrated.

Daily Variety. 6404 Sunset Blvd., Hollywood, California 90028. Editor: Thomas M. Pryor. Issued five times a week, trade journal.

Etudes Cinématographiques. 73 Rue du Cardinal-Lemoine, Paris 5, France. Editors: Henri Agel and Georges-Albert Astre. Illustrated.

Famous Monsters of Filmland. 420 Lexington Ave., New York, N. Y. Illustrated.

Film. 42 Bloomsbury Street, London W. C. 1, England. Editor: Peter Armitage. Quarterly, illustrated.

Film. Krakowskie. Przdemiescie 21/23, Warsaw, Poland. Editor: Bolesaw Michaels. Illustrated.

Filme. Avenida Casal Ribeiro, 14–60, Lisbon 1, Portugal. Editor: Luis de Pina. Bimonthly, illustrated.

Film Comment. 11 St. Luke's Place, New York, N. Y. 10014. Editor: Gordon Hitchens. Quarterly, illustrated.

Filmcritica. Via Carlo Fea 6, Rome, Italy. Editor: E. Bruno. Monthly, illustrated.

Film Culture. Box 1499 B. P. O., New York, N. Y. 10001. Editor: Jonas Meksas. Quarterly.

Film Daily. 1501 Broadway, New York, N. Y. 10036. Editor: Gene Arneel. Issued five times a week, illustrated.

Film Journal. 53 Cardigan St., Carlton N. 3, Victoria, Australia. Editors: James Merralls and Sascha Trikojus. Quarterly, illustrated.

Filmkritik. Mittermaystr. 10, Munich 13, Germany. Editors: Enno Patalas and Wilfried Berghahn. Monthly.

Film News. 250 W. 57th St., New York, N. Y. 10019. Editor: Rohama Lee. Bimonthly, illustrated.

Film Quarterly. University of California Press, Berkeley, California, 94720. Editor: Ernest Callenbach. Quarterly, illustrated.

Films and Filming. 16 Buckingham Palace Road, London S. W. 1, England. Editor: Peter Baker. Monthly, illustrated.

Films in Review. 31 Union Square, New York, N. Y. 10003. Editor: Henry Hart. Monthly (bimonthly in summer), illustrated.

Hollywood Reporter. 6715 Sunset Blvd., Hollywood, California 90028. Editor: Mac St. Johns. Trade journal, daily.

Image et Son. 3 Rue Recamier, Paris 7, France. Editor: François Chevassu. Published ten times a year, illustrated.

International Film Art News. 165 West End Ave., New York, N. Y. 10023. Editor: Harry K. McWilliams. Monthly, illustrated.

International Film Guide. 7 Sedley Place, London W. 1, England. Editor: Peter Cowie. Annual, illustrated. A mine of useful up-to-date information on all aspects of films.

Kosmorama. Vestergade 27, Copenhagen, Denmark. Editors: Paul Malmkjaer, Ib Monty, Jorgen Stegelmann. Quarterly, illustrated.

Modern Screen. 750 Third Ave., New York, N. Y. 10017. Editor: Judi R. Kesselman. Monthly, illustrated.

Monster World. 301 East 47th St., New York, N. Y. Illustrated.

Motion Picture Daily. 1270 Sixth Ave., New York, N. Y., 10020. Editor: Sherwin Kane. Issued five times a week, trade journal.

Motion Picture Magazine. 205 E. 42nd St., New York, N. Y. 10017. Editor: Lawrence B. Thomas. Monthly, illustrated.

Movie. 3 Cork St., London W. 1, England. Editor: Ian Cameron. Quarterly, illustrated.

Moviegoer. Box 128, Stuyvesant Station, New York, N. Y. 10009. Editor: James Stoller. Quarterly, illustrated.

Il Nuovo Spettatore Cinematografico. Via Fabro 6, Turin, Italy. Editor: Paolo Gobetti. Irregular, illustrated.

Photo Screen. 260 Park Ave. S., New York, N. Y. 10010. Editors: Ruth Marroff and Morris S. Latzen. Monthly, illustrated.

Premier Plan. B. P. 3, Lyon-Préfecture, France. Editor: Bernard Chardère. Monthly, illustrated.

Présence du Cinéma. 25 Passage des Princes, Paris 2, France. Editors: Jacques Lourcelles and Michel Mourlet. Monthly, illustrated.

Sight and Sound. 81 Dean Street, London W. 1, England. Editor: Penelope Houston. Quarterly, illustrated.

Télécine. 155 Bd. Haussmann, Paris 8, France. Editor: Gilbert Salachas. Published ten times a year, illustrated.

Contributors

MARTIN C. BATTESTIN
is professor of English at Rice University. He was educated at Princeton University and has also taught at Wesleyan and at the University of Virginia. He is the author of *The Moral Basis of Fielding's Art* and has edited the Riverside text edition of *Joseph Andrews* and *Shamela*. As one of the editors of the complete Fielding edition being published by Clarendon and the Wesleyan University Press, he is editing *Joseph Andrews, Tom Jones,* and *Amelia*. His scholarly and critical articles have appeared in numerous journals and anthologies.

JONATHAN BAUMBACH
received his Ph.D. degree from Stanford and has taught at Ohio State, New York University, and Brooklyn College. He is the author of *The Landscape of Nightmare,* a critical work which deals with the writing of Bellow, Malamud, Ellison, Salinger, Warren, and others. His first novel, *A Man to Conjure With,* was published in 1965 by Random House. Mr. Baumbach lives in New York City and is finishing a new novel, *What Comes Next.*

JOSEPH BLOTNER
is a native of New Jersey; he attended Drew University and Northwestern University and received the Ph.D. from the University of Pennsylvania. He has held a Guggenheim Fellowship and two Fulbright Teaching Fellowships as Lecturer in American literature at the University of Copenhagen. His books include *The Political Novel, The Fiction of J. D. Salinger* (with F. L. Gwynn), *William Faulkner's Library: A Catalogue,* and, most recently, *The Modern American Political Novel.* With F. L. Gwynn he edited *Faulkner in the University.* Mr. Blotner makes his home in Charlottesville, Virginia, where, under a second Guggenheim Fellowship, he is working on the authorized biography of William Faulkner.

R. V. CASSILL
was born, raised, and educated in Iowa and has long been associated with
the Writers' Workshop at the State University of Iowa. He now teaches at
Brown University and has also taught or been writer-in-residence at Columbia, the New School, the University of Washington, and Purdue. During
World War II he served for four years with the U.S. Army in the South
Pacific and in Japan. He is the author of four novels—*The Eagle on the
Coin, Clem Anderson, Pretty Leslie,* and *The President*—and a number of
original paperback novels. His collections of short stories include *15 x 3* (with
Herbert Gold and James B. Hall), *The Father and Other Stories,* and, most
recently, *The Happy Marriage and Other Stories.*

FRED CHAPPELL
is a member of the Writing Faculty of the University of North Carolina at
Greensboro. He was born in 1936 in Canton, North Carolina, and was
educated at Duke University where he studied writing with William Black-
burn. His stories, poems, and articles have appeared in many magazines including *Holiday, Saturday Evening Post, Paris Review, Transatlantic Review,
The Archive,* and *Red Clay Reader.* Two stories have recently been published in the anthologies *Southern Writing in the Sixties: Fiction* and *The
Girl in the Black Raincoat.* His novels are *It Is Time, Lord; The Inkling;*
and *Dagon.* He has also written science fiction under a pseudonym.

R. H. W. DILLARD
teaches at Hollins College. Born in Roanoke, Virginia, he graduated from
Roanoke College and received his M.A. and Ph.D. degrees from the University of Virginia. Author of bibliographical, scholarly, and critical articles, he
is known chiefly as a poet and a writer of fiction. His first collection of poems,
The Day I Stopped Dreaming About Barbara Steele, was published in November, 1966, by the University of North Carolina Press as part of their Contemporary Poetry Series. His stories have appeared in magazines and anthologies, including *Southern Writing in the Sixties: Fiction* and *The Girl in the
Black Raincoat.* He is co-author of the horror movie *Frankenstein Meets the
Space Monster.*

GEORGE E. DORRIS
was born and raised in Eugene, Oregon, and attended the University of
Oregon. He received his M.A. and Ph.D. degrees from Northwestern University and spent a year in Rome on a Fulbright. His book, *Paolo Rolli and the
Italian Circle in London,* is a recent publication. Mr. Dorris has taught at
Duke, Rutgers, and Queens College, and is currently teaching at York College
of the City University of New York.

ALAN S. DOWNER
is professor of English at Princeton University and has been chairman of the department since 1963. A native of Syracuse, New York, and once a professional actor, he was educated at Harvard University. He has lectured extensively in this country and in Europe. His most recent work, *Contemporary American Drama*, has been widely translated; among his other books are *British Drama, Fifty Years of American Drama, The Art of the Play, Twenty-Five Modern Plays, Recent American Drama, Seven American Plays,* and *On Plays, Playwrights, and Playgoers.* In 1967–68 Mr. Downer will initiate Princeton's first official course in the movies—Movie Appreciation. A shorter version of his essay was originally published in *University Magazine,* Summer, 1966.

ARMANDO FAVAZZA
is a psychiatrist with the Neuropsychiatric Institute of the University of Michigan. A graduate of the Medical School of the University of Virginia, he comes from Brooklyn. He has written articles for medical and psychiatric journals, as well as travel articles and short stories. He has traveled widely in Europe and writes out of a longtime interest in the film medium.

LESLIE FIEDLER
is professor of English at the State University of New York at Buffalo. Widely known for his distinguished critical works—*Love and Death in the American Novel, Waiting for the End, No! In Thunder,* and *An End to Innocence*—he is also a poet and the author of four works of fiction, *The Second Stone, Pull Down Vanity, Back to China,* and, most recently, *The Last Jew in America.* Professor Fiedler has written film criticism and comment for a number of magazines.

GEORGE GARRETT
was born in 1929 in Orlando, Florida, and was educated at Princeton University. Since the publication of *The Reverend Ghost: Poems* in 1957, he has published three novels, three collections of short stories, two other collections of poems, and a play; he also edited the anthology *The Girl in the Black Raincoat.* Currently professor of English at Hollins College, Mr. Garrett has taught at Wesleyan, Princeton, Rice, and the University of Virginia. He was recipient of the Sewanee Review Fellowship in Poetry, the Rome Prize of American Academy of Arts and Letters, and in 1960 a Ford Foundation Grant in Drama, through which he worked for a year with the Alley Theater in Houston. He has written a number of movie scripts, among them *The Young Lovers* and *The Playground,* and he was co-author of *Frankenstein Meets the Space Monster.* His next novel will be called *"Life with Kim Novak Is Hell."*

O. B. HARDISON
is professor of English at the University of North Carolina. He was born in

1928 in San Diego, California, and received his B.A. and M.A. degrees from the University of North Carolina, where he helped to found and edit the magazine *Factotum;* he earned his Ph.D. at the University of Wisconsin. *Practical Rhetoric,* his most recent book, follows two works of scholarship, *The Enduring Monument: The Idea of Praise in Renaissance Literary Theory and Practice* and *Christian Rite and Christian Drama in the Middle Ages,* and a volume of poetry, *Lyrics and Elegies.* He is editor of Goldentree Bibliographies and Crofts Classics for Appleton-Century-Crofts, was associate editor of the *Encyclopedia of Poetry and Poetics,* and has edited two widely used anthologies—*Modern Continental Literary Criticism* and *English Literary Criticism: The Renaissance.*

G. C. KINNEAR

was born in 1940 in Seattle, Washington, and was educated at Stanford and Princeton. He has written and published poetry and essays, and he is currently writing a book on the early writings of William Butler Yeats. Of his interest in Bergman Mr. Kinnear writes: "I first fell in love with Bergman when a French teacher offered as a theme topic a choice of *The Seventh Seal* or a story by Jules Supervielle. I wrote on the story, which I have altogether forgotten. The film has stayed with me ever since."

WALTER KORTE

has written on the cinema for various university and civic newspapers and magazines for the past four years. He spent the 1965–66 academic year in Milan on a Fulbright Fellowship, during which time he did work on a study of the films of Mauro Bolognini and Valerio Zurlini. At the time of this writing, he is completing an M.A. thesis on the *Ideological Elements in Eisenstein* at the University of Virginia, and he will enter Northwestern University in the fall of 1968 for work on a Ph.D. in cinema.

LARRY McMURTRY

was educated at North Texas State College in Denton and at Rice University. Still in his early thirties, he has already established himself as one of the leading novelists of the Southwest. His first novel, *Horseman, Pass By,* published in 1961, won the Jesse Jones Award as the best book of Texas fiction and was successfully filmed as *Hud.* Since then he has published two more novels—*Leaving Cheyenne* (1963) and *The Last Picture Show* (1966). He has written extensively for various publications including *The Texas Observer* and *Holiday.* He held a Wallace Stegner Fellowship at Stanford and has taught at Texas Christian University and at Rice University. Mr. McMurtry lives in Houston.

RICHARD E. PECK

is assistant professor of English at Temple University. When he was commissioned in June, 1956, he became the youngest officer and pilot in the

U.S. Marine Corps. After military service he finished college in two years and received his Ph.D. from Wisconsin five years after enrolling in college as a freshman. He is the author of many articles in American literature and editor of the forthcoming *Poems: Nathaniel Hawthorne.* Mr. Peck has also written a number of television scripts and for a time appeared as a standup comedian on the nightclub and coffeehouse circuit.

W. R. ROBINSON
is associate professor of English at the University of Florida. He was educated at Kentucky and Ohio State, where he took his Ph.D. He is author of *Edwin Arlington Robinson: A Poetry of the Act* and co-author of a forthcoming critical study of the Southern short story, together with a number of critical articles and many book reviews. For several years he has served as chairman of the William Faulkner Novel Award Committee. He was a paratrooper in the U.S. Army and has taught at Ohio State and at the University of Virginia. Mr. Robinson is now completing a study of the work of John Osborne and is editing an anthology of contemporary Southern short novels.

NATHAN A. SCOTT, JR.,
is an Episcopal priest and currently professor of theology and literature in the Divinity School of the University of Chicago. Born in Cleveland, Ohio, in 1925, he was educated at the University of Michigan, Union Theological Seminary, and Columbia University. He is co-editor of *The Journal of Religion* and book review editor of *The Christian Scholar.* Among his books are *Modern Literature and the Religious Frontier, Albert Camus, The New Orpheus: Essays Toward a Christian Poetic, The Climate of Faith in Modern Literature,* and, most recently, *The Broken Center: Studies in the Theological Horizon of Modern Literature* and *Ernest Hemingway: A Critical Essay,* both published in 1966. Dr. Scott has contributed a large body of articles to literary, philosophical, and theological journals in this country and abroad.

DAVID SLAVITT
was educated at Yale and Columbia and taught English for a while before joining the staff of *Newsweek.* He is author of two books of poems, *Suits for the Dead* and *The Carnivore;* two novels, *Rochelle: Or, Virtue Rewarded* and *Feel Free;* and two plays, *King Saul* and *The Cardinal Sins.* Forthcoming is a new collection of poems, *The Woods Are Full of Naked Ladies.* For several years he worked as movie editor of *Newsweek* and also wrote movie criticism for the *Yale Review.* Mr. Slavitt was born in White Plains, New York, in 1935 and now writes full-time and lives in the only southern mansion in Harwich, Massachusetts.

RICHARD WILBUR

is professor of English at Wesleyan University. Since the publication of his first collection of poems, *The Beautiful Changes and Other Poems,* he has been recognized as one of the major American poets of the postwar generation. His other collections of poems include *Ceremony and Other Poems, Things of This World* (which won the Pulitzer Prize), *Poems 1943–56, Advice to a Prophet,* and *The Poems of Richard Wilbur;* in addition, two of his translations, of Molière's *The Misanthrope* and *Tartuffe,* have been frequently staged. He is editor of *A Bestiary* and *Poe: Complete Poems* and serves as general editor of Dell's Laurel Books. Currently lyricist for the musical version of *The Madwoman of Chaillot,* he also wrote the lyrics for the Lillian Hellman–Leonard Bernstein musical *Candide.* Mr. Wilbur was born in Manhattan in 1921, grew up on a farm in New Jersey, and was educated at Amherst and Harvard.

Index of Names

Index of Films

369